The Life-boat Service

Also by Oliver Warner

A PORTRAIT OF LORD NELSON (Chatto and Windus)

THE GLORIOUS FIRST OF JUNE (Batsford)

WILBERFORCE AND HIS TIMES (Batsford)

ENGLISH LITERATURE: A PORTRAIT GALLERY (Chatto and Windus)

THE SEA AND THE SWORD: THE BALTIC 1630–1945 (Cape)

THE LIFE AND LETTERS OF VICE-ADMIRAL LORD COLLINGWOOD (Oxford University Press)

GREAT BATTLE FLEETS (Hamlyn)

The Life-boat Service

Oliver Warner

A History of the Royal National Life-boat Institution 1824-1974

With a Foreword by H.R.H. The Duke of Kent
President, R.N.L.I.

Cassell · London

CASSELL & COMPANY LTD
35 Red Lion Square, London WC1R 4SG
Sydney, Auckland
Toronto, Johannesburg

First published 1974

I.S.B.N. 0 304 29061 0

Printed in Great Britain by
The Camelot Press Ltd, London and Southampton
F. 174

Foreword by H.R.H The Duke of Kent
President of the Royal National Life-boat Institution

In a modern highly organized society there are certain functions which the average man tends to take wholly for granted, at least until they fail. Among these, at any rate in this country, the life-boat service is one whose reliability is regarded as absolute, whose efficiency is unquestioned—and should he or she be unlucky enough to need help at sea, they will not find their confidence misplaced. This book, which marks the 150th Anniversary of the Royal National Life-boat Institution, should help to remind the thousands of people who now use the sea for pleasure of just what the life-boat service is and how it originated.

The history of saving life at sea is of the greatest antiquity. In all ages people have been prepared to risk their own lives when the sea has threatened the lives of others. The shore-based life-boat was an invention of the late eighteenth century, but it was not until 1824 that a national organization came into being anywhere in the world for the sole purpose of saving life at sea. This was the body known today as the Royal National Life-boat Institution, which was founded at a meeting held in the City of London on 4 March 1824. Later in the same year a life-boat service organized in a similar way came into being in the Netherlands.

To commemorate the 150th Anniversary of the foundation of the Institution, Mr Oliver Warner was commissioned to write a new official history. The story he tells is that of one of the great voluntary services in the history of man; it is a fascinating and inspiring one. Here is a story of dedication and courage, of professional skill and adaptability to changing circumstances. Moreover, the changes chronicled by Mr Warner in this work are continual. The early pulling and sailing life-boats, many of them drawn into the water by horses, have been replaced by powerful boats driven by diesel engines, equipped with radio communications, radar, direction-finding apparatus, echo-sounders and other devices of technology. What is more, in recent years the Royal National Life-boat Institution has brought into being an additional fleet, that of the inshore life-boats, which today save more lives in a year than do the conventional boats. Yet through all these changes in equipment and techniques there runs the thread of a quality continuously maintained, the quality which inspires a volunteer to give time, effort and, if need be, his life in the service of other people. Perhaps one of the most striking features of the life-boat crews is that they so often contain several members of the same family, and that these families have supplied crewmen for two or three generations. Such is the meaning of totally dedicated service.

In telling this story the author has given due prominence to the gallantry the life-boat crews exhibit, at times in circumstances of extreme peril; to the dedicated efforts of those who raise money for a service which, in spite of fiercely rising costs, is still supported entirely by voluntary contributions; and to the administrators and others who provide the essential continuity.

As this account clearly shows, the life-boat service in this country belongs to the nation as a whole. It is one for which every member of the nation may feel responsible, and in which all should take part if the service is to continue as it has always done.

As President of the Royal National Life-boat Institution I have had the privilege of visiting many stations and meeting many people engaged in the life-boat service. It has been a profoundly inspiring experience.

EDWARD

Dedicated to the R.N.L.I.
upholding a great tradition of humanity

*

This history, while in no way officially inspired, would have lacked authority without guidance from those who serve the Royal National Life-boat Institution, or without access to its archives.

This dedication, which appears in place of what would be a very long list of individual and corporate acknowledgements, signifies the writer's debt to the many, at headquarters, at life-boat stations and elsewhere, who have so generously helped to give the book what flavour it may possess. It is also a tribute to those who continue a work of mercy requiring as high a degree of courage as any in the world.

O. W.

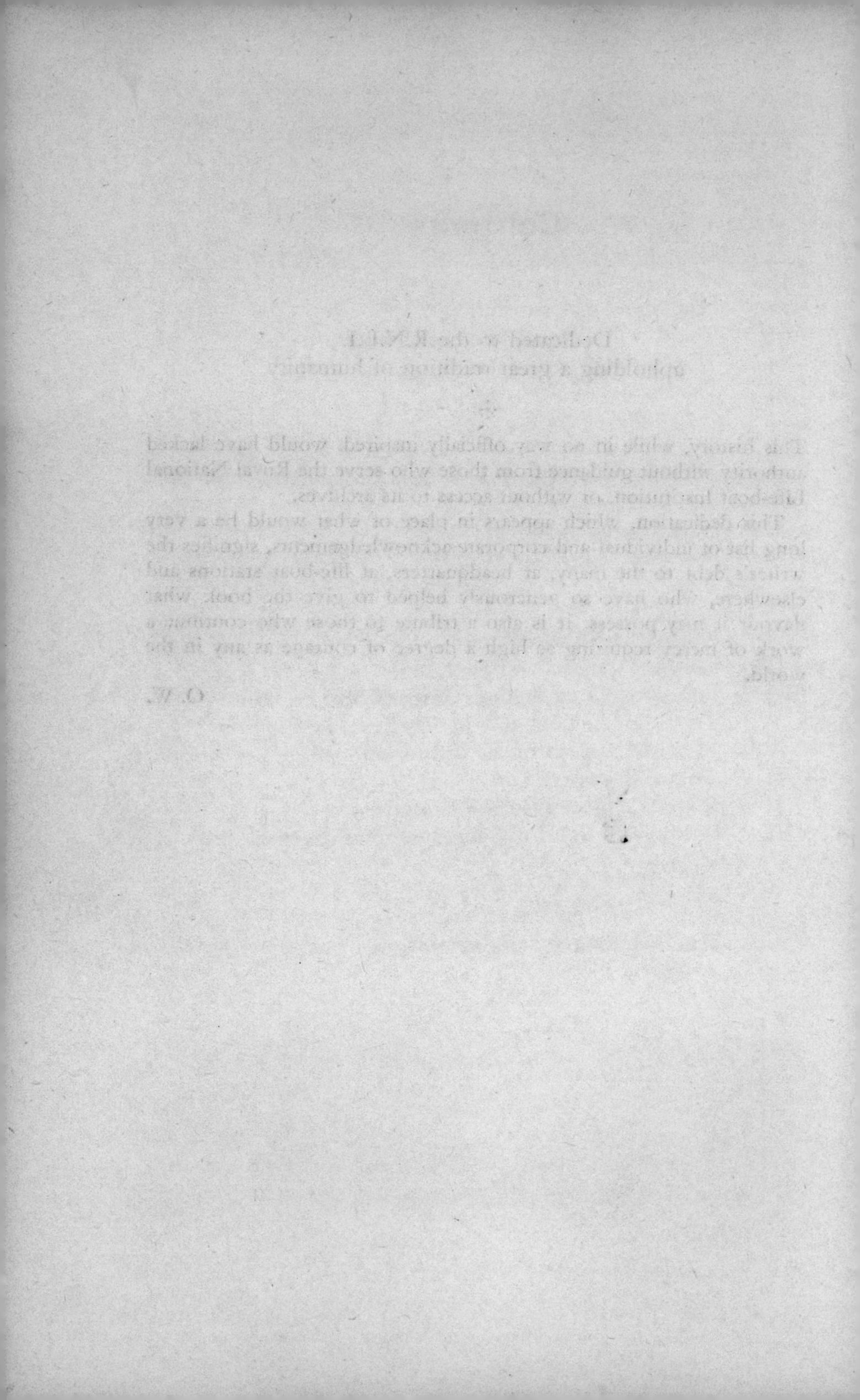

Contents

List of Illustrations

Except where stated otherwise, reproductions are by courtesy of the Royal National Life-boat Institution.

Line drawings in the text

1
'The Shipwreck Institution'

Anyone who in a sophisticated age is still moved by the words of William Whiting's well-known hymn 'Eternal Father, strong to save . . .' will have at least some idea of how powerfully the thought of being 'in peril on the sea' affected former generations. In an era when sea travel depended on wind and sail, dangers were ever present. Whiting spoke of 'rock and tempest, fire and foe'. If he had added collision, fog and human frailty the list would have been reasonably complete. Even today, despite every kind of technical advance, the sea engenders tragedies which stir not one country only, but all mankind. A century and a half ago, when the Royal National Life-boat Institution came into being under the title of 'The National Institution for the Preservation of Life from Shipwreck', these were so frequent as to be accepted as one of the sadder facts of life, just as road accidents are now.

Although tragedies have not ceased, and will not do so, alleviation is possible. This record is concerned with how the rescue of lives at sea has been carried out by one particular organization in one particular realm. It is a story which has called for the exercise of most of the more positive and creative characteristics possessed by men and women, ranging from selfless resolution in the face of death, to the most humdrum activities, pursued without thought of reward in order to further the work of the life-boat service.

Emphasis is, and always has been, on its voluntary nature. The crews are volunteers, and the whole organization depends upon the generosity of the public. The principle is of paramount importance, and has never been lost sight of. It extends to every sphere and it engenders a spirit not easily matched elsewhere.

While coxswains and crews are often drawn from amongst inshore fishermen and boatmen who have been familiar from childhood with a particular stretch of coast, others from very different sides of life have also been attracted to the service. For instance, Major-General J. E. B. Seely (1868–1947), who later became Lord Mottistone, was at one time a Secretary of State, the only such person ever to have been a regular member of a life-boat crew, and for three years a coxswain, as well as being on the Institution's Committee of Management. He wrote of those with whom he served—and he knew them well:

> . . . the British people are peculiar in many ways, and British seamen and fishermen are the most peculiar of all. They are capable of almost anything, even what seems to be the impossible, if you will let them do it their own way.

That remains so; and Arthur Marder's words on the British seamen of the First World War have an equally general application: 'Sailors are very quick to detect when they are trusted. When they are, they respond to every demand.'

General Seely wrote in *Launch*, which was an account of his experiences over many years: 'Perhaps the most surprising thing about the life-boat service, and it is very surprising, is the effect it has in abating the anger, hatred and malice of mankind.' Is this perhaps because the dangers of the sea are cleansing as well as daunting? Those who brave them, in the service of others, certainly add to their stature, though they would themselves be the last to say so.

In general terms, there are various types of people who have given, and continue to give, a valuable proportion of their energies to the Institution. There are the august patrons, the honorary officers, subscribers and members, who in most instances are far more than that, in so far that they show sustained enthusiasm for the work, and influence others in the cause of life-saving at sea. There is the Committee of Management, originally called the 'London Central Committee', made up of men of eminence and skill in various fields, and in which there is invariably a strong representation from the Royal Navy. Upon it devolves the direction of affairs, and the general policy of the Institution. There are the administrators, the inspectorate, the designers and many others to whom the Institution offers a career in which they take pride. There are the local committees, representative of their districts, and the coxswains and crews by whom rescue is achieved, upon whose seamanship and courage everything hinges, many of whom have the sea as their full-time calling. Finally there are the essential fund-raisers and helpers, men, women and children (with their pets), who are the means of providing the money by which the Institution is enabled to do its work.

Neither way of life, nor sex, nor age is any bar to humanitarian effort in which aptitudes of diverse kinds may be employed. This has, in fact, been one of the strongest appeals of the Life-boat Institution. It has attracted thousands, in successive generations, who find one of the more durable satisfactions in life to be work in a cause which transcends national boundaries.

One of the conclusions to be drawn from the lives of those who furthered the efforts of the rescue service, particularly in its earlier days, was how much personal experience and direct observation played in inspiring their activities. In this connection it may be appropriate to quote a passage concerning J. M. W. Turner, an artist who, though not connected with the Life-boat Institution, did as much as anyone of his time to make people visually aware of the facts of shipwreck. As Ruskin wrote in *Harbours of England*:

> I am perfectly certain that Turner had *seen* a shipwreck, and moreover one of that horrible kind—a ship dashed to pieces in deep water at the foot of an inaccessible cliff. Having once seen this, I perceive also that the image of it could not be effaced from his mind. It taught him two great facts, which he never afterwards forgot; namely, that both ships and sea were things that broke to pieces. He had . . . heard what a storm-gust sounded like that had taken up with it, in its swirl of a moment, the last breaths of a ship's crew. He never forgot either the sight or the sound.

What was true of Turner was true of many others, and certainly of Sir William Hillary (1771–1847), a man whose career was memorable in many ways, not least because he founded what in course of time became the Royal National Life-boat Institution, and by his personal courage three times won the Institution's gold medal for saving life at sea. Inspiration, drive and example have seldom been found so well combined in one man.

Locally run life-boats were no new thing in Hillary's day. There was an established life-saving station at Bamburgh in Northumberland, and records show that life-boats had been in use at North and South Shields at least since 1789. Many places such as Montrose and St Andrews in Scotland, St Peter Port in Guernsey, Douglas in the Isle of Man, Lowestoft, Ramsgate, Rye, Liverpool, Exmouth and elsewhere on the coast of England had rescue boats in regular use from the earliest years of the nineteenth century and, in some cases, certainly at Liverpool, well before that time. For instance, by 1776 Liverpool even had a system of awards for lives saved by a boat stationed 'on the strand about a mile below Formby lower landmark'. But to Hillary belongs the credit of advocating a *national* organization. From him derived much of the impetus which led to the establishment of a voluntary rather than a State-run service, such as has continued ever since. In a pamphlet issued in 1823 he wrote:

> In the nineteenth century, surrounded by every improvement and institution which the benevolent can suggest, or the art of man accomplish for the mitigation or prevention of human ills, will it for a moment be capable of belief, that there does not, in all our great and generous land, exist one National Institution which has for its direct object the rescue of human life from shipwreck?

Hillary's pamphlet, the full title of which was: *An Appeal to the British Nation on the Humanity and Policy of Forming a National Institution for the Preservation of Lives and Property from Shipwreck*, was among the most effective ever printed. Not only did it succeed in its object, but it laid down the lines of the work on which the Institution has been engaged ever since.

The purposes were announced as follows: the preservation of lives in peril, 'which should always be considered as the first great and permanent object of the Institution', help to ships in distress; safeguarding of property; prevention of plunder; the succour and support of those rescued; 'the people and vessels of every nation, whether in peace or war, to be equally objects of this Institution'; the offering of appropriate rewards to those who carried out rescues; and 'providing for the widows and families of those who lost their lives in attempting to rescue others'.

Besides proposing the establishment of a public body to administer a life-saving service, Hillary was brimful of ideas for making use of new or existing inventions of all kinds which might help in the saving of life. There was, for instance, the rocket and the mortar, which he knew could be employed effectively for shooting rescue lines to those in distress, and by means of which they could reach a lifeboat or the safety of the shore. Hillary followed every development in boats and life-lines, and in his pamphlet he referred specifically to those 'enlightened and highly patriotic officers, Sir W. Congreve, Captains Marryat, Manby, Dansey and various other meritorious individuals'. He had named some exceptional men.

Congreve's rockets had been used on active service at Boulogne, Copenhagen, Leipzig and Waterloo, in operations against countries dominated by Napoleon, and they were soon employed more peacefully. Captain Marryat, who was to become a popular writer, had devised a code of signals for merchant ships which was in wide use. He had also designed a life-boat, a model of which he had presented to the Royal Humane Society, whose life-saving medal he had won at sea. This Society, which had been in existence for half a century, primarily 'for the recovery of persons in a state of suspended animation', had aims akin to those of the 'Shipwreck Institution', and co-operation was valuable to both. George William Manby was a tireless experimenter in life-saving apparatus, including a line fired from a mortar, and he also wrote on the subject. His inventions were to prove of great benefit and they became extensively known. Being human, he had his faults, and among them was acute jealousy of the honours accorded to Hillary. Captain Dansey's unrewarded ingenuity was directed to trying to make use of kites for taking lines to ships.

Perhaps the most remarkable technical advocacy deriving from Hillary was directed to the application of steam to the life-boat. In 1824, following hard on his plea for a national body to concern itself with sea rescue, Hillary published *A Plan for the Construction of a Steam Life-boat, also for the Extinguishment of Fire at Sea.* Recollecting that, at the time Hillary wrote, steam, as applied to seafaring, was in its infancy, this little work is astonishing both in imagination and prophecy. Hillary had perceived the enormous advantage of steam in that it could enable a vessel to proceed directly to windward, which was beyond the capacity of sail.

> The principle I propose is to combine the safety and the incapability of being submerged which the life-boat possesses, with the commanding power of being impelled against both the wind and a heavy sea which the steam vessel alone can effect to any great extent . . . . Perhaps the boat might be about forty feet long, but varying in all her dimensions according to the nature of the service for which she may be intended: it would be both desirable and requisite that her beam should be considerable, and hence it would become nearly impossible for her to be overset.

Further suggestions put forward by Hillary were to fit the boat with 'masts which might be raised or taken down at pleasure', oars for use 'when requisite', and 'strong curved timbers' to protect the paddles when going alongside ships in trouble. At that time paddles were the usual means by which steamships were driven: the day of the screw propeller came later.

No detail was too small to engage Hillary's attention. His steam life-boat should, so he thought, 'have valves, or small ports, opening outward only', to clear her of water, and she should have powerful pumps. 'I would suggest,' he said, 'that she might, when thought advantageous, be fitted with forcing pumps or engines to throw water by her own steam power.' Practical application of most of these ideas was so far in the future that the first steam life-boat was not in the service of the Institution until over sixty years later in 1890. When at last she appeared she was at one stage stationed in the very area, that of Liverpool, which Hillary had thought of as providing a good opportunity for steam to show to advantage.

One of the curiosities about Sir William Hillary is that nothing in his earlier life had seemed to foreshadow the work for which he was to become famed. He was born in 1771 of a family which claimed to be of French descent, and which drew wealth from sugar plantations in Jamaica. As a young man he had the means to launch out into society with prospects of ease and enjoyment. At an early age he became equerry to the Duke of Sussex (an appointment later to be held by Captain Marryat), the Duke being the most versatile of the sons of George III. With his master, Hillary made an extensive tour of the Mediterranean. It was there that he first became attracted to seafaring—he circumnavigated the two islands of Sicily and Malta in an open boat—and there he began that interest in the fortunes of the Knights of St John of Jerusalem which became a life-long study.

Hillary is sometimes referred to in the rank of lieutenant-colonel, and there is reason for this. Soon after war with France began in 1793, a conflict which was to continue, with only one short break, for more than twenty years, Hillary, who was then living in Essex, raised the '1st Essex Legion of Infantry and Cavalry' at his own expense, which amounted to more than £20,000. He commanded the 1,400 men in person, and in 1805 he was made a baronet in recognition of his patriotic endeavour.

But the war seriously affected Hillary's West Indian sugar interests, and overstrained his resources in England. By 1808 he had lost most of his money. He thereupon left his home in East Anglia and settled at Douglas, Isle of Man, where he was safer from duns. There he lived for the twenty-five years which remained to him. Although his financial circumstances became more and more difficult, he was very active in Douglas, where he took a regular part in sea rescues, both before and after he had succeeded in enlisting public sympathy for the foundation of what was to become the Life-boat Institution.

The Isle of Man has various memorials to Hillary, the most conspicuous being what is known as the Tower of Refuge. This was built on Conister Rock in Douglas Bay in 1832 at a cost of £254. 12. 0. of which sum Hillary himself supplied £73. 6. 0. It was intended to give shelter to those who, when wrecked in the bay, were able to scramble to the building and stay there until the weather moderated and they could be taken off. The Tower—'Blest work . . . of love and innocence' as Wordsworth described it in a sonnet of 1833 referring to 'noble Hillary', and to the life-boatmen whose 'dread service nerves the heart it warms'—suggests a miniature castle. This refuge, set upon a rock, within a bay where storms are not infrequent, still seems today a reassuring feature of the seascape.

Hillary's appeal to the nation for a life-boat service was helped towards a flying start by his contacts and friendships. He had the entrée to Court circles by reason of his former post with the Duke of Sussex, and his pamphlet of 1823 was dedicated to George IV. The interest of Parliamentarians was also essential, and here too he was lucky. He found a warm supporter in George Hibbert, who had at one time been M.P. for Seaford, was a Fellow of the Royal Society, and had been active in the establishment of London's West India Docks, his fortune deriving from the same quarter as Hillary's. Still more important was the help of Thomas Wilson, M.P. for the City of London. It was on Wilson's initiative that a meeting was held at the City of London Tavern on 12 February 1824, when a resolution proposing the adoption of Hillary's plans was carried with acclaim.

The London Tavern, scene of the two original meetings which led to the founding of the Institution, was in Bishopsgate. By the time of the second, on 4 March 1824, the Sovereign had consented to become Patron. He had also persuaded the Prime Minister, Lord Liverpool, to become President, and five Royal Dukes to be Vice-Presidents. Support was also promised from the Archbishops of Canterbury and York, and from the Bishops of London, Durham, Bath and Wells, Chester, and Bristol. The Institution's archives also contain handsome letters from such notables as the Marquis of Hertford in his capacity as 'Vice-Admiral of Cornwall and the Coasts of Suffolk'; Lord Camden as 'Vice-Admiral of Kent'; Viscount Melville; Viscount Exmouth, better known as Admiral Sir Edward Pellew, famed as a fighting sailor in the Napoleonic Wars; Sir Robert Peel: George Canning; Frederick John Robinson, the Chancellor of the Exchequer; the Chairman of the East India Company; the Deputy Master of Trinity House; the Chairman of Lloyd's; the Lord Mayor of London; and the Governor of the Bank of England. No effort had been spared to enlist the most illustrious people.

The Establishment was so well and truly represented that the Archbishop of Canterbury, Dr Manners Sutton, actually took the chair at the inaugural meeting. The Bishops of London and Chester were present, also William Wilberforce, who had spent so much of his life fighting for the abolition of the slave trade, Captain Manby, and many distinguished naval officers and Members of Parliament.

The Archbishop moved the first and principal resolution:

> That an Institution be now formed for the Preservation of Life in cases of Shipwreck on the Coasts of the United Kingdom, to be supported by donations and subscriptions, and to be called the 'National Institution for the Preservation of Life from Shipwreck'.

Among the provisions agreed upon, which included every single one mentioned in Hillary's pamphlet, were that maritime countries and seaports should be invited to form Branches, and that the decisions reached should be reported to representatives of foreign countries.

The original premises were at 12 Austin Friars, within the City boundaries and not far from the Bank of England. This was a brick building which still survives. In 1826 the quarters were moved to No. 18, and in 1832 to No. 20, but no details have survived as to their extent. In 1846 there was a migration to No. 8, Great Winchester Street, still within the City. It was not until the virtual refounding of the Institution in 1851 that a move was made to the district of Charing Cross.

Resolutions and prominent supporters were all very well, but other ingredients were just as necessary. The first was money; the second, adroit management. In a voluntary and charitable organization, the two factors must obviously run together, and it was here that difficulties would arise. At first, in the initial burst of enthusiasm, the 'Shipwreck Institution', to give it the rather unfortunate name by which it first became known, had an encouraging start. The Archbishop of Canterbury was authorized to announce, as early as 20 March 1824, that the King had signified that the new Institution might have the prefix of *Royal*—and contributions had flowed in.

A total of £9,706. 6. 6. was in fact received in subscriptions and donations during the first year. A handsome proportion came from Trinity House. It included an initial gift of £500 from the Brethren, and fifty guineas from Joseph Cotton, Deputy Master. The Committee recorded that such munificence was all the more appreciated 'as coming from a body peculiarly competent to judge of the value of the Institution, and whose example may have the most important influence on its permanent establishment'.

Lloyd's subscribed £200. This was in line with efforts which the Corporation had made over many years to stimulate interest in designs for an efficient life-boat. John Julius Angerstein, who had died in 1823, had suggested the appropriation of £2,000 from the Fund to further this purpose. It was clear that the aims of the new Institution would be likely to increase efforts to improve standards of safety at sea. Although it had early support from Lloyd's, contributions were at first made irregularly, and at the request of the Institution. Previously, Lloyd's had, on their own initiative, arranged for rescue stations on various parts of the coast. The £2,000 originally set aside had in fact been used to supply life-boats to Hartlepool, Redcar, Whitby, St Andrews, Lowestoft, Bantry Bay, Ayr, Bideford, Christchurch, Aldeburgh, Newhaven, Arbroath, Exmouth and Mounts Bay.

If a flow of revenue had continued and increased, all would have been well, for the money was suitably laid out on life-boats, on rewards for rescue or for attempts at saving life at sea, on the care of the shipwrecked, and in sending the mortar rocket-throwing apparatus devised by Captain Manby to certain parts of the coast where it was thought that it would be most likely to be useful.

The rewards were headed by a medal which was to be struck in gold and silver, bestowed according to merit. A bronze variety was not issued until 1917, although there happen to be two bronze proofs or specimens of later versions in the Museum of the Royal Mint. The original Committee made a good choice of executant, for they turned to William Wyon, the leading member of a dynasty of medallists, the first of whom had come to England from Cologne soon after the Hanoverians were established on the throne of Great Britain.

William Wyon made engravings for the Institution during 1824 and the following year, one of them being considered by his son and successor in the service of the Mint, Leonard Charles Wyon, as among his finest work. The obverse showed the head of George IV, as Patron. The reverse, comprising a scene of rescue from drowning, was sketched by Henry Howard, the Secretary of the Royal Academy, who had advised the Committee that Wyon was the right engraver to approach. In point of fact, a figure to the left of the reverse design was that of Wyon himself. The legend ran: 'Let not the Deep swallow me up.' This was an adaptation from Psalm LXIX, verse 15, the words of the Authorised Version being: 'Let not the water flood overflow me, neither let the deep swallow me up.' Howard asked seven guineas for his original sketch, but took five because the cause was charitable. Wyon received £105 for engraving the dies, and another £102. 16. 0. was paid for the first batch of medals.

George IV's head was retained throughout the reign of his brother and successor, William IV, and indeed until 1860, when Leonard Charles Wyon engraved a new obverse die with the head of Queen Victoria. This was in use by the Institution for the rest of the Queen's long reign, the reverse of the original William Wyon medal being retained.

The text from the Psalms which appeared on the medal was most apt, not only for the rescued, but because it was not long before the Institution itself had need of succour. This was mainly owing to increasing claims and responsibilities, and to very fluctuating revenue which was never enough for its needs.

There was no doubt about the assiduity of Wilson in his capacity as Chairman, or of that of the first Secretary, Thomas Edwards, or the two or three members who regularly gave time to the Committee meetings—the minutes of their proceedings survive, and are proof of it. And if difficulties were manifest, so was ingenuity in meeting them. Technically, Wilson relied much on two naval officers, Captains Foulerton and Saumarez, the former sometimes taking the chair in Wilson's absence, unless Sir William Hillary happened to be in London. Saumarez, who belonged to a famous Channel Island family, was prepared not only to advise, but to experiment. For instance, in 1828 he took the Institution's Brighton boat out in a heavy sea to investigate its qualities. He also tested, in the water, the characteristics of an inflatable 'calico shirt life-preserver' which had been devised by a Lieutenant Kennedy and made by his wife. Saumarez was impressed, and in 1829 the Committee ordered £5 to be paid to Mrs Kennedy, a very early instance of a reward to a woman.

Such people as the Kennedys were welcomed, but there was a stream of cranks to be headed off, like the gentleman who would insist that iron life-boats were the answer to everything; and there were the grumblers, known to every committee assembled to deal with awards, who considered that their services had been undervalued. There was also Sir William Hillary, who had the drawbacks of his sterling qualities, and who never hesitated to trumpet his achievements and those of the Manxmen whose interests he fostered, so that there was a danger that disproportionate attention would be paid to their work.

This trait in the Founder was amusingly illustrated in the matter of medals. In the early distributions Hillary, as was proper, had been voted one in gold, as the 'original projector' of the Institution, as had the Archbishop of Canterbury, Captain Manby, and a few others whose services were considered to warrant it on general grounds. Not content with this, as early as December 1825 Hillary wrote to the Committee suggesting a second medal for himself, this time for gallantry in going to the aid of the ship *City of Glasgow*.

In the most tactful way possible, the Committee sent word back saying, wisely in the circumstances, that they 'felt themselves bound to husband their resources, and to grant rewards sparingly to men, for services, to whom a very small amount would be of consequence'. They went on to point out that Hillary already possessed the medal in gold, and that they hoped he would understand their attitude.

The answer did not content Hillary, and he very soon made this known, though in an indirect way. The Duke of Sussex had been persuaded to preside at an anniversary dinner in 1826, a ceremony which was additional to the Annual General Meeting. It was remarked that in his speech he recommended the award of a 'second medallion' or a 'bar to the first' when instances of sufficient merit had been brought to the notice of the Institution. As Hillary had been one of the Duke's equerries, it was not hard to deduce the source of this idea, particularly as the Duke knew little of the affairs of the organization before being briefed for the occasion of his speech. Hillary got his 'bar', or what would later be called a 'second service clasp', in 1828 for services in Douglas Bay to the Swedish ship *Fortroendert*, and two more in 1830. Originally the bars were in the form of a boat.

* * *

Many threads in the earlier history of the life-boat come together on the coasts of Northumberland and Durham, though their relevance to Hillary's National Institution was mainly indirect. The Tyne Life-boat Society, the best-known and one of the first local organizations for saving life from shipwreck, had been inaugurated as early as 1789 by Nicholas Fairles and a committee known as 'the Gentlemen of the Lawe House' who were in fact public-spirited citizens of South Shields. The Society remained independent of the Institution and made a great contribution to the design of the life-boat by ordering a craft, christened the *Original*, from Henry Greathead, a local builder. Their impetus derived, as has so often been the case, from a particular incident. This was a disaster to the *Adventure*, which occurred on 15 March 1789 when the entire ship's company perished one by one within full view of thousands ashore who were powerless to give them help, because no boat then available could live in the sea which was running at the time.

Further north, at Bamburgh Castle, which commands a view of the Farne Islands and of a dangerous stretch of sea, a Trust had been established, on the death in 1772 of Nathaniel Crewe, Bishop of Durham, which was concerned, among other matters, with sea-rescue. One of the later and abler administrators of the Trust was Dr John Sharp, Archdeacon of Northumberland, who in 1772 succeeded to the living of Bamburgh on the death of his younger brother.

Dr Sharp noted that 'the melancholy sight from the Castle of persons wrecked on the Islands, and starving with cold and hunger, together with the savage plundering of such goods etc, as were driven on shore, induced the Lords of the Manor to give every assistance to vessels in distress, and premiums for the saving of lives'. He could fairly have added that he himself made contributions from his own purse.

At Bamburgh an elaborate system of signals was in use. A gun was fired from the tower when a ship was seen to be in trouble, which was a sign for the local inhabitants to rally round. In periods of storm two men patrolled the shore on horseback from sunset to sunrise. One was to stay where he was, if signs of a ship in difficulties were observed out to sea, while the other was to report back to the Castle. A bell on the south turret served as a fog warning; a speaking trumpet was in readiness for communication with shipmasters; rooms were set apart to shelter the shipwrecked; and there was even provision for coffins and funeral expenses for the unlucky. The regulations of the Crewe Trustees, devised to meet conditions which obtained on many other parts of the coast, in fact gave a preview of most of those adopted in course of time by the Institution.

In one further matter the Institution became indebted to the Trust. It was the encouragement given by the active-minded Dr Sharp to the design of a life-boat, built for that special purpose. Sharp asked Lionel Lukin, who was known already to the Royal Humane Society for an idea for a raft for rescuing those who had fallen through the ice on rivers and ponds, to adapt a Northumberland coble in accordance with his own ideas. Lukin, by trade a coach-builder, was a man of varied inventive powers who, together with Henry Greathead and William Wouldhave, both of South Shields, has a very eminent place among those whose aim has been to perfect designs for rescue craft. His converted coble was at Bamburgh by 1787, and was one of the prototypes of the modern life-boat. And it was in a coble that Grace Darling took part in the rescues from the *Forfarshire* which brought her publicity and fame.

In the notice of Grace Darling which appears in the *Dictionary of National Biography* she is classified as a 'heroine'. Neither she, nor her family on her behalf, would ever have claimed this distinction; nevertheless, that is what she became for she was certainly one of the few women who have taken part in a dangerous and successful sea-rescue.

Grace Darling's people served Trinity House; her father and grandfather were lighthouse-keepers. William Darling, her father, was given charge of the Longstone Light, which had been brought into service in 1826. His wife Thomasin was the daughter of Job Horsley, gardener at Bamburgh to the Crewe Trustees, and Grace, who was born in 1815, was her seventh child. When the *Forfarshire* was wrecked during the night of 6–7 September 1838 William and Thomasin Darling, together with Grace, happened to be alone at the Longstone.

The *Forfarshire*, which had been built at Dundee two years earlier, plied between her home port and Hull with passengers and freight. She was of about 366 gross tons, was rigged as a topsail schooner, and she had a two-cylinder engine of 190 h.p., the boilers of which had been giving trouble. On her last journey they developed serious leaks. These, together with bad deterioration in the weather, and the master's decision to carry on under sail rather than to make for shelter immediately, led to her being driven in the darkness on to the Big Harcar rock. There, pounded by the seas, she broke in half just abaft her paddle wheels. The stern part sank, drowning all but one of the passengers and all the the crew who chanced to be aft at the time. Captain Humble, who had his wife with him, was washed overboard with her. Some of the remaining crew had managed to get away in a boat, leaving thirteen people, including a woman, Mrs Dawson, and two children, still on the wreck. By daylight, the children were dead from exposure and only their mother and eight men survived.

The evening before, William Darling, in view of the heavy weather, and in the expectation of an abnormally high tide, worked for some hours with Grace making everything outside the lighthouse as secure as possible. The two then went to bed, though not to sleep. On such a night, a wreck was probable, and indeed before sunrise on 7 September Grace, looking to seaward, made out what she believed was a ship ashore on the Big Harcar. Despite 'the glass incessantly applied', in Darling's phrase, it was almost seven o'clock in the morning before father and daughter were certain that there were living people aboard, and in dire need of help. They acted at once. As his coble was too big for Darling to manage on his own, Grace—slight as she was and not much over five feet tall—took an oar. The Darlings would have to depend on the muscle of survivors if it proved necessary to make more than a single journey to the wreck.

Mrs Darling helped to launch the coble. Father and daughter, the father on the midship thwart pulling an oar with each hand, Grace on the thwart abaft him, using both hands on an oar on the starboard side, then pulled away. The rudder was not shipped, Darling depending on his close knowledge of the reefs to reach the Big Harcar safely. As measured on the Admiralty chart, the direct distance was a little short of a thousand yards. By the route followed, the journey was perhaps as much as a mile, the first leg exposing the boat to the full force of wind and sea.

On reaching the *Forfarshire*, Darling scrambled to the rock, leaving Grace to manage the coble. He decided that two trips would indeed be necessary, since there were nine to be taken off. On the first he took Mrs Dawson, in deep distress for her two dead children, together with an injured man and three others. Two of the men, and Darling, had the oars. Grace, who had put blankets into the boat, looked after the passengers.

When the Longstone had been reached Darling, again with the aid of survivors, at once went back to the rock, where he picked up the remaining people. Although the coble was full of men in varying stages of exhaustion, the second journey had been completed by nine o'clock. It was a feat made possible through Darling's experienced knowledge of a formidable area of rock-strewn sea, and through superb handling of his boat. Grace and her mother meanwhile made the strangers as comfortable as confined quarters allowed.

A rescue attempt was also made in a coble from North Sunderland. Her coxswain was William Robson, and William Brooks Darling, one of Grace's brothers, was in the crew. On reaching Big Harcar and finding he had been forestalled, Robson moved some bodies out of reach of the sea and went on to the Longstone. There the men remained, short of food and with no dry clothes, for two weary days.

In the earlier days of Queen Victoria news took time to travel, and it was not until a fortnight after the rescues that trumpets began to sound. 'Is there,' asked *The Times*, 'in the whole field of history or of fiction, even one instance of female heroism to compare for one moment with this?' If there was, it signified nothing, for the public had found a new favourite, and it made the most of her.

The episode of the *Forfarshire* was taken up in a big way. Grace Darling, at the age of twenty-three, became a national figure, almost as much so, in her lowly sphere, as the still younger Queen, upon whom the hopes of so many were centred. She had much to endure for the remaining six years of her life. She became exposed to every kind of artist, writer, publicist and crank. Her cult was to continue long after her early death, which was probably due to consumption. This took place in 1842 at the cottage at Bamburgh where she had been born.

Wordsworth, who was by then Poet Laureate, reserved a tribute until after Grace's demise. It is in pedestrian verse, though there are passages with a blend of actuality and fancy which make them worth remembrance.

> Together they put forth, Father and Child!
> Each grasps an oar, and struggling on they go—
> Rivals in effort; and, alike intent
> Here to elude and there surmount, they watch
> The billows lengthening, mutually crossed
> And shattered, and re-gathering their might;
> As if the tumult, by the Almighty's will
> Were, in the conscious sea, roused and prolonged
> That woman's fortitude—so tried, so proved—
> May brighten more and more!

From the shower of rewards by which Grace Darling's courage was recognized, two stand out, for differing reasons. At the instigation of the third Duke of Northumberland, Grace and her father were given gold medals by the Royal Humane Society, while the 'Shipwreck Institution', then as always glad to honour life-saving at sea, even when undertaken in boats not under its control, gave them its silver medal. Furthermore, the Committee subscribed £100 to a general fund for the Darlings and the boat's owner from North Sunderland.

The interest of the Duke of Northumberland, whose predecessor had ordered a life-boat from Greathead for North Shields, was natural in the most influential nobleman of the region in which the Darlings lived, and it was perhaps on the suggestion of the Duchess, who had once been Queen Victoria's governess, that a gift of £50 was sent to Grace as royal bounty. Although the affairs of the 'Shipwreck Institution' itself were then somewhat in the doldrums, the interest of the ducal family in life-saving at sea was to continue, and was to be a principal factor in their revival.

Today, although there is no longer a life-boat station at Bamburgh, the Institution has charge of the Grace Darling Museum, founded in the centenary year of the rescue, and of the 21-foot coble in which the journeys were made. If the Institution, at the time when the affair was headline news, failed to seize a great chance of making its wants known, at least it recognized Grace's fortitude, and it is appropriate that it should help to keep her memory alive.

* * *

The lowest period in the whole history of the organization, when it had become a question of whether or not it could survive at all, was between 1841 and 1850. The impetus given by the Farne Islands rescue had, perhaps, some effect in keeping the Institution in being, but no appeals for funds were made to the public, and although each year awards were given, these had shrunk to a total of 123 in 1838, whereas nearly four times that number had been known in earlier years. In general, times were difficult, and for some years they continued to be so.

The one gleam of hope in the situation also contained dangers. In 1839 there had been founded a body, which happily still exists, known as the Shipwrecked Fishermen and Mariners Royal Benevolent Society. In addition to work in caring for distressed seamen, and in helping the families of those who had lost their lives afloat, the Society's funds ran to the provision of a few life-boats. It seemed, in fact, that there might be serious risk of duplication, as well as the possibility of a confusion of name, which could adversely affect the 'Shipwreck Institution'. For some time the affairs of the two organizations did run parallel but all was happily cleared up when the older body was completely reorganized during the course of the 1850s.

Meanwhile, there was to be a shock, of a kind such as has so often galvanized people or concerns in danger of becoming moribund. It came in December 1849. On the 4th of the month the locally run South Shields life-boat, after reaching a wreck not far from the mouth of the Tyne, capsized. Twenty out of her double crew of twenty-four men, chiefly pilots, were drowned. Mourning for their loss was made all the sharper because of the pace at which the volume of British shipping was growing, with attendant risk of loss, in every part of the world.

Within a few months of this episode, Richard Lewis, an energetic young barrister, became Secretary of the 'Shipwreck Institution' at a salary of £120 a year, 'to be increased annually ten pounds till it shall amount to £150 provided he continued to give satisfaction and the funds of the Institution would justify it'. Lewis was to hold office for more than thirty years. In the opinion of his successor, Charles Dibdin, who was himself at the heart of things for almost as long, he 'made' the organization, wrote the first history, and saw the annual income rise from a few hundred pounds to £58,000. Such a change was eloquent, not to say astonishing.

Lewis's appointment coincided with the final years of the Chairmanship of Thomas Wilson, who had been voted into office at the time of the original foundation. He was by now in his eighties, but was as regular in attendance, and as conscientious and interested in all the proceedings, as when in his prime. Although the elevated post of President remainded unfilled, early in 1851 Wilson had the idea of approaching the Duke of Northumberland, known for his expert knowledge of maritime affairs, to see whether he could be persuaded to take over. The Duke agreed.

This proved to be a turning-point. Wilson chaired a meeting very shortly before his death, in October 1852, and it was fitting that he, who had done so much for the Institution, should have lived to see a man presiding who would revitalize all its affairs.

Wilson's successor as Chairman of the Committee, Alderman Thompson, iron-master, shipowner and a former Lord Mayor of London, was not long in office. He died in 1854. Thomas Baring M.P., a member of the well-known financial house, Chairman of Lloyd's, and twice Chancellor of the Exchequer, took his place. With such men in control, who could have doubted that the Institution would enjoy a vigorous revival?

2

The Royal National Life-boat Institution

Although Sir William Hillary did not survive to see the great renewal of interest in his Institution, he lived until 1847, continuing almost to the last with his personal efforts to save life at sea. His record of three gold awards was unequalled until, during the present century, Henry Blogg of Cromer, who by general consent was the most outstanding life-boat coxswain of all time, won three gold medals and four silver. Blogg had to encounter peril not only from the sea but from dangers arising from two world wars which were mercifully unknown to Hillary: moreover, by Blogg's era the standard of gallantry, in the life-boat service always high, was still higher than during the era when Hillary was active.

In a single year, 1828, Hillary, his son Augustus (who was to receive the silver medal), and a Manx coxswain, Isaac Vondy, took part in saving a total of 62 people from three different ships. In 1830 the mail steamer *St George* was driven on to the rocks in a November gale. During the course of the rescue which followed Hillary was washed overboard from the life-boat and badly hurt. He was hauled back by the crew, which was fortunate as, like many rescuers of his own time and later, he could not swim. He helped to save 22 from the steamer.

At the age of over sixty Hillary took part in a sortie in which 54 men were saved from the *Parkfield*, a Liverpool ship which had gone aground in Douglas Bay in a south-easterly gale: and when over seventy he was still able, according to one who knew him, to launch a boat single-handed in an appreciable swell, jump over the stern, pick up the oars and take her out to sea. By the time of his death he had helped in the rescue of well over three hundred people. Although Hillary set a high value on his own services, for he was without false modesty, many surviving letters show him to have been generous in his praise of the courage of his crews. He was able to ensure that their efforts were recognized by the Institution.

Of the many testimonials Hillary received, perhaps none was

more valued than a letter to him from Teignmouth in 1831 from the hand of Admiral Lord Exmouth. This officer, in his earlier years when he was Sir Edward Pellew, had won a reputation for bravery second to none even in the classic era of the sailing Navy, and particularly for his spectacular efforts in saving life from shipwreck. Hillary had sent him an account of the *St George*, and on hearing about it, the Admiral wrote as follows:

> When I reflect on your Age, and see with what promptitude, energy and perseverance you eagerly embrace the dangers which would have appalled the boldest heart of Youth, I feel lost in admiration, wonder and surprise, and ask myself if your heart must not have received the Noble impulse from Divine inspiration, in the cause of Humanity and Christian exertion.

If, today, such sentiments may seem to have the flavour of hyperbole, there is no doubt that they were sincere, and that they were addressed by one fine man to another.

Manxmen greatly value their association with Hillary, and his influence is very much alive in Douglas. The life-boat flag flies above the Tower of Refuge in the bay and, on occasion, above his old home, Fort Anne, which is now an hotel, and is set in a fine position overlooking the busy harbour and the slipway down which the life-boat is launched. Sir William's tomb, in St George's churchyard, has been restored by the Institution and bears its insignia, while in the Manx Museum there hangs a vivid oil painting, unsigned but almost certainly by the hand of the Liverpool marine painter Samuel Walters, of the notable rescues from the *St George*. This painting has a claim to be the first of a whole succession of works of art commemorating deeds performed since the founding of the Institution. (See illustration following page 36.)

There are currently five life-boat or sea rescue stations in the Isle of Man and, as everywhere within the sphere of the rescue service, family tradition continues strongly. The same names recur again and again in records of crews and operations, a fact which makes the life-boat world as intimate and close-knit as any other worth-while specialization. This fact had been apparent from the first, particularly during the formative years of the nineteenth century, when for the first time works of humanity and charity began to have an impact far beyond anything known to earlier generations, and could be shared in by an ever-increasing number of people of an altruistic and benevolent turn of mind.

Life-saving was much in the news in mid-century. This is well illustrated by the references to the subject in the work of the most popular writer of the day, Charles Dickens. For instance, *David Copperfield*, published during 1849 and the following year, contained, in a memorable scene, the drowning of the villain Steerforth after shipwreck, and the death of Ham Peggotty in trying to save him. And in *Household Words*, the weekly journal started in 1850 by Dickens, he paid a spirited tribute to the boatmen who made rescues from ships lost on the Goodwin Sands.

> These are among the bravest and most skilful mariners that exist. Let a gale rise and swell into a storm; let a sea run that might appal the stoutest heart that ever beat . . . let them hear through the angry roar the signal guns of a ship in distress, and these men spring up with an activity so dauntless, so valiant and heroic, that the world cannot surpass it.

Yet nothing, not even the encouragement of the Press, helped forward the affairs of the Institution more than the activity of the fourth Duke of Northumberland. In 1851, the year he took office as President, he offered a prize of a hundred guineas for the best model of a life-boat, and a further sum towards the cost of construction. This was to have much influence on design, and it was to attract 280 entries, some of which came from abroad. It was also an advantage that the competition took place in the year of the Great Exhibition, which would provide a platform of publicity for new ideas, inventions and designs of every kind.

The Duke, who was born in 1792, was an exceptionally able man. Independently of the rank and wealth to which he succeeded in the year of Sir William Hillary's death, he had shown himself to be a practical seaman. He had joined the Navy as a youngster, had served under Collingwood in the Mediterranean, won the approbation of that highly critical Tynesider, who called him 'a fine young man', and had risen, by the year 1815, to the rank of post-captain. Although he had no operational command at sea after the Napoleonic wars ended, he accompanied Sir John Herschel's scientific expedition to the Cape of Good Hope in 1834, and reached the admirals' list by seniority in 1850. Two years later, during the short administration of Lord Derby, he was for some months First Lord of the Admiralty, thus doubly justifying the name by which he was often known, the 'Sailor Duke'. The life-boat service was not the only enterprise to benefit from his informed enthusiasm: he was the patron, friend and munificent supporter of Edward William Lane, the leading Arabic scholar of his day.

The life-boat, as a type, already had a respectable history, and one fact about it had been proved: there could be no single ideal, the best for all conditions. The reason was that the beaches from which boats had to be launched, by manual strength, or from a horse-drawn platform, or by a combination of these, differed widely. What would do for one stretch of coast would not necessarily suit another.

It is usual, in considering the life-boat's evolution, to dip a flag in salute to Monsieur de Bernières, Controller-General of Roads and Bridges in France. He devised a craft which, with nine men aboard, would neither sink when filled with water nor capsize when hove down so that the top of the mast was submerged. The date was 1765, but no evidence exists that the boat was ever put to practical use. Other countries besides France may claim to have produced pioneer life-boat designers, but what is beyond doubt is that before the close of the eighteenth century three Englishmen, Lionel Lukin, William Wouldhave and Henry Greathead, were involved in life-boat design or construction.

Lionel Lukin, who was not only the senior but much the longest-lived of the three, was born in Essex in 1742. By trade he was a coach-maker. He became Master of the Worshipful Company of Coachmakers in 1783 and some years later recorded how, when engaged in the study of what he believed would prove an 'unimmergible' boat, he had been encouraged by the interest shown by the Prince of Wales, afterwards George IV and the first Patron of the Institution.

Lukin bought a Norway yawl with which to experiment, tested her, and took out a patent in 1785. The main features of his conversion were a projecting cork gunwale, air-tight cases fore and aft as well as along the sides above and below the thwarts, and an iron keel. He entrusted the boat to a Ramsgate pilot to be tested in bad weather, but to his consternation never saw or heard of her again. It was believed that she crossed the Channel when nothing else would venture out, and he surmised that she had been engaged in smuggling and been captured or destroyed. Lukin then built a similar boat for himself. This he called the *Witch* in recognition of her prodigies of sailing in rough weather.

Although Lukin worked far away from the Northumbrians Wouldhave and Greathead, their paths sometimes crossed. When Archdeacon Sharp of Bamburgh asked Lukin to incorporate his ideas in a coble, the work of the southerner became known on the coast where Wouldhave and Greathead worked. Wouldhave's contribution was the idea that life-boats should be self-righting. He was not a shipwright but a house painter, a teacher of singing and a parish clerk. Greathead was a practical man who had the yard at South Shields from which the *Original* had come. The bow and stern of this craft were alike; she had no rudder but was steered by oar. She could be rowed in either direction, was clinker-built, that is, with overlapping planks, had a gunwale of cork held in position by copper fastenings, and a curved keel. She was not self-righting, had no air chambers, and no means of getting rid of water except by bailing. Greathead's later products incorporated many improvements. One of them, the *Zetland*, which was built in 1800 and sent to Redcar in 1802, was considered incomparable by her crew. She was in service for over eighty years, and is now preserved at Redcar as an historical relic. Another was bought for Bamburgh, where it was in competition with Lukin's converted coble. Yet another was ordered by the Duke of Atholl for Douglas, Isle of Man, where it was used when Sir William Hillary first settled there.

It was on the coast of Suffolk that Lukin had an opportunity to investigate Greathead's designs. In 1800 efforts were made to establish life-boats at Lowestoft, Bawdsey and elsewhere, Lord Nelson subscribing five guineas towards the Bawdsey boat. The Lowestoft boat was ordered from Greathead and she arrived in February 1801. She had a beam of 10 ft. 6 in. and was very like the *Original*. So was the Bawdsey boat, which was ready a month later.

The local beach men did not take to the design, which they said would not suit local conditions. So decided was their view that although in 1804 the Bawdsey boat, under the charge of a naval lieutenant serving with the Coastguard, rescued seven seamen and a woman from the brig *Pallas,* bound from Shields to London with coal, it was clear that, in Suffolk at any rate, Greathead would not make a fortune. Lukin was in Lowestoft in 1807 and examined the matter for himself. When discussing sailing with the beach men he was shown their favourite craft, broad-beamed, lug-rigged, and much used by pilots and for salvage work. He was assured that if a life-boat were built on similar lines and made unsinkable the Suffolk people would probably take to it.

The Suffolk Humane Society was now in being, and a boat was ordered from Batchelor Barcham of Lowestoft, to be built under Lukin's superintendence. She was named *Frances Ann*. She cost £200, lasted for over forty years and saved three hundred people. Her length was 40 ft. (keel 37 ft.) her beam 10 ft. and her depth of 3 ft. 6 in. was increased by an 8-inch movable wash-strake. She was a precursor of the Norfolk and Suffolk type of boat in which magnificent work was done during the course of the century.

Lukin had from the first been alive to a matter which soon became a precept with the Managing Committee of the Institution. He wrote: 'It is particularly advisable that all life-boats should be built of the form most approved by the pilots and seamen on the coast where they are to be used; as no one form will fit all shores.'

To these wise words should be added those of Coxswain Blogg of Cromer who, according to his biographer Cyril Jolly, stated, towards the end of his career: 'I have been a seaman all my life, and forty-five years of it have been spent as a life-boat man. From that experience it is impossible to guarantee any boat against disaster. It does not matter what type of boat it is, you cannot insure against accidents. All depends on the force of the storm and the judgement of the crew.'

Lukin lived until 1834, so that he was able to give his blessing to Hillary and the Institution. A tombstone at Hythe, Kent, bears the inscription that Lukin—

> Was the first who built a Life-boat, and was the original Inventor of that principle of safety, by which many lives and much property have been preserved from Shipwreck; and he obtained for it the King's patent in the year 1785.

It was Samuel Johnson who said that 'in lapidary inscriptions a man is not upon oath', and perhaps Lukin would have been too magnanimous to have been worried by the fact that there was already a memorial to Greathead, who died in 1816, stating that he was 'very generally. . . credited with designing and building the first Life-boat'. Actually Greathead had received a grant of £1,200 from Parliament for his work, as well as a gold medal from the Royal Society of Arts. There was yet another memorial, this time to Wouldhave, in St Hilda's church, South Shields, stating that he was the 'Inventor of that Invaluable blessing to Mankind, the Life-boat'. Wouldhave lived until 1821. Three distinct claimants at least signified the value of the invention.

Actually both Wouldhave and Greathead had been closely concerned with the first of various competitions for the design of an efficient life-boat. For, as a result of the overwhelming of the *Adventure* on the Herd Sands in 1789, the 'Gentlemen of the Lawe House' at South Shields, the moving spirit amongst whom was Nicholas Fairles, decided to offer a prize of two guineas, a modest enough sum even at that time, for the best model of a boat adapted for saving life at sea.

The model submitted by Wouldhave, roughly made from tin, and still preserved at South Shields, is an historical relic of much interest. Wouldhave had noticed on a country walk a woman who had been drawing water from a well. Her pail was full, and on the surface of the water floated a circular wooden dish which she had used to fill it. He tried to turn this dish over, but every attempt failed. It simply would not stay upside down. Its shape suggested the idea of the self-righting boat.

Wouldhave's model is 22 in. long, 9 in. broad, 4 in. deep amidships outside and 3 in. inside. It has a straight keel, and high peaked ends filled with water-tight cases containing cork, with cork along the sides. When the ingenious inventor took his creation to Lawe House, Mr Fairles held it up and said: 'What advantage do you say this thing possesses?'

Wouldhave, nettled at the tone in which the remark was made, answered: 'I say it will neither sink, nor go to pieces, nor lie bottom up. Will any others do as much?'

The Committee would not give the prize to the model as sent in, but the chairman offered Wouldhave the honorarium of a guinea, which he is said to have refused with contempt, saying afterwards (unless the local historian has credited him with a greater smoothness than was probable in the circumstances): 'Never mind, never mind; I know they have sense enough to adopt the good points of my model, and, though I am poor, if they refuse to give me the reward, I shall have the satisfaction of being instrumental in saving the lives of some of my fellow-creatures.'

Greathead, who also entered the competition, offered a model shaped like a raft, which was useless: however, although given no prize, he had the compensation of a chance to build a life-boat incorporating some of Wouldhave's ideas. It was not self-righting, was the same both ends, was steered by oar, had no air chambers and no water-relieving valves, and was given a cambered keel. The cost was £76. 9. 8. The boat, named the *Original*, appeared in January 1790 and became famous. She was 30 ft. by 10 ft., with ends 5 ft. 9 in. She gave admirable service for forty years, and was the means of saving many lives. Then, in 1830, having rescued the crew of the brig *Glatton*, which had been wrecked on the Black Middens, she was caught by a sea and driven against the rocks. She split in half, with the loss of two of her crew. Two years later Nicholas Fairles, who had been chiefly responsible for her construction, was murdered during the course of a riot concerning Parliamentary reform. His successors replaced the *Original* by the *Tyne* in 1833. This boat, after a rebuild in 1845, survived until 1887 and helped to save over a thousand people. Incidentally, Greathead had been of service to Lloyd's underwriters in reporting suspicious circumstances concerning the wreck of a ship off Calais in which he had served as carpenter. Lloyd's, in their turn, made Greathead's work known to the Duke of Northumberland.

In this time of experiment and practical rescue work at South Shields, matters had not been allowed to rest elsewhere. In 1807, the year that Lukin and Barcham's *Frances Ann* came into service on the East Anglian coast, the Royal Society of Arts, which had rewarded Greathead, gave a gold medal to Christopher Wilson of London for a 'self-balanced' boat which was stationed at Newhaven, where she did good work. The sides of Wilson's boat had outer and inner planking, with an air space between, the outer planking being carvel-built, the inner clinker-built.

Shortly after the founding of the Institution, George Palmer, M.P., who was Deputy Chairman, and enthusiastic about life-boat affairs, designed a craft which, although in essentials not in advance of Lukin's, was in demand for at least twenty years. It was so highly regarded by the Committee of Management that they later voted the designer the Institution's gold medal, together with a bar or 'boat' appended to it. Palmer, like the Duke of Northumberland, had had active experience at sea, and had been impressed when young by a narrow escape he had had from drowning, when in charge of a boat. After promotion, he not only made a fortune, but showed courage and initiative in fighting off some French frigates which attacked his ship. He had also, like Sir William Hillary, raised a land force in Essex, in his case one of yeomanry.

Palmer's boat had nine air-cases, three on each side, one in the bow and two in the stern, and four gunwale-cases made of tin. There were four scuppers, placed on either side. The length was 28 ft. 8 in. The boat could be steered by rudder or by oar, and she was fitted with two lug-sails. She could be made for £60, and this was one of the reasons why the type was popular. Some were ordered by the French Minister of Marine for use on the opposite side of the Channel.

Palmer, who lived until 1853 and was active in the affairs of the Institution until the time of his death at the age of eighty-one, was among those who considered the report of the committee appointed to adjudicate in the matter of the prize offered by the Duke of Northumberland. This folio appeared at the Duke's expense in 1851, a copy being presented to all the competitors, as well as to other interested people. The committee was chaired by Captain (later Rear-Admiral) John Washington, F.R.S. He had suggested the idea of the competition in the first instance, and a better choice could scarcely have been made. Washington, who as a young midshipman had served under one of Nelson's favourite captains, Sir Thomas Louis, was the originator of the wreck charts which were later to be published annually by the Institution and by the Board of Trade. He was a hydrographic surveyor, had been assistant to Sir Francis Beaufort, author of the well-known Beaufort Wind scale, and succeeded him as Hydrographer to the Navy. After his work for the Northumberland prize committee, the Government made use of a report he sent in, resulting from a visit to Denmark, Sweden and Russia, where he had gone on life-boat business.

Those who compiled and signed the competition report included, besides Washington, Isaac Watts, Assistant Surveyor of the Navy, John Fincham, Master Shipwright in H.M. Dockyard, Portsmouth, Commander W. Jerningham, R.N., and James Peake, Assistant Master Shipwright at H.M. Dockyard, Woolwich. The recommendations were endorsed by Sir Baldwin Walker, Surveyor of the Navy. It was a very official body, and although this lent it weight, it could have been criticized on the grounds that no representative of any organization outside the control of the Admiralty was included. Indeed, Captain John Ross Ward, R.N., the Institution's first Inspector of Life-boats, later remarked that none of the members had had actual experience of handling a life-boat in heavy surf.

The committee were able to reduce the number of entries worth sending to the Great Exhibition to fifty. The prize was given to James Beeching, then of Great Yarmouth, for his model of a righting boat which incorporated some of Wouldhave's ideas. She was to cost £250. She pulled twelve oars double-banked—i.e.. with rowers on six thwarts seated side by side—was fitted for lug-sail, being 'more efficient for sailing than for pulling', and was steered by rudder. A 6-inch cork fender ran round 7 in. below the gunwale. She was a heavy boat, weighing 67 cwt. including gear.

Judged by any standard, Beeching was a successful and versatile designer. After an apprenticeship at Bexhill he went to Flushing, where in 1819 he built a smuggling cutter *Big Jane*, which justified her name. At Great Yarmouth he built fishing boats, and even before the Northumberland committee awarded him the prize he embarked on the construction of a boat based on his model. She was 36 ft. by 9½ ft. by 3½ ft. and she could carry about seventy people. The self-righting characteristic was obtained by the height of the end air-cases, by the absence of side air-cases amidships, by 2½ tons of water ballast in tanks, and by an iron keel. Beeching sold his boat to the Ramsgate Royal Harbour Commissioners, who had earlier made use of a Greathead boat. Under their management she did sterling service for many years. She was much improved, after two years on station, by having her water ballast removed and solid ballast substituted. This was in accordance with recommendations from the Institution.

The Northumberland committee, while giving Beeching the prize, were not prepared to accept his design in every detail. Among their reservations they thought that, with the tanks knocked about by the seas, water ballast would somehow make its way into the air chambers. They therefore asked one of their members, James Peake, to design a boat which would include what they believed to be the best features of the various models they had had before them. It was to have cork instead of air chambers along the bottom, and no water ballast. Peake's boat underwent various changes in the course of time. As first built, at Woolwich Dockyard, she was 30 ft. long (length of keel 24 ft.), beam 8 ft., depth 3½ ft. She had both ends alike, and was steered by oar. She had a slightly raking stem and stern post, and was of rock elm, copper fastened. She pulled ten oars double-banked, or twelve if required, with eyebolts and rope grummets. There were side air-cases under the thwarts; raised ones 4 ft. long at the ends of the boat up to gunwale height, the tops covered with cork to prevent them being stove in if jumped upon. The cases were made of gutta-percha between two layers of thin wood. The boat could free herself of water in fifty-five seconds by means of eight tubes 6 in. in diameter, closed by self-acting valves, and she was self-righting within seven seconds. Her iron keel weighed 7 cwt, and her total weight was 46 cwt. Her draught when light was 15 in.—with crew, 18 in.—and her capacity was estimated at thirty people in addition to oarsmen, coxswain and bowman.

The boat did her trials at Brighton, where she was towed by an Admiralty tug in February 1852. She was in the charge of Captain John Ross Ward and a crew of coastguards. Among the numerous spectators were the Duke of Northumberland, and James Beeching. This was because, when taking office as President, the Duke had 'guaranteed to complete the coast of Northumberland from Berwick on Tweed to Tynemouth with life-boats and rocket apparatus . . . independently of the funds of the Institution', and he was keen to see that he acquired the best. The trials were satisfactory. The boat brought her crew ashore through heavy rollers without shipping water. She was then sent to a North Country station, where she did well.

The Duke ordered three of Peake's boats in addition to one of Beeching's. As knowledge began to accumulate, there was a reversion to many of Beeching's ideas, which was proof of his sagacity. Even so, two of his smaller boats, which had been ordered by the Shipwrecked Fishermen and Mariners Royal Benevolent Society, capsized with loss of life in 1852. The trouble was partly due to the fact that at the time of the accidents they were carrying too much sail, partly because the end air-cases had not been made properly water-tight. Moreover, as water ballast escaped, Peake's experiments were justified.

The winning model was given eighty-four marks out of a possible hundred, and it is interesting to note the drawbacks which the committee felt to be most apparent in earlier life-boats, and what points they were prepared to give for various features. The drawbacks were that boats 'did not right themselves in the event of being overset'; that they were usually too heavy to be readily launched, or 'transported along the coast in case of need'; that they did not rid themselves of water fast enough; and that they were 'very expensive'.

Considering the importance attached to self-righting, it is surprising that the committee did not grade this quality high in the order of marking. This was as follows:

Qualities as a rowing boat in all weathers	20
Qualities as a sailing boat	18
Qualities as a sea-boat; as, stability, safety, buoyancy forward for launching through a surf	10
Small internal capacity for water up to level of thwarts	9
Means of freeing boat of water readily	8
Extra buoyancy; its nature, amount, distribution, and mode of application	7
Power of self-righting	6
Suitableness for beaching	4
Room for, and power of, carrying passengers	3
Moderate rate of transport along shore	3
Protection from injury of bottom	3
Ballast, as iron (1), water (2), cork (3)	3
Access to stem or stern	3
Timber heads for securing warps to	2
Fenders, life-lines etc	1
	100

A note was added: 'It will be seen by the above formula (table of Values) that the committee consider it an essential requisite in a life-boat that she should be a good rowing-boat, able to get off the beach in any weather in which a boat can live at sea, as without the power of doing this, other good qualities are of no avail. To this, then, is awarded the highest number. As on the coast of Norfolk and Suffolk, where the wrecks generally occur on outlying sands, all the life-boats go off under sail, and as it was evident some of the best models were prepared with this view, it was considered that these also were entitled to be placed on a par with the boats built chiefly for pulling; but as rowing is the general rule around the coasts and sailing the exception, a slight difference was made in favour of the former.'

Apart from the successful James Beeching, other designers who got special mention in the report were Henry Hinks of Appledore (78 marks); J. & E. Pellew Plenty of Newbury, Berkshire (77 marks), who were increasingly specializing in ships' life-boats, and who had already, within Sir William Hillary's time, supplied the life-saving station at Douglas; William Teasdale of Great Yarmouth (75 marks); Harvey and Son of Ipswich (74 marks); George Farrow of South Shields (72 marks); Semmans and Thomas of Penzance (72 marks); George Palmer of Nazing Park, Essex (70 marks), who was of course already well known to the committee for his popular design; and William van Houten of Rotterdam (70 marks). Among the total of 37 designs specially noted appeared one from T. & J. White of Cowes who—with 62 marks—were fairly low down in the order. This firm, like that of Pellew Plenty, had experience with ships' life-boats and was much employed by the Admiralty. It was later to build a succession of fine boats for the Institution.

Next to those of Lukin, Greathead and Palmer, Pellew Plenty's boats were probably the best known to the Institution, which had at one time ordered several. In appearance they suggested miniature Norfolk wherries. They were very broad in the beam and had a straight keel. A thick cork lining on the bottom gave some protection on stony beaches. They were not self-righting, but they had six scuppers or draining valves which helped to free them of water. Two of the most successful were stationed at Skegness and Appledore. They cost £160.

Another type whose name has survived was the so-called Liverpool boat, built by Mr Costain of that port and favoured by the Liverpool Dock Trustees, who managed a number of life-boat stations. The Liverpool boat weighed only 37 cwt. and was easily transported. The length was 30 ft., the same as Greathead's *Original*, it pulled twelve oars double-banked, and was supplied with two sprit-sails and a jib. Extra buoyancy was given by twelve airtight casks secured along the sides of the craft, and a cork fender, leather-covered, ran all round, 6 in. below the gunwale.

The committee had therefore a very fair range of existing life-boats of one sort or another with which to compare Beeching's, and upon which to improve. As the choice fell upon what was in fact a development of existing practice, not upon a novelty, it could scarcely have been expected that the decision would please everybody. In fact it generated a certain amount of controversy, with as much heat in it as light. For example, among the ideas submitted but rejected was one for a tubular life-boat, which was sent in from Bala, North Wales. The boatmen of Rhyl were said to favour such a design, which could be described as a variation of the principle of the pontoon. It was at Rhyl that one of the two accidents to Beeching boats had occurred, the other being at Lytham. It was scarcely surprising therefore that the Rhyl men were on the lookout for something different.

The originators were two army officers, Henry Richardson, once of the 2nd Dragoon Guards, and his son Henry Thomas. They built a craft according to their own plans and sold it to the Portuguese, who placed it at Oporto as a successor to a Greathead boat which had been presented in 1800 by the second Duke of Northumberland. They then got William Lees of Manchester to build another, and this they sailed round the coast from Liverpool to Ramsgate, afterwards publishing *The Cruise of the Challenger Life-boat* with a dedication to 'The Life-boatmen of Great Britain and Ireland'. The journey, made in 1853, took eight weeks, and as these were during April, May and June they did not include the most tempestuous times of year.

The Richardsons were emphatic in their assertions that theirs was the best solution and, in accordance with local requests, a boat of the tubular sort was supplied in 1856 to Rhyl at a cost of £200. Seven years later another was sent to a newly opened station at New Brighton. The boats were 40 ft. and 42 ft. long respectively, and their two iron tubes were 3 ft. apart. They were divided into watertight compartments and their ends were curved so that they met at stem and stern. A platform or raft, with rope network surrounding it, was placed on top, and the crew rowed from this elevation.

The boat was not self-righting and it did not find general

favour. A special sort of carriage was required to transport it; a severe measure of exposure was entailed for the crew; and the boat was hard to manœuvre to windward. It was altogether an odd-looking experiment, and it is perhaps surprising that the New Brighton example was in use for as long as thirty-five years, and that Rhyl, which was supplied with another 34 ft. tubular boat as late in the century as 1896, remained so faithful. In fact, the type had a good record of life-saving.

* * *

While immense pains had been taken, ever since the early years of the nineteenth century, to evolve satisfactory designs for life-boats, much consideration had also to be given to their conveyance from the buildings where they were usually kept, to the most practicable places for them to be launched. These were generally to windward of the wrecks. Sometimes long distances were involved, and there are many cases on record of extraordinary journeys across country made by heavy boats on transporters. The most celebrated of these occurred in Devonshire at the end of the nineteenth century, when the Lynmouth life-boat was taken thirteen miles overland by men and horses. This exploit included the negotiation of a hill of 1,400 ft. with at times a gradient of one in four and a half. The journey was made by night with only oil lamps for light, and it took 10½ hours before the life-boat could even be launched.

Lord Henry Cholmondeley, a prominent subscriber to the Shipwrecked Fishermen and Mariners Royal Benevolent Society, devised a two-wheeled carriage for them but it did not prove satisfactory, too much weight having to be borne by the shaft horse. Much was expected, for these specially constructed carriages were essential in conditions which did not allow launching down a slipway, where boats could not lie afloat in sheltered water, or if beach conditions were exceptionally variable. In recent decades motor tractors have proved a satisfactory answer for towing these transporters, but in days when they had to be hauled by horses and human helpers, losses were not unknown among both before the boats were successfully got to sea. The process nearly always entailed risk, and there was the certainty of cold and drenching.

The competition of 1851 had shown little of value in the way of promising new designs for life-boat carriages, so, early in 1852, the Institution's Committee of Management asked the Master General and Board of Ordnance to permit an experimental transporter to be made at the Royal Arsenal, Woolwich. This was agreed to, and one was constructed, without charge on the Institution's funds, under the superintendence of Colonel Colquhoun of the Royal Artillery. It was sent to Cullercoats in Northumberland, but although practicable it was unnecessarily heavy, and it had been costly in material. However, as the local committee reported that it 'moved easily' on its four wheels, and as there was nothing better, three more were ordered for North Country stations. The carriages were built so that the limber or fore-carriage was detachable, and could serve to convey equipment. This also facilitated launching.

In 1856 the Royal Arsenal produced another design, from the hand of Lieutenant-Colonel Tulloch, which was executed by Ransomes and Sims of Ipswich. Tulloch also devised double harness for four horses, for use with the transporter. The Tulloch–Ransomes product was not only more satisfactory than Colquhoun's, but it incorporated a remarkable feature: wheels were fitted with what was described as 'Boydell's patent self-laying or endless railway' for use over the shingle at Dungeness, for which station the carriage was destined. This embodied the principle familiar today in the caterpillar tractor. Strong, flat plates attached to the wheels prevented them from sinking too far into certain types of difficult surface.

Boydell's was not a new idea, but it was important from the point of view of the Institution, and later in the century, it was improved upon by one of their own Inspectors, Lieutenant-Commander T. H. Gartside Tipping. The invention can be traced back at least as far as 1770 when Richard Lovell Edgeworth, father of Maria Edgeworth the novelist, propounded the notion of a 'footed wheel'. This was taken up some thirty years later by Thomas German, who patented a 'jointed track'. The device proved of little use at the time, but James Boydell's adaptation was the first of a continuing series which was to prove particularly useful when allied with mechanical propulsion. It was an early instance of the Committee of Management's eagerness to make use of advanced techniques where these were appropriate to its needs. The main difficulty with the system was that breakages were all too frequent.

* * *

Within two years of the advent of Richard Lewis as Secretary of the Institution two events took place which were to be of great importance to its future, and they were linked. The first was the issue, in March 1852, of a journal, the *Life-boat*; the second was the decision to appoint Captain (later Vice-Admiral) John Ross Ward as Inspector of Life-boats. Ward was the son of a naval officer who had served in the Napoleonic wars and later helped to develop Southampton Docks. The captain himself, expert in handling boats in heavy seas, was also an inventor who very soon designed an efficient cork life-jacket which became standard equipment. He had various useful contacts inside and outside the Navy and the Admiralty, and he and Lewis made an almost ideal combination for producing a specialist periodical. Lewis looked after the general editing and administration; Ward supplied authoritative technical backing.

More surprisingly, Ward had a turn for verse. Later on in life he composed a 'Life-boat Song' which had a vogue for some years. It was set to music by C. H. Purday. The first verse ran:

> Fine ships and boats of many kinds
> There are upon the sea;
> Some worked by sail, and some by steam,
> And other sorts there be.
>
> *Chorus:*
> But of all the bravest ships and boats
> That stem the briny wave,
> The Life-boat is the boat of boats
> Built human lives to save. . . .

The first number of the *Life-boat* was published by Charles Knight of Fleet Street, a pioneer of inexpensive literature. It was priced at 1½d, 'so as to place it within the reach of every boatman around our shores'. The editorial and general offices of the Institution were then in John Street, Adelphi, off the Strand in London, at first, from 1851–1855, at No 20, and later from 1855 to 1904, at No

14. It was stated that it was 'proposed to issue monthly, or occasionally as circumstances may seem to point out'. Like all vigorous journals the *Life-boat* was in fact subject to fairly continual change, not only in price—the first suggestion was optimistic: the charge was soon raised to 2d. and was later stabilized at 3d.—but in content, size and times of issue. A monthly appearance soon proved impractical, and within a few years the journal had settled down as a quarterly. The April issues, priced at a shilling, included the Institution's Annual Report, with details of rescues, stations, local committees and subscribers. There were annual Wreck Charts of the kind devised by Rear-Admiral Washington, and, in course of time, line drawings of approved types of life-boat, transporters, and many others items of equipment appeared regularly. News of incidents afloat was a regular feature, and so were lists of awards. The continuing series of the *Life-boat* has in fact provided the source for a whole library of recorded instances of bravery and devotion at sea.

Lewis sometimes signed obituaries, and Ward was undoubtedly responsible for a succession of articles on the techniques of life-saving and other relevant subjects, though he generally published them anonymously. He and Lewis were jointly responsible for attracting contributions from outside the ranks of the Institution's full-time service. Among the most notable was a series by Vice-Admiral Robert Fitz Roy (nowadays usually written as Fitzroy) a member of the Committee of Management, on weather forecasting. This began in 1862 and continued intermittently until Fitz Roy's death three years later. Even then, Lewis was able to secure a paper, which appeared posthumously, on Storm Warnings. Besides explaining how the weather operated, Fitz Roy included in his first article a sentence as relevant today as when it was written: 'These forecasts,' he said, 'are not prophecies: they are carefully drawn estimates of average possibilities, obtained by inter-comparison of facts, observed, telegraphed, and duly weighed, according to known laws.'

Fitz Roy was responsible for the issue of barometers to life-boat stations, made to his specification by Negretti and Zambra. One of his most important articles, published in October 1862, was illustrated with drawings of storm-cones and night lantern signals, both of which types of warning stood the test of time. The great hydrographer-meteorologist, always associated with Charles

AN APPEAL

TO THE

BRITISH NATION,

ON THE

HUMANITY AND POLICY

OF FORMING

A National Institution,

FOR THE PRESERVATION OF

LIVES AND PROPERTY FROM SHIPWRECK.

BY SIR WILLIAM HILLARY, BART.

LONDON:
PRINTED FOR G. AND W. B. WHITTAKER,
AVE-MARIA-LANE.

1823.

Title-page of Sir William Hillary's
'Appeal to the British Nation . . .' 1823

Medal of the Royal National Life-boat Institution.

Obverse: portrait of Sir William Hillary as Founder, by A. G. Wyon. Reverse: Scene of rescue, by William Wyon, R.A.

'Sir William Hillary and Manx Life-boat going to the help of the steamer *St George* in Douglas Bay, 1830.' Painting probably by Samuel Walters of Liverpool

Grace Darling (1815–42), by William Joy (1803–67)

Lord Prudhoe, later Duke of Northumberland, President of the R.N.L.I., 1851–65. Miniature of 1844 by Sir William Charles Ross, RA, hitherto unpublished

'Life-boat and Manby Rocket Apparatus Going to a Stranded Vessel Making a Signal of Distress, 1827.' By J. M. W. Turner, R.A.

Model of Beeching's prize design life-boat, 1851. She was 36 feet in length, with an iron keel and raised air cases fore and aft. She pulled 12 oars and was rigged with a lug foresail and mizen

Life-boat of 1872 built by Forrestt of Limehouse for the United States Revenue Marine Service. Length 30 feet, pulled by 12 oars, and built of double diagonally planked mahogany. The cost was about £250

Vice-Admiral J. Ross Ward,
Chief Inspector of
Life-boats, 1852–83

Richard Lewis,
Secretary, R.N.L.I., 1850–83

Sir George Shee,
Secretary, R.N.L.I., 1910–31

Charles Dibdin, Secretary,
R.N.L.I., 1883–1910,
in Court dress

Darwin and his voyage in HMS *Beagle*, was not the only distinguished Fellow of the Royal Society to enrich the earlier years of the *Life-boat*. In October 1863 Staff Commander F. J. Evans, Superintendent of Compasses to the Admiralty, contributed a paper on the subject in which he was most expert.

There were also to be found in the pages of the journal the first announcements of approved ways of doing things, some of which in course of time became traditional. For example, as early as the issue of July 1862 there was a description of how the Institution's life-boats should be painted.

> *Outside:* floor white to the load-water-line, and sheered upwards at bow and stern; upper-works, sky blue to gunwale; moulding or wale, vermilion. *Inside:* deck, thwarts and air cases, white.

Sixty years later, a protest signed by a number of eminent artists noted that the particular tone of supposedly 'Oxford' blue then in use was in fact excruciating!

The Annual Reports were by no means entirely factual, for it became the custom of the Institution to invite addresses from eminent people who were not necessarily honorary officers, though in most cases they were so. For instance, in 1861 the Chair was taken by Admiral the Earl of Hardwicke; in 1864 by Sir John Pakington, who was twice First Lord of the Admiralty; and three years later the Prince of Wales agreed to preside. This encouraging mark of royal interest was strengthened by the appearance in the Chair of the Duke of Edinburgh a few years later. The Duke, who made a full-time career in the Navy, became a member of the Committee of Management in the 1880s in his capacity of Admiral Superintendent of Naval Reserves.

* * *

There has been only one period in its history when the Institution has not relied entirely on its own exertions, backed by the generosity of the public, to maintain its service. This was between 1854 and 1869, fifteen years out of a century and a half. Self-help was a precept of the Victorian era, and it has always been applied in the affairs of the Institution. Had it not assumed the task of life-saving at sea, the cost would have fallen on the Board of Trade and thus, ultimately, on the tax-payer.

In 1854 however, and for some years after, its finances were not such that the organization could afford to forgo the benefit of an annual subsidy, at first of £2,000, payable from the Mercantile Marine Fund. This Fund was administered by the Board of Trade, which was also given charge of the rocket and mortar stations. The money was used for retaining fees for coxswains, and for rewards to crews in cases where these were merited.

The acceptance of State help was one of the results of a Merchant Shipping Act which became law in 1854, and was for the better regulation of maritime affairs. It was stipulated that the Board of Trade should assist in life-saving 'proportional to private and local exertions'. It was also emphasized that finance should be channelled through one central agency, 'which . . . would be one of the Societies already established'. This was an indication that the functions of the Shipwrecked Fishermen and Mariners Royal Benovelent Society and of the 'Shipwreck Institution' would need to be more clearly defined.

The two bodies, which had long been in close touch, agreed that the older body should be primarily responsible for life-saving measures, the Benevolent Society taking charge of people after rescue. The possibility of confusion in name was cleared up by the suggestion, which was readily agreed, that the Institution should be known as 'The Royal National Life-boat Institution founded in 1824 for the Preservation of Life from Shipwreck'. The Benevolent Society thereupon gave the Institution charge of its nine life-boats, nine boat-houses, and five boat carriages. The boats had been at Teignmouth, Llanelly, Tenby, Portmadoc, Rhyl, Lytham (two), Hornsea and Newhaven. Close liaison continued, and members of the Institution were encouraged to join the Benevolent Society.

The last issue of the *Life-boat* as the 'Journal of the National Shipwreck Institution' appeared in October 1854, and in January 1855, following the decision to change the name, it appeared as the 'Journal of the Life-boat Institution'. Six years later, it was able to print the text of the Charter of Incorporation authorized by Queen Victoria and dated 24 April 1860, which seemed to set the seal on everything which had gone before.

In the same year, the firm of Ransomes and Sims, which had made the special life-boat transporter for Dungeness under Colonel Tulloch's superintendence, subscribed the sum of £500 for a life-boat station and a boat to be called the *Ipswich*. She was the first to be sponsored for the Institution's service by an inland town. She was launched on the River Orwell on 29 May and was sent to the station then at Thorpeness, Suffolk. The originator of this gesture was W. Bateman Byng, and a letter written on behalf of the clerks, foremen and workmen addressed to their employers stated:

> We believe . . . that if the claims of this truly excellent Institution were taken up by the Principals of similar establishments throughout the Kingdom, in the same spirit which we are happy to recognise in you, the result would be such as we should all truly rejoice at.

With such evidence of public interest in life-saving at sea (and it was clear that this was growing yearly), it might have been anticipated that the effect of the acceptance of a State subsidy would not be wholly good. This was so, even from the point of revenue. For instance, Trinity House and the Committee of Lloyd's, which had been contributing handsomely, did not continue the same support. They feared an increasing measure of Government control, of which they were wary.

One of the Board of Trade's conditions of help to the Institution and to independent life-boat stations supported by other bodies such as Harbour Commissioners, was that a senior Coastguard officer or an official of the Board itself should be a member of the local committees, and that all applications for payments should be counter-signed by him. Another enjoined that continued efforts should be made to raise funds voluntarily. If the Institution's own Committee of Management had needed any stimulus to free itself as soon as possible from any measure of control from outside, it would have been this. Fund-raising became a primary task, and in the end it was successful. The spirit was very different from that which rules today, when a subsidy of some sort for voluntary Societies is generally a desideratum and often a necessity. But it was a very different age.

The case of Whitby provides as good an example as any of the passionate determination to be independent as long as possible. This Yorkshire sea-port, once the home of Captain James Cook, had had a life-boat service at least since 1802. In 1854, when the question arose of help from the Board of Trade, the local committee stated:

> . . . that they have at this port two efficient life-boats and boat-houses with an ample fund for contingencies—that hitherto they have not met with any difficulty in manning the boats or compensating the crews, and that the only objection they have to offer to the scheme proposed arises from the fact that any compulsory addition to their Board might create jealousy and affect the unanimity which has hitherto prevailed.

For nearly sixty years, from 1802 until 1861, the people of Whitby financed and managed their own rescue service, including a life-boat called *The Fisherman's Friend* which was afloat for forty years. The great trial came on 9 February 1861 when some half-dozen ships were seen to be in distress near the dangerous entrance to the harbour, in the course of a very heavy gale. A new life-boat, built only the previous year, went out under the command of Coxswain James Storr.

At least five times the life-boat was called for. Each time she returned with the crew of one or other of the vessels in trouble. At last, only a final journey seemed necessary. The coxswain put out again, but, when the boat was sixty yards from the pier, she was overset by a huge sea. Every member of the crew was drowned except one. His name was Henry Freeman, and he owed his life to the fact that, unlike his companions, he was wearing a cork life-belt of the kind designed by Captain Ross Ward, which had been sent to Whitby a few years earlier as an example of the belts worn by the Institution's own crews.

Shortly after the disaster—news of which had shaken the country—the Whitby committee recorded a resolution that 'the utility of the Whitby Life-boat Association would be much increased by unity with the Royal National Life-boat Institution'. This resolution was welcomed in London, and in April 1861 a new 32 ft. self-righting boat was sent to Yorkshire for use at Whitby, Henry Freeman later becoming coxswain. If it had taken a tragedy to cause Whitby to link up with the Institution, the association became so firm with time that the station has maintained a life-saving record of splendid achievement, including the award of six gold medals. Moreover, as within eight years the Institution had itself reasserted its independence, the 'unanimity which had hitherto prevailed' on the local committee was in no danger of disturbance.

The increase in the number of life-boat stations was gradual, and the measure of control exercised by the Institution itself varied much, since its policy has always been as flexible as possible. A Select Parliamentary Committee, of which the Chairman was George Palmer, was told in 1843 that there were 85 life-boats in existence, under numerous authorities and in widely different states of efficiency. Eight years later, when the Duke of Northumberland's prize was awarded, there were said to be 95, 19 of them run by the Institution, but many in a sorry state, including four in the Isle of Man which had 'been allowed to fall into decay', eight in Scotland (some 'quite unserviceable') and eight in Ireland which were all 'inefficient'.

By 1853, just before the Board of Trade subsidy began, there were 108 in England, 7 in Scotland, and 10 in Ireland. By 1865 the Institution could claim to be running 144 boats, but sometimes this was only partially true. For instance, the annals of the Suffolk Humane Society, which had made such interesting experiments with the earlier types of life-boat, show that in 1855 the managers asked the Institution to meet the cost of new boats, but they themselves still financed the running of the stations. It was not until 1873 that the Society handed over completely, and not until 1892 that it held its final meeting. Similar situations were to be met with all over the country.

The Institution's own total of stations and boats rose steadily, and growth was continuous until, during the course of the present century, the capabilities of the marine engine enabled the number to be reduced, since the modern life-boat had far greater range and scope than its rowing and sailing predecessors.

Receipts varied greatly. The Institution got £2,468 covering the time of the Great Exhibition; then there was a sudden drop until, from 1856 onwards, the curve rose fairly steadily from £4,893 to no less that £41,718 in 1866—a ten-fold increase within a decade, but a total which was not exceeded for many years. Although the number of boats in service rose irrespective of income, it was certain that in course of time the Institution would need to tap new resources if it was to keep pace with ever-growing commitments, to say nothing of extending them.

That this extension was necessary was indicated by the siting of stations, as noted, for instance, in the chart published by the Secretary, Richard Lewis, in 1874, fifty years after the original foundation. Although there were Institution life-boats shown in plenty along the southern and eastern coasts of England, the areas of dense traffic and continual calls, there were none between Margate and Aldeburgh. Another gap was in the north of Scotland between Lossiemouth and Thurso. A huge distance divided the easterly Thurso station from that of Ardrossan in south-west Ayrshire, showing that the whole north-west coast of Scotland was not provided for. Although the south and east coasts of Ireland were well taken care of, the north was not well off. Indeed there was no station run by the Institution between Greencastle at the sea entrance to Loch Foyle and Valentia in County Kerry.

Expansion had been among the principal aims of the fourth Duke of Northumberland during his term as President, which extended from 1851, when the prize he offered did so much to improve the life-boat, until his death in 1865. Although his loss was felt severely, the interest of his family was to be continued, for the position of President was taken over by Earl Percy, heir to the fifth Duke, who had succeeded to the title at an advanced age. The new President became sixth Duke of Northumberland in 1867. In addition to his work for the Institution he held public office, successively, in the Admiralty, as Vice-President of the Board of Trade, and as Lord Privy Seal.

* * *

To mark the granting of the Institution's Charter in 1860, Captain Ross Ward delivered a lecture on 17 January 1862 at the the Royal United Service Institution. He gave details of the types of life-boat in use in the years during which he had been responsible for ensuring their efficiency. The address was most timely, for the decade 1850–60 had been a particularly appropriate one for a vigorous policy in life-saving matters. In 1851, partly as the result of a disaster involving the heavily laden passenger ship *Royal Adelaide* off Margate, in which no fewer than 428 lives were lost, the Board of Trade prepared figures of marine casualties for the entire coast-line, and submitted them to Parliament. They showed a total for the previous year of 692 vessels wrecked and, in 1851, of 701. This rose to the appalling total of 1,115 ships lost, of which a high proportion were colliers, together with 900 lives, in

1852. These figures did not include British-registered shipping lost outside territorial waters, which would have nearly doubled the tally. The losses were categorized into 'total wrecks', 'sunk by leaks or collisions', 'abandoned', and—the largest class—'stranded and damaged so as to require them to discharge cargo', and all 'within the seas of the British Isles'. In January 1852 alone, a disastrous gale which lasted five days caused the loss of 257 vessels, together with 486 lives.

It was small wonder that public interest increasingly focused on rescue work at sea. The matter was re-emphasized with particular force in 1859. In October of that year the coast of Great Britain was hit by what became known as the '*Royal Charter*' gale, one of the worst on record. The name derived from the tragic loss of the Liverpool and Australian Steam Navigation Company's passenger vessel *Royal Charter* in Moelfre Bay, North Wales, in which 459 out of a total of 498 on board perished. The gale was at its height on 24 October, and during a twenty-four hour period 195 vessels were shattered and strewn round the coast, or were sunk. Neither wind nor sea returned to anything like normal until 1 November, when the country was shocked to learn from the newspapers that during a ten-day period the sea had claimed 248 ships and 686 lives.

The Institution recognized an act of gallantry which occurred during the *Royal Charter* wreck by awarding its gold medal to Joseph Rodgers, a Maltese seaman who at the utmost risk swam ashore from the ship through the boiling surf with a line. Unfortunately the vessel broke up in the huge seas before many could be saved by this means, but it was one of the many instances when the Committee were able to reward bravery outside the ranks of the Institution's own service.

By the time he gave his lecture, Captain Ross Ward had decided the relative importance of the special qualities essential to a life-boat. They were:

1. General lateral stability
2. Speed against heavy seas
3. Facility for launching and for taking the shore
4. Immediate self-discharge of water
5. Self-righting if upset
6. Strength
7. Stowage room

This was a somewhat different emphasis from the characteristics stressed by the adjudicators at the time of the Northumberland prize, but Ross Ward's observations were the result of experience of a range which no one else could then equal.

In surveying the Institution's resources, the lecturer listed first what he described as the 'North Country Life-boats'. These were Greatheads and later adaptations. There were eighteen still in service, the oldest being the Redcar *Zetland*, of which he was able to say 'no accident has happened to her, the boatmen have unbounded confidence in her, and would not exchange her for any other boat that could be given to them'.

Then came the 'Norfolk and Suffolk type', the oldest among which, a boat dating from 1833, had only recently been condemned. 'As exclusively sailing boats,' said the lecturer, 'I believe them to be unequalled. Yet, for various causes, there is perhaps scarcely any other part of the coast for which they could be useful, unless on Deal Beach, for service on the Goodwin Sands.'

Third came the Peake boats, to which Ross Ward referred as 'Beeching's life-boat, improved by Mr Peake'. There were a hundred of these in service, and they had become the standard self-righting type approved by the Institution. Regular though not exclusive arrangements had by then been made with a firm of builders, Messrs Forrestt of Limehouse. They were so successful and so reasonable in their charges that within a very few years they were asked to supply a number to the French Government. Later on, in 1872, they supplied a 30 ft. self-righting boat to the United States Revenue Marine Service. This survives at the Mariner's Museum, Newport News, Virginia. (See illustration following page 36.)

Other types which were given mention were the Richardson tubulars, and a ship's life-boat built by Messrs White of Cowes. Of this product, Ross Ward said: 'I believe it to be the best ship's life-boat yet adopted; but as a coast life-boat it is not considered to possess sufficient extra buoyancy or means of self discharge of water.'

Ross Ward concluded that as the result of the Institution's ceaseless experiments, mainly with Peake's boats, it was entitled to claim as its own, and as a matter of justice to those concerned in improvements, a design which he described as 'The Self-Righting Life-boat of the National Life-boat Institution'. This would in future be supplied to any station which did not specifically request a different type.

A typical nineteenth-century life-boat house, in the Early English tradition of Gothic architecture. For all its functional purpose it had a distinctly ecclesiastical appearance. Some still survive.

Concurrently with the lecture, and as a regular item at the time and for many years to come, the *Life-boat* printed line illustrations of this standard boat, which was usually 33 ft. by 8 ft., but occasionally larger, including a sheer plan, a deck plan, a body plan and a midships sectional view. Transporters were also regularly shown, with details of their arrangements, and with plans showing top, side and rear views. At times a life-boat house was also illustrated. This was something of a curiosity. It had three narrow side windows, with arches in the Early English style of Gothic Architecture, and a number of small buttresses. For all its secular purpose, the building was distinctly ecclesiastical in appearance, and very much of its period. A few survive; for instance, there is a good example at Wells in Norfolk, but such rarities have to be sought out. As a rule, they have disappeared and have been replaced by efficient modern structures.

* * *

The work accomplished for the Institution by Captain Ross Ward and Richard Lewis was of such importance that it is perhaps appropriate to consider, after Ross Ward's lecture, the principal work to come from Lewis, which followed twelve years after the Chief Inspector's review. This was his *History of the Life-boat and its Work*. It was published in 1874 to mark the fiftieth year of the Institution. It also marked the author's first twenty-four years in office. Although Lewis's book was largely technical, it included an account of the organization which the author served. Moreover it set out, in the form of appendices, the current regulations. These had been evolved over many years and had been published from time to time in the *Life-boat*, as well as in separate form, and were subject to continuous amendment in detail. Practical advice on such matters as resuscitation was also included. The steel engravings with which the book was illustrated were evocative of what may be regarded as an heroic era of sea-rescue. Life-boats were shown under oar in the frontispiece and on the title-page, and the vessels in distress were sailing ships, which at the time of publication were still predominant, certainly in the coastal trade, which provided the occasion of so many incidents. There was, however, one life-boat shown under canvas, and a drawing of a two-funnelled steam tug towing a life-boat to windward of a ship in trouble.

Lewis was careful to emphasize, in his preface, a tradition which endures—the fund of good-will which the organization had in newspaper offices, and thus 'the immense assistance rendered to this Institution by the Press'. He was able to include some accounts of well-known rescues from printed sources.

The Press had direct contact not only with headquarters, but with the local committees, on which devolved the management and maintenance of life-boat stations. The regulations stated that these were to consist, if practicable, of not fewer than five residents, to be elected annually. The Inspecting Commander of the particular Coastguard Division, or the nearest Coastguard officer, was to be invited to join, but did not, as during the years of the subsidy, claim membership as of right.

Crews were to consist of a coxswain superintendent, an assistant coxswain, a bowman, and as many boatmen as the boat pulled oars. Whenever possible, double the number of men required were to be invited to become crew members, to ensure an adequate reserve. They were to consist of local fishermen or other boatmen. Subject to Admiralty permission, any Coastguard who might volunteer was to be welcomed.

There were regulations for salvage, remuneration, exercises, signals, committee meetings, and for the form of reports to the Institution. It was made clear that while the method of approach to a wreck was left to the coxswain's judgement, the preservation of life was to be his *sole* consideration, and that he was 'on no account to take in goods or merchandise which might endanger the safety of his boat, and the lives of those entrusted to his charge'.

The section on towing belongs to a particular and fairly short span of life-boat history, when steam on occasion supplemented oar and sail. Crews under tow were recommended to sit well aft, 'to weight the boat by the stern, excepting one man well forward with a small hatchet by him, ready to cut the tow rope in a moment if it should become necessary'. The Liverpool boats, which were often in tow of paddle-tugs and other steamers, 'usually sheer off and tow well on the quarter, so as to be out of the way of the paddle-wheels'. Tows were always easier 'against a heavy head-sea than away from one', the Liverpool coxswains stating that 'in a long, heavy sea, they considered a boat more safe in tow than under sail, but in a short sea with irregular break, as at the meeting of currents or on the edge of banks, the contrary'. They added: 'The danger when towing a Life-boat before a heavy sea may be much lessened by towing a drogue astern of the boat, to prevent her running ahead in front of a sea (at risk of damage against the towing-vessel), and to keep a more equable station on the tow-rope.'

Regulations with regard to salvage were most explicit. The Institution's boats were not, as a general rule, 'to be employed to save property, so as to interfere with private enterprise'. But when other aid was not at hand, crews might consider that the life-boats were loaned for that purpose. Those participating 'will look to be paid by the owners of the property saved, and not by the Institution'. Here a clear distinction was made from the rewards normally given by the Institution for life-saving.

Boats were never to be launched expressly for salvage purposes without the sanction of the local committee or its representative. 'When, however, a Life-boat has been launched to save life, and on reaching a wrecked vessel, it is thought that the latter may also be saved with the aid of the Life-boat's crew, the coxswain will use his own discretion in allowing his crew to afford such aid or not.' But on such occasions the boats were not to be exposed to serious risk of damage or destruction' nor were 'exorbitant demands' to be made of the owners of property.

Finally, to cover the risk of harm to the boats, two shares of all salvage payments received—'that is, a sum equal to the shares of two men'—were to be made over to the Institution.

In an explanatory statement to the owners of distressed vessels with regard to these regulations, the Institution emphasized that as its first object was always to save life, preference in the matter of salvage would always be given to private enterprise. Nevertheless, where from circumstances the life-boat was the only likely means by which vessels or property could be saved

> . . . it is considered that such an arrangement cannot but be beneficial to all parties:—the owners or insurers of a valuable ship and cargo are fortunate in having their property saved at a small percentage—the crew of the Life-boat, always poor men, receive a handsome payment, calculated to increase their attachment to the Life-boat service—whilst the Institution obtains a sufficient amount to cover the risk of damage to its boat.

It so happened that within a few years of the appearance of Lewis's treatise, the Institution gave an example of how it would deal with any serious transgression of its salvage rules. On 25 November 1883 the Eastbourne life-boat rescued eleven of the crew of the Norwegian barque *New Brunswick,* which was wrecked off Birling Gap in Sussex in a south-westerly gale. The Institution gave the crew double pay, and they also received £20 from the donor of their boat and some £70 collected in the town. Still not content, the men claimed on the owners of the barque for life salvage. Although warned by the Institution that such an act was 'in direct contravention of the rules', they persisted, and they were paid £105. The Institution thereupon dismissed the coxswain and crew, with the concurrence of the local committee, and published an account of the affair in the *Life-boat.*

Afterwards, a life-boat house keeper was appointed to take charge of the station, 'with instructions that, in the event of a wreck or of a vessel being in distress, he is to give the keys of the

House to any responsible seafaring or otherwise competent body of men demanding them'.

Such incidents were so uncommon as to demand firm treatment, well publicized. It was essential, in salvage awards as in every other respect, to preserve the good name of the Institution, since once word got around that a crew was interested in money rather than in saving life, untold harm could be done to the vast majority who not only obeyed the rules, but fully approved of them.

* * *

In considering the era before mechanical power was brought to the aid of the sea-rescue service, even a moment or two spent on a shelving beach in the face of a high sea would convince the most purblind of the extraordinary dangers regularly faced by the earlier life-boat crews. Special interest therefore attaches to Lewis's notes 'on the Management of Open Rowing-boats in a Surf, Beaching them, etc.'. These and other practical memoranda had been compiled from information received from 128 different coastal areas over a period of at least twenty years, as well as from conclusions largely resulting from correspondence in the *Life-boat*. They were useful enough to be reprinted, often verbatim, in various manuals of seamanship of their own and later times. They owed much to the observations of Captain Ross Ward.

The notes were under four main heads: I. In Rowing to Seaward. II. On Running before a Broken Sea, or Surf, to the Shore. III. Beaching or Landing through a Surf. IV. Boarding a Wreck, or a Vessel, under Sail or at Anchor, in a Heavy Sea.

'Before stating the course to be pursued under each head,' so Lewis stated, 'we may remark that it is an axiom almost universally acknowledged that there is, as a general rule, far more danger when running for the shore before a broken sea, than when being propelled against it on going from the land; the danger consisting in the liability of a boat to broach-to and upset, either by running her bow under water, or by her being thrown on her beam-ends, and overturned broadside on.'

Launching, and the initial effort of rowing to seaward, depended for its success on speed. 'Indeed,' ran the note, 'under some circumstances safety will depend on the utmost speed being attained on meeting a sea. For if the sea be really heavy, and the wind blowing a hard on-shore gale, it can only be by the utmost exertions of the crew that any headway can be made. The great danger is, that an approaching heavy sea may carry the boat away on its front, and then turn it broadside on, or up-end it, either effect being immediately fatal.'

Three general rules were deduced from experience in meeting a head sea.

1. If sufficient command can be kept over a boat by the skill of those on board her, avoid or 'dodge' the sea if possible, so as not to meet it at the moment of its breaking or curling over.
2. Against a head-gale and heavy surf, get all possible speed on a boat on the approach of every sea which cannot be avoided.
3. If more speed can be given to a boat than is sufficient to prevent her being carried back by a surf, her way may be checked on its approach, which will give her an easier passage over it.

The best procedures for running before a broken sea to the shore demanded the utmost consideration. The object in this case was to ensure inertia at critical times, so that the boat would 'in succession pass through the descending, the horizontal and the ascending positions, as the crest of the wave passes successively her stern, her midships and her bow, in the reverse order in which the same positions occur to a boat propelled to seaward against a surf'.

It was recommended that in some conditions a boat's head should be turned to seaward before entering broken water, and then backing in stern foremost, pulling a few strokes ahead to meet each heavy sea, and then again backing astern. If approaching bows first, the use of a drogue was recommended, as being 'in common use by the boatmen of the Norfolk coast. . . . Drogues are chiefly used in sailing boats, when they serve both to check a boat's way, and to keep her end on to the sea. They are, however, a great source of safety in rowing boats, and the rowing Life-boats of the National Life-boat Institution are all now provided with them.'

It was further recommended that the principal weights in the boat should be brought 'towards the end that is to seaward, but not to the extreme end', and that if sail were employed, this should be taken in before entering broken water, and only oars used. 'If she have sails only, her sails should be much reduced, a half-lowered foresail or other small head-sail being sufficient.'

The rules quoted applied to a shelving beach: the case was different on a steep one, where 'the first heavy fall of broken water will be on the beach itself'. In such cases 'it is the general practice, in a boat of any size, to retain speed right on to the beach, and in the act of landing, whether under oars or sail, to turn the boat's bow half round towards the direction from which the surf is running, so that she may be thrown on her broadside up the beach, where abundance of help is usually at hand to haul her as quickly as possible out of reach of the sea. On such situations, we believe, it is nowhere the practice to back a boat in stern foremost under oars, but to row in under full speed as above described.'

As regards boarding a wreck, the circumstances were likely to vary so much that it was impossible to draw up any general rule for guidance. 'Nearly everything must depend on the skill, judgement and presence of mind of the coxswain . . . who will often have those qualities taxed to the utmost, as undoubtedly the operation of boarding a vessel in a heavy surf is frequently one of extreme danger.'

It was clear that boarding was best done from the leeward position, when the distressed vessel acted in some sort as a breakwater. The larger sailing life-boats, chiefly on the Norfolk and Suffolk coast, were, however, 'usually anchored to windward . . . and then veered down to 100 or 150 fathoms of cable, until near enough to throw a line on board. The greatest care under these circumstances has, of course, to be taken to prevent actual contact between the boat and the ship; and the crew of the latter have sometimes to jump overboard, and to be hauled to the boat by ropes.' It was emphasized that crowding or 'rushing headlong into the boat should be prevented as far as possible, and the captain of the ship, if a wreck, should be called on to remain on board to preserve order until every other person has left her'.

Finally, crews of stranded vessels were recommended to stay aboard them as long as possible, rather than to entrust themselves to the ship's boats. 'Viewed from to seaward,' it was noted, 'a surf has never so formidable an appearance as when seen from the land; persons in a boat outside the broken water are therefore apt to be deceived by it.'

At night particularly, 'it will in general be much safer to anchor a boat outside the surf until daylight, than to attempt to land through it in the dark'. An anchor and cable, buckets and a bailer should always be kept in ship's boats. These, it was pointed out, 'may ride out a heavy gale in the open sea, in safety, if not in comfort, by lashing their spars, oars etc. together, and riding to leeward of them, secured to them by a spar. The raft thus formed will break the sea; it may either be anchored or drifting, according to circumstances.'

A seaman who attended to the details of the Institution's regulations and notes could, in fact, form a shrewd idea, not only of the problems and perils of life-boatmen, but of how best to help himself when in trouble.

* * *

During the course of the 1880s the Institution received one of those legacies to be devoted to a specified object which, though often of great benefit, are rarely as satisfactory as those to which no provision is attached. It came from Admiral Sir George Back, who had been accustomed to spend holidays at Ramsgate, where he had formed a particular admiration for the life-boat crew, notably for the coxswain, Charles Fish, a character renowned among seafaring people. The admiral's bequest, amounting to £300, was for the provision of a 'substantial dinner' to the crew, at 'periodic intervals'.

The trustees made the occasion triennial, and invitations went not only to the crew but to launchers, to the captain and crew of the harbour tug which so often towed the life-boat, and to the harbour-master and others. The Secretary of the Institution was usually in the chair, and although there were always appropriate references to current services—the station being an exceptionally busy one—commemorative allusion was usually made to one of the more notable rescues in the history of the Institution. This occurred in January 1881 and included some of the classic ingredients of such an episode—terrible cold, fearsome seas, continuous danger, and more than one touch of the macabre.

There were sometimes complaints that the Ramsgate men got more than their share of publicity, and certainly there could be no greater mistake than to try to assess the relative merits of some of the finest rescues, such as have occurred on most parts of the coast-line of the United Kingdom and Ireland, but there is no doubt that the episode of the *Indian Chief* had a flavour of its own. It derived in part from the enterprise of the *Daily Telegraph*, with its reputation for good coverage of maritime affairs, and from its contributer William Clark Russell, who had been preceded at Ramsgate by another popular writer, aiming at a younger audience, R. M. Ballantyne. This enterprising Scot had drawn upon the experiences of an earlier Ramsgate coxswain, Jarman, to give colour to his spirited and frankly propaganda story, *The Life-boat*, published in 1864.

Clark Russell had in his day a wide reputation as a journalist and novelist specializing in sea matters, and with reason, for he had himself served for eight years in sail. It was through Russell that accounts of the *Indian Chief* appeared, giving two sides of the same story, that of rescued and rescuer.

The *Indian Chief*, a sailing ship of 1,238 registered tons, was four days out of Middlesbrough, Yorkshire, bound for Yokohama with a general cargo. She had twenty-nine aboard, including a North Country pilot. Early on 5 January 1881, with the night black and a high sea running, she grounded hard on Long Sand, part of the network of shoals near the mouth of the Thames, and it was soon clear that nothing could save her. The men sent up rockets, and these were seen and answered by two lightships, the Sunk and the Knock. There was little to do but wait, in the freezing cold, until daylight, and as there was then no electric communication between the lightships and the shore, the crew realized that their only hope of rescue was through visual signal with any ships which daylight brought into the area. One ship did in fact see them next day, but although she made efforts to approach through the confused seas at the edge of the sand, she failed. The *Indian Chief* soon broke her back, and the crew then took to the rigging. There they stayed all day, lashed to the swaying masts and spars.

During the night following the wreck, the main and mizen masts crashed into the water, drowning the survivors who had trusted to their security, their cries agonizing their ship-mates. But to them, with the coming of daylight, hope came as well, for those on the fore-mast saw the smoke of a small steamer, and then a life-boat. It was, said the Mate, who told the story:

> . . . under a reefed top-sail heading direct for us. It was a sight to make one crazy for joy; and it put the strength of ten men into every one of us. We could see her crew—twelve of them—sitting on the thwarts, all looking our way, steady as carved figures; and there was not a stir among them as the boat leapt from the crest of a huge sea right into the monstrous broken tumble. The peril of those men who were risking their lives for ours made us forget our own situation.

Being sailors, the men on the mast knew what to do even before being directed by Coxswain Fish. They unlashed themselves, bent a number of ropes' ends together and, making a piece of wood fast to the line, heaved it overboard and let it drift down to the boat. It was seized, a hawser was made fast, and the heavy rope dragged aboard. By its means, the life-boat's men were able to haul their craft under the quarter of the wreck, and the work of rescue began.

Fish pointed first to the body of the captain, who had his arms fast round the mast, his head erect, his eyes wide open. One of the crew called out: 'He's been dead four hours' and this was true. Knowing he would not survive the cold and exposure, he had handed over his personal treasures to the mate, giving him messages for home. His stark figure was long to haunt Fish, so the coxswain said later. The second mate, who was alive when taken off, died shortly after reaching the life-boat.

Once away, the seas off the Long Sand were so appalling that the mate felt at first he would have been safer on the wreck than in the boat. Seas breaking all ways in a storm on the edge of a sand-bank defy the most skilful seamanship, since their direction, behaviour and violence are unpredictable. The mate said:

> Never could I have believed that so small a craft could meet such a sea and live, yet she rose like a gull to the great roaring waves that followed her, draining every drop of water from her bottom as she hove up, and falling with terrible suddenness into the trough, only to bound like a living creature to the top of the next gigantic crest.

The mate's account concluded:

> What do you think of such a service? Our own suffering came to us as part of our calling as seamen. But theirs was courted and endured for the sake of fellow men they'd never seen. . . . . Nothing grander in its way was ever done by Englishmen.

Coxswain Fish's boat, which had replaced one of Beeching's, was named the *City of Bradford* after her donors, and he considered her as good as any afloat. When the news had come that a ship was aground on Long Sand, Captain Braine, the Ramsgate harbour-master, had ordered the tug *Vulcan* to take the life-boat out in tow. All concerned soon knew what was coming. Coxswain Fish said:

> I had my eye on the tug when she met the first of the seas, and she was tossed up like a ball; you could see her starboard paddle going round in the air high enough for a coach to pass under; and when she struck the hollow she dished a sea over her bows that left only her stern-post showing.

And the cold! 'I never remember a colder wind . . . it was more like a flaying-machine than a natural gale of wind. The feel of it in the face was like being gnawed by a dog.' The tug was little better off, 'the waves striking her bows and flying pretty nigh as high as her funnel, to blow the whole length of her and fall aft like a tumble of cart-loads of brick. I want to tell what they went through, for the way they were knocked about was something fearful. . . .'

The *Vulcan* could not get the bearing of the wreck from either of the light-vessels before night-fall, and lay to, all through the hours of darkness, the life-boat crew huddling together for warmth. Rum helped a little, though Fish himself was teetotal. Cold as they were, he said, the thought of the men on the *Indian Chief* 'made our own hardships small'.

Reward came with the morning, when one of the men, who had exceptional eyesight, caught a glimpse of the top of a single mast, about three miles away, 'sticking up out of the white water as thin and faint as a spider's line. Yet that was the ship we'd been waiting all night to see'.

The Coxswain continued:

> I reckon it was well there was something in front to keep our eyes that way, or the sight of the high and frightful seas that raged astern of us might have played Old Harry with some tired nerves. Some of the seas came with such force that they leapt clean over the boat, so that the air was dark with water flying a dozen yards over our heads in broad, solid sheets. They would fall with a roar like the explosion of a gun, a dozen fathoms ahead.

Slipping the tow and hoisting a storm fore-sail, Fish anchored at last near the wreck. As he veered out cable:

> . . . there was a horrible raffle of spars and canvas and rigging under her lee; but we couldn't guess what a fearful sight was there, until, our hawser being fast to the wreck, we had hauled the life-boat close under her quarter. There looked to be a whole score of dead bodies washing about among the spars. It stunned me for a moment, for I had thought all hands were in the fore-top, and never dreamed of so many lives having been lost. Seventeen were drowned.

By the time life-boat and tug got back to Ramsgate, the tug, said a local reporter, 'looked a hundred years old'. As for the rescued men:

> They were all saturated with brine; they were soaked with sea water to the very marrow of their bones. I had often met men newly rescued from ship-wreck, but never remember having beheld more mental anguish and physical suffering than were expressed in the countenances and movements of those eleven sailors.

Coxswain Fish received the Institution's gold medal and the life-boat's silver medal for the rescue, which was one of the most remarkable ever made with the aid of a tug, without which it could never have been achieved. The tugmaster and his crew were given the silver medal (as were the life-boat men). The episode emphasized the value of seamanship on the part of the rescued, for the life-boat's task would have been far harder but for the action of the survivors in the matter of the hawser, and for the orderly way in which they left the wreck. The whole affair gave point to many of the precepts laid down by Richard Lewis for rescue work.

* * *

Richard Lewis's book of 1874 remained standard for many years, and the author himself continued his service with the Institution until his death in 1883. This event coincided with the resignation of his close friend John Ross Ward, by then a Vice-Admiral on the retired list, from the Inspectorate of Life-boats.

Lewis's successor, Charles Dibdin, came from the Post Office, which was then an integral part of the Civil Service. He was to continue the example set by his two predecessors as Secretary in holding the office for a long period. Thomas Edwards was

Secretary for twenty-six years, Lewis for thirty-three, and Dibdin for twenty-seven. Dibdin's personal involvement with life-boat affairs was even longer, for before taking up his full-time appointment, he had done the Institution notable service as organizer of the Civil Service Life-boat Fund, which has since become the Civil Service and Post Office Life-boat Fund. It had been started in 1866.

Dibdin, who had been employed in the Savings Bank, became Honorary Secretary of the Fund in 1870. Even after his transfer to the Institution he continued to direct its affairs, and the consequences of the movement he did so much to help have been such that the Fund has provided, through voluntary gifts, a whole series of new life-boats—36 to date—at the cost of well over half a million pounds and it is now the largest single contributor to the life-boat service. Dibdin, when taking the chair at one of the Ramsgate dinners, told his listeners that he 'did not take an interest in the work because he was a paid officer of the Society, but he was its paid officer because he took an interest in the Institution'.

Dibdin had a highly individual way of combining both sides of the Institution's work—efficiency in sea-rescue, and pertinacity in helping to raise funds to carry this out. It showed in everything he did, and certainly in official memoranda issued to stations.

The Dibdin touch was apparent from the first. An example dating from 1888 is typical of many. Dibdin had to issue a general circular about life-boat exercises. He infused this with purpose.

> The boats are to be taken afloat for exercise fully manned, on a suitable day in each quarter, whether it has been out on service or not. . . . It is very desirable that one of the exercises should take place after dark.

Then came a characteristic Dibdin touch:

> . . . by the term suitable day is meant a day when there is a sea sufficient to test the capabilities of the Boat—but at Stations where there are many visitors during the summer months, the local Committees will doubtless consider that a suitable day in the *third* quarter is one in the month of August.

If Dibdin brought a breath of new life to the offices in the Adelphi, it was not long after his advent as a full-time employee that further stimulus came from elsewhere, this time from Lancashire: the dynamism derived from Charles Wright Macara, later to be made a baronet. He was born in Scotland in 1845, just within Hillary's lifetime, and he lived to see the Institution's centenary.

Macara was managing partner of a big firm of cotton spinners, and in the 1880s he was at the beginning of a long period of influence in the industry he represented. He benefited the cause of the life-boat men as only a handful of individuals had done up to that time. This was the result, as so often in the past, of direct experience.

Macara, to give himself some relief from continuous pressure of business, took a house at St Anne's-on-Sea, then a little-known resort not too far from his work in Manchester. It was his habit to engross himself in the life around him, and he soon had many friends among the fishermen, including those who made up the life-boat crew. He sometimes accompanied them on their exercises, and he became chairman of the local committee of the Institution. Macara gravitated towards chairs. In due course he was to become President of the Master Cotton Spinners' Federation and Chairman of the Committee of the International Cotton Federation.

In stormy weather during the early days of December 1886 Macara actually watched from the shore the rescue of survivors from a coaster driven on to Salter's Bank, in the estuary of the Ribble. That same evening, a concert was being held in aid of the funds of the Institution, and while this was in progress, the crew of the life-boat entered, together with the five men whose lives they had saved. 'I shall not soon forget that night,' wrote Macara, 'or the simple, moving story of wreck and rescue told by the Scottish master.'

Macara had the first telephone ever to be installed at St Anne's, and he was prompt to use it. 'After the concert,' he continued, 'I invited the coxswain and sub-coxswain of the life-boat to my house and induced them to describe their thrilling experience in their own words to the Manchester Press by telephone.' This must have been one of the earliest news-stories of its kind to be told in this particular way, and it was well that the chance was taken, for there was to be a terrible sequel. Within five days the entire life-boat crew were dead: not only so, but other crews were involved in what proved to be the greatest life-boat disaster recorded.

The coxswain had remarked to Macara that there had not been

a wreck for some time, but that such events seldom came singly. He was right. On 9 December there was a further storm of exceptional violence. The *Mexico*, a barque from Hamburg bound for Guayaquil out of Liverpool, struck on a sand-bank between Southport and Formby. Three life-boats put out in answer to her distress signals, which were seen at nine o'clock at night. They were those of Southport, Lytham and St Anne's. Among the volunteers for the St Anne's boat was the Scots captain who had recently been rescued, but as there was a full complement without him, he was not allowed to go.

Macara shared in the all-night vigil ashore; that it would be one of great anxiety was apparent from the difficulties the crews had had in getting afloat. The Southport boat, the first to reach the barque, had to be pulled by horses and helpers three and half miles along the shore on her carriage before she could be launched to windward of the *Mexico*. It was four hours before she reached the ship, and it was apparently the intention of the coxswain to let go an anchor and veer down on to the barque. In the process, a heavy sea struck the boat and instantly capsized her. Two hours later she was found three miles from Southport with only two men alive out of her crew of fifteen.

The St Anne's boat made for the barque under oars for the first 500 yards of her passage. Then she hoisted sail and reached a point about two miles from Southport. What happened afterwards will never be known, for nothing more was seen or heard of her, except two red lights. At a quarter past eleven the next morning the boat was found ashore, bottom up, with three dead bodies hanging on the thwarts, head downwards. The entire crew was lost.

The Lytham boat, which was new, had never before been launched on service. Her crew took her down to the Ribble under oars and then set a sail, but the seas were such that she filled four or five times. Before she reached the *Mexico* the barque was on her beam ends and the crew had lashed themselves to the rigging, but the Lytham men succeeded in their mission. They saved twelve, at the cost, to the life-boat service, of twenty-seven. 'News came by telephone to my house,' wrote Macara, 'as the bodies were washed upon the opposite shore, and one by one the drowned men were recovered from the sea and laid in the churchyards of St Anne's and Lytham.'

There had been many earlier life-boat disasters, but this one struck home with peculiar force. A public subscription for the sixteen widows and the fifty orphans was opened at once. Contributions came from Queen Victoria, from the German Emperor, and from the port of Hamburg. The Institution itself appropriated £2,000: an anonymous donor gave the money for a new Southport boat, and a man living at Rochdale paid for another for St Anne's. In little over a fortnight £33,000 had been collected, and the total rose eventually to £50,000.

Macara was chairman of the St Anne's Lifeboat Disaster Committee, and the success of the appeal decided him to do something further for the cause. 'I made a rough estimate,' he wrote, 'that not more than 25,000 people out of many millions who constituted this great maritime nation contributed to the support of the Institution, and the average of the branches, including all the large cities and towns in the country, did not amount to more than £35 a year.' The position was indeed as Macara stated; in fact an analysis made at the time when he wrote showed that two-thirds of the Institution's regular income came each year from about a hundred people. Macara's calculation was that an income of £100,000 a year would be needed to meet the requirements of the service efficiently, 'and yet the sum I asked was under three farthings a head of the population . . . a very small item indeed for a nation that owned such a vast proportion of the world's shipping to spend upon this voluntary organization for the saving of life at sea'.

On 23 July 1891 Macara sent an appeal to the Press. He pointed out that 35,000 lives had already been saved by the Institution's boats, and that the heartening response to the call for help which had been made after the disaster on the Lancashire coast 'emboldened me to appeal on national grounds, as, if generous help were not forthcoming, the operations of the Institution would have to be very seriously curtailed'.

The call was answered, particularly so in the north of England, where the newspapers were enthusiastic backers. A fund opened by the *Yorkshire Post* totalled £2,500 within a fortnight, and another, sponsored by the *Sheffield Daily Telegraph*, was also generously supported.

Macara, encouraged by this public interest, decided to make an even wider appeal than could be achieved through newspapers. In the words of his biographer, W. Haslam Mills, he had an idea which 'brought charity into the streets and the streets into charity'. This was to make direct contact between life-boat crews and the public of the great inland towns. It was the genesis of what were to become known as Life-boat Saturdays. These were the forerunners of the modern flag-day.

Macara called on the Mayors of Manchester and Salford and on a number of prominent business men, and got together an organizing committee. Under its auspices the first Saturday street collection was made on behalf of the Institution in October 1891. The whole affair was staged with imagination, and after very careful planning. On Thursday and Friday two Lancashire life-boat crews paraded cities and suburbs: they were, in fact, drawn from stations which had more than one life-boat as well as an adequate reserve of volunteers. On Saturday began the serious business, life-boat crews and bands parading, life-boats on their carriages, detachments from fire brigade and ambulance units. Life-boats were actually launched in the artificial lake in Belle Vue Gardens, Manchester, and in the evening a rescue by rocket apparatus was staged. This was watched by a crowd estimated at 30,000.

There was great enthusiasm. Money was thrown from upstairs windows and from the tops of tram-cars into the collecting carts which followed the life-boats in the procession. More than £600 was taken in the streets, mostly in coppers, and altogether more than £5,000 was raised as a result of the experiment, which quickly extended to Bolton, Oldham, Stockport and then beyond the borders of Lancashire. In 1892 a Life-boat Saturday was organized in Dundee, and soon the idea spread south.

Certainly the results were remarkable. For instance, Manchester and Salford, where the experiment had started, had only averaged a yearly contribution of about £200 to the funds of the Institution. This was increased to £4,000, whilst the counties of Lancashire and Yorkshire raised their collections from about £3,000, as the previous best, to £21,000 in the first year of the movement.

So it went on, a demonstration in Edinburgh in 1894 being especially successful. This time the Navy and Army were to the fore, including a detachment from H.M.S. *Galatea*, the band of the Black Watch, and that of the 12th Lancers, mounted. Today, such demonstrations might seem unsophisticated, but there were fewer diversions in the nineteenth than in the twentieth century.

Macara was greatly helped by his wife, whose support at St Anne's, Manchester and elsewhere could always be relied upon in the life-boat cause. 'Great as was my enthusiasm,' wrote the admiring husband, 'it did not exceed hers.' Mrs Macara was a principal means of establishing the first Ladies' Auxiliary Committee in Manchester and Salford. The idea soon spread to other parts of the country. Six districts were organized on lines suggested by Macara to cover the whole of Great Britain and Ireland, and every section of the community was encouraged to take an interest in life-boat work.

By the end of the 1890s the Duke of York, later George V, had become President of the Saturday Life-boat Fund. There were eighty collecting districts in London alone, and there was an office at 3 Adelphi Terrace, Strand, not far from the headquarters of the Institution in John Street.

Macara ceased to play a very direct part in the movement he had originated some time before it was formally taken over by the parent body. This came about on 31 December 1910. He had had disagreements with the Committee of Management, as we shall see, although he never ceased to take a keen interest in the Institution's work.

* * *

Macara was to some degree involved in a significant event which took place during the closing years of the nineteenth century. This was a detailed investigation of the Institution and its work, leading to a Parliamentary Report. It was published at a time when the country was celebrating the Diamond Jubilee of Queen Victoria's accession, and it proved to be a vindication so thorough as to have realized the hopes of the most enthusiastic supporter.

As a result of serious charges of various kinds which had been made in the Press and elsewhere against the Committee of Management, those with the life-boat cause at heart requested an official inquiry, and this was agreed to by the House of Commons. On 17 March 1897 a Select Committee was approved. Fifteen members were nominated, their mandate being 'to inquire into the Administration of the Royal National Life-boat Institution, and into the adequacy of its organization for Saving Life on our

Coasts'. Four months later, on 15 July, the Report was ready.

It consisted of over a thousand closely printed pages. The Committee's conclusions were preceded by a succinct history of the Institution, an examination of its workings, and the answers to no fewer that 11,864 questions asked of fifty witnesses examined on oath. Also presented were the analysed results of a questionnaire which had been addressed to more than 800 Lloyd's Agents and Receivers of Wreck. An elaborate index rounded off a monumental work.

When the complexity of the material is considered, the thoroughness and speed with which everything was digested compels admiration, indeed astonishment. Efficiency and drive were shown by all concerned, great credit being due to the Chairman, C. J. Darling, Q.C., who later became a High Court judge well known for his highly individual comments from the Bench.

The Committee held twenty-five sittings to hear evidence, and others took place in private. The Report upheld the good name of the Institution in every particular, and gave such praise to its work as must have raised the spirits of all who took part in it.

Moreover, a series of facts was revealed during the inquiry which would have caused much discomfort, not least to the critic-in-chief. This was Mr E. H. Bayley, who had at one time been elected M.P. for North Camberwell, and who had been a persistent cause of trouble to the Institution for some years. Perhaps Mr Bayley was lucky to have escaped without being involved in a series of actions for libel, and he could scarcely have relished the concluding words of the findings, which were that the Committee regretted 'that it was not in their power to suggest some protection for charitable institutions against the attacks of irresponsible persons, which attacks may, as in the present case, turn out to be unfounded and untrue'.

Mr E. H. Bayley, it seemed, had been head of a carriage-building business which seven years earlier had done some work for the Institution, supplying transporting platforms according to tender. The items had been much delayed, a fact which was noted at the time in the pages of the *Life-boat*, and the Institution actually rejected certain of them on the grounds of bad workship. Mr Bayley's riposte was first to try to bribe one of the Institution's employees to pass work as satisfactory, against the man's better judgement. Then, having received the answer he deserved, he channelled his energies into blackguarding the Institution in articles, lectures, and by other means including gossip. His malice and activity equalled his ignorance in many matters about which he pontificated, and his temerity in offering his opinions was as remarkable as his verbosity. The Committee's patience, although sometimes strained, held good for long stretches, which provided some lively though not always edifying reading in the Report.

Mr Bayley's charges were that the published accounts of the Institution had at one time been misleading; that legacies had not always been applied as intended; that the existing life-boats were dangerous and slow, and should be replaced wherever practicable by steam-driven craft; that the crews were undisciplined, underpaid, and allowed to recoup themselves by claims on those assisted, resulting in cases of extortion; and that Great Britain was 'behind other nations, and that the life-boat service if transferred to the Government might be made efficient as well as profitable to the nation'. This was by no means the full extent of the original charges, but a few were withdrawn, sometimes reluctantly, and never with any grace. They included aspersions on Sir Edward Birkbeck, who had been a most active Chairman of the Committee of Management since 1883, and these Mr Bayley attempted to laugh off on the ground that they were 'chaff'. Chaff from such a quarter could only have been looked upon coldly, and there is no evidence that this glib explanation carried any weight.

Other critics included Colonel H. M. Hozier, Secretary of the Committee of Lloyd's. Although in a private capacity the Colonel was a supporter of the Institution's work, he was the channel of information derogatory to life-boat crews with regard to salvage claims. The evidence provided by Lloyd's did not stand up to close scrutiny, and it was clear from the start that Colonel Hozier himself was a reluctant witness. 'It is only in consequence of the summons of the Committee that I am here,' he said, 'not as a volunteer.'

Mr Bayley had relied heavily on evidence supplied to Lloyd's for many of his charges, but no witness could have been more responsible than Colonel Hozier, or less persistent in pressing matters which could not be proved. There had indeed been differences between Lloyd's and the Institution, but the Colonel's main wish was that the organization he represented should come to an agreement about the conditions and operation of future salvage claims by life-boat people. In this respect, by removing grounds for suspicion and acrimony, the Committee's Report did good by making consultation easier between the various interested parties. This could hardly have happened when one of them was under a number of accusations which had not been publicly disproved.

In the upshot, the Report was severe on the evidence supplied through Lloyd's, being 'emphatically of opinion that the attacks made upon the Institution in respect of property salvage have been as unfounded as they have certainly been mischievous'. But, they added: 'Your Committee recommend that the Institution should only allow their crews to use the Institution boats on condition of the crews agreeing to such terms, as to remuneration, and arbitration in case of dispute, as the Institution may prescribe. These terms your Committee think the Institution should settle in consultation with the Committee of Lloyd's and the Board of Trade.' In due time, consultations took place, and the Institution's regulations were agreed as being satisfactory.

The principal remaining critic was Charles Wright Macara, whose drive and powers of organization had done so much for the financial benefit of the Institution's service. Macara's grievances were of a different order from Mr Bayley's. It was mainly that he wanted everything done *his* way. Because it had not been, he deemed himself to have been treated with less than justice by the managing Committee, of which he had at one time become a member. At the back of it all, as he wrote many years later in his *Recollections*, was the decision to move the headquarters of the Life-boat Saturday Fund from Manchester to London. In Lancashire, Macara had been the king-pin: in London, even as a member of the Committee of Management, he could not be so important.

Among the witnesses was Mr H. J. Palmer, editor of the *Yorkshire Post*. Palmer had been an enthusiastic publicist for life-boat work, and had written a leading article in which he asked: 'When will the shillings and half-crowns of the gentlemen of England who live at home at ease . . . be forthcoming with half the readiness with which these gallant men tender their lives?'

In life-boat matters, when they had been associated, Mr Palmer had not found Mr Macara an altogether comfortable ally. When he was asked by a member of the Parliamentary Committee whether he did not view Mr Macara as being 'somewhat masterful in his methods', the answer was an emphatic: 'Yes, I did.' Mr Macara himself, when his own turn came to be examined, was asked at one point whether it was true that he could not conceive any other view but his own on a certain matter: 'Quite so,' was the reply.

'Consequently,' the questioner continued, 'you cannot admit that it resolves itself into a matter of opinion?'

'I do not think so,' replied the witness.

The Report concluded that suggestions of the mishandling of the Saturday Life-boat Fund brought by Mr Macara could be dismissed. 'Your Committee,' it was stated, 'are of the opinion that the charges of mismanagement brought against the Institution are entirely without foundation.'

The critics thus being disposed of, the Committee wound up with a general benediction. They stated that they 'cannot conclude their Report without recording their opinion that the thanks of the whole community are due to the Committee of the Royal National Life-boat Institution for the energy and good management (often in very difficult circumstances) with which they have for so many years successfully carried out the national work of life-saving, and this without reward or payment of any sort'.

Very little sympathy was shown by most witnesses for Mr Bayley's idea that the work of the Institution should be assumed by Government, or that crews should be specially recruited, or else drawn mainly from the Coastguard, which not only formed a principal reserve for the Royal Navy, but was responsible for life-saving apparatus ashore. As for steam life-boats, so strenuously advocated by Mr Bayley, the Institution already had experimental boats in service, while in many cases, since they had to be maintained afloat in sheltered waters instead of being drawn up ashore, they were impracticable. Steam tugs, on the other hand, had long proved their value as life-boat auxiliaries.

One hostile witness, Mr G. H. Little, who held a Board of Trade master mariner's certificate and who had become, after a good many years at sea, a nautical journalist, distinguished himself by saying, in answer to the question whether he had any complaints against the Institution: 'When you have an organization like that, and when their doings are tinctured with flabby piety, it is open to suspicion.'

This brought the question, which must surely have raised smiles: 'Do you think that a misanthropic society would work it better?'

Mr Little's answer was: 'No, I believe in State Control for all these things.' He was declaring himself one of a very small minority.

In this respect, he had two eminent men closely concerned with the Board of Trade against him. Upon this Department would have fallen the task of maintaining a life-boat service had not a voluntary organization already been in existence. Sir Courtenay Boyle, Permanent Secretary of the Board, expressed the view that 'the public, with that fair-mindedness which generally distinguishes it, would be more tolerant of a voluntary organization than a Government institution, and rightly so'. And four years earlier, in a public speech, Mr Anthony Mundella, when President of the Board which Sir Courtenay was representing, had gone still further:

> No Government Department could ever do the work as well as the National Life-boat Institution; no Government Department would ever maintain that alertness and alacrity which the Governors of that Institution have always exhibited; and no Government Department could ever evoke that generous sympathy with the heroism that has characterized the work of the Institution. . . . I trust the time will never come when the English public will abdicate their duty and their highest privilege of supporting such a noble Institution.

For all his criticisms, Mr Little did make one forward-looking suggestion, and remembering that this was in the infancy of the internal combustion engine, it was memorable. When asked his opinion of steam life-boats, he answered: 'I am very doubtful as to whether steam is the proper motive power to use. I think very much might be accomplished by adopting some form of petroleum motor.' In that respect he was indeed prophetic, though the first motor-driven life-boats, after experiments which began as early as 1904, did not come into service until still later.

Mr Little was the only witness examined who, though often misguided, and having what could be described as extensive areas of ignorance, was full of that protesting spirit with which society has since grown so familiar, and he was all for revolutionary change. 'You want something totally new, do you?' asked Sir John Colomb, one of the Committee, referring to the witness's ideas for new construction. 'You want to replace the steam motor by a petroleum motor?

'Yes,' said Mr Little.

'And in fact you want to revolutionize everything, do you not?'

'Exactly,' came the stout reply.

If the Institution had been angered by the attacks which had resulted in the official inquiry, and if its members had been gratified by a Report which had vindicated them so thoroughly, there might have been some danger from complacency. This, however, would have been an unlikely mood to continue for any length of time, and for a very good reason: every major tragedy at sea led to inquiries, and these ensured that the Institution was kept constantly up to the mark, because of the inevitable criticisms which arose when, for instance, rescue failed, or when life-boat crews were drowned on duty. Such criticisms were often based on false assumptions, but they had to be met. Just as Question Time in the House of Commons is a valuable means of making Government Departments realize that they are the nation's servants, not its masters, so even the most misguided comment, requiring as it did a reasoned answer, kept the Institution alert. As tragedies at sea were then still of frequent occurrence, there was rarely a time when there could be no occasion for comment in the Press on the working of the life-boat service, and it was in the nature of things that this comment would not automatically be favourable.

What the Parliamentary Report of 1897 had done was to make clear that the main ideas behind the organization, all of which had been formulated by Hillary more than seventy years earlier, held good, and were carried out well.

3
The Marine Engine

Among the results of the Institution's investigation into the disasters off the Ribble Estuary in 1886 had been a protracted and critical re-examination of the various types of life-boat then in service. This had eventually led to a series of trials, which took place in February 1892 at Lowestoft, and in March of the following year at Montrose, to test the qualities of boats in sailing and pulling.

These trials, in which the Norfolk and Suffolk life-boats, various types of self-righting boat, a new boat modified from one which had been built for Southport, designed by Mr George Lennox Watson, and the tubular boats all took part, yielded valuable information. Much remarked was the difficulty, found at Montrose, of getting some of the larger boats launched from carriages on a flat or open shore.

The most immediate outcome was the abandonment of the practice of having open water-ballast in the Norfolk and Suffolk type. This feature, said the report, was

> . . . a weakness long known by the officers of the Institution . . . but the men who worked the boats would have no alteration made in them: however, since the trials they have withdrawn their objection and these boats have been enormously improved by confining the water-ballast in tanks.

The entry into service of a boat designed by Mr G. L. Watson was an event of much significance, for the recommendations of the Southport inquiry had included a proposal that the Institution should appoint a Consulting Naval Architect. Mr Watson accepted the post in 1887, and as he was internationally renowned, and was later to be responsible, among other achievements, for the royal yacht *Britannia*, which was and still is regarded as the finest vessel of her size ever built, he was a great addition to the technical strength of the Institution.

From the outset, Mr Watson thoroughly identified himself with life-boat design, and in spite of his exceptionally busy private practice he gave a great deal of time to the work, far beyond what could reasonably have been looked for. He addressed himself particularly to the problem of a satisfactory steam life-boat, which in the 1870s had seemed so baffling that it was at one time reported that the Committee of Management 'did not feel able to expect that steam life-boats will ever come into general use'.

Although this remained true, and although a special sub-committee at first found itself 'unable to recommend at present'. yet, stimulated by Mr Watson, during the summer of 1887 the Institution announced that it had

> . . . resolved to offer a gold and silver medal for drawings or models of a mechanically propelled Life-boat best adapted to meet the conditions under which life-boats are called upon to perform their work. Also a gold and silver medal for models or drawings of a propelling power suitable for the self-righting boats of the Institution.

A panel of judges was nominated, but the members were not called upon for a verdict, no awards being made. However, not many months after the decision that nothing practical was yet in view, the firm of J. and F. Green of Blackwall put forward a scheme which seemed promising enough to follow up. It was the idea that what is now generally called the 'hydraulic' principle should be employed. A powerful centrifugal pump sucked water through an inlet in the bottom of a boat and expelled it under water via outlets at stem, stern or sides, the craft being driven by reaction in the direction required—in effect, it was driven by water jets. It was a development of a notion first put forward in the eighteenth century by an American, James Rumsey, which, though discarded, had been revived from time to time with varying success. The principle was sometimes referred to as that of the 'turbine', but modern usage of the terms 'turbine' and 'jet propulsion' has been so much affected by later developments that it will be convenient to refer to it by its original name.

Screw propulsion was not then favoured owing to the likelihood of damage to the screw, particularly when the boat was in the midst of wreckage; and for smaller craft the paddle-wheel system had never been very practical. So Sir William Hillary's project of a steam life-boat, though realized in the course of time, was, in the outcome, to be on rather different lines from those he had envisaged so imaginatively.

The issue of the *Life-boat* for November 1890 carried the first details of the *Duke of Northumberland*, which made one of her first trial trips from the builder's yard up the Thames to the President's estate at Syon House, opposite Kew Gardens. She was 50 ft. long; her moulded breadth was 12 ft., extreme breadth 14 ft. 3 in., and her depth 3 ft. 6 in. She was made from the finest steel, had 72,000 rivets and 15 water-tight compartments, and she cost £5,000. In addition to her powerful main pump she had two bilge pumps and steam ejectors. Although not self-righting her sea-worthy qualities were, theoretically, exceptional. It was stated that 'her stability vanishes at 110°, that is to say, when the mast is sufficiently far below the surface of the water to make an angle of 20° between it and the surface'. She was decked all over, and could hold between thirty and forty people below. Her engines were of the 'horizontal direct-acting compound surface-condensing type, with cylinders of $8\frac{1}{2}'' \times 14\frac{1}{2}''$ diameter, and a 12″ stroke'. The boiler was a 'Thornycroft's patent tubulous pattern'. The highest speed attained on the measured mile was 9·17 knots. She was heavy, just over 30 tons displacement, and would be expensive to maintain—£800 per annum was estimated—since she needed a technical crew of four, consisting of a chief engineer, an assistant engineer, and two firemen. She must be ready to get up steam immediately her services were likely to be required, a process which took about 15 minutes when the boiler had been warmed, and from 20 to 25 minutes from cold. Finally, she would need to be moored in sheltered water, since she could not be launched from the shore.

By May 1891 the boat was on trial at Harwich, and she soon proved useful not only on her own, but for her ability to tow a sailing or pulling boat or to assist a ship in trouble. A few weeks after entering service it was reported that she had been 'throughly tried in bad weather and heavy seas, and has proved a complete success, having already contributed to the saving of 33 lives'.

The Prince of Wales (later King Edward VII), whose concern for the life-boat cause was so far from being perfunctory, or confined to formal occasions, that he once said it was 'one of the finest and noblest to which a human being can belong', took a strong interest in the *Duke of Northumberland*, just as he was to do with the earlier motor-cars. During the course of the boat's passage round the coast from Harwich to Holyhead and New Brighton in 1897—the move was made for purposes of experiment in a different area of sea—the Prince had a run in her at Cowes, as did his nephew, the Emperor Wilhelm II of Germany.

Curiosity on the part of the Kaiser possibly arose from the fact that in 1895 the South Holland Life-boat Society had taken the step of ordering Messrs Thornycroft of Chiswick to build them an 'hydraulic' boat on the lines of the *Duke of Northumberland*, with some modifications suggested by Mr G. L. Watson. Their boat was five feet longer than the British prototype and had a proportionately wider beam. What might suit the Dutch coast might well be useful on the German, and the Emperor, whose passion for matters nautical was strong and increasing, would not have let the chance of gathering useful information go by.

By the time of these royal visitations other steam life-boats were in the service of the Institution. The second was the *City of Glasgow* and she had been christened by Mrs Bell, the wife of Glasgow's Lord Provost, in June 1894. Her builders were once again Messrs Green of Blackwall, and she resembled the Dutch boat more closely than she did her English predecessor. It was hoped that experience would help to overcome certain difficulties of operation, for example, the tendency of the main pump to become partly choked or even to stop, as happened once on service through a stray rope, and there was the need for better lateral propulsion when close alongside a wreck. This time there were two pumps; the intakes were flush with the skin of the craft; there was an increase in horse-power, and (a characteristic which answered closely to one of Sir William Hillary's ideas), 'a novel feature of this new design is that it has the power of using the turbine for pumping out of the vessel any water that may enter by leak or otherwise, and, in fact, utilizing this very water to assist to drive the boat along'—this according to a description which appeared in the *Life-boat*.

The *City of Glasgow* cost less than the *Duke of Northumberland*, for her building charge was £3,250. She was slightly larger: length overall 53 ft., beam 16 ft. Her carrying capacity was much the same, and so were her weight and speed. There was bunkerage for four tons of coal, and she could carry half a ton of fresh water.

Her machinery was built by Messrs Penn, and she was in service with the Institution for seven years. She was sent to Harwich, but although she did useful work, her record was not the equal of that of the first of her type.

One more 'hydraulic' boat was ordered. She was the *Queen*, and in most characteristics she resembled the *Duke of Northumberland*, though she was faster. Much thought was given to the question of fitting her to burn oil in her furnace, which would have been an enlightened step considering the future of this fuel as serving the marine engine, but in the end coal was retained. The boat was sent to New Brighton in 1897, where she proved exceptionally popular with her crew. Although in due course the motor life-boat was to replace steam and indeed all other types of life-boat completely, it is worth remark that the *Duke of Northumberland* had an active life of over thirty years, and the *Queen* of twenty-six.

The *Queen* was built by Messrs Thornycroft at a cost of £5,000, of which sum over £2,000 came from Liverpool sources. This was particularly gratifying because only three years earlier the Liverpool authorities had handed over the management of their life-boats, which were extremely well run, to the Institution. The name of the new boat was commemorative of the Jubilee of Queen Victoria. Her length overall was 55 ft. and her extreme breadth 16 ft; her depth moulded was 5 ft 6 in., her draught amidships 3 ft. 1½ in., her displacement 31 tons. She had stowage room for 3½ tons of coal or two tons of oil, and her mast was fitted to carry a lug-sail or jib. In 1897 the *Queen* relieved the *Duke of Northumberland* at New Brighton, the pioneer steam life-boat being re-stationed at Holyhead.

The experiment of burning oil in the *Queen*, after the furnace had been started up with coal, followed a series of tests which had been successfully concluded by James Holden, the Chief Mechanical Engineer of the Great Eastern Railway, for locomotive firing. The oil was sprayed into the life-boat's furnace by compressed air; but the process involved skill and judgement on the part of the firemen, even if it relieved them of labour. Although proved to be practicable, the system was not persisted with, nor was it tried on any other boat belonging to the Institution. However, as had been the case so many years earlier in the matter of the Boydell wheel-fittings for life-boat transporters, it was a clear sign of how alert was the technical staff to what was being tried out elsewhere. Mr Holden, incidentally, was a particular friend of the life-boat men and he lent one of his experts to superintend oil firing at sea. He was following an admirable railway tradition of helpfulness, for as early as the 1860s it had become the custom of all the leading companies to transport life-boats over their systems free, though they usually occupied at least three flat trucks.

After the completion of the *Queen* the hydraulic system was given up in favour of the screw, whose disadvantages in a life-boat could, it was thought, be overcome. One of the handicaps of hydraulic boats had, in practice, been found to be speed. Although on her trials the *Duke of Northumberland* had slightly exceeded 9 knots, in service 7 knots proved to be the maximum attainable in rough weather or for any length of time, and this was not considered good enough in relation to power output. After deciding to adopt screw propulsion, the Committee of Management ordered two boats from the firm of J. Samuel White & Co. of East Cowes, whose high standard of workmanship was already well known to the Institution. An ingeniously built tunnel was designed to protect the screw itself, which was placed further forward than would have been the case, for instance, in a naval picket-boat of the time. A third screw-propelled boat replaced the hydraulic-powered *City of Glasgow* in 1901.

The Cowes boats, which were christened *James Stevens No. 3 and James Stevens No. 4* were 56 ft. 6 in. in length overall. They had a beam of 14 ft. and a mean draught of 3 ft. 5½ in. They had side-by-side twin funnels, like the hydraulic boats, and it was found after trials that the screw steamers, while satisfactory in other ways, were economical on fuel. The engines, of 180 horse power, were described as 'miniature vertical inverted compound surface condensers'. The boats were in service in 1899. The *James Stevens No. 3* was sent first to Grimsby, was transferred in 1903 to Gorleston, where she gave great satisfaction, and then, in 1908, she went to Milford Haven. The *James Stevens No. 4* was sent to Padstow, North Cornwall, to an area where there had recently been an alarming sequence of marine disasters, which decided the Institution on special measures. It seemed that there was truth in the local rhyme—

> From Padstow Point to Lundy light
> Is a watery grave by day or night

The Padstow boat went out on her first operational mission on 4 April 1899, watched by spectators on the cliffs as she breasted the huge seas which rolled in, unimpeded, from the Atlantic. She returned safely; but a year later, on 11 April 1900, there occurred the first tragedy associated with the steam life-boats. When outward bound, with a hard west-north-west wind blowing, the boat was struck by a huge wave rolling up on her port quarter. The sea broke as it struck her, and she turned over. She became a complete wreck, and was washed up on the rocks. Of those on board, eight were drowned, including her four engine-room staff. The Institution set aside £1,000 for the immediate relief of dependants.

The *James Stevens No. 4* was replaced by a sailing life-boat, the *Edmund Harvey*, but in view of the special conditions prevailing at Padstow, Mr Watson designed a tug for the Institution's service, which was used for getting the *Edmund Harvey* to sea under bad conditions. She proved a remarkable tribute to her designer, for she did good service for nearly thirty years. She was of 231 tons and had twin screws. Her name was *Helen Peele*.

It had been the custom for the *Duke of Northumberland* to return to Liverpool for periodical overhaul. On 26 June 1901, when the boat was in the Mersey preparing to return to Holyhead, there was an explosion in the engine-room which killed the two firemen and badly scalded the assistant engineer. The boat was repaired, and she continued to give valuable service until 1922, so much so that to her belongs the credit for what was perhaps the finest rescue made under steam.

On 22 February 1908 an unusually strong gale swept the country, causing havoc. The *Duke of Northumberland*, which had just returned from giving help to a disabled steamer, received news that another ship, the *Harold*, was in danger. She was small, 75 tons, and was bound from Teignmouth in Devon to Runcorn in Cheshire loaded with china clay. She was drifting with the tide towards the rock-bound shore of Anglesey, between the North and South Stacks. The wind was at hurricane force at the time, and the *Harold* had come to anchor close under the cliffs, but in seas so violent that it was at first impossible for the life-boat to get near her. Then, helped by the slackening tide, the coxswain, after two hours of intricate manœuvring, at last succeeded in getting a line across, by means of which seven were saved. A huge sea then washed the *Duke of Northumberland* right alongside the

Harold, and the remaining two men were able to jump to safety.

This service was attended by exceptional risk, owing to the nearness of the shore. The slightest misjudgement on the part of Coxswain Owen would have brought instant destruction. Conditions for the engine-room crew, battened down below in the appalling seas, beggared description. For this exploit Owen was given the Institution's gold medal, and all eleven members of his crew received the silver medal. Owen himself already held the silver medal, as well as one awarded by the Royal Humane Society. The rescue was considered of such note that the Prince of Wales, as President, commanded Owen's presence at Marlborough House to receive his award.

* * *

In January 1899 the sixth Duke of Northumberland died at Alnwick, after holding office as President for thirty-three years, the longest tenure in the history of the Institution. Although towards the end of his life the Duke had not taken a very active part in life-boat affairs, which were conducted from day to day by Sir Edward Birkbeck as Chairman, by the Secretary, and by the managing and other committees, he had remained the final resort or court of appeal, and his counsel was never looked for in vain. The Duke had become concerned in life-boat affairs nearly a decade before his term as President began, and even in his later years he was anything but a figure-head, as was seen by his keen interest in the first steam life-boat.

The question of a successor was settled in the most satisfactory way, for three months after the Duke's death the Prince of Wales agreed to accept office. Successive sovereigns had been Patrons of the Institution from the earliest days, but this was the first time that a member of the Royal Family had signified that he would be glad to take a prominent part in its affairs.

The Prince had already taken the chair at three Annual General Meetings, those of 1867, 1884 and 1893, and Sir Edward Birkbeck could rely upon his support with the same confidence with which he had looked to his predecessor, with whom he had worked for so many years.

The Prince's tenure was brief, for in 1901 he succeeded Queen Victoria on the throne of Great Britain, and the Presidency was thereupon taken over by the Duke of York, who was already President of the Saturday Life-boat Fund and who, as a professional naval officer, followed maritime activity of every kind with a keen eye. But, as King, Edward VII gave many indications that the work of the Institution was near his heart, and he made at least one typical though private gesture showing his pride in having been associated with sea rescue. On one occasion, when he was the guest of Mr Dorrien-Smith of Tresco Abbey on board the Tresco yacht, Mr Dorrien-Smith, who was Honorary Secretary of the Isles of Scilly Life-boat Committee, told him of a particularly fine rescue made by one of the local boatmen. Shortly afterwards, this very man was seen at the tiller of a boat which was steering a course close to that of the yacht. Mr Dorrien-Smith remarked on the coincidence, and the King, with one of those spontaneous acts of recognition which so became him, saluted the boatman as they passed.

In 1904, not long after the Duke of York, who was now Prince of Wales, had taken over the Presidency from his father, the Institution made a move from the premises at 14 John Street, Adelphi, which it had occupied since 1855, to Nos. 20 and 22 Charing Cross Road. In view of the rise in prices of London property since that time, the terms may be of interest. £10,000 was paid for a sixty-five-year lease of the new premises, on which an annual ground rent of £385 was due. The buildings were more spacious than the old ones, and just as central.

In the same year that the move was made, a change took place in the form of the Institution's gallantry medal. A design was produced by Mr G. W. de Saulles of the Royal Mint, the obverse showing the head of Edward VII as Patron, and the reverse, departing from the original design by William Wyon, showed, in the words of the official description, the

> . . . Figure of Hope assisting a Coxswain-Superintendent of a Life-boat to buckle on his life-belt, and wishing him and his crew 'God speed' with a Life-boat manned in the distance ready to launch, and awaiting the Instructions of the Coxswain-Superintendent.

It was not to have as long a vogue as its predecessor. In 1913 the head of George V by Sir Bertram MacKennal was shown on the obverse, and William Wyon's reverse was restored.

* * *

Two practical problems concerned the Institution at the time of the move to Charing Cross Road, both of which, in time, were to be solved satisfactorily. The first was the provision of direct communication, electrically, between lightships and isolated lighthouses and the shore, a matter which had first been raised in Parliament in 1892 by Sir Edward Birkbeck. It was one to which the Post Office and other authorities had responded, and by the end of the nineteenth century the situation had been transformed for the better, to the great benefit of the life-boat service. Far quicker and more detailed warning could now be given when vessels appeared to be running into danger, and their position could be notified without delay.

The second problem was the provision of satisfactory petrol-driven motors as auxiliary to sail in life-boats. Considering the stage of evolution which the internal combustion engine had reached at the time, which could be described as one of infinite promise but uncertain course, much experiment would be entailed.

Mr Watson, who had been so closely involved with the design of the steam life-boat, had been among the first to realize the limitations of steam-propulsion for rescue work, not only on the ground of expense, which was disproportionate to utility, but in other ways. The great majority of rescues continued to be made under sail, and this would be so for many years to come. What was looked for was a reliable *secondary* source of power. The question had been engaging Mr Watson for some time before his death, at the comparatively early age of fifty-three, in November 1904. The loss of the services to the Institution of this distinguished man was acknowledged by all who had worked with him, and it was fortunate that Mr J. R. Barnett, a partner in the yacht-building firm which Mr Watson had founded, agreed to succeed him as Consulting Naval Architect. Both Watson and Barnett were to give their names to successful types of life-boat, and both have a notable place in the history of the Institution.

From the start, the active co-operation of a specialist firm was necessary. This was obtained from Messrs Thelluson, one of whose directors, Captain E. du Boulay, supervised the pioneering processes. There were certain specific requirements to be considered, the first being that the engine had to be inside a water-tight casing which would be unaffected by seas breaking inboard.

This casing could not be air-tight because the motor would need a supply of air to the carburettor. The condition would have to be met by a specially contrived pipe and valve which, while letting air in, would keep sea-water out.

The engine would have to be as nearly automatic as possible. This was because, once he had started it up, the mechanic in charge would not be able to give close attention to it, particularly on a dark night with a high sea running. It meant, among other things, that lubrication must be self-renewing. Again, power output must be steady, and unaffected when the life-boat was standing more or less on end.

If the boat was a self-righter, this property must not be jeopardized by the fitting of a motor. But it was also essential that if the boat capsized, power should be cut off. The sailing and pulling qualities of the boat would have to be as little affected as possible. She must be unsinkable, and must retain the ability of ridding herself of water immediately.

There were two further conditions: the engine must be as simple as possible, so that in an emergency it could be controlled by an unskilled member of the crew; and it must always be ready to start, winter or summer, even after standing idle for some time.

All this was asking much, though not quite the impossible. Indeed, some of the requirements were met with greater speed and satisfaction than could reasonably have been expected when experiments began at Cowes in the early months of 1904.

The boat picked upon was the 38 ft. self-righter *J. McConnell Hussy,* which was normally stationed at Folkestone in Kent. She was fitted with a two-cylinder two-stroke Fay and Bowen engine, developing about 9 h.p. The trials were promising: the boat attained a speed of 6 knots, with the motor running at 450 revolutions per minute and using 1½ gallons of petrol per hour. Stability was carefully tested and found to be as good as ever. Although the centre of gravity had been slightly raised by the necessary alterations, the life-boat righted herself satisfactorily.

After work had been completed to the Institution's instructions, the boat was not returned to Folkstone but was sent to Tynemouth in Northumberland. Here an army officer, Captain H. E. Burton, was well known for his interest in and knowledge of life-boat matters, and was a leading spirit on the local committee. He was to hold a very special place in the history of the Institution. whose gold and silver medals he won.

At first the Northumbrian crew, who like most seamen regarded major changes with suspicion, would have nothing to do with the *J. McConnell Hussy* and her petrol engine. Burton therefore got together a volunteer crew, drawn from his own men, soldiers one and all. This state of affairs did not last long. What transformed them completely was a successful rescue by Burton and his team, without benefit of local help. Thereupon, shown to be wrong-headed, the regular crew expressed themselves happy to serve aboard the *J. McConnell Hussy* provided that Burton, in whom they had great faith, would continue in charge of the station and would take responsibility for looking after the engine. All being agreed, matters remained harmonious and indeed within a few years a Tynemouth motor life-boat—not, however, this experimentally converted craft—with Burton aboard as well as the regular coxswain, took a leading part in a spectacular war-time rescue which will be described later.

As a result of the technical success with the *J. McConnell Hussy,* three other boats were put in hand, the Newhaven 38 ft. self-righter, which was given a 24 h.p. Thornycroft motor, the 43 ft. Ramsgate self-righter, into which was put a 30 h.p. Tylor, and the 43 ft. Walton-on-the-Naze boat, which was of the Norfolk and Suffolk type and thus not self-righting. She was equipped with a 32 h.p. Blake motor.

Tests continued during 1905 and 1906, and the results were scrupulously noted and compared. They were thought good enough for the fitted boats to be returned to stations for operational service. For the time, trials were confined to larger boats, as it was held that the risk of damage to machinery and propellers was too great to allow petrol engines to be fitted to craft designed for launch from transporters. But optimism was such that as early as 1905, the year after the very first experiments, a design was prepared for the first boat in which the engine would be an integral part of the structure, even though it was considered subsidiary to sail.

Work proceeded cautiously, as lessons from the various trials were assimilated. The boat, which was destined for Stromness in the Orkneys off the far north of Scotland, was not ready until 1909, but the wait had been worth while, for she proved to be soundly designed. She was 42 ft. and self-righting. Considerable use was made of the experience gained from the screw-driven steam craft. In the steamers the protective propeller shaft tunnel had been made of steel. In the Stromness boat, which was wooden, still further ingenuity went into the construction of the tunnel, which had a bronze frame inside. A single drop keel replaced the two which were usual in this type, and an ingenious method was worked out whereby the screw could be made accessible from inside the boat, so that it could be cleared at once if fouled. It was reached by way of a watertight trunk-hatch.

The wood used for all the earlier motor-fitted boats was Honduras mahogany for the diagonal, double-skinned planking, the framing being of oak and elm. A Tylor motor was chosen for the Stromness boat.

Another boat had been ordered for Stronsay, also in the Orkneys. This was a 43 ft. Watson type, not self-righting. The pair left London together on 15 April 1909, together with a sailing life-boat destined for Thurso, Caithness, in the north of Scotland. After a voyage of seventeen days, during which there were enthusiastic receptions at ports on the way north, the motor-fitted boats reached their stations under their own power, though not without incident.

The convoy was in charge of Commander Harold Rowley, R.N., Inspector of Life-boats for the Northern District. During most of the journey, which was not by any means trouble-free, sail was set wherever useful. The Stromness boat, although her engine was of 10 h.p. less than the 40 h.p. engine provided for the Stronsay, towed the larger boat, which in turn towed the Thurso sailer. Speed was 7½ knots at best, and at Grimsby, Scarborough and Tynemouth the mechanics became busy with minor faults.

Near Aberdeen, head winds reduced the convoy's speed almost to zero, and Commander Rowley was glad to accept a tow into and out of the port by the harbour authority's tug. When the Pentland Firth was reached, tows were slipped in the turbulent water and the Stronsay mechanic, no doubt chagrined at having been for so long behind Stromness, let his engine out, and at first outdistanced the Stromness men. Alas, he was too impetuous, for he met trouble and had to return to Thurso, while the Stromness boat went on, in her steady way, reaching her station during the evening of 30 April. The Stronsay boat, helped by a tow from the steamer *Ola,* was at Orkney by next day, after an instructive trip.

Two years later another such convoy of three powered boats, one for Tynemouth, one for Seaham and one for St Abbs, Berwickshire, the latter two boats equipped with 34-h.p. Wolseley engines and the Tynemouth boat with a 40-h.p. Tylor, spent most of a day at Gorleston when one of the motors refused to start, so that it continued to be a wise directive by the Institution to coxswains that 'the motor is an auxiliary to the sails, which latter are the principal motive power'. This emphasis held good for a few years more, since it was only gradually that the petrol-fuelled marine engine became sufficiently reliable to be depended on without reserve. The Institution had, indeed, the best engines it could find but, considering the conditions which they were liable to be called upon to meet, it would have been misguided, to say the least, to encourage in coxswains and crews any idea that engines were infallible.

As if to make the matter crystal clear, the first issue of the *Life-boat* for the year 1906, when so much hope was being aroused by the extending use of mechanical propulsion, featured an account of the standard sailing rigs, and these were to serve the majority of boats up to and including the period of the First World War.

Pulling-and sailing life-boat types

Norfolk and Suffolk type, fitted with dipping fore-lug and standing mizen sail with outrigger

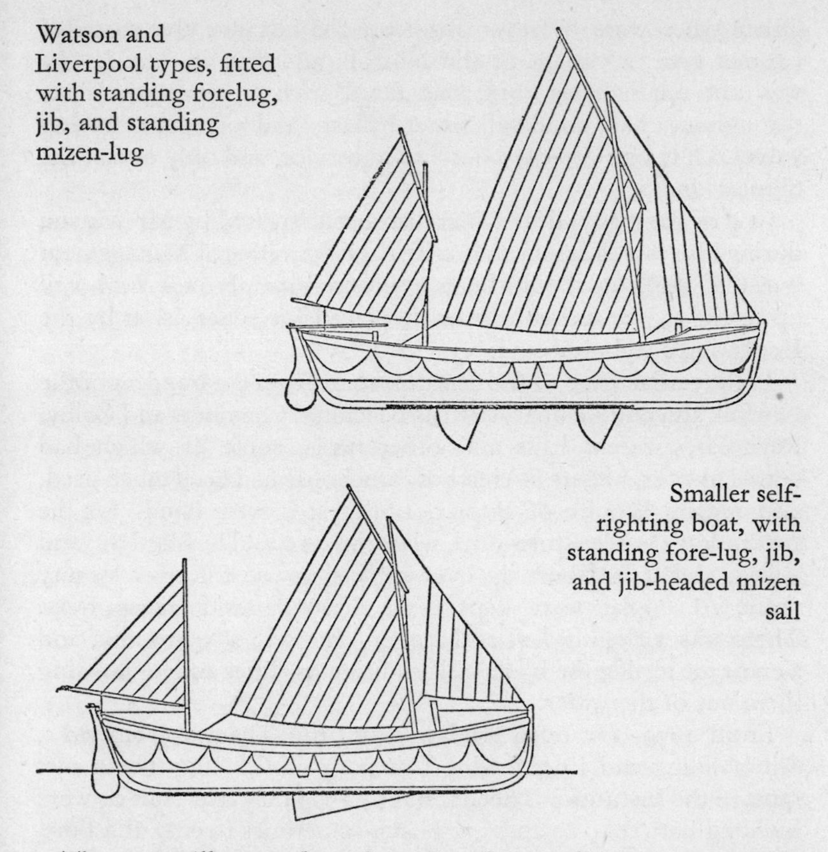

Watson and Liverpool types, fitted with standing forelug, jib, and standing mizen-lug

Smaller self-righting boat, with standing fore-lug, jib, and jib-headed mizen sail

The types illustrated, each with a fore and mizen mast, were three in number. The first included the Norfolk and Suffolk boats, which carried a dipping fore-lug, and a standing mizen-sail with outrigger. The second, represented by the Watson and Liverpool boats and the larger self-righters, had a standing fore-lug, a jib and a standing mizen-lug. Here there were two qualifications: 'Some of the large self-righting boats,' said the account, 'are also rigged with a dipping fore-lug, but in their case the mizen mast is stepped at the second thwart from aft, and there is no outrigger for mizen sheet or bumpkin for fore-tack.' Also, 'the larger Watson boats carry a mizen boom with their standard rig, but the boom is not fitted in the other boats of their type.'

The remaining type, consisting of the smaller self-righters, carried a standing fore-lug, a jib, and a jib-headed mizen sail.

Other types were by now obsolete; for instance the so-called Cromer boat, a variant of the Norfolk and Suffolk breed. She was not self-righting, but was fitted with a watertight deck throughout, had confined water-ballast, and adequate freeing valves. Only one Cromer boat was in service, and only one of the tubular kind.

One of the many ideas which had been stressed by Mr Watson during his years of association with the Committee of Management was that building should be concentrated mainly in a yard well up to the work, and conveniently placed for supervision by the Institution's technical staff.

In the earlier years of the century, apart from the builders of the Norfolk and Suffolk boats such as Beeching, Chambers and Colby, Reynolds, Critten, Ellis and other firms, some of which had ceased to exist, Messrs Forrestt of Limehouse had been much used, also Messrs Woolfe of Poplar. Both yards were handy for the Institution's Poplar store-yard, where boats could be fitted out and tested, and it had been in ever-increasing use for over twenty years. At Poplar were kept spare life-boats and transporters. There was a rigging loft and riggers' houses; store-rooms; and a crane for testing the boats' self-righting qualities and for hoisting them out of the water.

From 1899, for over twelve years, the Thames Ironworks, Shipbuilding and Engineering Company of Canning Town met most of the Institution's needs, and by 1909 they had built or were building between 160 and 170 boats, sometimes twenty at a time. Smaller boats took from six to eight months; the larger types occasionally took as much as a year. In general, such a concentration of effort and expertise meant that a representative of the Institution could usefully be in the yard all the time, ensuring that all material and workmanship was up to the high standards specified.

The Norfolk and Suffolk boats were clinker-built, but 90 per cent of the fleet were planked diagonally, the layers of the inner skin being reinforced by an outer skin arranged cross-wise. Between these two skins, which were of Honduras mahogany (as were the bulkheads, decks and end boards), there was a thick layer of stout unbleached calico, coated on both sides with a mixture of white lead and raw linseed oil. The skins were fastened with copper clench nails.

Canada elm was used for the keel and keelson, bilge keel, floors, gunwales and rudders. English oak was used for the stem and stern-post and for the quarter bollards, the towing bollards being of 'clean straight Danzig fir'. The masts and yards were of 'best selected Norway spars, sound, clean and close-grained, and free from injurious knots'. The air cases were of 'clean white pine Deal board'. The drop keels were of mild steel plate, the fixed metal keels of cast iron, in the smaller boats the weight being between 9½ and 25 cwt., and in the larger boats from 2 to 3½ tons.

No boats anywhere in the country underwent more careful scrutiny during building, or such thorough testing afterwards. If the Institution could not insure against stress of weather, it could see that the life-boatmen were given everything the best of its kind, made from thoroughly seasoned wood. Mishaps which occurred during sea-rescues were seldom due to failure of material, and for this, builders and inspectorate could share the credit. Each type of wood used resulted from experiments showing that it was best fitted for its purpose.

* * *

Every flourishing organization owes its condition to team-work. Just as the combination of Richard Lewis as Secretary and Admiral Ross Ward as Chief Inspector had led to such a remarkable consolidation and expansion of the work begun by their predecessors, so the co-operation between Sir Edward Birkbeck as Chairman, Charles Dibdin as Secretary, and Commander St Vincent Nepean as Chief Inspector was the mainspring of the Institution between 1883 and 1907. Sir Edward Birkbeck died in 1907, and Dibdin, though he survived until 1910, waged a losing battle against ill health in the later stages of his life.

Both men were hard to replace, but Sir Fitzroy Clayton, who succeeded as Chairman, had an almost unequalled record of long service, since he had joined the Committee of Management as far back as 1863 and had been Deputy Chairman since 1883. Dibdin was succeeded in 1910 by George, later Sir George, Shee, who had been an outstanding success as Secretary of the National Service League.

In paying tribute to the late Secretary, who died in his sixty-first year, the editor of the *Life-boat* stated that 'it was with melancholy satisfaction that we read the intimation that His Majesty had intended to confer on his birthday a knighthood on Mr Dibdin'. This recognition would indeed have been likely and appropriate, for the Institution's President had succeeded his father in 1910 as King George V, and no one knew better the value of Dibdin's work.

There were to be two other important changes: as the King could not be, simultaneously, both Patron and President, the office of President was offered in 1911 to the seventh Duke of Northumberland, who thus became the third member of his family to be closely associated with the life-boat cause. The final change resulted from the resignation of Commander St Vincent Nepean as Chief Inspector, after thirty years with the Institution. He was succeeded by Commander Thomas Holmes, R.N.

It was not long before a new emphasis was apparent in the *Life-boat,* and this was not before time. Hitherto the journal, while giving excellent if often succinct coverage to the numerous episodes at sea, had in its main articles confined itself to general or official themes. But in the issue for February 1912 there appeared the first full-page feature on a life-boatman. The subject was John Owston, who for forty-one years had been coxswain of the Scarborough boat. The text was accompanied by a photograph, the first of a gallery of splendid faces which, if it had extended back into even the nearer past, must surely have included some memorable characters now lost to posterity except for brief printed records.

Owston, a fisherman, had then just retired, at the age of well over sixty. He had been born in 1844 and during the course of his life he had helped to save 230 people from shipwreck. In 1880, when he was a coxswain of seven years' standing, he had gone out on five separate missions in a hard October gale, rescuing twenty-eight men, services for which he had been awarded the silver medal. In December 1911 he sailed on his last operation. Some cobles were seen to be in trouble in the broken water not far from the entrance to Scarborough harbour. In going out to them, the life-boat was swept by a huge wave which washed Owston and a young crew member overboard, though they were both pulled back. But Owston was suffering from shock and the effects of immersion and was taken to hospital. There he realized that his days of active service were over.

The writer of what would now be called the 'profile' was careful to emphasize that 'this fine old man would be the first to recognize that it is as an example of the spirit and achievement of many another coxswain and member of a life-boat crew around our coasts', and not because he was pre-eminent, that he had been chosen for special notice.

In the issue for August 1915, some three years after the article on Owston had appeared, there was a long obituary of Charles Fish of Ramsgate, who had died the month before at the age of seventy-six, and who during a quarter of a century as second coxswain and coxswain at Ramsgate had helped in the saving of 877 lives. The article included a reprint of the entire material concerning the rescues from the *Indian Chief*. Following on this tribute, notices and photographs of coxswains became a regular, popular and most appropriate feature of the journal.

There were also some lighter touches: for instance, in March 1913 the Archbishops of Canterbury and York happened to be staying at the Lizard together on holiday. Recollecting, no doubt, that it was one of his predecessors who had set the Institution on its course, the Archbishop of Canterbury considered a visit to the life-boat station an essential part of his duty, and there he addressed the local committee and members of the crew. The Archbishop of York went further: he put out in the life-boat on exercise. Judging by the published photograph, the launch must have been rough, though not so bad that the prelate had not breath enough for a few words afterwards to the men.

The years immediately preceding the First World War were marked by the manifold services to the Institution of Sir John Cameron Lamb. A Civil Servant by profession, and for eight years Second Secretary at the Post Office, Lamb had been enlisted by Sir Edward Birkbeck for his specialist knowledge of telegraphic matters, and he had been a member of the Royal Commission which had investigated the question of electrical communication for lightships.

Lamb became a dedicated life-boat man. He combined the offices of Deputy Chairman of the Committee of Management with the Chairmanship of the Royal Society of Arts, being renowned for his rapid and efficient handling of business. During Dibdin's years of illness, Lamb shouldered much of the day-to-day work of the Institution, and he was chairman of sub-committees on Building, Finance and Correspondence, Wreck and Reward, and Organization. He also mastered the history of the life-boat itself, and his consideration of the subject, which was given as a lecture before the Royal Society of Arts, and which was published for the Institution in 1911, remains the best short account up to and including the steam-driven types and the first experiments with the petrol engine. Lamb, who died during the earlier days of the war, was one of those rare people who, immensely able, industrious and scholarly, combined these characteristics with a winning kindness.

* * *

Just as the programme of mechanization was thoroughly under way and being extended every year, with confidence growing on the part of the crews in the capabilities of the powered boats, the Institution had news that, from 31 December 1912, the Thomas Ironworks yard would close, so that it would have to look elsewhere in the future. This was a serious setback, for the Thames work-people had answered every call made upon them with skill and enthusiasm, but the firm had over-extended itself in big-ship construction, with resulting heavy loss. Fortunately, as the Institution had never been entirely dependent on London or indeed any other resources, it was not long before the Committee of Management found that many of its needs could be met by Messrs S. E. Saunders of East Cowes, a firm which was later to become famous in the field of aircraft and general engineering, under the name of Saunders-Roe.

At the time of the change-over there were seventeen motor-fitted boats on station, with five buildings at an average cost of about £3,000 each. The new construction, although it could not be completely standardized, was mainly of large Watson-type boats, 43 ft. by 12 ft. 6 in., which were given 50 h.p. Tylor motors. The Tylor engine had emerged very successfully from trials, and within the next few years all new motor-boats of large size had either 60 or 40 h.p. Tylor engines, the smaller self-righting boats being given one of 35 h.p. which was found adequate for a speed of about 7½ knots.

The current construction programme was in line with life-boat development abroad, where motorization was going ahead.

Leading the field was the United States of America with over a hundred such craft in service, but of these thirty-nine were known as 'motor surf boats' and even the largest was only 36 ft., equipped with what was described as a '6-cylinder four-cycle Holmes auto-marine engine'. The Germans had by now four motor life-boats, France and the Netherlands three apiece, and there was a solitary example in Spain.

One of the problems of the Committee of Management was that if, as was soon likely, the motor was to become the main rather than an auxiliary source of power, it must be maintained in perfect order at all times, ready to start up in any weather, however bad. This would involve more expense, for it entailed the employment of a full-time mechanic. This solution had been recommended as early as the summer of 1913 by a delegation to St Abbs, where the practical question had arisen. In course of time, it became an accepted principle.

One of the happier events, before the curtain fell upon the older Europe, was a visit in 1913 by King George V to the motor life-boat *Frederick Kitchen,* which was destined for Beaumaris. He embarked at Cowes, as his father had done on the *Duke of Northumberland* sixteen years earlier. He was accompanied by Sir Godfrey Baring, a future Chairman of the Committee of Management, by Commander Thomas Holmes, R.N., as Chief Inspector, and by the District Inspector. The *Frederick Kitchen* was of the largest type, and one of the last products to come from the Thames shipyard. The King, who showed a keen interest in everything, completed the occasion by visiting the yard at Messrs Saunders which was to build so many fine boats for the Institution.

4
The Impact of War

On the day the First World War began for Great Britain, 4 August 1914, there took place a little ceremony at Fraserburgh, in North Aberdeenshire, which was to symbolize much of the immediate future of the life-boat organization. A 40 ft. self-righting boat, equipped with a 40 h.p. Tylor motor and designed for a crew of twelve, was presented to the Institution by Mr T. Dyer Edwardes. She was named *Lady Rothes*, 'as a thank-offering to Almighty God', in the donor's words, 'for preserving the life of my only child from a great peril, in the foundering of the White Star liner *Titanic*'.

The Countess of Rothes, who named the boat herself, had behaved with great courage when, on the night of 14–15 April 1912, the liner sank in collision with an iceberg in the North Atlantic, with the loss of 1,513 lives. The Countess took the helm of one of the ship's life-boats for some eight hours, until she and other survivors were picked up by the *Carpathia*.

Within a few days of the presentation, the *Lady Rothes* was the means of rescuing fourteen people from the steam-ship *Glenravel* of Belfast, which was sunk by a German submarine fifteen miles from Fraserburgh.

The effect of war on the Institution could have been catastrophic. The gravest matter was immediate loss of revenue, for all financial appeals were abandoned, except where they would directly serve the war effort. Most Coastguards were withdrawn, to be replaced by some 1,400 Boy Scouts. In the course of time they grew remarkably efficient, but needed experience to prove their value. Crews, shore committees, headquarters staff, all were depleted by calls to the colours, and five out of seven District Inspectors joined the Fleet.

With both human and financial resources reduced, at times almost to nothing, matters were also difficult at sea. For when life-boats were called upon, they had to operate under unprecedented conditions. All coastal lights were extinguished; buoys and beacons were removed; defensive minefields were sown offshore, with the result that traffic was sometimes forced to make use of dangerous inshore channels. Lightships were forbidden to report casualties by gunfire or wireless. Finally—a rule which grew increasingly irksome and was occasionally defied—life-boats could not proceed on missions without the sanction of the naval officer in charge of the district. These officers were often inexperienced about life-boat matters, and sometimes actively obstructive.

Inevitably there were changes in the sort of crew which was available. Older men gallantly filled the places of sons, grandsons, nephews and friends who were with the armed forces. As far as possible, experience had to make good any diminution in physical fitness. Even the types who volunteered began to change, and it was no uncommon event for bluejackets, soldiers, and sometimes army horses, to help at launches and fill gaps. Two horses, loaned by a farmer, were actually drowned at Bridlington in 1915, as well as a helper, Robert Carr, aged sixty-five, when the life-boat was swept sideways off its carriage by a huge wave as she was being got to sea.

In the 1890s it had been remarked that there were, in the main, four sorts of people from whom crews were drawn. There were the old 'beach companies', whose traditions and unwritten rules and customs went back far beyond memory, who lived not by fishing but by salvage and what was known as 'hovelling', which meant giving help in various ways to ships and boats in need of it.

Then there were the regular and part-time fishermen, who formed the majority of the sailing and pulling crews; the boatmen of the pleasure resorts; and finally, the Coastguard volunteers, those who could be spared from working the life-saving apparatus ashore. The war was to alter the old pattern to some extent. There were places where fishing was restricted or impossible; the communities of beach-men were slowly decreasing; there was no call on boatmen for pleasure trips; and, as time went on, crews were drawn more and more from other than professionally seafaring men. The process was gradual, and many of the more notable rescues of the war were made by those who would have done the work under conditions of peace.

This was certainly so in the case of the wreck of the hospital ship *Rohilla*, which drove ashore at Saltwick Nab near Whitby in Yorkshire, in a tremendous south-easterly gale, in the early hours of the morning of 30 October 1914. The *Rohilla*, of 7,400 gross tons, was registered at Glasgow. She belonged to the British India Line, and was on her way from Queensferry to Dunkirk with 229 people on board, including medical staff and five nurses who were to attend the wounded when embarked.

The events which followed make up one of the more dramatic stories of the sea. As the writer of the account which appeared in the *Life-boat* put it: 'The conditions, being extraordinary, do not lend themselves to ordinary comparisons.' This was nothing less than the truth.

Whitby had two life-boats, the coxswain of the first being Thomas Langlands. He had come from Seahouses, near Bamburgh, and had joined the Whitby crew at the age of eighteen. He had already won the Institution's silver medal for a rescue carried out in his own coble at the harbour entrance. Now some difficult decisions were before him.

It was clear that there was no hope, under prevailing conditions, of being able to launch the No. 1 boat to go to the help of the *Rohilla*. No. 2 boat was moored in the haven, but to get her to sea with the wind as it was would entail an overland journey. She would have to be hauled manually, on skids, from the east pier till she was near the wreck. Here the cliffs fall almost sheer to the sea, and some of those to whom Langlands explained his plan thought it would be impossible to carry it out. All the same, there was no lack of helpers, and the task began. It proved as stiff as the most pessimistic had feared, and even before the boat had reached the water's edge she had been stove in, in two places. Undeterred, Langlands resolved to make an attempt at rescue.

The *Rohilla* lay about a quarter of a mile from the shore, among rocks which seemed impenetrable. Yet Langlands knew the coast well enough to think he had a hope of saving life, and after great difficulty he was able to launch. Better still, he reached the wreck and took on board twelve men and all five nurses. They were brought ashore safely.

That was a first success, and soon there was another. Langlands put out again. Although this time the crew found it nearly impossible to reach the ship, yet they did so at last, in spite of huge seas which were breaking over the steamer and which, sweeping through her, filled the life-boat. Eighteen more were taken on board, which was as many as could be carried under the circumstances.

During the hair-raising course of their second return journey the crew realized what was facing them. Even if they reached the shore alive, their boat would be no further use, for she was by now too badly damaged. Langlands managed to beach, but Whitby No. 2 was indeed out of action. She had had two almost miraculous successes, and it would be many hours before there was a third.

At that time there was a life-boat station at Upgang, just to the west of Whitby, which has since been closed. The Upgang people brought their boat overland, horse-drawn, and it was then lowered down the cliffs by rope. But by the time she was at the edge of the sea, ready to launch, the gale was such that the crew knew they would stand no chance. They waited all night, and even next morning, 31 October, when they were able to make an attempt at rescue, they were forced by the seas and the strong current to return without having been able to get to the wreck. Seeing the Upgang boat approach led some of the men on board the *Rohilla* to jump into the sea in an effort to reach her. Several were drowned, but a few, helped by onlookers who dashed into the surf, were brought ashore exhausted.

By this time stations other than Upgang had been alerted by telephone. The Scarborough and Teesmouth boats put out. The Scarborough boat, towed to sea by the steam trawler *Morning Star*, arrived at 6 p.m. and stood by for hours in the dreadful weather, though all her attempts to close the wreck failed, and she was forced to return. The Teesmouth boat put to sea in tow of the local Harbour Commissioner's tug, but she sprang a leak and her crew had to abandon her, though the tug was able to get the half-submerged boat back to Middlesbrough. There was one more gallant attempt by Langlands, who at last succeeded in getting to sea in the Whitby No. 1 boat, but he still could not reach the wreck.

It was a motor life-boat which turned apparent failure into triumph, against heavy odds. There was one at Tynemouth, to which a telegram had been sent asking for help. Through the raging sea, and with all coastal lights extinguished, the Tynemouth life-boat made the 44-mile journey. She reached Whitby harbour at 1 a.m. on the dark morning of Sunday 1 November.

Her coxswain was Robert Smith. With him was Captain H. E. Burton of the Royal Engineers, the Honorary Superintendent of the Tynemouth station. 'The music of the engine,' said a Whitby onlooker, 'was sweet to the ear.' Smith poured oil on the surface of the sea to help calm the water, and he took on board Commander Basil Hall, who was at Whitby helping to co-ordinate the rescue efforts. Hall was now to verify the truth of some prophetic words spoken to him a few years earlier by Commander Charles Cunninghame Graham: 'It is not small boats, as at present, stationed in the *bights*, but large ones in the *horns* of bays which the future will see successful.'

All Whitby turned out to watch the effort of the Tynemouth boat to reach the *Rohilla* at daybreak. When she came within two hundred yards of the wreck it seemed that she too had been defeated. Gallons of oil were then released, and the effect was decisive. A reporter was there from the *Yorkshire Post*, and he wrote:

> . . . the life-boat turned about, raced at full speed outside the line of breakers, past the stern of the wreck, and then turned directly towards the shore. The most dangerous moment came when she was inside the surf and broad-side on to the waves; but, guided with splendid skill and courage, she moved forward steadily, and a cheer of relief went out from the shore when she reached the lee of the wreck, immediately beneath the crowded bridge. The feelings of those on board as they saw salvation at hand can only be imagined.

There were still fifty men on board the *Rohilla*. Within a quarter of an hour more than forty were transferred to the life-boat. Then two huge waves swept over her, and she disappeared from sight completely. After a moment of terrible suspense, she reappeared, went once more alongside the *Rohilla*, and saved the rest. The last to leave was the captain, wearing an overcoat and pince-nez, apparently quite unruffled. Some of the survivors were in pyjamas, and one of them had a black kitten on his shoulder.

For this exceptional service, recognition was on a fitting scale. It included gold meals for Coxswain Smith and Captain Burton of Tynemouth, and for Langlands of Whitby, who had been in charge of the only pulling boat which had succeeded in reaching the wreck. Silver medals were given to Commander Basil Hall, to Richard Eglon, Langland's able assistant, to James Brownlee of Tynemouth, and to George Peart, who had been foremost among those who had dashed into the sea to succour the bold spirits who had tried to swim from the *Rohilla*. The Upgang crew received the thanks of the Institution inscribed on vellum, to honour their gallant attempt.

Before the close of 1914 the Institution added another notable rescue to its records. The Sunderland-built destroyer *Success* ran ashore in darkness, on 27 December, in a very high sea. This was at Kingsbarns, six miles from St Andrews on the coast of Fife. Her distress signals were seen, and the Crail life-boat was launched at once. The state of the sea was such that not only was she holed, but her coxswain, Andrew Cunningham, was washed overboard, together with one of his crew. Both were pulled back and then, in spite of the damage to his boat, Cunningham made two separate bids at rescue. On the first he saved twenty, and on the second, thirty-four, an extraordinary number considering the condition in which his boat then was. The rescue was completed by the St Andrews boat, which saved thirteen, and Cunningham was given the silver medal.

* * *

It was not long after the *Rohilla* and the Scottish rescues that Coxswain Henry Blogg of Cromer first appeared in the *Life-boat*'s gallery, in which he was to figure much in the future. He had become a member of the Cromer crew in 1894 and had been coxswain since 1909. In January 1916 he made a remarkable rescue of the only survivor from the Norwegian steamer *Havfru*, 860 tons. This little ship had gone aground on Haisborough Sands, some ten miles from the Norfolk coast and the village of Happisburgh. The Sands contain the fragments of more wrecks than on any other shoal round the British islands, not excepting the Goodwins. The lone seaman was Niels Nielson, the steamer's Danish donkey-man.

A year later Blogg's leadership resulted in further notable rescues, first from the Greek steamer *Pyrin*, and then from the Swedish *Fernebo*, which broke in half after a boiler explosion. The Cromer life-boat of that era was of the Liverpool type, and was launched off the beach. On 9 January 1917 there was a strong north-easterly gale blowing, and a high sea. Getting the life-boat away was a task of much difficulty. It was achieved with the help of a number of soldiers stationed in the area, some of whom waded up to their shoulders in the water before Blogg and his men could get afloat. The rescue itself was achieved at about two o'clock, the *Pyrin*'s crew of sixteen being brought safely ashore an hour later.

The accident to the *Fernebo* happened just as the life-boat was beaching, the crew by that time being in an exhausted state. Blogg himself was in his late thirties, but most of his men were much older, and to call upon them for a further immediate effort was asking much. None the less, they agreed to put out again, and for half an hour, pulling at their oars, they did their best to do so. They could not get their boat beyond the breakers, and at length were forced back, temporarily defeated.

Meanwhile, a small boat had left the *Fernebo*. She capsized in the surf near the shore, but all six occupants were somehow brought to land, some by the efforts of Stewart Holmes, a private soldier of the Seaforth Highlanders, who was awarded the silver medal for his bravery. By the late afternoon the two halves of the steamer had grounded, one abreast a long wooden groyne which projected about 400 feet into the sea the other a mile farther to the east. The rocket apparatus went into action, but the force of the wind was such that no line reached the survivors.

Commander Basil Hall, who by then had been recalled for service with the Fleet, happened to be in Cromer at the time. In the evening Blogg suggested to him that one more effort should be made, in the darkness, to take off the survivors. Hall gave his consent with great reluctance, and by half past nine the life-boat was away. Hall described the scene which followed.

> For half an hour these splendid men made the most gallant attempt to reach the vessel—over and over again the boat was swept back into the shallow water inshore, but each time they succeeded in keeping her head on to the sea and pulling her out again into the deeper water about halfway between the ship and the shore.
>
> Bathed in the brilliant beam of the searchlight, one moment standing on end as she mounted the crest of a huge breaker, at another with her nose buried in the trough of the sea, or completely lost to sight as a sea broke right over her, the life-boat made a sight which will never be forgotten by the hundreds of spell-bound spectators who lined the beach. I myself would not have believed it possible for even a strong and young crew to do so well with this heavy boat.

Five oars were smashed; three more were washed away, and Blogg was forced to return. Spare oars were then produced, and one last effort attempted. This time, against all likelihood, success rewarded resolution, and eleven men were taken off. It was for this outstanding feat that Blogg was awarded his first gold medal. Hall's report stated of the coxswain:

> Even more than is usually the case, it was thanks to him that this fine service was possible. It was his own remarkable personality and really great qualities of leadership which magnetised tired and somewhat dispirited men into launching, and when the boat was launched it was the consummate skill with which he managed her, and the encouragement he gave his crew which brought their efforts to such a successful conclusion.

The Duke of Connaught made special reference to the episode when he presided at the next Annual General Meeting. So impressed was he by the gallantry shown, and by the response of the troops who had helped in the rescues, that shortly after the war he addressed a letter to the officers and men of the regiments of which he was Colonel-in-Chief, asking their support for the Institution. The result, as might have been expected, reflected credit on the generous spirit of all concerned.

Enthusiasm, courage and energy, immensely helpful as they were in the business of launching and beaching, could, however, seldom make up for lack of local and professional experience in actual life-boat work, in pulling and sailing cases. This was shown with peculiar force a few weeks after Blogg had rescued Niels Nielson. The Norwegian barque *Auder*, loaded with pit-props for West Hartlepool, was wrecked in Blyth Bay. Both the life-boat crew and the rocket team were summoned, but the ship was too far out for rockets to be of use if fired from the shore. The life-boat crew exhausted themselves in saving five men, a task which was completed with great difficulty and only after several attempts. Later, two seamen struggled ashore through the surf, but there were still three left on board, the captain, an able seaman and a boy.

A volunteer crew of bluejackets then tried their hand in a strenuous effort to reach the wreck, but without success. Conceiving that failure might have been due to the muscle of those involved, another bluejacket crew was formed, but met with no better luck. At length the regulars, who had by now recovered, got their boat away a second time, and managed to put a line aboard the barque, by means of which the men were taken off. The *Life-boat* commented:

> It is a fairly common fallacy that, given a number of men pulling a good oar and, of course, the courage to face any risk, it is easy enough to form a successful life-boat crew. Nothing could be more erroneous, and the present case proves it, though it does not diminish by one jot or tittle the splendid conduct of the bluejackets who volunteered to man the life-boat.

Although this observation was true, the day-to-day occupation of a member of a life-boat crew, or even of a coxswain, was not necessarily of significance. This was well demonstrated in December 1916 when the Venerable Archdeacon J. R. H. Becher, who was Honorary Secretary of the local life-boat Committee, won a silver medal for his leading part in the rescue of sixteen men from the steam-ship *Alondra* which had gone ashore on Kedge Rock, off Baltimore, County Cork.

* * *

As the war went on with its interminable casualty lists recording death and wounds suffered by land, sea and air, the burden on the Institution seemed to increase. Nineteen-fifteen proved to be a record year for the saving of life. No fewer than 1,300 were rescued, more than equivalent, as many pointed out, to the strongest infantry battalion.

The cost was not negligible, particularly as in many cases the average age of crews rose to be as high as fifty, while it was not unknown for septuagenarians to handle an oar. One of the saddest losses occurred at Salcombe, Devon, on 27 October 1916 when, in crossing the harbour bar during an attempt to help the schooner *Western Lass*, thirteen out of the local crew of fifteen lost their lives. Salcombe was reputedly the scene of inspiration for Tennyson's lines 'Sunset and evening star . . .' though some hold them to have derived from a journey from Lymington across to the Isle of Wight. After this occasion, they were most appropriately quoted:

> Sunset and evening star,
> And one clear call for me!
> And may there be no moaning at the bar,
> When I put out to sea,

But such a tide as moving seems asleep,
Too full for sound and foam.
When that which drew from out the boundless deep
Turns again home.

So many instances of gallantry in this time of war were on record that in February 1917 the Committee of Management decided to authorize the issue of a medal in bronze, which could be awarded additionally to those which had for so long been given in gold or silver for services of special distinction. This gave much satisfaction, and it enabled crew members to receive recognition in cases where, previously, the coxswain alone might have been singled out for decoration. It should also be observed that it added to the difficulty, always present when medals are involved, of deciding, in an even more delicate way than before, what were the degrees of merit and risk in any given case.

It took some time for the ban on Life-boat Days to be lifted, but the authorities at last relented. Pin-stickers, with the R.N.L.I. house-flag in miniature attached to them, could then be seen once more on people's coats, reminding their wearers of a work of mercy that had never been more necessary than at a time when the sinking of merchant ships was continuing at a rate which threatened the entire war effort. The London Ladies' Committee, on whom fell the responsibility for organizing collections, included Mrs Lloyd George, wife of the Prime Minister, Lady Waldegrave, wife of the Chairman of the Committee of Management, and the wives of Admirals Jellicoe and Beatty.

In 1918, in days of ever-increasing shortages and hardship, a regular pensions scheme was established for the benefit of dependants of those who lost their lives on service. These were to be in line with those obtaining in H.M. forces, coxswains ranking with chief petty officers of the navy, second coxswains and bowmen with petty officers, and crew members with able seamen.

During the course of the same year the seventh Duke of Northumberland, who had been President of the Institution since 1911, died at the age of seventy-two. One of his last endeavours had been to inaugurate an annual essay competition on the work of the life-boats, with a prize of £100 and a district challenge shield. This was to be open to 'children still actually attending the senior classes in national elementary schools throughout the United Kingdom'.

At the Annual General Meeting, which was held in August 1918 under the chairmanship of Mr Asquith, who had been Prime Minister for the first two years of the war, it was announced that Edward, Prince of Wales, had agreed to accept office as President. This was momentous news, far more so than could have been realized at the time, when it was noted that the Prince, who was then serving with the army in France, would take up a post once held by his father and grandfather. It could not have been foreseen how soon that same young man would come to signify hope for the future to a country which was then enduring some of the darkest hours in its history. Victory was in sight, but the cost had been so high that it would soon seem a hollow word.

War had indeed taken its toll among the servants of the Institution. Inspectors, and a great many of the staff, had been called or recalled to the colours. The Inspectors had had extremely varied experiences. One of them, Lieutenant Commander H. T. Gartside Tipping, had been killed in action, his death being witnessed by a fellow Inspector, Commander W. G. Rigg, who was awarded the Distinguished Service Order for minesweeping with the Dover Patrol. Gartside Tipping, who at the age of sixty-six was believed to be the oldest naval officer actually serving afloat, was killed on 25 September 1915 when the ex steam-yacht *Sandra*, which he commanded, was hit by an 8-inch shell from a German coastal battery, and sank with the loss of over half her complement. The sound of the action, due to a freak of wind, could be faintly heard as far away as Hickling in Norfolk, where Gartside Tipping had long made his home. The survivors were picked up by Commander Rigg.

Commander F. J. Rowley, who in the immediate future was to start on what became in due course a most distinguished record as Chief Inspector, was promoted during the course of the war to the rank of post-captain for services with the Fleet, as was Commander Basil Hall. Commander E. D. Drury of the Western District was given charge of H.M.S. *Empress*, one of the early seaplane carriers, and Commander P. F. M. Fellows, who had assumed the task of District Organizing Secretary for the south of England after being invalided out of the Navy, managed to join the flying wing. He won the D.S.O. but was shot down off the Belgian coast. Fortunately for him, the enemy picked him up,

Depot at Poplar, East London, nineteenth century, showing life-boat transporters used on open beaches, once pulled by horses and later by tractors, to get the life-boats into positions from which they could be launched

Depot at Boreham Wood, Hertfordshire

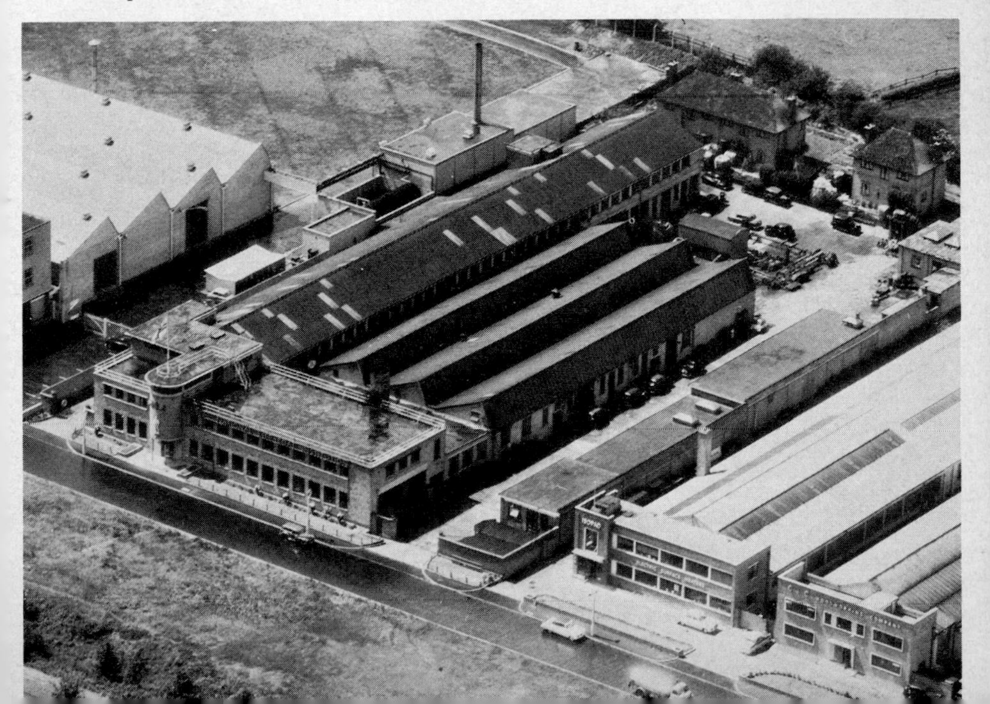

Hydraulically propelled steam life-boat *Queen* on trials in 1897 on the Thames, with Rennie's Waterloo Bridge in the background. Built by Thornycroft, 55 feet in length, the *Queen* had an active life of twenty-six years and was the means of rescuing 196 people

Lord Mottistone and the crew of the Brooke, Isle of Wight, life-boat preparing for a routine exercise

Famous coxswains;
Charles Fish of Ramsgate, leader of the *Indian Chief* rescue of 1881

James Cable of Aldeburgh, wearing old-pattern life-belt with knife-holder

Robert Smith of Tynemouth, conspicuous in the *Rohilla* rescue of 1914

Robert Cross of the Humber, outstanding in the Second World War

Steam paddle-tug towing life-boat to wreck, nineteenth century.
Painting by G. N. Nibbs (1816–93), hitherto unpublished

Famous coxswains:
John McLean of Peterhead,
gold medal, 1942

Patrick Sliney of Ballycotton,
gold medal winner for the Daunt
Rock light-ship rescue of 1936

Richard Evans of Moelfre, twice
awarded the gold medal of the R.N.L.I.

Herbert Petit of Guernsey,
awarded a gold medal in 1963

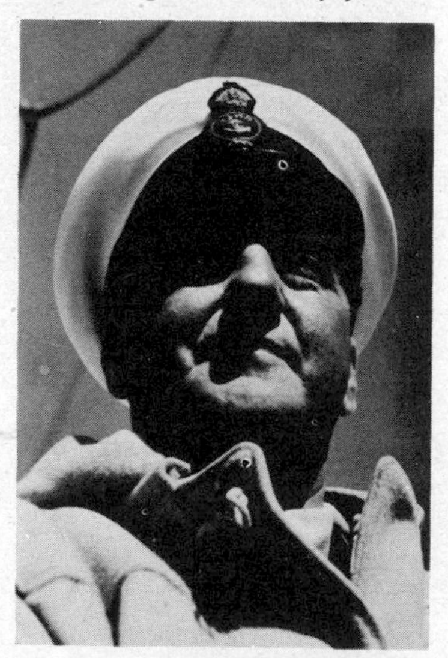

ail and motor: the Sheringham life-boat, 1936

Mrs Margaret Armstrong, of Cresswell, Northumberland, 1849–1928, who for fifty years never missed a launch of the life-boat

and he spent some time as a prisoner-of-war. Mr James Edward Martin, who had been the Institution's Chief Rigger, joined a seaplane carrier which had been converted from a Liverpool–Isle of Man steamer, but died in 1916 on active service. Another rigger, Mr John Nunn, served at the battle of Jutland as an able seaman aboard H.M.S. *Warspite*.

In the last war-time issue of the *Life-boat*, which was dated November 1918 and covered the period of relief and thankfulness which accompanied the signing of the Armistice, the price of the journal, which had remained at a modest 3*d*. for over sixty years, was unobtrusively doubled, an inflationary symptom which at the time was scarcely noticed.

Then and later, opportunity was taken to assess the size of the Institution's achievement during the years since 1914. There had been a total of 1,808 launches; 5,332 lives had been saved, and 186 vessels. Of the launches, 549 had been directly concerned with H.M. ships or those employed by the Government. Among the men saved were 22 from seaplanes, 16 of whom were picked up in a single year, 1918. Allied ships and seamen had greatly benefited. Two French ships and 98 Frenchmen had been saved, as had 91 Italians and at least one of their vessels. Ninety-eight seamen of the United States owed their lives to the British life-boat organization. And there was at least an occasional direct war service. For instance, on 24 November 1917 the North Deal life-boat was called on to take four naval officers to an abandoned German submarine. The record of this incident is tantalizingly brief, but certainly that particular U-boat would have done no further harm to Allied shipping.

Although comparisons are profitless when so much splendid work is concerned, there was a measure of agreement as to what had been among the greater feats. There had been the rescues at Whitby from the *Rohilla*, and in Scotland from H.M.S. *Success*; the rescues at Cromer from the *Pyrin* and other ships; and a series of rescues in November 1916 in which the Deal, Ramsgate and Kingsdown boats had all been involved, when a total of 82 had been saved during a storm of exceptional ferocity. And within a few weeks of the end of the war, Coxswain Swan of Lowestoft, with a scratch crew of eighteen men of whom two were over seventy, twelve over sixty, and four over fifty, rescued nine out of twelve men from the sloop *Pomona*, which was wrecked five miles from Southwold in Suffolk, the captain and the two remaining men having been swept away almost at once.

* * *

The war had opened, for the Institution, with the christening at Fraserburgh of the life-boat *Lady Rothes*. A sad tail-piece occurred in the same place in the summer of 1919, before the Peace Treaty was signed on 28 June. The patrol vessel *Eminent* of Burghead, which was on the Admiralty's list for disposal, was making for shelter in a heavy sea when her engines broke down. The captain tried to anchor offshore, but the anchors dragged, and distress signals were sent off.

These were answered by the *Lady Rothes*, in charge of Coxswain Andrew Noble, who put out with a crew of eleven. The life-boat was soon in trouble in the very heavy sea, and all but three of the crew were washed overboard when she suddenly overturned. As the boat was a self-righter most of her men managed to scramble back inboard, or to reach the shore on their own in their life-belts: but Noble, whose age was fifty-nine, and Farquhar, the second coxswain, who was fifty, died as the result of exposure. This was a very heavy loss, for Noble was senior pilot at Fraserburgh and the senior life-boat coxswain then active in Scotland. He had held the post since 1887. The *Eminent* eventually drove on to the sands, and her entire crew were rescued by rocket apparatus.

It was to be of significance for the future that the Institution had been concerned, during the war, in rescues from aircraft. Its work in this direction was in due course to multiply, and a time would come when aircraft would prove an invaluable aid to the life-boat service. It is also of interest to note that for a period of some two years the wireless station at Sheerness alerted the London air defence stations. A naval officer pointed out that among the Coastguard stores were maroons used for summoning life-boats. A supply was sent to London, where they became the first public air-raid warnings. Winston Churchill once referred to later warnings as 'banshee wails', but their mournful sound was the means of saving many lives.

5
A Century of Service

The Institution had sustained spells of poverty, a Parliamentary inquiry, and war. The problems of peace and reconstruction were now before it, with the prospect of centenary celebrations in a few years' time. The transference of motive power from oar and sail to mechanical means, which had begun so promisingly, had been interrupted and must be resumed. Conflict in Europe gave place in newspaper headlines to trouble in Ireland, as they had done so often before. There the Institution, because it was one of the few bodies with interests on both sides of the Irish Sea, could look for understanding.

Sir William Hillary, active in his day in the Isle of Man, soon found that the Irish Sea presented as many challenges to rescuers as the North Sea or the English Channel. 'Those of us who have daily to do with it,' wrote Dr de Courcy Ireland, historian of the Irish life-boat service, 'know it alike for its fathomless malice and for the unsurpassed skill of so many of the seamen who have learned their trade on its perfidious waters.'

There was a life-boat at Dublin at least as early as 1801, although, as in the case of so many Irish stations, whether run by the Institution or not, there were gaps in its continuity. There had even been an Irish Grace Darling—two in fact. For when, towards the end of the eighteenth century, a ship was wrecked in Dublin Bay, two women who were managing their father's business at Pidgeon House Dock (which later became the mail terminal), rowed out and rescued a man and a child. Their names were Rachel and Mary Pidgeon. The man proved to be a widower from Philadelphia. He married Mary, whereupon she and Rachel went out to North America to live.

The original Irish stations, which were run by the organization set up in 1786 which is now known as the Dublin Port and Docks Board, were around Dublin Bay. They included Dun Laoghaire and Howth, which still exist. John Clements of Dublin built the first Irish life-boat, which cost £115. 18. 9.

The first Irish station to be managed by the Institution was at

Arklow, County Wicklow. It was established in 1826. It has remained important: so much so that although it was Wicklow itself which in 1911 was given the first Irish motor life-boat, Arklow was equipped with one three years later. It was among the few which were delivered during the course of the war. The first of the Institution's gold medals awarded in Ireland went in 1829 to a Ballycotton coastguard, Sam Lloyd.

Between the Easter Rebellion in Dublin of 1916 and the first Irish constitution of 1922, the island was in a state of disturbance, sometimes fiercely active, sometimes dormant, but always threatening. One of the few organizations about which there was a measure of agreement was the R.N.L.I. The Irish stations continued to be administered from London so far as related to equipment and policy, and they received a small annual subsidy therefrom, since the results of local fund-raising proved insufficient to meet the full costs of the service. Even so, they were gallant and sustained, and there is evidence that the ladies of Dublin, collecting for the cause during the summer of 1921, came under fire, although they were not the targets. They actually raised £572, exceeding their previous year's total by £80.

Great efforts were made to continue the link with the United Kingdom, and they were successful, so much so that after the establishment of Irish independence, the name of the Institution was retained at stations, including the prefix Royal. Even differences of religion could at times be forgotten, as occurred, for instance, at what was then known as Kingstown, but which has since become Dun Laoghaire, just south of Dublin. There, the motor life-boat *Dunleary*, which had been sailed from Cowes in charge of Commander S. C. Douglas, R.N., the Inspector for the Irish District, during the previous winter, was officially blessed on 17 April 1920, in brilliant weather.

The 500-mile journey which the boat had made from Cowes to reach the station had not been without incident. Off St Albans Head in Dorset the crew were nearly swamped by the tide-race. At Plymouth there had been some difficulty in finding enough petrol for the lap round Land's End. At Padstow, the crew were piloted in by the local coxswain. At Pembroke, a tremendous wind blew the golden weather-cock down from the church, and people could barely stand upright. Off Rosslare Point the local coxswain, as at Padstow, brought the boat in. Off Wicklow, on

21 December 1919, the *Dunleary* met with such a gale that, even with the 60 h.p. Tylor motor at full power, 'it took an hour,' according to Commander Douglas's account, 'to do the two short miles from Wicklow Head'. Kingstown was in sight on 22 December, and it looked as if there might be a chance of making a rescue even before reaching station, for a man and a boy were distantly sighted in a dangerous situation offshore in a small boat. Commander Douglas was, however, forestalled by a steam launch in the service of the Commissioners of Irish Lights, whose men got matters in hand just as the life-boat was about to alter course to help. The journey was typical of many in the earlier days, when motor life-boats had to be delivered to their stations by sea during the winter.

Kingstown had had a tragedy on Christmas Eve, 1895, which was still all too well remembered. Fifteen life-boatmen had been drowned and their boat wrecked in an attempt to save the crew of the barque *Palme* of Finland, which drove aground in Dublin Bay in a south-easterly gale. Kingstown had also produced a hero, Captain Thomas McCombie. At the time of the disaster this officer was master of the SS *Tearaght*. Two days later, as the people on board the *Palme* were seen to be still alive, McCombie put off in a boat with members of his ship's company, and rescued the captain of the *Palme*, his wife, and the crew, after their long ordeal. He was awarded the Institution's gold medal for this feat. He already held the silver medal for a gallant service some twenty years earlier when, as second officer of the SS *Princess Alice*, he had saved three men from the brig *Hampton* of Dublin, which had been wrecked during a heavy gale.

The arrival of a new motor life-boat was particularly welcome at a station of fine traditions, which was also among the oldest in Ireland.

* * *

If disturbances on the far side of the Irish Sea might have caused special difficulties for headquarters, many other matters were then engaging the energies of the Secretary, George Shee, who as the servant of the Committee of Management was to steer the Institution through some critical years. He was among the foremost in recognizing that, in the last resort, it was the fortitude of their womenfolk which nerved the life-boat crews as they battled with the sea.

Women began to appear in the *Life-boat* gallery. They were drawn from three sorts of people: there were those who lived on the coast, who helped their men to launch the boats, and who sometimes took part in rescues from the beaches. There were the voluntary workers everywhere, who not only raised funds but who, by means of lectures and discussions, made the life-boat cause more widely known; and there were those who, from their position in society, gave prestige to the Institution, and this not in a tepid or a formal way.

Among such women, the Northumbrian Mrs Margaret Armstrong was outstanding. She lived at Cresswell, a small coastal village facing Druridge Bay, which for some seventy years had a life-boat station of its own. It was a place where at one time most of the inhabitants, many of whom were of almost giant stature, were called Brown. This was Mrs Armstrong's maiden name. From her earliest years she helped her family in their fishing, but in 1873 their coble was overturned, and Margaret had the tragic experience of seeing the bodies of her father and three of her brothers brought ashore.

Three years later, after the life-boat station had been established, the Swedish ship *Gustaf* ran ashore near the village during a fierce, snow-laden January gale, with fourteen on board, including three women. Margaret formed part of a living chain to try to pull from the sea those who had put out in one of the ship's boats and been overset, and in so doing she was at times out of her depth and in acute peril. The *Gustaf* lay where the life-boat could not be of immediate use, such was the state of the tide, and it was soon clear that a message must somehow be got through to the coastguards at Newbiggin, asking them to bring their shore apparatus to the scene. Newbiggin was five long miles away, by any practicable route, and most of it was very rough going. Margaret and Mary Brown, and Isabella Armstrong of Cresswell struggled through the storm, determined to get help. The younger girls had to give up from exhaustion, but Margaret herself reached the coastguard station, her feet bleeding, and by that time speechless. But the men knew her, knew why she had come, and knew what to do. They got their life-saving equipment post-haste to Cresswell, horse-drawn, although by the time it arrived the life-boat had been able to reach the wreck and to take off the remaining survivors, a man and three women.

The coastguards were so struck with the pluck Margaret had shown in reaching them that they gave her a silver tea-pot, and the two other girls received inscribed mementoes. To the end of her life, Mrs Armstrong remained one of the Cresswell life-boat launchers, and on 14 January 1922 Sir Godfrey Baring, Deputy Chairman of the Committee of Management, presented her with a gold brooch and a record of thanks for her fine example over so many years. Even after her marriage, Mrs Armstrong had not been allowed to forget the dangers of seafaring, for her son was drowned, and yet another of her brothers, as the result of storms.

On the very next day after Mrs Armstrong had been honoured, there occurred yet another instance of particular service on the part of women. It took place at Holy Island, where the trawler *James Graham* of Hartlepool went ashore in darkness. Her distress signals were seen, and sixty islanders, the great majority of them women, were called upon to get the life-boat launched. The trawler was wrecked in one of the most dangerous spots on the north side of the island, but, after a great struggle, her entire crew was taken off. For this successful feat the Holy Island coxswain, George Cromarty, was given a clasp to the silver medal he had won during the war for rescues from the Swedish barque *Jolani*. Bronze medals were awarded to the second coxswain and the bowman. The women concerned in the launch received a special letter of thanks, Miss Daisy Cromarty being chosen by the others as their representative.

Pride of place in the gallery among women workers inland went to Miss Alice Marshall, the Honorary Secretary of the Institution's Oxford Branch, in recognition of the fact that Oxford had done more by way of fund-raising than any place outside the London area except for great cities such as Edinburgh, Glasgow, Liverpool and Birmingham. Miss Marshall would certainly have subscribed to the view, expressed by a seasoned collector, that while people in general seldom lacked goodwill, they were lazy, sometimes almost unbelievably so, and, in her words, 'you have to go and *take* it from them!'.

There was also example, and this was not lacking. A Ladies' Life-boat Guild was formed in 1921, absorbing earlier organizations, with the Duchess of Portland as President. The qualification for membership consisted of readiness to help, by personal service. A badge was authorized, with a bar for office holders. This was fulfilling the idea, which had been approved before the war by King George V, of giving tangible recognition to those who performed 'distinguished, exceptional, or long and faithful services other than those for which the medals of the Institution are given'.

In 1923, Princess Louise, Duchess of Argyll, became Patron of the Guild, the Duchess of Norfolk and the Marchioness of Milford Haven also accepting office. Already by that time the Prince of Wales had actively associated himself with the cause. He took the chair at the Annual General Meeting on 28 April 1921 and the stimulus he gave was soon apparent. It was well illustrated two years later when, on what he had agreed should be called 'Prince of Wales's Day' the London collectors exceeded all records. The Prince, radiating enthusiasm, visited many London boroughs in person, and the results were memorable. Stepney, for instance, a poor district with much unemployment, raised £163 as opposed to a mere £10 the previous year, and Lambeth £311 as against £49. More than £5,500 was raised during the course of the day.

* * *

If the war and its immediate aftermath had curtailed life-boat building and strained resources sometimes to the limit, there had been side-effects which proved beneficial. The smaller type of marine engine had been improved, though it had a long way to go before it could be considered reliable under all conditions. There had even been some tentative experiments in assisting survivors with inflated rafts dropped from aircraft, a process which was investigated by the Institution.

There was also the development of the caterpillar tractor. This had proved valuable for military purposes, and it was seen as affording an exciting possibility in assisting life-boat launches. And there was a new line-throwing gun which, after development by the Birmingham Small Arms Company, was shown to be effective at between sixty and eighty yards. This contrasted strikingly with the old cane line, with lead weight attached, which was thrown by hand. In a high wind, this could carry only a trifling distance. The gun was adopted, and soon became standard equipment.

Captain Rowley, as Chief Inspector, made initial experiments with a 35 h.p. caterpillar tractor at Hunstanton, Norfolk. The machine itself weighed three tons. The transporter, fitted with Tipping plates, and the life-boat, together weighed 7 tons 3 cwt., a load which proved to be well within the tractor's capability. Where the ground was favourable, a speed of 6 m.p.h. could be maintained. A 25-foot long pushing pole was intended to facilitate matters. When the tractor and its tow had got to a point on the beach where the sea covered the tracks to a depth of about two feet, Rowley gave the order to launch. The coxswain had other ideas and did nothing, with the result that, as the tide came in, the tractor became totally submerged. Captain Rowley, the mechanic, and the Institution's Deputy Surveyor of Machinery were taken off by the life-boat, which by that time was afloat.

In spite of this initial contretemps, the tractor suffered no lasting damage, and a later effort at Hunstanton was successful. The Clayton was also tried out at Heacham, a little farther along the Norfolk shore. There, the shingle proved too much for it, but later trials at Worthing, Sussex, were promising, and it was soon shown conclusively that the tractor was a practical ancillary. Like the line-gun, it was duly adopted, and it continues to be of the utmost value at many life-boat stations.

The next important step was to develop a marine engine under the immediate eye of the Institution's own experts. This had become necessary because Messrs Tylor, who had proved so useful in supplying efficient motors over a good many years, discontinued marine work. Thereupon, the Institution made use of facilities offered by the Weyburn Engineering Co. of Godalming, Surrey, and they would have gone on so doing but for a fire at the works which damaged the engine under construction. This was, however, duly completed, and it was installed in a boat destined for Penlee in Cornwall. It developed 76 h.p. and was the prototype of a successful series. The Penlee crew made their first rescues in their new boat in January 1923. They saved 27 from the Yugoslav ship *Dubrovka* which was wrecked not far from Land's End.

On the test bench, the engine looked a beautifully neat and workmanlike job. It weighed 37 cwt., and its power-to-weight ratio was considered excellent by contemporary standards. Those who worked on it remarked on the extraordinary number of fittings, particularly those which concerned controls, which had to be designed without any guidance from previous experience. It could have been said without exaggeration that the Institution's staff, in evolving their motor, had done much for the advancement of marine engineering in general.

Work on the engine was particularly important, since even before it had proved itself in service the Institution had released the fact to the Press that its Consulting Naval Architect, Mr J. R. Barnett, had designed a twin-screw boat, 60 ft. by 15 ft., with a draught of 4 ft. 6 in. which, with her 40 tons displacement, would be the largest life-boat in the world except for one on trial for the North and South Holland Life-saving Society which was due to replace the steam-powered *Brandaris*.

The artist working at that time for the weekly *Graphic*, Mr Clatworthy, was allowed to publish a diagrammatic impression of the boat, which had many new features, including a searchlight, a life-saving net, and the line-throwing gun. She was to have two motors which would, so it was expected, give her a service speed of about 10 knots. For the first time, two cabins were provided, and although the boat was not self-righting she was considered almost unsinkable. She was built of teak, double-skinned, and she had eleven transverse and three longitudinal steel bulk-heads, forming fifteen main water-tight compartments. Her capacity was 150, and so much did the idea of the safety which lay in the two separate engines impress the Institution's technicians that she was provided with only a jury rig, consisting of a small triangular fore-lug and jib, which could be set on the single mast. When completed in 1923 the Barnett boat was sent to New Brighton, where she replaced the steam-powered *Queen*.

* * *

A matter which had long worried fund-raisers at headquarters was the very small amount of the Institution's total revenue which came from British shipping companies. Certain firms were, and had long been, subscribers, but the majority, even when they had benefited more than once from the Institution's activities, remained oblivious of its claims. The stricture applied more rarely to individual officers and men, who were well aware that they might owe their lives, in any crisis, to the skill and seamanship of volunteers who went out to them in trouble.

Over a period of years, the Secretary conducted a regular campaign, as did representatives of shipping interests on the Committee of Management, to try to remedy the matter. Every form of persuasion was employed, from straight appeals to justice and generosity, through cajolery, to attempts to shame the unresponsive into doing their duty. Lists were published of lives saved and services rendered over a given period, with an indication of where reciprocation had taken place, and where it had not. Just after the war, it had been shown by statistics that British ship-owners contributed under 1 per cent of the money needed to maintain the rescue service. Three and four years later, things were no better, and it was shown that, as at May 1922, while 290 British shipping firms subscribed to the funds, some 1,610 others did not, although no fewer than 125 foreign concerns were on the regular list of benefactors.

The situation continued to be unsatisfactory, and it was perhaps partly in the hope of improvement that in November 1922 an officer belonging to the Merchant Navy was elected to the Committee of Management. By any reckoning, this was a belated step, and it would have caused the historically inclined to recall criticisms which had arisen, sometimes within the Institution itself, when, at the time of the award of the Northumberland Prize in 1851, the adjudicating body had been drawn exclusively from naval or official circles. The Royal Navy continued to be well represented, as was proper, and the officer who joined the Committee from the sister service, Captain G. C. Holloway, could hardly have been better qualified. Apart from his professional attainments, he held a commission in the Naval Reserve, and he had received three life-saving awards from the Royal Humane Society.

One further step was taken to make the Merchant Navy more aware of the achievements of the Institution. This was the happy inspiration of inviting Joseph Conrad, master mariner, and the most distinguished living writer about the sea, to the platform at the Annual General Meeting which was held on 14 April 1923. On this occasion the Chairman was Admiral of the Fleet Earl Beatty, and it was hoped that Conrad might speak after him. The meeting was also attended by an influential Labour politician, Miss Margaret Bondfield, who at the time was Secretary of the Women's Section of the National Union of General Workers.

Earl Beatty made the point that 'the life-boats are essentially a fighting service. The men in it train their courage and acquire their skill in seamanship in a daily struggle with the elements. It is a struggle which lasts all their lives, and so we can conclude that they are a fighting service in the best sense of the word.' He had a very stirring episode to which to refer.

Between 19 and 21 October 1922 both the Gorleston and the Lowestoft life-boats had been concerned in attempts to rescue the crew of 24 of the SS *Hopelyn* of Newcastle, which had driven on to Scroby Sands in a high sea. Efforts were made almost continuously, over two nights and a day, to get the men off the wreck. The Gorleston life-boat, which was not mechanically powered, failed, after an heroic fight by her coxswain, William Fleming, and his crew. But Fleming was able to second the work of Coxswain John Swan of Lowestoft, who with his motor life-boat was at last able to get all the survivors to safety. Both coxswains were awarded the Institution's highest honour, their gold medal.

To Joseph Conrad, this feat was of special significance, for, as he recalled in his speech, he had himself served under the red ensign in ships manned by East Anglians, for whom he retained the warmest affection. He referred to the Institution as 'this national organization, so universally known and trusted, that a seaman of any nationality, directly he has sighted our shores, feels himself the object of its sleepless care'. He added that the first words he ever heard about the life-boat service 'were on the lips of a Breton seaman in the West Indies. He had been, it seems, wrecked on our east coast at one time, and what he said was: "On those men you can always depend. They don't give up. . . ." I now know, of my own knowledge, that a life-boat crew may fail sometimes (there is no shame in being defeated by the sea), but that it does not give up.'

It may have been that in preparing this part of his speech Conrad was influenced by the memory of another event of the East Anglian coast which had long been famous. On 14 November 1901, one of the two life-boats at Caister, a 36-foot pulling and sailing boat of the Norfolk and Suffolk type, capsized in cold and darkness and a high sea, not far from where she had been launched, with the utmost difficulty, to answer a call. Having done their duty most of the helpers, wet through, left the beach for a change of clothes. One who did not do so was James Haylett, a man of seventy-eight who, when younger, had been second coxswain.

Haylett had two sons, a son-in-law and a grandson in the boat. When, at some point in her struggle, she turned over, many of the crew were pinned beneath her, and nine of them lost their lives. As the upturned boat neared the beach Haylett, at the greatest risk, dashed into the surf with one of his grandsons, and they succeeded in rescuing three men, one of whom was the old man's son-in-law, George Knights, and another his grandson. Both his sons perished. Gallant old James Haylett received the gold medal, and his grandson Frederick the Institution's thanks inscribed on vellum.

At the inquest, the suggestion was put forward that the lifeboat might have been returning, after abandoning her mission. James Haylett would have none of it. 'Caister men never turn back,' he said, and his words reverberated. They are commemorated in local folklore, and what could be a better fate?

This was exactly the sort of incident which would have appealed to Conrad, with his extreme and justified reverence for 'fidelity'. Recalling his own early days at sea, he said his Lowestoft and other shipmates 'may have been amused at me, but they taught me the elements of a seaman's duty, below and aloft, and the very terms of our sea speech, which has been mine now for many years'. The rescued 'looked to them for their lives with that absolute confidence which is the due, and, after all, the greatest reward of men who never give up'.

Conrad's speech was made just a week before he sailed on a triumphant tour to the United States, the last protracted excursion of his life.

* * *

Any organization dependent not upon Government resources or commercial interest, but solely upon the voluntary support of the public, is in duty bound to take every occasion to remind people of its continuing needs; to seize every chance, in a competitive world, to make its aims and wants known; to keep its image fresh in popular imagination. Tragedy at sea always generates its own macabre publicity, and a successful rescue, the more spectacular the better, has generally been considered newsworthy. More certain in its effects, because it can be planned well in advance, is the appeal of a jubilee or centenary occasion. The servants of the Institution had long been aware of the significance of the year 1924. So much was this so, that plans had been in train for the centenary even before the end of the war. The result of such foresight was a many-sided celebration whose effects were lasting, since they added to the usefulness of the Institution to nations other than Great Britain.

Sir William Hillary's precept—'the people and vessels of every nation, whether in peace or war, to be equally the objects of this Institution'—had never been overlooked. But it had long been felt that there could be far more profitable exchange of information between life-boat Societies in the countries which possessed them. A start was made by inviting authoritative brief histories or descriptions of affairs abroad, as contributions to the *Life-boat*.

The closest ties were with Holland, and as early as 1836 a Willem van Houten of Rotterdam had been awarded the Institution's silver medal for a model of a life-boat and carriage, the latter being described by the Committee as 'the best they have ever seen for the purpose'. In his country, two separate organizations had been founded in 1824, within a very short time of Hillary's. They were the North and South Holland Life-saving Society, and the South Holland Society for Saving the Shipwrecked. Liaison had been frequent between Dutch and British experts, and it was not therefore surprising that the first account of a foreign service was written (in admirable English) by H. de Booy, the Secretary of the North and South Holland Life-saving Society. This was followed up by others, in a series which was to continue over several years, and which has to some degree remained a regular feature.

Soon after the war had ended, the Secretary, the Chief Inspector and the Surveyor were welcomed personally in Holland. They went on an exercise in the steam *Brandaris*, British-built in 1910, which was to be tragically lost in October 1921 off Terschelling. Help and advice had been sought by Denmark, Spain, Turkey, Romania, Mexico and Uruguay, and had been gladly given. Inquiries had also been received from revolutionary Russia, through the Trade Commission in London. This had been of special interest, for there had been a Tsarist rescue organization, dating from the 1870s, which by 1891 was reported to have 125 stations, 60 on the banks of rivers and 65 on the coast. In that year, British residents in St Petersburg had presented two boats, of similar design to those in use by the Institution, to the Duke of Edinburgh and the Grand Duchess Marie of Russia when they married. It was a practical gesture which had appealed to the Duke, with his interest in life-boat matters.

Invitations to the centenary celebrations were extended abroad, not just as a matter of courtesy, but with the hope of initiating an International Life-boat Conference. Eight countries sent representatives: Denmark, France, Japan, Holland, Norway, Spain, Sweden and the United States, each with its own maritime interests and traditions.

Another preliminary was the appearance of an authorized history of the work of the Institution, which was written by Major A. J. Dawson at the request of the Committee of Management. Its title was *Britain's Life-boats: the Story of a Century of Heroic Service*. It had an Introduction by the Prince of Wales, and a Foreword by Conrad. 'The first maritime nation in the world,' wrote the Prince, 'has made it a point of honour that the Service which embodies the Brotherhood of the Sea, should be a Service supplied and maintained by the people itself.' It is suggestive of the changes which have taken place during the past fifty years that the ordinary cloth-bound edition of a work of some 282 pages, lavishly illustrated, could be sold at 7*s*. 6*d*.

Conrad's tribute is worth quoting both as an example of how well he put things, and because it was among the last work he published, for he died some ten months after its appearance.

> No voluntary organization for a humane end has the reputation and the prestige of the Royal National Life-boat Institution, or a clearer record of efficiency and, one may say, of brotherly devotion. But it is only those who have followed the sea for their livelihood that know with what confidence the Life-boat Service is looked upon by those for whose benefit it has been founded by the generosity of people who live ashore.
>
> Myself a British seaman, with something like twenty years' service, I can testify to that feeling, and to the comfort the existence of Life-boat Stations, with their ever-ready crews, brings to the hearts

of men on board ships of all nations approaching our shores in dangerous weather.

I can bear witness to our unshakeable belief in the Life-boat organization and to our pride in the achievements of our fellow seamen, who, husbands and fathers, would go out on a black night without hesitation to dispute our homeless fate with the angry seas. I remember well how affectionately we looked at those white and blue boats of characteristic shape into which (through a slot in the deck) we used to drop a little silver on paying-off days; feeling that we could do but little in that way, but daring to hope that we, too, serving the overseas commerce of this generous country, were not upon the whole unworthy of the assistance given us for the preservation of the property under our care and for the saving of our obscure lives.

* * *

The events of the centenary would necessarily place a burden on the Chairman of the Committee of Management, and employ a great deal of his time, because, next to the Secretary and the permanent staff, he had always been the Institution's most active officer. Lord Waldegrave, who had been on the Committee since 1877 and Chairman since 1911, was in ever more uncertain health, and his duties had in recent years often fallen to his Deputy, Sir Godfrey Baring, who took on the Chairmanship in 1923. Sir Godfrey had been present at an act of piety which had taken place at Douglas, Isle of Man, not long after the war, when he had placed a wreath on the tomb of Sir William Hillary. This had fallen into disrepair, and was restored by a local architect, Mr J. H. Royston, and was given an appropriate inscription, the Institution's badge being incorporated. The design of this badge, which is still in use, had been submitted to the King in 1910 for his approval. This had been given. Sir Godfrey was a highly experienced administrator. He had been on the Committee for twelve years, and was to show himself as enthusiastic a Chairman as the most energetic of his predecessors.

The formal centenary plans included an Annual General Meeting which, so it was decided, should be held on 3 March 1924 in the City of London, this time at the Mansion House with the Lord Mayor as host and with the Archbishop of Canterbury present. In June, there would be a Life-boat Ball, and in July an official dinner of welcome to the foreign delegates, which would be attended by the Prime Minister, James Ramsay MacDonald.

The centenary coincided with the Empire Exhibition at Wembley, where the Institution would erect a handsome pavilion, close to a replica of Old London Bridge. This would include a modern life-boat with all its gear, earlier types and models, a diorama of the *Rohilla* rescue (see pages 91–5), and such features as a wax figure of a life-boatman, operationally equipped.

A Thames life-boat flotilla would include two of the latest type, one a 60-foot twin-screw Barnett, the other a 45-foot Watson with a single 76 h.p. engine. There would also be on view the new twin-screw *Brandaris* from the North and South Holland Society; the steam-driven *Prins der Nederlanden* from South Holland; a Danish boat fitted with an auxiliary motor; a Norwegian cruising ketch used for life-saving; a Swedish boat fitted with sail and motor; and a French 36-foot twin-screw boat, whose normal station was at Calais. When assembled, these boats created much interest, and to many, including the present writer, they recalled the Thames pageant of 1919 (the last occasion of its kind), when the Institution had been represented by a steam-driven boat.

King George V's resonant voice was heard for the first time by thousands of his subjects when his welcoming speech at Wembley was broadcast on what was soon to become known as the radio. The King made a special gesture in honour of the Institution when he personally invested seven of the eight living holders of the Institution's gold medal with the Empire Gallantry Medal, at Buckingham Palace. They were Captain Thomas McCrombie of Kingstown; Major Burton and Robert Smith of Tynemouth; Coxswain Blogg of Cromer; Coxswain Howells of Fishguard; Coxswain Fleming of Gorleston; Coxswain Swan of Lowestoft; and the Reverend John O'Shea of County Waterford.

Much the youngest was Blogg, who survived, as did Fleming, to receive the George Cross when, during the Second World War, holders of the Empire Gallantry Medal were given the Cross in substitution. The oldest was Robert Smith of Tynemouth, who had retired and was almost blind. He was seventy-five, and as he also held the Institution's silver medal and clasp, it was remarked by one of the other recipients that 'he got most of the talk'. The Reverend John O'Shea would have completed the party, but he was unable to be there.

Major Burton appeared in uniform, and presented his sovereign with the highly unusual spectacle of a military officer with seven medals on the left side of his tunic and four (all for life-saving) on the right. Coxswain Howells, who like Smith was over seventy and had also retired from the Institution's service, had been concerned in a particularly gallant rescue, on 3 December 1920, from the schooner *Hermina* of Rotterdam, which had been wrecked on Needle Rock, Fishguard, during a north-westerly gale. Swan, like Smith and Howells, had also retired. He held the Institution's silver medal and clasp for two rescues made during the war. The Reverend John O'Shea, who had formerly been a pillar of the life-boat station at Ardmore, had shown exceptional initiative and courage in leading attempts by a small boat to save the lives of the crew of the schooner *Teaser*, wrecked on 18 March 1911 during the course of a north-easterly gale.

The Institution had awarded only 109 gold medals and bars, during its hundred years of existence. Of these, all but fifteen, which had been bestowed for 'special services', most of which had been rendered many years earlier, had been given for great courage in rescue operations, some successful, others not. As the living recipients indicated, medallists had not in all cases been direct servants of the organization. Indeed the first gold medal for gallantry had gone to Commander, later Admiral, Sir Charles Fremantle who, when employed on coastguard duties, had in March 1824 swum with a line to a Swedish brig wrecked off Christchurch, Hampshire. As the Institution had been the means of saving 59,998 lives up to the end of its centenary year (the 60,000 mark was reached and passed on New Year's Day 1925 at Tenby), its severest critic could scarcely have held that its rewards were cheap.

At the Mansion House the Archbishop, Dr Randall Davidson, who had obviously made a careful study of the records of the original meeting at the London Tavern, where his predecessor, Dr Manners Sutton, had presided, moved a suitable resolution. It was read and carried with acclaim, in the following terms, as desiring to show

> . . . hearty appreciation of the gallantry of the Coxswains and Crews, to pay a tribute of respect and admiration to those who have sacrificed their lives in the attempt to save others, and gratefully to acknowledge the invaluable help rendered to the life-boat cause by the Local

Committees, Honorary Secretaries and Honorary Treasurers, and many thousands of seafaring men and women who have helped to maintain that cause in the hearts of the British people.

The dinner to foreign guests took place at Lancaster House. The toast was proposed by Sidney Webb, who was then the President of the Board of Trade, but who was far better known as an historian of the poor. He was replied to by the President of the North and South Holland Life-saving Society, who spoke 'as a representative of the younger brother, though not quite the twin brother, of the Institution, for his Society was founded in the same year as the British, eight months later'. A characteristic passage of rhetoric was supplied by Winston Churchill at another dinner which took place at the Hotel Cecil. He was at the time not merely out of office but temporarily out of Parliament. He spoke of the life-boat which

> . . . drives on with a courage which is stronger than the storm, it drives on with a mercy which does not quail in the presence of death, it drives on as a proof, a symbol, a testimony that man is created in the image of God, and that valour and virtue have not perished in the British race.

The most constructive business—and it proved very constructive indeed—was done at the meetings of the 'Conference on the World's Life-boat Service', which were held on 1 and 2 July in Westminster City Hall. These set a pattern for the future, and the fact that there was a fairly restricted attendance helped to make the reading of papers, which were kept admirably concise, and the resulting discussion, both intimate and effective. 'We want to learn,' said Mr Barnett, 'and we are anxious to give what information we have.' This feeling was general.

It was a tribute to Continental and Japanese education that those from abroad spoke English so well. The societies or bodies involved, in addition to the two Dutch organizations which were already so close to the R.N.L.I., were the Royal Danish Government; the Central Society of France for Saving the Shipwrecked; the Imperial Japanese Life-boat Society; the Spanish Society for Saving Life from Shipwreck; the Royal Swedish Government; the Swedish Society for Saving the Shipwrecked; the Norwegian Society for Saving the Shipwrecked; and the United States Coast Guard.

The possibility of making such a Conference a regular event was raised by Count Yoshii of Japan, who put forward a resolution, which was carried unanimously:

> That an international Life-boat organization be formed on the lines of the Red Cross Society, with all the National Life-boat Societies as its members, and that copies of this resolution be sent to all maritime countries, the headquarters of the League of Nations at Geneva, and the League of Nations Union of all countries.

The papers included 'Life-boat Signals' by Captain Rowley; 'Self-righting and non Self-righting Life-boats', by Mr Barnett; 'Petrol and Heavy Oil Motors for Life-boats', by Mr Arthur Evans, the Institution's Surveyor of Machinery; 'Tractive Power or other Mechanical Means for Launching Life-boats over Flat, Open Beaches', by Commander S. C. Douglas; 'Some Inside Aspects (Wages, Pensions and Distribution of Money) of the Life-boat Service of Denmark', by Captain Jorgen Saxild of the Danish Ministry of Marine; 'The Question of the Desirability of an International Distinguishing Mark for Life-boats', by Captain Ottar Vogt, the Secretary of the Norwegian Society; and 'Line-Throwing Appliances', a further contribution by Commander Douglas.

Much was learnt in a practical way: for instance, that the French had twice tried the hydraulic principle for life-boat work, and twice given it up in favour of internal combustion; that the Dutch had fitted a heavy oil motor in a new boat, the *Insulinde*, and that they believed, rightly as it proved, that heavy oil was the key to the future; that they had a higher opinion of all-steel construction than British experts, though it was admitted that Dutch and British coastal conditions differed, sometimes radically; and that the Swedes had found teak, which had proved so useful in wooden construction, could suffer severely from prolonged frost.

Before the end of the year, delegations from the Institution were invited to Holland to the festivities organized by the Dutch Societies. Although their centenaries followed very closely upon one another (North and South Holland, 11 November, South Holland, 20 November), the celebrations were kept strictly apart. With respect to the South Holland Society there was a special call for thankfulness in that the very first steam-powered Dutch life-boat, the *President van Heel*, which was still active at the Hook after nearly thirty years' operational service, had in October 1923 saved 29 British lives when the SS *Stuart Star* was wrecked near the south pier.

A Service of Thanksgiving, attended by the Prince of Wales and Princess Louise, Duchess of Argyll, was held on 14 December at the Central Hall, Westminster. To this came representatives from all parts of the United Kingdom and Ireland, where enthusiastic and successful efforts had been made to ensure that the centenary would be properly honoured.

In reviewing the results of the year, it was clear to the Institution that one of the most significant events had been the Conference. Its recommendations were duly presented by the Secretary to the Advisory Technical Committee for Communications and Transport of the League of Nations. This body showed sympathy, and gave assurance of support, resolving to ask the Governments concerned to induce their national organizations 'to keep in constant touch with each other'. It also expressed its willingness 'to assist in realizing these aims'.

So far, so good; but nothing concrete came out of the idea of trying to persuade official bodies to help in liaison work. Life-boat Societies would have to rely on each other for exchange of information. This fact has been realized in very early days by both British and Dutch. For in February 1826 the Secretary of one of the Dutch Societies had written to London suggesting that 'a friendly intercourse or correspondence between different Institutions established for the same object would be of great service'. Thomas Lewis, who was then the Secretary of the Institution, had answered that his Committee 'would have great pleasure at all times in reciprocating information on the very interesting subject which both Institutions have in view'. The idea was at last to be fully implemented, but through self-help.

* * *

Of the Life-boat Areas (see foldout map) among which the work of the Institution is distributed, the North of Scotland is No. 1. And within that district, which contains stations as well known as Montrose, Stromness and Stornoway, none is more important than Aberdeen, the area headquarters.

As a station, Aberdeen's history has been unusual. The thriving port had a life-boat at the service of its Harbour Commissioners at least as early as 1802. But Aberdeen, as had been the case at Liverpool and Ramsgate, continued to be independent long after the founding of the Institution, and it was in fact the last of the more important stations to hand over responsibility to the specialists. This was in 1925.

The Commissioners had been approached many times on the matter, and had been interested enough in the Institution to watch the trials at Montrose in 1893, but they decided to continue to run their own two boats, and they also held the view that a transporter invented in Aberdeen was better than anything they had seen elsewhere for use on a particular type of beach.

When the question was mooted once more in 1912, the Commissioners came to the same conclusion as before. 'No better boats propelled by oars,' wrote the Harbour Master, 'could be obtained for the requirements of this port.' There was also the difficulty that the Commissioners were responsible for running five rocket stations, and that the life-boat crews were all either pilots or served the rocket apparatus. The arrangements caused no difficulties locally, and change seemed pointless, though the life-boats themselves were getting old, not to say ancient: one dated from 1875 and the other from 1853.

Matters came to a head when in 1923 the trawler *Imperial Prince* was wrecked near the port with the loss of two of her crew. A public inquiry was held, and although the court found that every reasonable step had been taken to prevent loss of life, a rider was added. 'In our opinion,' this read, 'a motor life-boat would have obviated the heavy labour of the men in rowing.' Hearty agreement was expressed by all who had been involved.

Soon after this episode negotiations were reopened between the Harbour Commissioners and the Institution, and agreement was reached. The Institution would send two pulling and sailing life-boats to Aberdeen at once, and order a 60-foot Barnett type motor life-boat, powered by two of the Institution's 76 h.p. engines, the estimated cost being £14,000. It was considered that the Harbour Master should act as Honorary Superintendent of the station, and that fund-raising should remain the responsibility of the Honorary Secretary of the local branch of the Institution.

One unusual aspect of the arrangement was that, since the

Aberdeen life-boat crew were drawn largely from men who served the rocket apparatus, and since the same body controlled the rocket and the life-boat stations, the Institution assumed responsibility for manning the rockets, in consideration of an annual subsidy from the Commissioners. In this one instance, therefore, the Institution became involved in work of a kind with which it had regularly been concerned in its earliest days, but of which it had divested itself when, in the 1850s, agreement had been reached about the division of duties between the Institution, the Board of Trade and the Shipwrecked Mariners Society.

The Barnett boat was delivered to Aberdeen in October 1926, and an inauguration ceremony was arranged for September of the following year. Eleven days before the date fixed, at 10.30 p.m. on 6 September, the new boat was called out, and proved how valuable she could be. The steam trawler *Ben Torc* ran ashore among the rocks in a dense fog. Her crew of six were rescued with the help of the life-boat's searchlight, the whole operation being completed in an hour.

It was partly the events at Aberdeen which led the Committee of Management to review the entire situation in Scotland, for it was felt that, while the country was equipped with some of the Institution's best and most modern boats, and while it was clear to all that the record of the Scots in the adventure of saving life at sea could challenge comparison with any, there was insufficient awareness of the parent body's own ever-increasing needs. The service to Scotland cost some £17,000–£18,000 yearly at that time, but the totals of contributions raised north of the Border fell well below that figure. Even in the centenary year, when special efforts had been made, it was not more than £12,993, a sum which, though creditable, was not much above the yearly average.

It was generally felt that in a country so sea-minded, whose sons had always contributed so much to seafaring, it only needed better organization to ensure that appeals brought in more money. That this view was justified has been shown by Scotland's more recent record, and the change for the better was immeasurably helped by the formation, in 1927, of a Scottish Council, which has done invaluable work ever since.

The proposal for such a Council was first put forward at a conference held in Dowell's Rooms, Edinburgh, on 15 January.

This was attended by, among others, Sir Godfrey Baring, General Seely, the Duke of Montrose, the Secretary and his Deputy, Major C. R. Satterthwaite, together with seventy representatives from all over Scotland. A resolution was carried that the Council should be formed:

> . . . to promote and further the life-boat cause in Scotland, and to make recommendations to the Committee of Management in London on matters pertaining to the organization of the Institution in Scotland, provided that the Council should not deal in any way with the management and control of Station Branches.

At the first meeting of the Council itself, which was held on 15 February, the Duke of Montrose accepted the Chairmanship and Miss May Connell, who had done admirable work for the Society of Friends, was appointed District Organizing Secretary. Lady Findlay became the Council's Honorary Secretary.

Having set the Council on its appointed course, under enthusiastic officers, the occasion was marked by a statement of general policy which remains as true today as it would have been in 1824.

> The Committee of Management were anxious there should be no misunderstanding with regard to the attitude of the Institution in this matter. It will provide and maintain the best and most efficient life-boat service wherever it is required, whether the particular district can and does contribute a sum sufficient to cover the cost of maintenance or not. . . . The Institution has never hesitated and will never hesitate to spend whatever is required so long as the British people continue to accord to the Life-boat Service the confidence and the generous support which has been given during the last century.

* * *

Just before Scottish affairs had been put on a better footing, a national crisis had occurred, the course of which showed that it would be an exceptional catastrophe indeed which could inhibit the Institution. The industrial and general unrest which had marked the years immediately following the war rose to its climax in the General Strike, which brought most of the productive work of the country to a standstill between midnight on 3 May and noon on 12 May, 1926.

The Institution carried on, not as if nothing had happened, for that was impossible, but because its business, and the dedication of those who served it, transcended such disputes, even when they occurred on such a widespread scale. One member of the staff walked twenty miles to Charing Cross Road and back on the first two days, and nine miles on the others, and although he was exceptional, there were many instances of determination defeating lack of transport. And there were four operational launches.

The first two were concerned with French ships. On 5 May the steamer *Montauban* of Nantes went aground on the Goodwins, and was got off with the help of three tugs, the North Deal life-boat standing by. Later the Kingsdown boat stood by the *Toulouse*, also of Nantes, which was able to get off under her own steam.

On 8 May the New Brighton motor life-boat brought in a yacht which was in danger of sinking, though her people had been drowned before warning of danger reached the station. Four days later, a crew were at sea for six hours going to the help of the Bideford cutter *Curlew*, which was found to be in trouble seven or eight miles off the north Devon coast. The launch itself was difficult and the men were all soaked before they even put to sea. Three were found on board the *Curlew*, and they and their cutter were brought in to Clovelly.

* * *

The first gold medals to be won since the rescues from the *Hopelyn* in 1922 were awarded to William Roberts and Captain Owen Jones of Moelfre, for gallantry during the course of a gale which swept over the country, and was particularly severe in western districts, between 27 and 29 October 1927. The life-boat was called out at 3 p.m. on 28 October to go to the help of a ship in distress some 3½ miles from Point Lynas. It was exceptionally cold and the Moelfre boat was of the pulling and sailing type, offering no protection to the crew.

As the regular coxswain was not available, the boat was in charge of the second coxswain, William Roberts. With him as a crew member was Captain Owen Jones, who was experienced in local conditions and able to give expert advice.

After a search of more than two hours, Roberts found the auxiliary ketch *Excel* helpless and waterlogged. She was made fast to a German steamer, which cast off the lashings when the life-boat came in sight, heading away from the scene. In the very difficult circumstances, and with the ketch sinking, Roberts decided to proceed under full sail right over the almost submerged wreck. This he did, and although his boat was stove in in three places, three men were rescued just as the ketch foundered. By this time it was pitch dark, and one of the survivors died of injuries almost immediately after being picked up.

Shortly afterwards the life-boat's jib was blown to ribbons, but somehow Roberts managed to beat against the gale towards such shelter as was afforded by the Menai Straits, which he reached during the early morning of 29 October after more than fifteen hours in the open sea. A crew member and namesake, William Roberts, collapsed and died of exposure before the Beaumaris motor life-boat was able to find the Moelfre boat and tow her to safety.

Roberts had been at the tiller the whole time, and for some hours after landing he was completely blind from the effects of salt spray, wind, and the strain of his vigil. All the Moelfre crew received bronze medals, as did the widow of the man who lost his life on service.

The effect of spray on Roberts is an illustration of the way in which the hazards of sea-rescue may occur. At about the same time as the Anglesey episode the Italian steamer *Isabo* ran ashore on Scilly Rock, due west of the island of Bryher. At the time of the grounding, dense fog added to the dangers of a high sea, but the ship's siren was heard by the Bryher boatmen, who put out at once and made a series of what the Institution knows as 'shore boat' rescues in their own craft, for which a silver and a bronze medal were awarded.

Coxswain Matthew Lethbridge, bearing a name famous in the annals of Scilly, took the life-boat out from St Mary's and completed the work of the Bryher men. One of his more remarkable rescues was of an Italian, an expert swimmer, who had managed to reach a nearby rock and find some shelter thereon, though he was almost naked. He was actually asleep when he heard the life-boat approach! The steamer happened to be loaded with grain, and the rescued men one and all complained of the intense pain caused by grains of wheat being blown in their faces by the high wind. Matthew Lethbridge was awarded a silver medal, and his elder brother James, who was second coxswain, received a bronze.

Less than a month after these two episodes from the westerly regions, a number of East Anglian coxswains were once again in the news: for in the darkness of the evening of 21 November 1927, and to the roar of an easterly gale, the Great Yarmouth and Gorleston life-boat, in charge of William Fleming, was launched to go to the help of a ship in distress. She had been reported by wireless from the SS *Trent* as being in trouble on Haisborough Sands. The victim was the Dutch oil tanker *Georgia*, and in the seas which were then running she soon broke in two. The after part drifted towards Cromer, where it eventually stranded, though not before the *Trent* had taken off the sixteen men who were aboard.

Fleming was out with his crew for twenty-one hours, trying to save the remaining Dutchmen. At first he had some help from the *Trent*, which was still standing by, and later from the destroyer *Thanet*, which supplied hot tea to a very cold crew, and water for the life-boat's circulating system, which was giving trouble to the mechanic. But line after line parted; the seas grew worse; and eventually Fleming had to give up. Attempts to help were also made by the Southwold boat, whose crew had the advantage of the destroyer's searchlight, but they had no better luck. The Lowestoft life-boat would also have been present had not her coxswain, Albert Spurgeon, damaged his boat so badly in making rescues a little earlier from the fishing-boat *Lily of Devon* that he could not get to sea.

It was Blogg of Cromer who succeeded, after a long struggle, in saving the remaining fifteen Dutchmen. His was a feat so masterly as to earn him a second gold medal, making him the only living man so honoured. All the Cromer crew received medals in bronze, and so did Coxswain Fleming for his valiant attempts, Fleming being the only man at that time to have been awarded medals in gold, silver and bronze. Spurgeon received the silver medal for his rescues from the *Lily of Devon*.

These were events which could be alluded to proudly by the Prince of Wales when, on 28 March 1928, he once again presided at the Annual General Meeting of the Institution, this time in the additional capacity of 'Master of the Merchant Navy and Fishing Fleets', a title which had been given him by his father to show appreciation of those seafarers who, in peace and war, were so vital to an island nation.

A point concerning the life-boat service made by the Prince was that

> . . . one of its difficulties lies in the fact that the work of its crews is carried out mostly in the darkness of a winter's night at some remote spot on our coast; and quite often little more is heard of that splendid work than is contained in a short paragraph in the newspapers (and maybe only in the local newspapers) the following day. So I can understand why it may require some imagination to enable some people to realize what the life-boat service means.

He later made an appeal (doubtless prompted by the Secretary) for greater consideration to the Institution on the part of the shipping lines. His words bore fruit, when so many earlier exhortations had not. Six firms of the first rank, the Cunard Line, the P. & O., the Royal Mail Steam Packet Company, the Union Castle, the Canadian Pacific and the White Star Companies allocated money to present life-boats, a most welcome gesture and an admirable example to others.

The Prince also gave a special word of praise to the work of the women, which was so essential to the success of any approach made direct to the public. 'I know,' he said, 'it is not the slightest bit of good to make an appeal if we do not enlist the help of our women. You cannot get any distance without it. *With* it you can do almost anything.'

There had seldom been anyone of his eminence who worked more successfully for the cause than the Prince. The following year he went to Edinburgh, to cheer on the work of the Scottish Council. There the Scots silver medallists since 1905 were presented to him, and he had a talk with each of them. The ceremony over, he went by special train to Glasgow, where he attended a life-boat ball held aboard the Anchor liner *Transylvania*. This was the means of raising £1,350, whilst Scotland's general total for the year leapt from £16,000 in 1929 to over £28,000 in 1930.

The Prince once again took the chair at the Annual General Meeting in 1931, when he put the case of the life-boat service to trawler owners, emphasizing that, all through the Institution's history, it had been fishermen who had benefited most through the gallantry of the life-boat crews, who were so often of their own kind. It should be added that over the years fishermen themselves proved far more consistent and generous supporters than most of those who owned trawler fleets—but then, they knew the sea and its peril in a way that no landsmen could.

In a speech in support of the appeal, Sir Godfrey Baring said words about the Prince which were as true as they were deserved. 'There has never been anything which we have asked His Royal Highness to do that he has not done, and what he has done for the life-boat service really beggars description.' That fact was recalled by many on the Prince's death in 1972, after he had been many years Duke of Windsor.

* * *

The Institution's representatives much looked forward to the second International Life-boat Conference. This was held in Paris, the hosts being the Société Centrale de Sauvetage des Naufragés. For two crowded days in June 1928 a wider gathering than had been present at the inaugural conference attended meetings for papers and discussions.

Seventeen nations actually participated, which was nearly double the representation of 1924, and an eighteenth, Norway, submitted a paper on a line-throwing gun. Those concerned were the German Life-boat Society; the Belgian and Danish Governments; the Spanish Society; the Governments of the U.S.A., Finland and Greece; France; the Italian Society for Saving the Shipwrecked; Japan; Latvia; the two Dutch Societies; the Polish and Turkish Governments; the Swedish Society and the Society for the Succour of the Shipwrecked of the U.S.S.R. The delegates from the R.N.L.I., were Sir Godfrey Baring, the Hon. George Colville, Deputy Chairman of the Committee of Management, the Chief Inspector of Life-boats, Captain H. F. J. Rowley, and Mr Barnett.

The conference was offered one very pleasant excursion. This was to Villenes-sur-Seine, about twenty-five miles from Paris, where members were shown a newly designed twin-screw boat shortly coming into service, and a line-thrower which was then being tried out. Many useful suggestions and valuable information resulted from the circulation and discussion of the technical papers, particularly as Mr Barnett was able to give details of British experiments with twin screws, and Captain Rowley could report favourably on the good work done at launches by caterpillar tractors. Not the least important paper was one submitted by the Germans on the heavy oil diesel engine, of which they were to make such good use.

It was clear that the Germans, the Dutch and the Swedes were well ahead in the development of their marine engines, and the Dutch and Germans in satisfactory wireless equipment for life-boats. Continental engineers were in advance of their British counterparts in the attention they gave to the smaller types of power unit. The Germans had had the twin-screw *Hindenburg* in service by 1927 with heavy oil machinery, and the Dutch the self-righting *Insulinde*. Both countries claimed that their motors could be started up with far less difficulty than the French, for instance, had experienced with this type.

There was much interest in the paper read by Mr Lachkevitch, the Legal Adviser to the Russian Embassy in Paris. He dated the Tsarist service from 1872, and claimed that by 1914 it had had some 1,890 'life-saving units', 800 life-boats, two cruising boats and 1,000 'line-throwers'. He stated that since the Revolution an average of 2,500 lives had been saved annually, as against 800–900 before 1917, and he gave the information that there was even a Caspian service which employed 'two steam vessels, principally to protect fishermen and their equipment'. The appearance of this Russian delegate was of considerable note, and his audience would have realized the difficulty of obtaining reliable figures from such an enormous country as the U.S.S.R.

The impressions made by the Paris deliberations had scarcely been assimilated before the Institution was faced with one of those seemingly inescapable tragedies which have marked its history. The seventeen-man crew of the Rye pulling and sailing life-boat was drowned on 15 November 1928, after trying to go to the help of the Latvian steamer *Alice*. The loss was additionally sad because it was unnecessary. The life-boat had been launched just before 7 a.m. and she was scarcely at sea before news came through to the Coastguard station that the *Alice*'s crew had been taken off by another steamer. It was before the days when life-boats had standard equipment of wireless or radio-telephone, and although signals of recall were fired three times they were not heard by the Rye men. This was not surprising considering the weather.

The boat returned at 10.30 a.m. under sail, and capsized near the harbour entrance in a terrible sea. The men were all wearing kapok life-belts as approved by the Institution and the Board of Trade, but in the opinion of the committee which investigated the accident, they had been beaten to death by the surf before they were swept ashore. 'No belt ever designed,' the verdict concluded, 'would have saved men subject to these conditions.' The crew was typical of many in its family links. The coxswain, Herbert Head, had two sons with him. Henry Cutting, the bowman, had two brothers in the boat. There were three brothers Pope, two brothers Clark, and two Downing cousins.

Within a fortnight of the Rye disaster the Institution's steam-vessel *Helen Peele* of Padstow made her last rescues. Operating on her own, she took off five men of the fishing-boat *Our Girlie* of Port Isaac, a feat for which her master was given the bronze medal. In April 1929 the well-tried tug was withdrawn from service. She had been concerned in saving 78 lives when working with one or other of the Padstow life-boats, and she had rescued ten others on her own.

The *Helen Peele* had been at the Cornish station since 1901, the continuity broken only between December 1917 and January 1919, when she had acted as a rescue tug with the Navy. Even in the course of that temporary duty she had saved eleven lives and helped to salvage many ships. She was to continue her useful life, being still classed 100 A1 at Lloyd's, as tender to big yachts on the Clyde, where she had been built.

As the last remaining steam life-boat, the *James Stevens No. 4*, had been withdrawn a few months earlier, it is appropriate to record the total of services by steam craft in the years (1890–1928) during which they were employed, never more than four being operational at any one time. They made 468 launches and saved 673 lives. The record was held by the first of her kind, the *Duke of Northumberland*, which saved no fewer than 295. Next came the *Queen*, with 196; then the second *City of Glasgow* with 87; then the *James Stevens No. 3* with 54; the first *City of Glasgow* with 32, and the ill-fated *James Stevens No 4* with nine. They were creditable figures for a class of life-boat whose limitations had always been recognized, but whose characteristics had been exploited to the limit.

It is sad to note that the Dutch steam-driven *Prins der Netherlanden*, which had represented her country at the Institution's centenary, was lost with all hands a few months before the *Helen Peele* went to the Clyde.

* * *

The decade which was to end in the cataclysm of another war was eventful for the Institution, not least because of a change of premises. Between the years 1921 and 1930 the headquarters of the High Commissioner for India had been at 42 Grosvenor Gardens, near Victoria Station, and this was the building leased as the new headquarters, the move being completed during the summer of 1931. The rooms at Charing Cross Road had since 1904 grown steadily more congested and ever more noisy from the traffic of a busy artery—although the flag which flew amid the bookshops of the area had become familiar to thousands who in the ordinary way might have known little of the Institution's work. The Grosvenor Gardens house offered scope and dignity.

Almost concurrent with the move were two retirements. Captain Rowley relinquished the Chief Inspectorship, and George Shee, who was knighted in the Birthday Honours of 1931, the Secretaryship. Captain Rowley had been twenty-eight years with the Institution, a period broken only by his temporary recall to the Fleet. During his eleven years as Chief Inspector he had seen motor life-boat numbers grow from 19 to 88, and every important technical experiment had been watched with care. He retired shortly before the change of headquarters, and was succeeded by Commander E. D. Drury.

The fruitfulness of the co-operation between Rowley and Shee recalls that partnership of Ross Ward and Lewis which had been so important in an earlier epoch. The gifts of the two men were as diverse as their personalities, but they were single-minded in dedication to their work.

In manner and appearance Sir George Shee had pre-eminent dignity. He once described himself as 'an English Catholic bearing an Irish name' and he was at home in any society which had service to the nation and the life-boat cause at heart. Very correct in his dress, it was his custom, so it is said, to put on a tail coat for meetings of the full Committee of Management. A short one sufficed for sub-committees! He had had as predecessors a city man, a lawyer and a civil servant. Each had had a long tenure of office, and Shee's would have been extended had he not taxed his strength severely by meeting calls for his personal appearance all over the country. Some of them he could fairly have left to others, but the results of his unsparing work were astonishing. Among them was the fact that in 1910, the year he joined the Institution, its revenue was £97,000. When he resigned it was £264,000.

Shee's successor, Lieutenant-Colonel C. R. Satterthwaite, had been for six years his deputy. He had originally held a commission in the Royal Engineers and had fought at Gallipoli. In a valedictory message to his former chief, the new Secretary emphasized three characteristics which had made everyone devoted to him: the first and most important was infectious enthusiasm; the second was an amazing power of work; the third was unfailing kindness. The affection was reciprocated. 'I would not have changed my staff,' said Shee, 'for any that I have known in London.'

One of the changes brought about by Shee's retirement was that Charles Vince, who since 1920 had been Assistant Secretary for Publicity, took charge of public relations and assumed the editorship of the *Life-boat*. This was a task with which he could easily cope, for he was a trained journalist, and in due time he was to record the achievements of the life-boat crews under the stress of war.

It was typical of Shee that, in spite of no longer having any official connexion with the Institution, he should have attended the third International Life-boat Conference. This was held in June 1932 in Holland. Sir Godfrey Baring, the new Chief Inspector, Mr Barnett, and Captain A. G. Bremner, the Superintendent Engineer, were also present. Included in the party were the Chief Inspector of Coastguard, and two representatives from East Anglia. Mr Riggs, the Honorary Secretary of the station at Aldeburgh and Lieutenant-Commander P. E. Vaux, Inspector for the Eastern District, sailed across the North Sea in a 15-ton yacht to join the delegates.

The Dutch Societies were, as so often before, the friendliest of hosts. In the case of the North and South Holland Society, with its headquarters at Amsterdam and its care of the coast from the Hook to the German frontier, the British delegates once again met two staunch allies in H. de Booy and his son H. Th. de Booy, who was then his assistant. Both de Booys in course of time became Honorary Life Governors of the R.N.L.I. This was a distinction shared later with Captain Hans Hansson of Sweden and Captain Olaf Bjornstad of Norway.

The first meeting was held at Rotterdam, and it was attended by representatives from twelve nations. Although this was fewer than those at Paris four years earlier, a valuable conference ensued. The South Holland Society, which looked after the Dutch coast from the Belgian frontier to the Hook, had supervised arrangements which were intended to show how aeroplanes might best co-operate in sea-rescues, and technically one of the most valuable papers was produced by the younger de Booy. This was on the radio-telephone system then in experimental use. One of the delegates who was particularly congenial to the rest was the veteran Herr Rösing, who was then celebrating his thirty-second year as Secretary to the German Society.

The personalities, and the maritime background and activities of the Dutch Societies, were already so well known to the British members of the party that the conference was for them more in the nature of a relaxation than the two previous ones had been. But the strength of the representation was proof of how close they felt to members of the senior Societies of the Continent. The delegates were shown some of the reclamation work proceeding at that time in the Zuider Zee, and they were able to see the special conditions and difficulties of the coast of Holland.

The energy, progressiveness and enthusiasm of the Dutch, who had advanced so steadily in developing mechanical and electrical equipment for their life-boat service, would have been a stimulus, had one been needed, to the British team. In fairness, they needed none. Life-boat design was going ahead as fast as resources allowed, as shown by the significant fact that by 1933 there were in service a number of comparatively light motor-powered boats which could be launched either from a transporter or an open beach.

The standard pattern was 35 ft. 6 in., self-righting, with a 35 h.p. engine which could maintain a service speed of just over

7 knots, and had a range of over a hundred miles without refuelling. A drop-keel, fore-lug and jib were fitted. The boats needed a crew of seven and could accommodate about thirty all told. Ten were placed on the English coast, four in Scotland, three in Ireland, and one in Wales.

There had also been built a highly interesting boat stationed at Dover. She was the forerunner of a type which was later developed for rescue work by the armed forces, particularly the Royal Air Force. She was 64 ft. long, had a beam of 14 ft., a mean draught of 4 ft. 2 in., and was the largest and fastest of the Institution's fleet. She was of 27 tons displacement, could accommodate about a hundred, and maintain 17–18 knots in a moderate sea. She had been designed primarily for air-sea rescue work, which required speed, since aircraft rarely floated long when forced down on water. The boat was powered by two 12-cylinder Thornycroft engines of 375 h.p. each, with twin screws. Her range was 78 miles at full power and she had a crew of seven. Her engines were not watertight as they were not expected to withstand such sea conditions as were met with by standard boats.

Experiments were started in 1934 with a 6-cylinder diesel engine running at 1,600 revolutions per minute and weighing 26½ cwt. This engine, which was specially built for the Institution, was put in a reserve 45-foot Watson cabin boat originally stationed at Tenby, and it was made watertight. Tests were satisfactory, and the boat was sent first to Weymouth, then to Falmouth and finally to Yarmouth, Isle of Wight. Her performance was such as to justify ordering two 40 h.p. engines which were to be installed in a Watson boat earmarked for Selsey.

After that, there was no looking back. Within a year eleven diesels were on order, to be placed in Watson cabin boats. Their engines would be 4-cylinder, developing 40 h.p. at 1,200 revolutions per minute. The weight problem had by then been solved, for these engines weighed one ton, which was only a hundredweight more than a petrol motor of equivalent power. They were safer from the risk of fire, and more economical in use than their predecessors.

Concurrently with the development of the diesel went the increasing use of radio-telephony. Experiments had begun in 1929 and, within a few years, 26 out of 53 cabin boats were thus equipped. This was the greatest help to coxswains, who for the first time could speak to those ashore.

* * *

The Institution's President had emphasized that, from the very nature of its activities, from the fact that its resources were rarely called upon except in times of crisis and then all too often in darkness and storm, the R.N.L.I. had to seize upon any and every occasion to make its wants known. It had no broad highway to public sympathy as, for instance, was the case with the hospitals, which were also then run on a voluntary basis, and which touched life continually at so many points. Hence the importance not only of the official centenary, but of particular anniversaries such as those of the founding or taking over of individual stations; hence too the value of celebrations concerned with the naming or inauguration of boats. In this direction no royalty had been more zealous than King George V's youngest surviving son, the Duke of Kent, who like his father, spent his earlier years in the Navy. The Duke's presence attracted many who would not otherwise have attended, and the cause benefited accordingly.

There had also come into being, as early as the 1920s, that regular series of BBC broadcast appeals, 'The Week's Good Cause' which over the decades has helped so many. The first appeal made on behalf of the Institution was put over the air in 1927. It had been in the form of a duologue entitled 'SOS' spoken by Sir Gerald du Maurier and Mabel Terry-Lewis. The text had been written by Commander Stopford Douglas, then Deputy Chief Inspector. It described the effect of an operational call on the destiny of some of those most nearly concerned. It had raised the sum of £376. 17. 2., which was a reasonable sum of money in those days to result from such an occasion.

The second had been made in 1930 by ex-Coxswain Swan of Lowestoft, one of the holders of the gold medal. This had raised £751. 4. 3. The third was made in March 1934 by Lord Mottistone, better known as General Seely and by then a senior statesman. In the life-boat service Lord Mottistone's name was of special renown, though the station he had served so long, that of Brooke, Isle of Wight, was shortly to be closed because of the greater area which could be covered by the motorized fleet.

Lord Mottistone had the splendid response of £2,443. 5. 3., but he had had a story of self-sacrifice to refer to in his address which had moved many at the time and has not been forgotten.

On 8 February the call had come at the Yorkshire station of Runswick for the life-boat to go to the help of the salvage steamer *Dispenser* of West Hartlepool, which was in tow of a tug, but was sinking. Seven out of the steamer's crew of eight had been taken off by the tug but there was an eighth, a lame man, who could not be persuaded to leave the ship.

When the life-boat had been brought alongside the *Dispenser* the crew called on this survivor to jump, but he refused. Instead, he lowered himself over the side and hung there. The coxswain, Robert Patton, seized him and told him to let go, but the man only clung on tighter, and the life-boat was soon carried away from the steamer in the stormy sea.

Patton knew that he himself still had time to loose his grip and stay aboard the life-boat, but had he done so the man would almost certainly have fallen into the sea. He held on therefore and was dragged overboard, but he still kept his hold on the man as they were both thrown into the water. Then a big wave flung the life-boat back towards the steamer, and Patton took the full weight of the blow on his life-belt. The crew dragged the lame man on board, but before they could rescue their coxswain he had twice more been crushed between the boat and the *Dispenser*, which sank shortly afterwards.

When the life-boat returned to Runswick, Patton was taken to hospital, very badly injured. Two days later he was able to talk to an officer of the Institution. To him he said: 'I could not let the poor man go, as he might have been drowned.' A week later he was dead. He was given the gold medal posthumously. He was forty-six and he had been a life-boatman for thirty years, a span broken only by war service in minesweepers. He had been the Runswick coxswain for three years and incidentally he had been among those who had dashed into the surf at Whitby to help in the rescue of people on the ever-memorable occasion of the wreck of the *Rohilla*.

Coxswain Patton's difficulty with the terrified man of the *Dispenser* was paralleled by an incident which occurred at the very end of one of the most protracted operations of its time. This has gone down in life-boat history as the Daunt Rock rescue.

It took place early in February 1936. The crew concerned was that of Ballycotton, County Cork, the district which had won the first Irish gold medal over a century before.

Calm weather with frost had been succeeded by winds from the south-east, the quarter most feared at Ballycotton as it drove the sea straight at them. On 7 February a gale began which did not blow itself out for five days, and by the 9th it had reached almost hurricane force. The local coxswain, Patrick Sliney, had to take every measure to protect the life-boat from being driven against the breakwater, and next day his own boat was in danger of being smashed up. It was made secure, not without trouble, and in the course of this Sliney injured his hand. By that time slates were flying from roofs, and people trying to walk were spun round or bowled over by the wind. Spray was flying over the lantern of the lighthouse, which was 196 feet high.

Everyone expected trouble, and it came on Tuesday 11 February, early in the day. A message was delivered, by word of mouth since all the lines were down, that the Daunt Rock lightship, with eight men on board, had broken from her moorings, and appeared to be drifting towards Ballycotton.

No one believed it would be possible to get the life-boat out; and no maroons were fired: but when Patrick Sliney heard the news, he passed word round to the crew. They were all of his own name or that of Walsh—John Walsh being second coxswain, Thomas Sliney, Patrick's brother, motor mechanic, Michael and Thomas Walsh, crew members, and John and William Sliney, who made up the complement of seven.

When the Ballycotton people saw the life-boat put out to sea they could hardly believe their eyes. No children went to school that day, and before Mass Father Thornhill, the village priest, asked the congregation to 'pray for the crew of the life-boat, which has gone out on an errand of mercy'.

Sliney searched the area of mountainous sea into which he judged the lightship might have drifted, but could find nothing. At last, with everyone battered by the force of the waves, he put into Cobh, once known as Queenstown, where he could get news of the situation. He reached the haven at about 11 o'clock, and put out again immediately he had the information he needed. Just after midday he found the lightship, which had an anchor down and was quarter of a mile south-west of Daunt Rock and half a mile from the shore. Two ships were standing by her: the destroyer *Tenedos* and the steamer *Innisfallen*. When the life-boat appeared the steamer left.

The crew of the lightship were unwilling to leave her, but they could not be certain that their anchor would hold and they asked Sliney to stand by. He did so for three hours, while continuous efforts were made by his men and those of the destroyer to pass a line to the lightship so that she could be towed. All efforts failed. The destroyer's captain said he would stand by all night, which enabled Sliney to return to Cobh. It was 9.30 before the life-boat had regained shelter, and new lines, a spare drogue and a much-needed supply of dry clothes were sent to Cobh from Ballycotton over roads made difficult by fallen trees.

Sliney put out again early on Wednesday the 12th. When the life-boat reached the lightship the *Tenedos* left, for she had had news that the *Isolda*, belonging to the Commissioners of Irish Lights, was expected from Dublin. All day long the life-boat stayed at hand, only leaving to warn vessels to alter course because the lightship was out of position. The vigil continued throughout the night that followed.

At dawn the life-boat, which had been at sea continuously for twenty-four hours, had little petrol left and was forced to return to Cobh. By that time Sliney's damaged hand was causing him considerable pain, his son, William, was suffering from continuous sea-sickness, and all the men were starving. The sea had given them what are known as salt-water burns, sores which can be excruciating, and they were so perished with cold that they could not wait for tea to be made in a pot. They had it infused in cups, and drank it as it scalded their throats. There was delay in finding enough petrol to get the life-boat out again, and it was dusk before Sliney once more sighted the lightship.

By that time the *Isolda* had arrived. Her captain told Sliney that he intended to stand by all night and then to try to secure a tow. But at 8 o'clock a huge sea carried away one of the lightship's two red lights, hoisted to show that she was out of position. The wind shifted and the lightship began to drift farther towards Daunt Rock. About half past nine Sliney took his boat round the lightship's stern while the searchlight played on her. She was now only sixty yards from the rock and if the wind shifted more to the west she would certainly strike.

The *Isolda*'s captain could do nothing, and he agreed that Sliney should try to take the men off. Seas were now sweeping right over the lightship, which was plunging on her cable, rolling from thirty to forty degrees and burying her starboard bow in the water. She had rolling chocks which projected more than two feet from her sides, and as she rolled these threshed the water. Because of the cable it was impossible for Sliney to anchor to windward and veer down: the only possible course was to approach from astern and make quick runs in on the port side, giving the crew a moment in which to jump into the life-boat. The lightship was only 98 feet long, and if the 52-foot Barnett life-boat, coming in at speed, ran too far, she would go over the cable and capsize. And every time the life-boat went alongside, the lightship, as she plunged and rolled, might well crash down on top of her. All these risks were clear to Sliney as he made his plan.

First he went ahead and pumped oil, though this had little effect on the sea. Then he went astern and drove at full speed alongside. One man jumped successfully. The second time, no one jumped. The third time, five jumped, leaving two remaining. On the fourth run the lightship sheered violently and her counter crashed down on the life-boat, smashing the rails and damaging the fender and deck. No one was hurt, but the man working the searchlight had to jump for his life. On the fifth run, still no one jumped.

The crew now saw what was happening. The two men remaining were clinging to the rails as if transfixed. Sliney gave orders to seize them next time the life-boat came alongside, and this was done at the greatest possible risk. The men were hurt, one in the face and the other in the legs, and the life-boat had hardly made away into the darkness before one of them, overcome by the effects of strain, became hysterical and wanted to jump overboard. Two men, themselves exhausted, had to hold him down by force. It was not until 11 o'clock on the night of 13 February that the life-boat put into Cobh harbour for the last time, and the crew could get a good night's rest. They had been away for 76½ hours, and had been on service for 63 hours. They had been in the open sea for 49 hours, 25 of them without food. Towards the end of that period of stress Sliney had had to carry out a feat of seamanship of the highest order, and ask services of his crew which would have taxed fresh men. His gold medal was a fitting recognition, and so were the silver medals given to John Walsh, second coxswain, and to Thomas Sliney, the motor mechanic. The rest of the crew were given bronze medals for a service which was the equal of anything in the Institution's history, and which had stretched the resources even of the most up-to-date boat and equipment to the limit.

Patrick Sliney survived to the age of eighty-seven, and when he died in June 1972, he was honoured with a leading obituary in *The Times*. His service at Ballycotton had extended from 1922 to 1950, and in addition to his gold medal, he held the Institution's awards in silver and bronze.

* * *

The Irish rescue took place a few weeks after the Prince of Wales's accession to the throne as King Edward VIII. His brother, the Duke of York, accepted the position of President of the Institution, but during the 325 days of the new reign, other preoccupations prevented him from taking any prominent part in its affairs. Happily, the Duke of Kent continued his enthusiastic interest, as was shown by his taking the chair at four successive Annual General Meetings, the first of these being in 1936. The Duke set the seal on his endeavours when, after King Edward's Abdication and the accession of the Duke of York as King George VI, he consented to become President. The association of the Institution with this branch of the royal family has been unbroken ever since.

King George VI, meticulous in everything which concerned honours and awards, extended his interest to the medals of the life-boat service. This implied no criticism of the way in which recognition for gallantry was granted, but his decision was that the sovereign's head should no longer appear on the obverse, where it had figured as 'Patron' since the time of George IV. This enabled a portrait of Sir William Hillary as 'Founder' to replace it, the original reverse, by William Wyon, being retained. The new medal was ready by 1938 and had the advantage of good design and permanence, Hillary's profile being rendered by Allan Gairdner Wyon, a member of the famous family of medallists. It prevented the occurrence of gaps in the series of sovereign's heads, as had been instanced by the fact that William IV, Edward VIII and George VI did not figure at all, while an effigy of Queen Victoria was not struck until 1860, nearly a quarter of a century after her accession, to mark the granting of the Charter of Incorporation.

Royal interest in life-boat affairs, which for so long had been an encouraging feature, was neatly illustrated by the fact that in the apartments of St James's Palace occupied by the former Prince of Wales, a life-boat collecting-box was the only object of its kind on view. Interest in high quarters was also made very plain, this time abroad, during the course of the fourth International Conference. Gothenburg was the meeting-place chosen, and many of the proceedings were attended by the Swedish Crown Prince, later to become King Gustaf VI. The Prince had married an English wife and spoke English perfectly. His zest for nautical affairs had long been as marked as it had shown itself to be for archaeology and Oriental ceramics.

There had been much to encourage the delegates since the conference in Holland. Although the Russians had held off since their unexpected participation at Paris in 1928, a Romanian service had been started. One of the Institution's inspectors, Lieutenant-Commander P. E. Vaux, spent some weeks there in the summer of 1933 advising on life-boat affairs, particularly in relation to Constanza, for which a 51 ft. Barnett and a 35 ft. 6 in. light Liverpool-type boat and carriage had been ordered, also a caterpillar tractor.

Sixteen nations sent delegates, Iceland being represented for the first time. Twenty-four papers were read and discussed. Many of the meetings were held in the Maritime Museum, the chair being taken by Commander Gibson, a descendant of one of the numerous Scots settlers who in times past had taken service under the Swedish crown. He referred to the delegates as 'friends' not 'foreigners' and no gathering could have been better arranged.

The British members included the Deputy Chairman, the Hon. George Colville; the Chief Inspector of Coastguard; the Deputy Chief Inspector of Life-boats, Captain R. L. Hamer; the Superintending Engineer; Mr Barnett, and the Institution's Secretary. The main subjects covered were coastguard rescues; the development of wireless equipment; light diesels, which were coming into favour wherever a rescue service operated, and tunnels and rudders in powered boats. There was also a discussion of the organization of the R.N.L.I.

When all was over, delegates greatly looked forward to the next opportunity to meet those of like mind. They were due for disappointment. The clouds of war were then beginning to gather ominously over Europe, and it was to be more than a decade before international discussion could be resumed.

* * *

'A life-boatman must possess great courage, a spirit of self-sacrifice, and a water-proof.' This sentence appeared in a schoolboy essay submitted in one of the competitions established by the seventh Duke of Northumberland. Certainly the trials which had been so constant a factor in pulling and sailing days were not eliminated with the advent of the motor. This was all too clearly shown by two accidents to the St Ives, Cornwall, boat which happened within a year of one another. They took place in mid-winter, in severe weather and high seas. The first was on 31 January 1938.

The boat was launched in darkness to the help of the SS *Alba*, loaded with coal from South Wales to Italy. She had driven ashore near the town and was in danger of breaking up. The ship flew the Panamanian flag, but she was owned by a Swiss and had a crew mainly Hungarian. This added to the rescuers' difficulties, for they were far more aware of the dangers of their own stretch of the Cornish coast than strangers could possibly be. So little did the steamer's crew realize their plight that they started passing down personal baggage, and as they knew no English it was over half an hour before they could be made to understand that they must abandon ship at once, if they valued their lives. When at last they agreed to be taken on board it was doubtful whether, in the state of the tide and sea, Coxswain Thomas Cocking could hope to reach safety.

In fact, through no fault whatever of his own, he had left it too late, for the life-boat overturned in the surf. She had taken on board all 23 men from the *Alba* and, thanks to the efforts of the crew and of those of many ashore, including the coastguards with their life-saving gear, all the life-boat's crew and all but five of the *Alba*'s men were rescued.

The boat, a 35 ft. 6 in. self-righter, was so badly damaged that her crew asked that the battered remains should be burnt, after the engine and other fittings had been removed. They did not want her to become a hunting-ground for the collectors of souvenirs who were apt to haunt the beaches.

Cocking won the silver medal and his men the bronze: the Coxswain himself would also have received a Hungarian decoration had he not met with tragedy just as this was about to be presented. For on 23 January 1939 he put out again, in the teeth of a north-westerly gale, to go to the help of a steamer believed to be in difficulties about eleven miles off the coast. She is almost certain to have been the *Wilston* of Glasgow which, from the evidence of wreckage and bodies cast ashore, disappeared about that time.

A crew of eight men were got together, five of whom had taken part in the *Alba* rescue. Cocking's son, John, was with him; so were two brothers, Matthew and William Barber; John Thomas, signalman; Richard Stevens, motor mechanic, who was the coxswain's son-in-law; and crew members Edgar Bassett and William Freeman. As on the earlier occasion, darkness added to the difficulties, the launch taking place at 2.30 a.m. with only an even chance of being able to find and help the ship. The life-boat, which had been temporarily transferred from Padstow, was self-righting, and her capabilities in this respect were to be tested to the limit, for she capsized three times.

After the first occasion the coxswain was never seen again; nor were William Barber, acting as bowman, John Thomas or Edgar Bassett. That left four surviving, including the motor mechanic who, although able to restart the engine when the boat was once more upright, could not engage the gear and concluded that something had fouled the screw.

An anchor was then put out, but the cable soon parted, after which it was not long before the boat turned over once again. This time only man man was left alive. He was William Freeman, who happened to be on his first operational service. There was nothing he could do but wait until the boat was flung ashore by the breakers. Before she was smashed against the rocks near the Godrevy lighthouse she turned over a third time and it was by a near-miracle that Freeman managed to claw his way through the under-tow to dry land and at last to reach a farmhouse, from which news of the full extent of the disaster spread.

It was the first time in the Institution's history that a double tragedy such as this had struck an individual station. It underlined the fact that neither experience, skill, gallantry nor the best equipment that could be supplied could prevent disasters during the course of work which is by its nature perilous in the extreme. If the lesson was driven home to the public, who responded generously to an appeal to supplement the Institution's pensions to the relatives of those who had lost their lives, it was no news to life-boatmen.

Even exercises could not always be undertaken without risk, as was shown at Cullercoats in Northumberland shortly after the St Ives catastrophe. Six lives were lost during a practice launch when the life-boat, which was close inshore, was overset by the sudden building up of a wave of exceptional size. Of the ten on board only four reached safety. Among those lost were the second coxswain, J. R. Armstrong, the Honorary Secretary, Lieutenant-Commander L. E. R. Blakeney Booth and his stepson, a naval cadet, aged sixteen, the motor mechanic and his assistant, and the bowman. The survivors were George Brunton, the coxswain, the Institution's District Engineer, and two crew members.

* * *

The last team of horses to be in regular use for launches was dispersed at Wells, Norfolk, in 1936, leaving only a pair at Hastings which turned the hauling-up capstan on the beach, a labour which was shortly to devolve upon an electric winch. Belonging essentially to the sailing and pulling era, horses had played a not ignoble part in the rescue service for well over a century, and the teams which had been lent so willingly by farmers, contractors and others had been a source of pride at many stations.

The principal change in personnel at this period concerned the retirement of Commander E. D. Drury as Chief Inspector, at the end of 1938. He had been on the technical staff, apart from war service, for thirty years and had been Chief Inspector for eight of them. His successor was Lieutenant-Commander P. E. Vaux, a character notable among other qualities for his love of sailing.

The new Chief Inspector had a fighting record which would have been hard to equal in an officer of his seniority. He had served with Beatty's battle-cruiser flagship, the *Lion*, at Heligoland and the Dogger Bank, and aboard the battleship *Warspite* at Jutland. Later he had won the Distinguished Service Cross for gallantry in H.M.S. *Iphigenia*, a cruiser which had been used as a block-ship in the raid on the submarine pens at Zeebrugge in 1918. In the employment of the Institution he had been awarded the bronze medal in 1926 when, as Inspector for the Irish District, he had gone in search of trawlermen wrecked in a gale. It was almost inevitable that an officer with such experience should, when the time came, be recalled for service with the fleet.

A foretaste of renewed war had come to life-boatmen of the North Sea in November 1938, twenty years to a month since the last shots had been fired in the First World War. The Cromer boat was called out after gunfire had been heard off the coast. It was the time of the Spanish Civil War, and the incident in fact concerned two vessels belonging to Spain. The auxiliary cruiser *Nadir*, employed by General Franco, was discovered to be attacking the steamer *Cantabria*, which had been loaded at a Russian port with a cargo consigned to the Spanish Republican Government.

After some preliminary shots, the *Cantabria*'s crew lowered two boats, in which the majority of them abandoned ship. One was picked up by the *Nadir*, the other by a British steamer, the *Pattersonian*, which happened to be in the area at the time. When the life-boat arrived there were still five on board the *Cantabria*, the master, his wife, two children, and one of the seamen. They were taken off, and landed safely at Cromer.

In view of such occurrences, rare in British home waters but then not uncommon off the Spanish and North African coasts and in the Mediterranean, it was well that the Institution had the foresight to plan an entirely new depot outside the capital. For it was clear to all but the most optimistic that the country might soon be engaged in a war which would result in devastation. Dispersal was in the air, and it was not too early.

Since 1882 the Institution's store-yard on the Thames at Poplar had been a centre for repair and replenishment. It had also harboured the reserve fleet. It had been enlarged in 1915 to include a graving dock, and had been extended farther between 1919 and 1922. The store-yard had always fostered *esprit de corps*, and the parties given by the staff to the children of the East End at times such as Christmas had long been known for their gaiety.

But with the increasing specialization which had come about as the result of a motorized fleet, and with far more complex and extensive equipment than in the past, the drawbacks of the place had become apparent. Repairs were more and more often done at shipyards, and Poplar had never been ideal for the swift dispatch of essential supplies by rail or road to various parts of the country.

The Committee's decision was to acquire a site at Boreham Wood on the A1 road, near Elstree in Hertfordshire, within easy reach of London. The foundation stone of a building designed by Herbert Kenchington was laid by Sir Godfrey Baring on 6 January 1939. Work proceeded quickly, and the place was in use by the following July. Just over a year later it was seen how providential the move had been. Huge areas of London's dockland had been by then reduced to rubble, and the country was facing the greatest crisis since the Spanish Armada.

6
War Renewed

If the Second World War gave Britain her finest hour, from the outset it provided the most severe strain ever suffered by the life-boat service. To the constant perils of the sea was once again added the malice of the enemy. This was all the more menacing because while the effects of the mine and torpedo, the gun and the bomb had become known to the older coxswains and crews in the earlier struggle, there seemed to be no limit to the refinement and ingenuity in making still more lethal an already tremendous armoury. And while in the first war the possibility of invasion, recognized as it had been at the outset, had receded after the saving of the French ports and the consolidation of surface supremacy by the Royal Navy, in the second, events turned out so differently that within less than a year Britain found herself, as she had done in the time of Napoleon, with an army ranged against her on the other side of the Channel.

The challenges, however formidable, were met in a spirit which, though it might have been looked for, was none the less remarkable, for there could be no general awareness of what the crews were doing. Although even in peace-time much of the more dangerous life-saving work, and all routine operations, were carried out without benefit of regular publicity, in time of national emergency secrecy was imposed, and restrictions of every sort continued to be applied vigorously throughout the struggle. The life-boatmen had therefore not even the compensation of being in the news, except on rare occasions. This certainly did not apply to the armed services, and the merchant fleet provided the closest parallel. Although the entire war effort depended on its courage and capacity, its ordeals and tragedies remained for the most part unknown to the public. When the war was over and the size of its achievement was at last made clear, the time had gone by for that *immediate* sympathy and recognition which is so heartening.

Even during what went by the name of the 'phoney' war, the period between September 1939 and the spring of the following year, when Hitler invaded Norway and Denmark, sailors and airmen were at full stretch, and they had to suffer one of the bitterest winters ever known in Britain.

The case for the life-boat people was put, succinctly and without exaggeration, by the Honorary Secretary of the Walmer station, towards the end of this preliminary phase.

> Frequent explosions are heard in the town, many in one day, of drifting mines striking the sands. Only very subdued navigation lights are permitted on the life-boat, searchlights not at all. The sea is dotted with sunken wrecks, unbuoyed and unlighted, and on moonless or overcast nights the men are without assistance to safety during their passages other than their trust in God and their own stout hearts. Add to all this, gales of wind, high seas, heavy rain or snow squalls, when the presence of floating or submerged dangers is much more difficult to detect. It is doubtful if any other section of the community has to contend with equal obstacles. Certainly there is no other section which carries out its duties so cheerfully and with such persistent heroism.

One great difference between the wars was the result of the policy of modernization which had been carried out so rigorously. In 1918 only nineteen life-boats were power-driven out of an active and reserve fleet of some 250 boats. Twenty-one years later, only fifteen pulling and sailing boats were in service. Of the coxswains, only six had been in command during the first war, though many others had war experience. Of those six, two, Robert Cross of the Humber, and Henry Blogg of Cromer, although they were in their sixties, became the outstanding life-boatmen of the new war.

Both were East Coast men, and it was significant that the very first wartime rescue, which took place on 10 September 1939, the eighth day after the outbreak of war, should have been off Suffolk. The steamer *Magdapur* of Liverpool struck a mine two miles offshore on a still afternoon, and broke her back. Five of her crew were killed by the explosion, but the Aldeburgh life-boat brought the rest ashore safely—seventy-four in all. Of these, twelve were wounded and most were smothered in black fuel oil. It took two and a half hours to clear the life-boat of oil and blood. A pattern had been established, for this was the prototype of a long succession of rescues in the waters of the United Kingdom and of Eire. They were to continue, in every kind of weather, by night and day, sometimes under immediate threat of air attack, for nearly six years.

Soon there came the toll of shipping taken by the weapon the enemy believed would paralyse all coastal traffic—the magnetic mine, dropped by aircraft. The threat was mastered, but not before estuaries and port approaches had been strewn with wrecks. Twenty-seven merchantmen, a total of 120,958 tons, were sunk in a single month, and many more were damaged.

Then came winter, so severe that spray froze as it fell. Life-boats returned from launches encased in ice; equipment had to be chipped off the crews. The Wells men searched for six hours for a missing boat, and then put into the Ouse to refuel. There they were first of all frozen fast, and then carried helpless up the river by the tide. They got back to their station after twenty-two hours away with an inch-thick coating of ice on their boat and with everyone frostbitten.

As in 1914, Whitby had its tragedy. Early in February 1940 the Belgian ship *Charles* ran ashore in storm and darkness at Saltwick Nab, not a hundred yards from the scene of the *Rohilla* rescues. In the deeper darkness under the cliffs where the life-boat was searching, two of the crew were washed overboard. The fact was unknown until the coxswain called the roll after a tremendous wave had nearly stunned him. They were John Dryden, who was acting as second coxswain, and the bowman, Christopher Wale, both with over thirty years of service and both of them officially 'retired'. Wale was taking the place of his son, who was with the Navy.

The first seven months of the war were in fact the busiest ever experienced since the founding of the Institution. Not only had there been nothing like them in the past, but there was to be nothing like them during the remainder of the conflict. They included the episodes which gave Henry Blogg the first of the Institution's medals to be awarded during the war, and his third in silver; also the action which brought Cross his first gold medal. Blogg took off twenty-nine survivors from the Greek ship *Mount Ida* in the autumn of 1939. And a few days after the loss of Dryden and Wale of Whitby, on 12 February 1940, when the weather was still tempestuous, Cross made some extraordinary rescues from the trawler *Gurth* which went ashore near the mouth of the Humber.

Cross, whose station was at lonely Spurn Head, had an exceptional record. He had joined the life-boat service in 1902 when the station was controlled by Hull Trinity House and had served six years there. Then he had taken charge of a herring drifter, but he kept his connexion with the life-boat service, and in 1909 he went out with the Flamborough boat to the aid of some cobles which were in trouble. Two were lost, and among those drowned were Cross's brother and two nephews. Three years later Cross returned to Spurn Head, this time as coxswain, so that by the time war broke out he had had thirty-two years' service, all but six in command. He had won two silver medals, the first in 1916 and the second ten years later, also the bronze.

Spurn Head, with its curved horn running out into the shipping lane of the third port of England, was, even in peace-time, a place demanding exceptional skill from pilots and others who navigated the waters around it. Under war conditions, as it was within an area bristling with land, sea and under-sea defences of every kind and complication, with no lights allowed and only the narrowest channel, where minesweepers were constantly on duty, it was not an enviable post for a coxswain and it required the closest knowledge of the tidal conditions of a dangerous area of estuary and sea. That was what Cross possessed, or he could never have succeeded in saving so many lives.

As Charles Vince wrote in a tribute to him: 'a difficult rescue by a life-boat is not only an act of courage, it is a work of art'. On the night that Cross was called upon to exercise every scrap of his powers, every circumstance might have seemed to combine to daunt him. There was a bitter onshore north-easter blowing, with snow falling which even in daylight would have made visibility low. A 4-knot tide was running out of the Humber almost at right-angles to the sea. The life-boat should have had a crew of eight, but when the call came there were only seven men on the post, and of these two were ill in bed. Maroons, which had been forbidden to the life-boatmen because they could have been taken for air-raid warnings, were not in use, and when Cross rang the assembly bell one of the sick men, the assistant motor mechanic, at once got up, put on his oilskins, not without help, and asked to be taken. Reluctantly, Cross agreed to do so, knowing that even so he would be two short of his proper complement, and that every available hand would be needed. The six on board were Cross, the second coxswain, the bowman, the motor mechanic, his assistant, and one other man.

A signal indicated that the *Gurth* was in trouble south of the estuary, and before the life-boat reached her she struck. The surf swept over her, and her stern disappeared. Only her forecastle remained above water, and it was there that her nine men clung to whatever they could find. The ship lay nearly stern to sea, with the tide running strongly against such lee as she could provide.

Cross anchored to windward 160 yards away from the wreck, and with his engines working slowly he began to move stern first towards her. Standing at his wheel, with the trawler behind him and the gale in his face, Cross stared over the bows at the seas as they thundered down out of the dark. When he judged that one might break over his boat he ordered the engines full ahead to meet it; then, the danger temporarily over, he edged backwards once again.

By the time Cross was within ten yards of the shore he was almost parallel with the wreck, but the tide then carried him 150 yards down the coast: he must now move up against it. He did so by means of a rope attached to the anchor cable and secured on a stern bollard, accepting the fact that he would be broadside on to the sea. As he gradually neared the *Gurth* he told his men that when he touched her they were to seize the men on the forecastle and somehow get them aboard the life-boat.

During the approach the crew were knocked down over and over again by the force of the seas, and the engine-room cockpit was flooded, the mechanic having to find his controls by touch under water, his chin being just above it. If a rope parted, all would have been quickly over, for the life-boat would have been beyond control and the men beaten or choked to death in the surf as she was driven ashore.

After twenty separate movements, six of the nine men had been rescued. At that moment one of the engines stopped, the propeller fouled by a rope. Cross had no thought of giving in, and the movements continued, rendered still more difficult by the serious loss of power. But at last the remaining three were taken off and the rope attached to the bollard could be let go. Then, as the life-boat's stern fell away before the wind, she struck the bottom. The rudder was split, but Cross found he could still steer. He then moved out towards his anchor and the men hauled it in. Next they opened the scuttle over the fouled propeller and cleared it. Then at last they could head through the night for Grimsby, with ten chilling miles to go.

Just outside the harbour boom, Cross hailed the examination vessel and her captain asked for the lights to be put on to guide the life-boat in. Although this was done, when Cross arrived at eight o'clock next morning it was still so dark, and the snow so blinding, that he had to use his forbidden searchlight to find the entrance.

After their eleven-hour ordeal, those who welcomed the crew said that they looked more exhausted than those they had rescued. As for the boat, her stern was pierced, her bow-pudding, the massive fender of plaited rope which was standard fitting, had been torn away, and most of the iron stanchions that held the guard-rails were beaten level with the deck.

Cross was sixty-four years old at the time, but, said one of his crew, he still moved with a step almost as light as a boy's. His touch on the wheel was as sure as ever, and, added the same admirer, 'he handled the life-boat as if she had been glass'.

Later the same year, the King instituted the George Cross and the George Medal. The Humber coxswain was given the George Medal, as well as the Institution's highest award, and there was no man who would have begrudged it.

* * *

After such an arctic winter came an unforgettable summer. During the splendid weather, Britain was called upon to face some of the greatest crises which had ever come upon her. First came the withdrawal of the Expeditionary Force from Dunkirk, following the defeat of the French army and encirclement by the advancing Germans, and then the Battle of Britain. Life-boats were involved in both these events.

On 30 May 1940 there came an urgent request to the Institution to send as many as possible of its boats to Dover, the main terminal for vessels loaded with returning troops. Eighteen stations between Gorleston in Norfolk and Shoreham in Sussex were asked to sail boats and crews for special duty, with full tanks and grass warps for towage. Two boats went direct to France, those of Ramsgate and Margate, and they soon made the Institution's colours familiar to the soldiers.

The *Prudential* of Ramsgate was the first away, with Coxswain Harold Primrose Knight in charge, at first in tow of a Dutch barge. She lay close off the beaches, under constant attack from the air, for over thirty hours, and helped to ferry 2,800 men to larger boats and so safely home. Once, out of the darkness as the crew neared the shore, a voice hailed them: 'I can't see who you are. Are you a naval party?'

He was answered, 'No sir, we are men of the crew of the Ramsgate life-boat.'

The voice called back: 'Thank you, and thank God for such men as you have proved yourselves to be. There is a party of fifty Highlanders coming next.'

The record of Edward Drake Parker of Margate, who arrived shortly after Knight, was equally gallant. His boat, the *Lord Southborough*, was close off the beaches for some twenty-four hours, and when he returned to his station it was just in time to prevent a destroyer, crammed with men, running on to the rocks in a mist. Both Knight and Parker were awarded the Distinguished Service Medal, and the house-flag of the Institution which had flown at the mast-head of the Ramsgate boat was later laid up in the parish church.

There was trouble too. The Hythe coxswain thought the conditions in which they asked him to operate, running his boat on to the sand rather than laying off and receiving troops as they were ferried out by smaller craft, were quite unsuitable for a heavy boat such as his. He also asked to have in writing the amount of pension families of life-boatmen could expect if they lost their lives during the withdrawal. The officers who were trying to organize matters bearing on immediate life or death could not spare even seconds over what they would have thought of as belly-aching. The coxswain was handed a railway warrant there and then, and he took his crew home, leaving his boat to be handled by a naval crew from Sheerness. As, by his example, he influenced not only his own men, but those from Walmer and Dungeness not to go over to Dunkirk, he and the Hythe motor mechanic were dismissed from the life-boat service. This was in spite of a record of gallantry, and, in the coxswain's case, twenty years' seniority.

On hearing the decision, the mechanic said: 'If the order had come from the Institution to "proceed to Dunkirk and do the best you can", there would have been no holding back.' He spoke for most of those concerned. No one could doubt their courage, and if the crews had indeed gone to the beaches, even in a protesting spirit, the conditions they would have found there would have made them realize why the authorities were apt to be short-tempered. 'I have a fishing boat,' said the coxswain to one of the Institution's staff, 'and will not see a man drown if I can get her off.' A few months later he had the chance to be as good as his word. He rescued two airmen from a crashed bomber.

The affair had very sad consequences, for when the next batch of life-boats, seven in all, arrived at Dover on 31 May, they were taken over by the authorities and the crews forbidden to sail. Protests were useless, and when the Navy, relenting slightly, said that motor mechanics could go, the answer was curt and natural under the circumstances—'All or none'.

Commander John Upton, Inspector for the East Coast, was at Brightlingsea in Essex when he heard of the difficulties. He went to Dover at once by road, and arrived just as the last of the dejected men were being sent away. He was able to organize and supervise the hasty training of naval stokers in the use of life-boat engines, and he, together with two of the Institution's reserve mechanics, formed themselves into a repair and maintenance party for all motor-boats sailing in and out of Dover for Dunkirk. They worked in shifts throughout the day and night, their number increasing from time to time till they mustered seven. They were on duty until 'Operation Dynamo' was over.

Nineteen life-boats took part in the withdrawal. The Ramsgate and Margate boats have been named already. The remaining roll of honour was as follows: the *Louise Stephens* of Great Yarmouth and Gorleston; the *Michael Stephens* of Lowestoft; the *Mary Scott* of Southwold; the *Abdy Beauclerk* and the *Lucy Lavers* of Aldeburgh; the *E.M.E.D.* of Walton and Frinton; the *Edward Z. Dresden* of Clacton-on-Sea; the *Greater London* (*Civil Service No. 3*) of Southend-on-Sea; the *Charles Dibdin* (*Civil Service No. 2*) of Walmer; the *Viscountess Wakefield* of Hythe; the *Charles Cooper Henderson* of Dungeness; the *Cyril and Lilian Bishop*, of Hastings; the *Jane Holland*, of Eastbourne; the *Cecil and Lilian Philpott*, of Newhaven; the *Rosa Woodd* and *Phyllis Lunn*, of Shoreham Harbour; the *Thomas Kirk Wright*, of Poole and Bournemouth, and a new, and as yet unnamed boat which had just been completed at the Rowledge Iron Works, Essex. This boat survived to be stationed at Cadgwith in Cornwall, a gift of £5,000 from the Girl Guides of the Empire being used to pay for her. She became *Guide of Dunkirk*.

These boats met with plenty of adventure. The Newhaven, Poole, Walton, Lowestoft and Clacton boats all worked in Dunkirk harbour itself, ferrying men to the ships outside, mainly during the hours of darkness. The Poole boat, loaded with French soldiers, came under fire from German troops at short range, though no one was hurt. The Walton boat went over in a string of boats in tow of a tug, to save fuel. Off Gravelines they were thrice attacked from the air. Blast broke the tow-rope and threw men into the sea. One boat was sunk, others turned back, but Walton went on. The officer in charge of her was killed by a shell, and she got back to Dover with a rope round her propeller. A diver went down and cut it away, and then she sailed again.

The Lowestoft boat was twice rammed by motor torpedo-boats, but she was able to continue her work, and to get home under her own power. The Clacton boat took out her last load at about daybreak on the final day, just before all ships left the harbour and it was closed by block-ships. On her way home, she attracted the attention of the Luftwaffe, but managed to evade machine-gun fire without serious damage. The Dungeness boat arrived at Margate with four sailors on board, one of them wounded, and two of her stanchions torn away. The Walmer boat came home with bullet-holes in both sides.

The naval officer who found himself in charge of the Southwold boat, Sub-Lieutenant Stephen Dickinson, had been one of the Institution's Inspectors. After taking off many loads of soldiers his engine stalled, but he was rescued by the Great Yarmouth boat which took him back to Dover, where he had his first sleep for several days. Refreshed, he volunteered for another trip, and Commander Upton was able to give him the Shoreham Harbour boat. By now a seasoned Dunkirker, Dickinson led a marauding party round the dockyard, found a large sheet of steel which he fastened behind the steering-wheel, built a screen of fenders on either side, and with a white ensign almost as large as the boat, was about to sail on his fourth journey when the shelling was reported to have become so heavy on the beaches that boats were forbidden to go across.

Another member of the Institution's staff, one of the Surveyors of Machinery, returned from Dunkirk and went over a second time in the new life-boat which had come straight from the building yard. He joined her by jumping aboard just as she sailed. She was towed across and arrived at dusk, but before she could cast off the tow-rope it was carried round her propeller. Next day the Surveyor stripped and went overboard with a knife, but the rope, drawn tight round the shaft, was immovable. He found he could not even cut it, so climbed aboard again, covered with fuel oil. The crew then made sail, using the life-boat's stumpy mizen and blankets sewn together with string, which they hoisted on two boat-hooks. The contrived sail only gave her two knots, but this was better than nothing. Later, by working the engine, they were able to loosen the rope a little and they then started on their journey home, moving slowly stern first, the only way they could get help from the engine. In the end they were found fast asleep on a lightship at the mouth of the Thames, and the life-boat was taken to Sheerness.

Among the most remarkable adventures were those which happened to the Eastbourne boat. Her naval captain had been off Dunkirk for several days in craft which had sustained every kind of damage, some of which had become unserviceable. He asked Commander Upton to find him something which was unsinkable. As the Eastbourne boat happened to be at Dover for servicing, he was given charge of her, and he set off once more for the scene of operations. Next day he was back again and told his tale. He had been rammed by a French motor torpedo boat. He had been sprayed with German machine-gun bullets. The engine had stalled in the open sea and he had been forced to abandon his command, but when last he saw her she was still afloat. Two days later she was found drifting in the English Channel and was brought in to Dover. Her fore-end box was stove in. She had over five hundred bullet-holes in her hull. She was full of water. But she had not sunk, and ten months later she was fully repaired and ready to go back to her normal duties.

Some life-boatmen went over to Dunkirk in their own boats, or in those of others. Among them was the Wells coxswain, by birth a Dane. He longed to get to grips with the Germans who had occupied his native country and were menacing his adopted one. He set out from Norfolk a simple fisherman, arrived at

Dover wearing his R.N.L.I. cap, but was then armed with a rifle and revolver and sent away on a secret mission in a boat in charge of an ex-captain of the Indian Army. There were two naval gunners, a twin Lewis gun, a bucket full of hand grenades and a gallon of rum. It was believed that the boat was to pick up a V.I.P., rumoured to be the Ambassador to Belgium, but he did not appear, and the Dane, through no fault of his own, had to return with nothing done.

During the last phase of the withdrawal the Shoreham Harbour boat was able to save a survey ship which was trying to embark two hundred French soldiers from the mole. Something under-water obstructed the screw, and the captain could not move her. There seemed no chance of getting away before the blockships were put in position, when he saw a life-boat nearby full of troops. He hailed her and, by valiant efforts, the officer in charge was able to give the survey ship a tug that freed her, saving her and the Frenchmen from capture. The life-boat was the *Greater London* of Southend.

There was a time when it seemed likely that several of the life-boats engaged off Dunkirk would never return home. The Honorary Secretary of the Margate station, who went over on board a destroyer, saw three of them ashore. But in the end, all but one were returned to the Institution. The exception was the Hythe boat. The Admiralty sent word that she had been damaged and abandoned. She had come to grief in exactly the way her coxswain had foretold when he protested at the manner in which he had been expected to use her.

* * *

The Battle of Britain, which followed closely on the withdrawal from Dunkirk, extended officially from 8 August to 31 October 1940. As a result of the defeat of the Luftwaffe, invasion had been postponed, if not abandoned.

Ever since the outbreak of war, the life-boats had been called upon to rescue airmen almost as often, and under as great difficulties, as seamen. This particular task intensified during the continuous air fighting, in the course of which there were 264 operational launches, 131 of which were concerned with aircraft. Ten British and eight Germans were picked up by the life-boatmen in the most critical weeks, the total being greatly swelled by 'shore-boat' services, by Royal Air Force and Royal Naval launches specially adapted for the purpose, which though faster than any life-boat except the specially built one stationed before the war at Dover, were less satisfactory in very rough weather.

The Margate and the Selsey stations were the most active during the eighty-five days when the issue of the battle hung in the balance. It was the Margate men who had the satisfaction of saving the life of Richard Hillary.

This pilot officer, one of the few to whom so many owed so much, was a great-great-great-great nephew of Sir William Hillary. Flying a Spitfire, he had been attacked above the Channel and his aircraft shot to pieces. He struggled to get out of the blazing machine, lost consciousness, and then came to. He found himself floating slowly downwards, with his parachute, which he had managed to open himself, doing its duty.

The day was calm and the wind light, but there was mist over the sea and the Margate crew searched for over an hour before they found him. He was terribly burned and near collapse. The life-boatmen bandaged him, sustained him, and made him as comfortable as they could as they headed for home at their best speed.

Hillary lived to write his own story, which appeared in 1942 as *The Last Enemy*, the title taken from the fifteenth chapter of the First Epistle to the Corinthians: 'The last enemy that shall be destroyed is death.' Before he was found, he had realized the extent of his wounds. He saw that the skin of his hands hung in shreds. He could see his lips, they were so swollen, and he felt sick from the smell of his own burnt flesh. He kept up a tuneless chant, stopping it from time to time to call for help. The sea grew colder; the sun went in. He looked again at his hands, but as he could not see them, he knew that he was blind. He felt certain then that he would die. He felt no fear, only curiosity, and thought to end things at once. He unscrewed the valve of his life-belt and his head went under water, but it rose again. His faithful parachute would not let him sink. When he realized this he laughed. Then he felt very lonely.

He was still conscious when he heard shouts, knew that he was being lifted from the sea, that a flask had been put to his lips;

that something had been put above him to keep the sun, which had reappeared, from his burnt face. In the sea he had been free from pain. In the life-boat it came upon him, and he could hardly keep from crying aloud during the waves of agony which swept over him. The time taken in getting ashore seemed to him endless.

The Margate men, who had searched so patiently for him, did not forget him once they had brought him to safety. They visited him, as he lay in his hospital bed. Slowly he recovered, and he even flew again, though this was against all advice, for he never had the full use of his hands. He was killed on active service in January 1943, while training as a night fighter, at the age of twenty-three. His ashes were scattered from an aircraft over the sea where he had been picked up.

* * *

Much information concerning this and other rescues, a substantial part of it dramatic, which might have been steered past the censor and been seen in the pages of the *Life-boat* had now to be withheld, or mentioned only briefly, in the news given to those accustomed to follow the fortunes of the stations. It would have included an account of the loss, for the remainder of the war, of the Channel Island boats at Guernsey and Jersey; the finding of an abandoned Belgian life-boat which was salvaged, repaired and sent to various stations including Plymouth, where she took the place of one commandeered by the Admiralty for use in Iceland; and of air attacks such as that on Ramsgate in August 1940. When the bombs fell, nine of the crew were in a shelter close by the harbour, and six of them were wounded. The station could not reopen until October. At Tynemouth there was a direct hit on the boat-house, destroying building, boat, and part of the launching slipway.

In peace-time the Institution's journal had used over eighteen tons of paper annually, and although, since the outbreak of war, it had been reduced in size to 48 pages, the continuity of eighty-eight years had so far been unbroken. This could be so no longer, and in the interests of economy, publication was suspended. The last number in the form so long familiar was dated April 1940, after which there was to be a break until the summer of 1947.

Publicity did not cease. Appeals went on. Use was made of broadcasting whenever the chance arose, and the Institution continued to support an illustrated annual, *The Story of the Life-boat*, which had been published on its behalf for some fifteen years by Felix Newbury of Shaftesbury Avenue. It was largely through this publication, in which photographs sometimes appeared, that the public were able to learn something of what the life-boats were achieving.

The headquarters in Grosvenor Gardens, which was damaged during air-raids in 1940 and in the following year (as was the depot), had only a skeleton staff, and for official news the Institution's members and well-wishers had to be content with a *Life-boat War Bulletin*. This was issued quarterly, edited from Boreham Wood. The first of these news-sheets—for they were scarcely more—appeared in September 1940, the last in December 1946. Over 100,000 copies were circulated, and they contained items not easily found elsewhere.

The last issue of the regular *Life-boat* had covered a period in which two losses occurred within a few days of each other. Sir George Shee died on 29 November 1939, and Princess Louise, Duchess of Argyll, who had closely identified herself with the cause, on 3 December. The Princess's work was undertaken by the Duchess of Sutherland, though for less than three years, as she herself died during the course of the war. The Presidency of the Ladies' Life-boat Guild was then accepted by Lady Louis Mountbatten, whose husband was at that time about to become Supreme Allied Commander, South-East Asia.

The staff, and more especially the Inspectorate, was heavily depleted by calls to the colours, as had been the case in the First World War. Commander Vaux, as could have been anticipated in the case of an officer with his experience, went to the Fleet, and saw active service in North Africa and elsewhere—but he was released to return to his pre-war duties before the end of the struggle.

A very sad loss occurred on 25 August 1942 when the Duke of Kent, who at the time was serving with the Royal Air Force in the rank of Air Commodore, was killed in Scotland in an air accident to a Sunderland flying-boat, from which there was only one survivor. He had indicated, at the Annual General Meeting held a few months before the war, that as he was going to

Australia as Governor-General, he would have to delegate his duties as President. Owing to the critical situation of international affairs the appointment was put off, and he remained in Britain, or on tours of inspection, until his death. His last act on behalf of the Institution was to present awards to life-boatmen at Plymouth for rescues from an aircraft, and it is certain that, had he lived, he would have continued his support as enthusiastically as had his elder brother, and so many other members of his family.

The Presidency was taken over in 1943 by the Duke's widow, Princess Marina. She was to continue in this office for the rest of her life, and she was the first woman to hold it. She shared many of the Duke's interests, and as head of the Women's Royal Naval Service identified herself wholeheartedly with matters relating to the sea.

* * *

It was not only the life-boatmen who were handicapped by the difficulties met with in the narrow, mine-swept channels used by coastal convoys. The merchantmen themselves suffered as badly, and if precautions against attack protected them more often than not, they could also lead to loss. A disaster happened off the Norfolk coast of a kind inconceivable in peace. It not only wrecked six ships, one of them new, at a time when every vessel that could float was precious, but resulted in a combined operation on the part of life-boats which was among the most notable in their annals. As so often in the past, the scene was Haisborough Sands.

During the early hours of 6 August 1941, a convoy was sailing down the narrow waterway, nicknamed E-boat Alley because of constant tip-and-run raids by German motor torpedo-boats. This was then a highway of the North Sea. It was not, however, the enemy that worried the commodore in charge that day so much as the darkness, and the gale from the north-west which was churning the nine square miles of Haisborough into a tumult of foam and spray. The course of the leading merchantman was in error, and as the ships had been ordered to follow one another closely, showing no lights, when the first of them struck the Sands, so did five more, all within a few minutes. This was just after 4 a.m. but not until 8 o'clock did the Navy seek help from the life-boats. Then it needed all it could get.

The message was received by Cromer and Great Yarmouth, Lowestoft and Sheringham. Within ten minutes the larger of the two Cromer boats, under Coxswain Blogg, was running down her slipway. She had seventeen miles to go, and she reached the Sands at 10 o'clock. There an astonishing scene met the crew. All six ships were in process of breaking up, with aircraft circling round them, and destroyers standing by in deeper water. The Navy had taken off most of the crew of one steamer in their sea-boats, but the greater number of the men, who had already endured the battering of the sea for six hours, were beyond the reach of seamen unskilled in local conditions. Some had already tried to swim for the boats and been drowned, and as the tide was ebbing, the shallow water over the Sands grew ever shallower, and made the work of rescue each moment more difficult. The wrecks were strung out along about half a mile of sea, though two of them were so close together that they looked like one.

Blogg chose a steamer whose decks were under water. He could see her crew on top of the engine-room clustered behind the funnel. For the time being they were just out of reach of the seas, but their ship was visibly going to pieces beneath them, and they had nothing secure to which a line could be made fast. But there was a great crack in the iron plates near where the men were gathered. Blogg decided to use it, instead of a rope, to hold his boat, and he sailed her right over the bulwarks on to the flooded deck, driving her bow into the crack. The breaking waters poured over the life-boat, filling her cock-pits: then they flowed away and she crashed on the deck. Again and again they washed her from her hold between the broken plates, but Blogg forced the bow into the crack again and his crew snatched sixteen men, one by one, from the top of the engine-room.

The second ship proved easier, for although she was more than half under water, the life-boat could lie alongside while her thirty-one men jumped or slid down ropes to safety. With forty-seven rescued men on board, Blogg's boat was too full to be of further use until he had transferred them to a destroyer. This he now did. It was noon by this time, and the second Cromer boat had just arrived on the scene. Blogg put his second coxswain aboard her to take command and then, with one man short, made for his third steamer. This looked as tricky a rescue as the first, for only the bridge was visible, and nineteen men were crowded on it. Once again Blogg sailed his life-boat right over the bulwarks on to the deck. He laid her alongside the bridge and, with her engines working first ahead and then astern, he held her there against the fierce wash of the seas until every man was safe.

Blogg then looked round for still more work. He saw that the second Cromer boat had just rescued the crew of the fourth ship in the line and that the Great Yarmouth boat had arrived and was alongside the fifth. There was one more. Once again he was able to lie alongside, while twenty-two men jumped into his boat. But the water was now so shallow that he was bumping on the Sands, and as he steered for deeper water the life-boat ran aground for her whole length, and was helpless. Had the next sea broken on her it would have rolled her over and washed away every man. Instead, it broke before it reached her, and lifted her off, just in time.

By now it was 1 o'clock in the afternoon, three hours since Blogg had arrived. Between them the two Cromer boats and the Great Yarmouth boat had saved 119 men, and Blogg's own share was 88. The boats from Sheringham and Lowestoft, which had farther to come, arrived when the work was over, but that was no fault of their own, and they might have been of great use in the final stages.

When the Cromer first boat was examined, the extent of her risks could be appreciated. There were three holes in the bow; her bow-pudding, eight feet of her oaken stem, and over twenty feet of her fender of rock elm were torn off. One of the rescued captains said afterwards that he had seen the fender float away and expected next moment to be in the water, with the life-boat sunk. A detail noted with astonishment by the shipwrights was that the brass bolts of the stem, left when it was broken off, had been driven inwards through eight inches of oak and had pierced the air-cases inside her hull.

For his magnificent achievement, Blogg received his third gold medal from the Institution, thus equalling the record of Sir William Hillary, though exceeding all others in terms of seamanship and risk. On the recommendation of the Admiralty, he was also awarded the British Empire Medal, adding this to the George Cross which he already held.

Scarcely had the Cromer men recovered from their summer

Coxswain Henry Blogg, G.C., B.E.M., of Cromer

'Coxswain Blogg making rescues from the barge *Sepoy*, 1933, in heavy surf: Cromer church in the background.'
From the painting by Charles Dixon, R.I.

Life-boat designers and their boats:
J. R. Barnett

52 ft. Barnett boat

R. A. Oakley

48 ft. 6 in. Oakley boat

Launching the Peterhead life-boat

Poster-stamps (1950) illustrating the work of the life-boat service. See pages 180–1.

ROYAL NATIONAL LIFE-BOAT INSTITUTION
1800
The ORIGINAL off Tynemouth Castle
3D
ROYAL NATIONAL LIFE-BOAT INSTITUTION
1900
Rescue from barque GLINT: Lizard
3D
ROYAL NATIONAL LIFE-BOAT INSTITUTION
1830
Wreck of ST. GEORGE in Douglas Bay
3D
ROYAL NATIONAL LIFE-BOAT INSTITUTION
Cromer life-boat & wreck of SEPOY
3D
ROYAL NATIONAL LIFE-BOAT INSTITUTION
1881
Ramsgate life-boat & INDIAN CHIEF
3D
ROYAL NATIONAL LIFE-BOAT INSTITUTION
1936
Ballycotton life-boat & Daunt Rock Lightship
3D
ROYAL NATIONAL LIFE-BOAT INSTITUTION
1890
A wrecked schooner & Southsea life-boat
3D
ROYAL NATIONAL LIFE-BOAT INSTITUTION
Rescue from crashed bomber: Wells, Norfolk
3D
FOUNDER
ROYAL NATIONAL LIFE-BOAT INSTITUTION
6D
LIEUT. COL.
SIR WILLIAM HILLARY, BT
POSTERSTAMPS LTD

Building life-boats at
Messrs Samuel White of Cowes

ordeal when they were called upon to face another, which in every way was more severe. It led to the only loss suffered by a crew commanded by Blogg, and to his own narrowest escape during the course of an attempt at rescue.

At 8 o'clock on the morning of 26 October 1941 the Cromer coastguard rang the life-boat station to say that a ship was aground on Hammond Knoll, a sand-bank twenty-five miles away. It was a grey, cold day, with a north-easter blowing, and with stinging squalls of hail. When Blogg reached the ship he thought he had never seen worse conditions, and that, from a man of his experience, said everything.

The wreck—she was the steamer *English Trader*—had already sunk when Blogg found her at midday. Only her masts, funnel and chart-house were above water, and the seas, as so often with a sand-bank, were breaking all ways, meeting at times with a clap like thunder, to rise mast-high and crash down on the sheltering men.

There were obstacles of every kind to be guarded against; loose wires from the ship; boats on her fore-derrick which had broken loose and which swung about in every sea; while the surrounding water was strewn with crates and cases which were being scoured out of the holds.

Blogg decided to wait for the slack of the tide, which would occur about 4 o'clock, but he watched for every chance which might enable him to get the men off sooner. After two hours tossing about, his patience wore thin, and he determined to make the attempt, though few in the life-boat beside himself would have considered that they had the slightest chance of success.

He approached the steamer very cautiously, at half speed, but, as the seas were then running, he had to do so broadside on. Suddenly a huge wall of water rose on the life-boat's quarter. Blogg heard one of the crew shout a warning, but before he could give a turn to the wheel to meet it, the advancing surge crashed down on the boat, lifting the coxswain bodily, and hurling him into the water. It did the same to the second coxswain, the bowman, and another of the crew. Two more would also have gone the same way, but as they were swirled over the side they clutched the guard rail, held fast to it, and managed to haul themselves inboard. The others on deck just had time to throw themselves flat, and the sea merely gave already drenched men a battering.

As the life-boat heeled over to the shock, those on the *English Trader* could actually see her keel, and thought that next moment she would be bottom up, with her men drowned, for she was not self-righting. But she slowly swung back, and long before the last of the water had drained from the scuppers the second coxswain's son had seized the wheel. Blogg and his second-in-command were floating some yards away, and the young man steered towards them. Then someone remembered that there was an aircraft's dinghy under the canopy. This was flung to Blogg, and he held on to it while those on board hauled in the second coxswain. Blogg himself was then fished out of the water, and he at once took charge again, set on finding the other two men.

They had been together at first—then a big sea separated them. The bowman was the first to be rescued, just when he had begun to give up hope. When the other, Signalman Allen, was found, he had been nearly half an hour in the water and was floating unconscious. His clothing was so weighed down that it took five minutes of hard struggle to get him aboard. Soon afterwards he seemed to revive. He even sat up, and spoke a few words. Then he collapsed, and was put under the shelter of the engine-room canopy.

It was by now three in the afternoon, seven hours since the boat had left Cromer. Everyone was spent. Several ropes had been washed overboard, and one of them had fouled a propeller. Blogg realized he could do no more for the time being, and he headed for the shelter of Great Yarmouth harbour. On his way there he actually passed the Yarmouth boat going out to the wreck, but the coxswains did not see each other. The Yarmouth men, on reaching Hammond Knoll, came to the same conclusion as Blogg. Five times their boat tried to approach the *English Trader*. Each time she came near capsizing. Once she got near enough to fire her line-throwing gun, and the steamer's men pulled in a rope and made it fast, but it snapped, and the seas carried the life-boat out of range.

By this time the force of the gale was actually increasing, night had almost come, and the captain of the steamer himself blew a whistle and waved to the life-boatmen to go. No more could be done that night, which the wrecked men must endure as best they could in their cold, wind-swept and sea-swept shelter, with the risk that the ship would break up beneath them.

Blogg reached Great Yarmouth at 6 o'clock, his men continuing to try to revive the signalman. They could not do so; he never spoke again. Ambulances and cars were waiting in the hope of being able to do something either for the Cromer crew or for any who might have been rescued, but Blogg felt well enough to go straight to the Sailors' Home with his men. He was seen by the port admiral and told that he was not to go out again without his permission. Blogg said nothing to this, but when his men had recovered a little they refilled the petrol tanks and telephoned to Cromer for dry clothes, fresh oilskins, and a spare man. Everything came at once, by road.

The Great Yarmouth life-boat did not return until after 10 o'clock and the coxswains then discussed their plans. Blogg intended to sail about 4 a.m., in the dark of the morning. Great Yarmouth would wait until day. Blogg then went to bed for a few hours' rest. He was up again at 3.30 a.m. and telephoned for reports on the weather to the local base, also to Cromer. Both said the same: wind and sea had gone down a little, but the weather was much as it had been the day before.

Blogg then asked for the harbour boom to be opened, roused his crew, and sailed, without objection from the admiral, just after half past four. He had about three hours of darkness before him, and ropes were still round a propeller, reducing the life-boat's speed by a third. But his optimistic view of the day's prospects was justified. When he reached Hammond Knoll he found that the north-easterly wind had backed to the north-west, and that wind and sea were lighter. So much was this so that Blogg was able to take his boat straight alongside the steamer. Within half an hour he had rescued forty-four men, and none of them ever wished to hear the words Hammond Knoll again.

If ever a feat deserved a fourth gold medal, it was this. But Blogg had come to be judged by different standards from most of his fellows, and he received a fourth in silver.

As if superlative fulfilment of their duties were not enough in itself, both Blogg and Coxswain Cross of the Humber, who incidentally won a second gold medal in 1943 before ill-health caused him to retire, were effective speakers. Being modest men, they had no love of giving tongue in public, but when called upon to do so on behalf of the service to which they belonged, they did not refuse.

Cross spoke for the R.N.L.I. in April 1940 in the series given to the Week's Good Cause, and the response amounted to a notable sum: £5,693. 10. 5. Blogg followed him two years later and raised £5,260. The Norfolk man in fact spoke six times altogether during the earlier years of the war, and was allowed to describe some of his own experiences in making rescues from coastal convoys and from the *English Trader*. Cross spoke twice, the second time being in the one o'clock news during the last few weeks of 1941. Other coxswains whose voices were heard over the radio were Albert Spurgeon of Lowestoft, Andrew Mearns of Montrose, Francis Mair of Buckie, Banffshire, James Coule of Broughty Ferry, Angus, and Patrick Murphy of Newcastle, County Down.

All such publicity helped the cause, but no contribution to the funds of the Institution was received with more pride than the sum of £28. 5. 10. which came to the Treasurer from the *Jervis Bay*. This armed merchant cruiser had been escorting an Atlantic convoy in November 1940 when she encountered a German pocket battleship. Her captain ordered the merchant ships to scatter behind a smoke-screen, while she herself faced the raider. The ship's few and antiquated 6-inch guns were no match for the 11-inch salvoes of her great opponent, but although the *Jervis Bay* went down fighting she had gained precious time. This enabled all but a handful of the convoy to escape destruction.

Two months later the Admiralty wrote to say that, by the wish of her crew, half the *Jervis Bay*'s ship's fund was to go to the Institution if she were sunk. Her self-sacrifice was of a kind which was well understood by the life-boat service—as well as by the wives of those who belonged to it. This was touchingly shown by the widow of Signalman Allen of Cromer, who in her will left half the value of her cottage to the Institution. She had been receiving the pension given to the next of kin of a leading hand who had lost his life on duty, and this was her way of repaying it.

* * *

The life-boats of the eastern coasts of England had no monopoly of distinguished war service, though they certainly had their full share of operational calls. It so happened that during the year following the Haisborough Sands and Hammond Knoll episodes, Scotland endured terrible conditions.

Typical of the early months was the weather experienced in January 1942 by the old-time whaling port of Peterhead. It was as violent as could be remembered, even in an area in which gales were commonplace. A high wind blew ceaselessly for three days, during which gusts were thought to have exceeded a hundred miles an hour. A hundred feet of the three-hundred-foot breakwater were washed away, and tons of solid masonry tossed about like pebbles.

Peterhead had had a succession of fine coxswains. Cameron and Strachan had both won the Institution's silver medal before the war. Now it was the turn of Coxswain John McLean. At one critical stage he and his crew stood by for fifty-four hours. They were actually at sea for nearly ten, going on three separate missions to the help of different ships, twice in pitch dark and blinding snow. They rescued 106 lives, and McLean won the first gold medal which had come Scotland's way for over a century. The average age of his crew was fifty.

The good work went on. Scottish life-boats were responsible for 357 out of a total of 596 lives saved by the rescue service that year. Peterhead could claim 135. Campbelltown in Argyllshire was next with 74. Scotland also had the lion's share of medals, eighteen out of thirty-eight awarded by the Institution, and three British Empire Medals awarded by the King.

As the war went on, shortages of every kind increased. As it had been a feature of more than one operation that the crews had gone hungry for long periods, the Committee of Management greatly welcomed the generous gesture of a number of firms in supplying emergency rations of chocolate and biscuits, suitably cased, to life-boat stations. The chocolate came from Messrs Cadbury, Fry, and Rowntree; the biscuits from Messrs Huntley and Palmer, McVitie and Price, and Peek Frean. In every area, they were put to good use, and as the war increased in complexity, so did the tasks assigned to the crews.

The boats served as fire-tenders to ships set ablaze by bombs, and they stood sentinel near floating mines, to warn sea traffic until they could be disposed of. They helped the Home Guard in their exercises, and landed mock invasion parties. They sometimes took the mail. They brought food to the starving, doctors to the injured, priests to the dying. They were ambulances to take sick and wounded to hospital, and hearses to carry the dead.

In Fraserburgh, during the third winter, heavy snowstorms blocked all railways and roads, and brought down telephone and telegraph wires. During ten snow-bound days the life-boat was at times almost the only form of transport free to operate. This she did continuously. More than that, she found a trawler which had run aground and been abandoned by her crew, and towed her into harbour.

One of the last and best of the war-time rescues took place off the coast of South Wales in March 1945. Four years earlier, Coxswain William Gammon had won a bronze medal for rescuing the crew of a steamer wrecked among the iron stakes of the coastal defences. Now it was a frigate belonging to the Canadian Navy which was in trouble. She had been torpedoed in the Atlantic, a thousand miles away, and had been towed into the Bristol Channel. There she had anchored in Swansea Bay. Her ordeal seemed over, and the rescue tug went away. Then a sudden squall blew up, and within a few hours the frigate was signalling for help. The life-boat found her lying, smothered in the surf, on Port Talbot Bar. There, forty-one years before, an earlier life-boat from the Mumbles, the station concerned, had turned over, drowning six of her crew. The average age of Gammon's crew was fifty-five. Two men were in their sixties and two over seventy. They included a survivor of the disaster of many years before.

Gammon took his life-boat into the surf twelve times, turned, and as he came seawards again, shaved the warship's side. On her forecastle, rolling to the seas, her men waited. They had only a moment or two in which to judge and make their dangerous jump into the boat, which one moment was level with the deck, and the next had dropped out of sight below the water-line. One man fell through the darkness on top of Gammon, bruising him against his wheel. Another fell into the sea between frigate and life-boat, but Gammon seized and dragged him aboard before the vessels crashed together. In this way, forty-two men were taken off; and no sooner was the life-boat back than she was called to another ship. She was at sea for over ten hours, and this was indeed, as was duly recognized, a gold medal operation.

Among the more notable wartime episodes was a service in 1943 by the Hastings crew. The naval trawler *Gaulonia* was reported to be in trouble in high seas near Jury's Gap, on the

Dungeness side of Rye Bay. Coxswain John Muggeridge and the motor mechanic, W. R. Hilder, were awarded bronze medals for saving seven men. There was a sad sequel, for a few days later the coxswain lost his life when his own fishing boat hit a mine and sank, and Hilder was killed in an air raid the same year.

Gammon's gold medal was the last of its kind to be given during a war in which the crews of all parts of the United Kingdom—never more united—and of neutral Eire, had shown their valour. For example, the many admirers of Coxswain Sliney of Ballycotton, the central character in the Daunt Rock rescue (who had requested that a plaque be put on his boat afterwards because he regarded her, not himself, as the real hero), were delighted that he added a silver medal to his earlier awards. Farther north, at Newcastle, County Down, Patrick Murphy won a gold medal in January 1942 which ranks among the best achievements.

Having taken 39 men off a wrecked steamer, at least eleven more than his boat could safely carry, Murphy found himself unable to turn. He had squeezed into a narrow channel to get alongside; now he was trapped there. The only way out seemed barred by the reef on which the steamer's stern was beached. Murphy, his decks nearly awash under the added weight of so many survivors, decided to try to cross it.

He took advantage of three big waves coming along together and with his engine at full speed, he let them wash him over the rocks, risking damage or disaster. The mate of the steamer said afterwards that if he had known what Murphy was up to he would never have left the wreck! But boldness paid off, and everyone reached safety.

That was often so, as records proved, for even the splendid total of 5,322 rescues made during the First World War had been handsomely exceeded. Exclusive of Dunkirk, 6,376 lives had been saved, more than during the last eighteen years of peace. But this had been an even longer struggle, and the life-boats had been far better equipped—a major factor in their success. The great similarity had been the contribution of those who, although too old for the fighting line, were prepared to face the sea at its most destructive in their efforts to save their fellows.

7

The Post-War Era

Those whose memory went back to the aftermath of both World Wars were agreed that, at least on the national plane, it was easier the second time than the first. War had been brought home more continuously to these islands; most civilians had withstood bombardment, and there was not that sharp division between the fighting men and others which had once led to bitterness. There was, moreover, little clap-trap about 'a land fit for heroes to live in', while, administratively, lessons had been learnt which eased the transition from emergency conditions to something which gradually approached the normal.

The Institution stood well. Its reputation remained high. Although it had lost a handful of life-boats, the majority of personnel casualties were from mine and bomb, and most of them had been sustained when the victims were not on rescue operations. Some seventeen boats had been completed during the war years, and they were all of types which had proved themselves in hard circumstances. It was true that in peace-time between sixty and seventy new boats might have been expected to enter service in the six years which had been taken up by the war, and that for some time many building yards would be engaged in the replacement of major losses—but there was no feeling of discouragement, rather the reverse.

The immediate post-war programme foreshadowed the building of twenty-nine new boats, all with two engines and two screws, for if recent experience has shown one thing more than another it was the value of double power equipment. Men such as Blogg and Cross would undoubtedly have lost their lives had they not had the advantage of a second engine. All future boats would be of the diesel type, which would increase their range by a third. But as the petrol engine had had so satisfactory a record, the number then on order would be completed, with the expectation of many years of useful life. There was also a trend in design to place the wheel amidships, which from every point of view was to a coxswain's advantage. Increased use was to be made of aluminium, and loudhailers were to replace the old speaking trumpets. One experiment which was not carried further was a reversion to water-jet propulsion, used in the early steam life-boats, which had been applied to the internal combustion engine in the *Kate Greatorex*. This was a life-boat sent to Padstow in 1939. She had Gill power units.

At the time the *Life-boat* reappeared, in June 1947, there had been a tragedy to record. It emphasized once again that, even when conducted by the most skilful and experienced coxswain, sea-rescue was in its nature so hazardous that no amount of success could conceal the fact that heavy odds were as often as not against the life-boatmen.

On 23 August 1947 the Mumbles boat, in charge of William Gammon, was called to the help of the steamer *Samtampa* of Middlesbrough. This ship was reported to be in trouble off Sker Point, about eleven miles from the station. The weather was appalling, and the exact sequence of events will never be known, for when Gammon reached the *Samtampa* she was already among the rocks and, in trying to approach her in the heavy surf to take off the crew, the life-boat overturned. All her men were drowned.

It was a scene of desolation rarely to be met with, for the entire crew of the steamer, forty-one in all, were also lost. Wreckage strewed the whole area. The life-boat was found bottom up, and the men who had done so much when the Canadian frigate *Cheboque* had foundered two years before had attempted their last service. This was in fact the third tragedy the station had suffered, for some twenty years before the disaster of 1903, when six men had been drowned, the life-boat had lost four of the crew including the second coxswain and the bowman, in weather and under conditions not unlike those of 1947.

As this was the first life-boat catastrophe which had occurred for some time, and was indeed the first that many younger newspaper readers had heard about, there was a great deal of Press comment, including much misinformation, and the raising of the demand, familiar to old hands, that all life-boats should be self-righting, and why were they not? The effective answer, that types of life-boat were in every case chosen by the crews, who in most cases preferred the additional stability given by non-self-righters, was not always readily accepted. The facts were that at that time there were only a few self-righting boats in the service of the Institution, these being of the lighter types. The majority of the crews were not only perfectly satisfied with what they had, but would not have exchanged their boats, even if given the opportunity, by reason of anything which might have happened elsewhere.

Within a few years of the episode at the Mumbles, there was to be a practical illustration of the fact that self-righting was not then universally regarded as a blessing. At Bridlington, one of the self-righters capsized and the bowman was lost. The crew asked for their boat to be replaced by a non-self-righter. This request was met.

During the summer of 1947, after an interval of eleven years instead of the usual four, it was at last found possible to hold another International Life-boat Conference, the fifth. This took place in July at Oslo. As if to make up for lost opportunities, it lasted a week, which was full of variety. The meeting-place was a particularly happy one for the British, for the western nations which had recently been allied had rarely seemed closer. The meetings themselves, attended by representatives from eleven countries, enabled old companionships to be renewed and new contracts established.

The countries which sent members were Belgium, Denmark, Finland, Great Britain, Holland, Iceland, Norway, Sweden, Turkey and the United States. It had been sadly remarked that ever since the meeting at Paris in 1928 the Russians had not permitted themselves even the courtesy of acknowledging invitations to attend. This made it seem likely that their sole appearance had been the result of a bureaucratic freak.

The delegates were welcomed by King Haakon and Crown Prince Olaf. The Mayor of Oslo, an Oxford graduate, took part in the proceedings, which were under the chairmanship of Dagfinn Paust, the President of the Norwegian Life-boat Service. The subjects discussed were of exceptional current interest. The Americans described what had been done with amphibious vehicles such as had played so important a part in combined military operations. They also suggested the value of the helicopter, of which a great deal more was to be heard within the next few years. The representatives of the Institution gave instances from their experience of the virtues of twin screws.

There was even some revival of friendly controversy with Holland over the respective merits of steel and wood.

A number of cruising boats had been made available to take delegates among the fjords and fishing-grounds, and when the Conference had been concluded it was agreed that there had seldom been a more refreshing gathering. The only disappointment was that more nations had not been present. This was not due to lack of goodwill, as was seen when the time came for the sixth conference. It arose from transport and other difficulties which in many countries were then severely felt.

Hardly had the British delegates settled to their normal work when they had news of one of the less ordinary rescues. H.M.S. *Warspite*, the battleship with the longest roll of honour in the history of the Navy, and a ship of special interest to the Chief Inspector, Lieutenant-Commander P. E. Vaux, since he had served in her in action, broke from her tugs while being towed round the Cornish coast on her way to be broken up, and after various adventures in Mounts Bay in heavy weather, ran ashore among the rocks just beneath the granite mass of St Michael's Mount. The working party aboard her had to be taken off in circumstances of difficulty and danger. Conditions were such as to justify the award of the silver medal to Coxswain Edward Madron of Penlee, and the bronze medal to his motor mechanic, John Drew.

* * *

Inevitably, there were changes and farewells in the years immediately following the war. The Secretary, Lieutenant-Colonel Satterthwaite, who had headed the administrative staff since the resignation of Sir George Shee and had guided the Institution for fifteen years, relinquished office at the end of 1946. He had succeeded a man much revered, and had himself been regarded with great affection. By temperament self-effacing, he had always been ready, particularly in times of difficulty, to shoulder responsibility which would have daunted other men. He had also been faced with a great burden of work, for Colonel A. D. Burnett Brown, who had been his deputy through much of his time in office, and was to succeed him, had rejoined the army at the outbreak of war. He had served with the British Expeditionary Force in France, and had later been appointed garrison commander in the Isles of Scilly, where he had many opportunities of appreciating the work of the service to which he belonged.

There were two notable retirements in 1947: Henry Blogg, and that great life-boat designer, J. R. Barnett. Blogg, aged seventy-one, gave up the Cromer coxswainship which he had made so famous, though he returned for one launch a year later, as a crew member—perhaps the call was irresistible. With his many distinctions, including his three medals in gold and four in silver from the Institution, and his recognition by the King, he had long been regarded as a paragon. Among the many other honours he received had been a medal from the Canine Defence League for the rescue of a Newfoundland dog from the *Monte Nevoso*. The animal had become his constant companion, and together they became a familiar feature of Cromer.

Tribute was universal, and Blogg even had a book written about him, though it was not published until after his death. Two remarks made by men who served with him deserve to be recalled: 'He never criticized the younger generation'; and 'Whatever line he had chosen, he would have been "the Guv'nor". He was that type of man.'

Blogg had taken part in 155 launches, which had been the means of saving 448 lives. He died on 13 June 1954, and one of those who attended the memorial service came all the way from Holland to do so. His name was Captain van der Hidde, and Blogg had rescued him twenty-three years before. Blogg's portrait by T. C. Dugdale R.A. was shown at the Academy in 1942. Less well known is the pastel, also painted during the war, by William Dring R.A., which was commissioned by the Admiralty and belongs to the Imperial War Museum.

The 46 ft. Watson cabin life-boat *H. F. Bailey,* in which Blogg made many of his rescues, including all those of the Second World War, went to Cromer in 1935. She was built by Groves and Guttridge of Cowes, and was in service for a quarter of a century —between 1935 and 1964 at Cromer, and then at Helvick Head, County Waterford. She was launched on service 198 times, and was the means of saving 475 lives.

The *H. F. Bailey* was in the reserve fleet until 1972 when she was bought by Leisure Sport Ltd for future use in a 500-acre water-park at Thorpe, Surrey. There she will be launched daily by ex-

R.N.L.I. men, and will help to raise funds. She sailed from Ireland to the United Kingdom in July 1973 under the command of Lieutenant-Commander Harold Harvey, R.N.R., the only Inspector of Life-boats ever to have won the Institution's gold medal. The rescue in which he was concerned took place in 1967, as will appear later in this narrative.

J. R. Barnett retired after forty-three years as the Institution's Naval Architect, and his name is commemorated in many fine boats. In earlier life he had seventeen years' association with his predecessor, G. L. Watson, a man of equal renown as a designer of yachts, so that Barnett's work on life-boats had extended over sixty years, a record unlikely to be surpassed. In some farewell reminiscences Barnett recalled one incident which might have been forgotten but for his retentive memory. He had been working at Cowes when the last of the steam life-boats had gone out on her trials. The weather had been extremely rough, and Queen Victoria had sent word from Osborne to inquire what boat was out on such a day.

Lord Mottistone died, in his eightieth year, a few months after Barnett's retirement. He had served on the Committee of Management for over forty years, and his experience as crew member and coxswain had combined planning and execution in a way which had been rare if not unique since the example set by Sir William Hillary. Captain Rowley, one of the ablest Chief Inspectors in the history of the Institution, did not long survive him, yet it was long enough to know that of the 158 life-boats then in operational service, the last of the sailing life-boats would shortly be disposed of. This would make the fleet entirely motorized, except for one harbour pulling boat retained, at local request, for the special conditions at Whitby.

The remaining sailing life-boat was the *William Cantrell Ashley*. She was stationed at New Quay, Cardiganshire, and was of the Liverpool type, rigged with jib, fore-lug and mizen. She pulled twelve oars. Her loaded weight, with a crew of fifteen, was nearly six tons. She dated from 1907, had been launched on service eighteen times, and had saved ten lives.

The *William Cantrell Ashley* was replaced by one of the modern Liverpool-type boats, 35 ft. by 6 in. long, with a breadth of 10 ft. 8 in., powered by two 18 h.p. engines, and with a crew of eight. Her loaded weight was 8½ tons and her name was *St Albans*, as being the gift of that place. When the old and new boats met at sea, they were televised together. This was the first chance the public had had of seeing life-boats on the screen in their homes. The old boat had not had an unduly hard life, and when she was presented to the Outward Bound Sea School at Aberdovey in Wales, her new owners pronounced her to be in first-rate shape. That is the description many have used who have been lucky enough to acquire life-boats considered to have completed their useful span of life in the role for which they were built.

If the day of the sailing life-boat was over, it was fast becoming the age of the amateur yachtsman. 'Believe me, my young friend,' runs a well-known sentence in *The Wind in the Willows,* 'there is *nothing*—absolutely nothing—half so much worth doing as simply messing about in boats.' Kenneth Grahame wrote in 1908. Forty years later, with roads congested and urban life seeming to have less and less appeal, large numbers of people had taken to the sea and were growing adventurous in their plans. Far too often enterprise outran skill, experience and local knowledge, so that whereas in former days it had been the fishing fleets which had made the most numerous calls on the life-boats, the smaller private yacht soon became a principal object of help.

Certainly it was a craft of modest size which was the cause of the award of the first gold medal since the war. This went to Coxswain Thomas King of St Helier, Jersey, for his audacious success in getting a ten-ton cutter, the *Maurice Georges*, out of danger. His skill set a standard for rescues of this type, though few have been so swiftly concluded.

On 13 September 1949 St Helier airport asked the life-boat to search for a French military aircraft which had come down in the sea, it was thought to the south-east of Jersey. King put out at 3.30 p.m. in the *Hearts of Oak*, a reserve life-boat which had been sent to the station while the regular boat was refitting. The Honorary Secretary, L. P. Stevens, was among the crew.

The day was rough, with a westerly wind and heavy squalls. As the position of the aircraft was uncertain, the Guernsey boat was also called out, but a search of six hours gave no clue as to the whereabouts of the casualty. It was learnt later that the plane had sunk with the loss of six men. The rest, three in number, managed to get ashore on the islet of Chausey.

The St Helier boat was recalled at 9.30 p.m. by which time she was getting low in fuel. At about midnight, when she had been well over eight hours at sea and was nearing home with very little in her tanks, the coxswain received a message to say that a light had been seen near Demie des Pas to the east of St. Helier. It was apparently close inshore, and could have come from a ship in trouble.

King turned to search, though the weather was still rough, and the 'point of no return' could not be far off, when, if she had not been successful, the life-boat would have to anchor until she could get more fuel. The *Maurice Georges*, when found, was indeed in a critical situation. She was anchored off a lee shore, with her engine useless and her cable about to part.

The wind was blowing against the tide, which was ebbing, and the dark was very dark. The cutter was already deep among the rocks and, to quote the official report on the incident, 'to go among them was to go blindfold into the dragon's mouth'. Things were not made easier by the knowledge that as the life-boat was a single-engined, single-screw type, any mechanical failure would have been disastrous.

King did not hesitate to take his boat right among the rocks, and luck was with him, though he had many narrow shaves and more than one bump. He threw a line to the cutter, which was seized. He then decided that it would be easier to try to tow the *Maurice Georges* out of danger than to try to take her crew off, so he passed a tow rope. This parted, but another one held, and the main task was completed within fifteen minutes. The boat was back at St Helier soon after 12.30.

When the District Inspector went to investigate the incident, it happened to be a calm day, with excellent visibility. He asked King to take him to the exact place where the rescue had taken place. The coxswain would not approach nearer than about a mile. 'I wouldn't like to go in there now,' he explained. 'We might hit something!'

Not only did the Committee of Management consider the award of a gold medal to King as thoroughly justified, but all who had taken part in the launch received one in bronze. It was a good instance of the fact that in considering the merit of operations, many factors had to be taken into account, including the state of the sea, the light or lack of it, the exhaustion of the crew, the danger from rocks—and any exceptional features. In this case, those who took part were in a boat unfamiliar to them, and they had no reserve either of fuel or power.

* * *

Among the ways of drawing attention to an organization or a cause is the commemorative stamp. So far as life-boat stamps are concerned, the Dutch had been pioneers. They had issued a pair in 1924 to mark their centenaries, and followed these up with a further four in 1933, partly to commemorate the third International Life-boat Conference in Holland. Just after the war the U.S.A. had honoured their Coast Guard Service in a similar way.

The R.N.L.I. embarked on philately in 1950. The Committee of Management ordered seventeen designs from Posterstamps Ltd to be produced in various colours. Technically, they were attractive, and they are still of interest as showing what were then regarded as the subjects most likely to appeal to the public. They were not intended or allowable for use as postage stamps.

The largest stamp, priced at *6d.*, showed Allan Gairdner Wyon's profile of Sir William Hillary, familiar on the obverse of the Institution's medals. The only other portraits were those of Grace Darling, based on the best contemporary version, that of William Joy, and Dugdale's portrait of Henry Blogg. These, and the remainder of the series, were priced at *3d.*

Greathead's *Original* was included, the reproduction being made from a contemporary print. There was a nineteenth-century pulling life-boat stationed at Padstow; another under sail; the steam-driven *Duke of Northumberland*; the successful motor life-boat *Sir Fitzroy Clayton* built in 1912 with a roll of honour of 107 lives saved; the first deck-cabin boat, built in 1948, with two 40 h.p. diesel engines and up-to-date fittings including radio, loud-hailer and searchlight.

The remaining eight stamps were concerned with actual rescues. The *Original* reappeared, manned by pilots of South Shields, going to the help of seamen wrecked off Tynemouth Castle. There was the rescue from the *St George* in 1830 off the Isle of Man in which Hillary took part; the Ramsgate boat at sea going out to the *Indian Chief*; rescues at Southsea and the Lizard; Blogg bringing the Cromer boat to the help of the London barge *Sepoy* in 1933; the Daunt Rock rescue three years later, and a war-time incident when the Wells coxswain climbed on to the wreckage of an R.A.F. Lancaster bomber down in the sea, and took off a survivor.

Unfortunately, in spite of a cardboard album in navy blue being available, it proved difficult to arrange any economical scheme of buying and selling, since the profit margin was so low, and the stamps have long since become a curiosity. There was, however, a revival of the idea some thirteen years later, when the Post Office authorized an issue of three stamps, designed by David Gentleman, to coincide with the ninth International Life-boat Conference at Edinburgh. Although these helped the Institution indirectly through publicity, there was no direct benefit to the funds. The stamps showed a Westland Widgeon helicopter winching a man from a 37-foot Oakley life-boat; a late nineteenth-century clinker-built life-boat based at Aldeburgh; and three life-boatmen in oilskins. The respective values were 2½*d.*, 4*d.* and 1*s.* 6*d.*

A retirement in 1950 which might have gone unmarked by ceremony in an organization less conscious of what it owed to its technical staff was that of Mr A. C. Butcher. He had twenty-eight years of service behind him, first as Surveyor of Machinery and then as Superintending Engineer. In actual achievement his record was rather longer, for he had originally been employed on the design and construction of the marine engines of the firm of Tylor, whose motors had been found so promising in the first days of internal combustion. When the firm had gone out of business, Mr Butcher had transferred to the Institution, and he had the principal hand in designing six types of engine, each of which had been ordered in some quantity.

In order of appearance, these were a 6-cylinder 80 h.p. motor of 1922; a 4-cylinder 40 h.p. motor of 1927; a 6-cylinder 60 h.p. motor of 1928; a 6-cylinder 35 h.p. motor of 1929; a light 2-cylinder motor of 12 h.p. in 1935 and, in 1945, a 4-cylinder 18 h.p. unit. The success of Mr Butcher's work may be judged best by the low failure rate of every type of power unit for which he was responsible. By far the greatest number of mishaps had not been due to mechanical faults, but to the fouling of screws by ropes, a calamity that no design could hope to eliminate entirely.

As the centenary of the 'Great Exhibition of the Industry of All Nations' which had been held in Hyde Park, and which had been so important in the history of the Institution, would fall in

1951, it was inevitable that there should be plans to celebrate it on a national scale. The effort was duly made, and so the Festival of Britain was born.

It cannot be said that the occasion repeated the far-reaching success which had been achieved in the distant era of the Prince Consort, or even that of the 'Empire Exhibition' at Wembley of 1924. This was inevitable. The Empire was fast dissolving, and although six years had passed since the end of large-scale campaigning, a Cold War was in progress in Europe and a very active one in Korea. In the circumstances it was not surprising that the country lacked that buoyant atmosphere which had been remarked of earlier occasions.

The Institution played its part. The principal item on show, named after the indefatigable Chairman, was the *Sir Godfrey Baring*. She was a boat of the Watson cabin type, 46 ft. 9 in. by 12 ft. 6 in., her weight being 22½ tons. She was powered by two 40 h.p. diesel motors, in the design of which Mr Butcher had been concerned, and her cost was £24,000, a startling rise from the £5,000 which had covered the construction of the pioneer steam life-boat some sixty years before.

A light Liverpool-type boat was also put on show, which was destined for Minehead. She was 35 ft. 6 in. long, 10 ft. 8 in. broad, and she weighed 8½ tons. She was given two 18 h.p. petrol motors, later replaced by more powerful diesels. She went on board H.M.S. *Campania,* an aircraft carrier which between May and September paid a round of visits to home ports.

In June, Commander Vaux retired as Chief Inspector. Most of his predecessors in the post had had a long career in the Navy before joining the Institution. Brilliant as his Service record had been, Commander Vaux had retired at the early age of twenty-four and had made life-boats his predominant interest. He had won a bronze medal in 1926 for his part in the rescue of trawlermen off the coast of Connemara when he had been in charge of the Irish District. He had himself been saved, in the bitter months of 1940, by the Bembridge life-boat, when a ship he commanded was about to sink in a blizzard. Apart from the earlier years of the Second World War his activity had been very much to the benefit of the stations. His successor was Commander T. G. Michelmore, who had had over twenty years' experience as an Inspector.

It was Michelmore, together with Earl Howe, now Sir Godfrey

Baring's very active deputy, the Secretary, and the Consulting Naval Architect, Mr W. Smart, who represented the Institution at the sixth International Conference, which took place in July in Belgium. It was heartening in that fifteen countries sent delegates, four more than at Oslo in 1947. Most had attended one or other of the earlier gatherings, and they came from Denmark, Finland, France, Great Britain, Germany, Greece, Iceland, Italy, Japan, Holland, Norway, Portugal, Spain, Sweden, and the United States.

In welcoming the occasion, Monsieur P. W. Segers, the Belgian Minister of Communications, said:

> While in other spheres scientists and inventors work too often in secret so as to keep the profit of their science and inventions to themselves, or to a very limited number of interested persons, you are acting exactly the opposite way, because you are eager to communicate to each other, without any restrictions, the last progress which has been realized, to your knowledge, in the ways and means of saving lives, and to give the benefit of your experience to everyone.

The subjects of papers included the protection of life-boats in time of war; the unification of signals, a matter over which there had, in the past, been more talk than agreement; and experiences in co-operation with helicopters, which were becoming more and more useful in life-saving at sea.

It was in Belgium that, at the request of the other life-boat organizations, the R.N.L.I. formally undertook the task of distributing information to all countries with life-boat organizations; in short, it became the central life-boat secretariat for the world. This was the most significant step taken at any Conference since the first in 1924.

Three months after the delegates had returned home, an incident occurred involving two well-known Yorkshire stations, Runswick and Whitby, such as are perhaps inevitable in any rescue service. It arose from possible failure to save life, and its interest lies in the way it was settled—by the application of reason and good-will to a situation which at one time had all the elements of serious trouble.

During the early morning of 22 October 1951 the Coastguard informed the Honorary Secretary of the Runswick station that a ship was firing red rockets about five miles north-north-east of his post. At the time, there was a northerly gale driving the sea on to the bar across Runswick Bay and across the harbour entrance at Whitby, and in the view of the coxswains at both places, it would not have been possible to launch a life-boat successfully.

The ship in distress was the coaster *Pandora* of Beaumaris, with a crew of six. She was seen by men of the Newcastle steamer *Gripfast* and ropes were thrown to her, but the two vessels drifted apart before anyone could be taken off the *Pandora*, which was presently seen to sink. The *Gripfast* tried to make a search for survivors in the water, but soon had to let go both her anchors as she was in difficulties herself.

The Coastguard had been under the impression that either the Runswick or the Whitby life-boat would go to the area, and it was not until nearly three hours after the first alarm that the services of the Teesmouth station were requested, where there would have been no serious difficulty in getting away. The Teesmouth men, once alerted, were out until 3.30 p.m. but found no trace of the missing crew. By that time the state of sea and tide had enabled the Runswick and Whitby boats to go to the help of the *Gripfast*, which had been blowing her siren, and to stand by her until tugs got her in tow.

Two days later, the District Inspector held an inquiry, from which it appeared that while the coxswain and second coxswain at Runswick had been against the early morning launch, five of the crew had thought it could have been attempted. The immediate outcome was the temporary closing of the station. This caused concern at Whitby, where the coxswain and second coxswain promptly resigned.

On 1 November the Deputy Chief Inspector, Commander S. W. F. Bennetts, visited the area and found that at Whitby there was a strong feeling that the decision to close Runswick was wrong. A week later, a statement was issued to the effect that while it had been confirmed that the Whitby boat could not have been launched successfully at the time, an attempt should have been made by the Runswick coxswain to launch into the bay, to make certain whether it was or was not possible to negotiate the passage of the bar. Meanwhile, the station was to stay closed.

As concern at Whitby continued, yet another inquiry was held, as the result of which it was proposed that Runswick should reopen as soon as possible, and that an election should take place to decide who should be coxswain. Although the original coxswain was persuaded to stand, he was not re-elected, and neither was his second.

Almost a year later, at the County Court, Newcastle-upon-Tyne, the Wreck Commissioner pronounced that while the crews both at Runswick and Whitby had been ready and willing to proceed, 'weather conditions were such that the Whitby boat could not be launched. Although the Runswick boat could have been launched into the bay, conditions were such as to preclude the crew from going to sea over the bar.' The procedure at Runswick had already been accepted by Whitby as settling the matter satisfactorily, and the resignations there were withdrawn.

The next event of importance, which happened much further south, was one of those characteristic Goodwin Sands rescues which, throughout the annals of the Institution, have made the area as well known to life-boatmen as the hazardous stretches off the coast of Norfolk.

The whole circumstances were typical. Shortly before 11 o'clock on the night of 13 January 1952 the Walmer coxswain was informed that there was a ship in distress and probably aground on the South Goodwin Bank. It was very dark, with patches of mist. A gale from the south-west brought stinging rain. The *Charles Dibdin* (*Civil Service No. 2*), veteran of Dunkirk, was launched at 11.10 p.m., but it was not until 1.30 a.m. next morning that Frederick Upton, searching the most likely places for a casualty, made out a light amid the confused sea. He could not get alongside the vessel, or even approach within reasonable distance, for more than an hour.

She was the French ship *Agen*, of La Rochelle, 4,000 tons, bound from Dakar to Hamburg, with a crew of thirty-eight. Already she had broken in two, and there was a 30-foot gap between the forward and after parts, all the crew being forward. The *Agen* was between 400 and 500 yards away from three other wrecks, from which the Walmer men had rescued 115 survivors during the previous six years.

As the tide was ebbing fast, Upton decided to wait until conditions were better for resue work. He judged the moment had come at 6.15 a.m. when he steered between the two parts of the French ship and took off everyone but the Master, who refused to leave. One man, but only one, was injured in the process, which considering the state of the sea was remarkable. Having landed the main contingent, Upton then returned to exercise a little persuasion on the captain. What good the captain could have done, alone and with half a ship fast on a notorious sand, defies conjecture. In time, he saw sense, and consented to be taken off, by which stage conditions were slightly better. Upton was awarded a second silver medal, and Percy Cavell, his motor mechanic, a second in bronze, both of them being seasoned rescuers.

In the summer of the following year, 1953, Richard Dimbleby of the BBC went out with Upton on an exercise, and a few months later spoke for the Institution in 'The Week's Good Cause'. The £3,302. 7. 5. raised by his appeal came from 3,943 different people. It was the first of its kind in the new reign, that of a Queen whose husband would be the second Duke of Edinburgh, trained as a naval officer, to serve on the Committee of Management.

* * *

All through their history, life-boats have had the chance to show their versatility during floods. Many stations have records of successful rescues made inland, up-river and across what were normally fields. The scale of these floods has varied enormously, but those which occurred at the end of January 1953 were disastrous. Among the areas most affected were the east coasts of England and Scotland, and Holland. In Britain, over three hundred people lost their lives either through these floods or the accompanying storms. Fourteen life-boat stations were damaged, and among the life-boats most often in demand were those of Southend-on-Sea and Clacton. They not only stood by ships, barges and boats, but gave help to scores of marooned people.

Concurrently, there was a tragedy at sea. It involved the motor ship *Princess Victoria*, owned by the Transport Commission. She was of 2,694 tons, was less than six years old, and she made a regular run between Stranraer in Wigtownshire and Larne in Antrim, being a much-used and speedy ferry.

The ship left Stranraer at a quarter to eight on the morning of 31 January with 127 passengers, a crew of 49, and a mixed cargo. She had been built to carry a number of cars, and had been given a large after-deck which facilitated loading and discharge. Heavy steel doors were fitted to keep this space water-tight.

The weather was extremely bad, with squalls of sleet and snow, and with winds gusting up to 75 m.p.h. The captain was accustomed to making the passage in rough conditions, but on that day, as soon as his ship lost the shelter of Loch Ryan and turned west into the North Channel which divides Scotland from Ireland, she met unusually heavy seas. One of them struck her aft, and the doors protecting the car deck were forced open. Water entered, causing immediate flooding to a depth of about two feet. The vessel began to list to starboard, and this list soon increased.

Two hours after she had left harbour, the *Princess Victoria* signalled for the help of a tug, giving her position as the entrance to the Loch. The nearest life-boat station was at Portpatrick and, on hearing the news, the crew assembled. Just after noon, when the motor-ship followed up her first message with an SOS, the life-boat was launched. The position of the ship was then said to be four miles north-west of Corsewell Point on the Scottish coast, roughly where she might have been expected, though the Portpatrick men, searching the area, found nothing.

Away in Ulster, at Donaghadee, where there was a life-boat station, the weather was awful, although no ships in distress had been reported. There was a big football match that day. Most members of the life-boat crew had arranged to go, but there was a feeling among them that they might be needed and at one o'clock, when it was announced in a BBC news bulletin that the *Princess Victoria* was in trouble off the Scottish coast, much happened in a short time. First there was a sudden power failure, widespread in Donaghadee, which prevented the broadcast message being taken in entire; then came a signal from the ship that her captain was preparing to abandon her. Seven minutes later the coastguard at Bangor, County Down, told the Donaghadee Honorary Secretary that the vessel was believed to be somewhere between Portpatrick and Belfast. The Donaghadee boat was launched into a very rough sea, with a full gale blowing. If there was too little precise news, there was not likely to be much time, if anything useful was to be done.

At first the Irishmen were as luckless as those from Portpatrick, but Coxswain Hugh Nelson of Donaghadee made contact with the destroyer *Contest* and at first decided to follow her course.

Then he spoke with the master of the SS *Orchy* who gave news, though it was distressing. Survivors had been reported in an area which was indicated. Nelson made for it at once. He reached it a little after three o'clock, when he heard that the *Princess Victoria* had sunk more than an hour before.

A number of people had managed to take to the ship's boats and rafts. In one boat there were twenty-nine, and Nelson got alongside and transferred them to relative safety. Then he picked up a lone man in another boat, and one on a raft. The Portpatrick crew, at last guided to the right place, had taken two others from rafts. Various ships picked up ten more.

Search continued, with the life-boat from Cloughey in Ulster joining in, until it was certain that everything possible had been done. Then the three crews, of Donaghadee, Portpatrick and Cloughey, steered for Donaghadee, and some who had set out early that raw morning reached Ireland in a very different fashion from what they had expected. The Donaghadee men actually made two more launches, but it was with the sad task of taking bodies on board.

The total number of survivors was only 43, while 133 people had lost their lives in the greatest disaster suffered by a British merchant vessel in peace-time for a quarter of a century. The initiative and thoroughness shown by the life-boatmen was appropriately recognized. The British Empire Medal was awarded to Hugh Nelson, and to Coxswain William McConnell of Portpatrick. Both of them also received the Institution's medal in bronze.

Although misfortunes rarely come singly they can sometimes be prepared for, but it was the unexpectedness as much as the shock of events at Fraserburgh, scarcely a week after the affair of the *Princess Victoria*, which caused consternation, also the fact that the tragedy was witnessed by so many.

There was a stiff easterly breeze on the morning of 9 February 1953, and a heavy swell across the harbour mouth foreshadowed a gale. As it was thought that some of the local fishing boats might have difficulty in getting to shelter, maroons were fired at 12.48 for the life-boat to escort them in.

Andrew Ritchie had had seven years' experience as coxswain, and twenty years with life-boats. Most of his men were veterans, and his motor mechanic, G. F. Duthie, had had no less than thirty years' service. The boat was of the 46 ft. Watson cabin type, with two 40 h.p. diesels, built in 1937. When close outside the harbour entrance, a sudden swell reared astern, broke inboard over the starboard quarter, and overturned the life-boat.

Ritchie himself was flung clear, but was hit on the head and killed by some wreckage. Six of the crew were trapped beneath the canopy, and the only man washed up alive, on to the rocks south of the harbour, was the second coxswain, C. G. Tait. The life-boat herself came ashore a hundred yards from the south pier, but for four days the weather prevented a full examination.

When the boat was refloated she was found to be so badly damaged from being pounded on the rocks, that repairs would have cost £10,000. Everything usable was salvaged, and a ship-breaker engaged to remove the hull within a week. She was the *John and Charles Kennedy*. She had been launched 98 times on service and had been the means of saving 199 lives. The incident inevitably recalled the fate which had overtaken the *Lady Rothes* in 1919. Among those lost was Charles Tait, a man of sixty-one and the father of the only survivor. The younger Tait at once re-engaged as a crew member.

The Sheriff's Court at Aberdeen recorded the verdict that the disaster was the result of 'one of those unfortunate risks which men called upon to serve in life-boats have to undergo'. This was all too sadly true, but it is also to be noted that of the 170 Watson-type boats which had entered service up to that time, the *John and Charles Kennedy* was only the second to capsize, the first being at the Mumbles six years earlier. The fact that many are still on station today is a proof that confidence in their qualities continued.

It was not that self-righting in itself could always provide much comfort, as was shown the following autumn, again in Scotland. The Arbroath and Anstruther boats were called out one dark night because rockets had been seen about three miles east of Fifeness. There was a gale from the south-south-east at the time, the worst quarter, with a very rough sea. Although the launches were successful, neither crew could report having seen anything, and at 4.20 a.m. on 27 October the Arbroath coxswain, David Bruce, signalled that he would return. In view of prevailing conditions an answer was sent that it might be better to consider making for Anstruther, but Bruce replied that he would wait for daylight and then see what the Arbroath bar was like. At

5.0 a.m. he signalled that he hoped to be in harbour in twenty minutes.

The sea was then such that the coastguard went to the east pier with three men and a rocket pistol, prepared for trouble. It came. At 5.47 the life-boat's light, which had been visible, disappeared in a steep cross-sea which swept abaft her beam on the port side, turning the boat over. The coastguards fired rockets at random, since they could see nothing, and by pure chance, or a miracle, one of them fell across the second coxswain, Archibald Smith, who was hauled ashore, the only survivor of a crew of seven. Like Tait of Fraserburgh, he signed on again for life-boat service.

The boat, the *Robert Lindsay*, was a 35 ft. 6 in. Liverpool-type built as recently as 1950 and with the standard two engines. She was found to be in perfect order and she had behaved just as she should. This was the first mishap of its sort, though it was not the last. During the course of the following year the *E.C.J.R.* of Scarborough, of the same type, met with an accident of much the same kind when going to the help of fishermen. She lost her first and second coxswains and her signalman. The coxswain, Sheader, was a man of sixty-three with forty-two years of service.

* * *

The first issue of the Institution's journal had appeared in March 1852. Just over a year after the centenary number, there was a change of Editors. This had always been a rare event, for one of the most consistent features of the life-boat service has been the way in which its officers, by their dedication, have brought a sense of continuity to its affairs. Charles Vince, who had been in charge for over twenty years, had joined the Institution after a spell in journalism, and, under Sir George Shee's guidance, had looked after the running of the *Life-boat* for some time before his official appointment.

The proof of the value of Vince's work lay in the goodwill which the Institution continued to enjoy with the Press in general, and in the attraction of the periodical itself. Vince had inherited from his predecessors the desire to keep it human. No one recognized more clearly than he did that it was personalities as much as the nature of their employment which helped to make so many life-boat stations, and the various regional offices and head-quarters, what many actually called them—'the best clubs we know of'. Contributions had been kept crisp and clear, and Vince had tried to ensure an ever better standard of photography. The words used of him on leaving, by the Chief Inspector, Captain Michelmore—'I have never in my life known a more collectively popular man'—would have warmed anyone's heart.

Vince's successor, Patrick Howarth, came with the training and experience of a Press officer in Government service at home and abroad. Vince left as his permanent memorial a published record of the services of the life-boatmen in the Second World War, *Storm on the Waters*. Within four years of his appointment, Howarth had absorbed the history and traditions of the Institution so well as to enable him to publish a conspectus of its work, from the very beginning. This was the first official account since the centenary volume. It appeared as *The Life-boat Story*.

This was indeed a time of change and renewal. It was typified by the splendour of the Queen's coronation. The ceremonies attendant upon this event culminated, so far as the sea services were concerned, in the latest of a long and historical succession of Fleet Reviews, which took place at Spithead in June 1953. The Institution was well represented. Four life-boats were anchored off Gilkicker Point, after they had cruised along the lines of shipping. There were two new boats, the *City of Glasgow II*, destined for Campbeltown, and the *Friendly Forester*, which was to go to Flamborough. There were also two veterans, the Dunkirkers *Lord Southborough, Civil Service No. 1*, formerly of Margate, and the *Prudential*, once of Ramsgate and shortly to be sold out of service, with a record of 276 operational launches and 330 lives saved, exclusive of troops brought back from France in 1940. The crews manned ship and gave three cheers as the Queen went by in H.M.S. *Surprise*, and the coxswains were delighted with a signal, sent by the captain commanding one of the destroyer flotillas, congratulating them on their turn-out.

* * *

During the last week in November 1954 a storm swept the country. Besides doing great damage at sea and ashore, it led to a number of rescues by life-boatmen and others, one of which was of much significance for the future.

The crisis came on 27 November, when three incidents occurred well separated in area if not in time. They called for a great measure of resource on the part of all concerned.

The first was a rescue, in the classic manner and in a very high and dangerous sea, of the crew of the auxiliary schooner *Vega,* a Danish vessel, about 25 miles south-south-west of Beachy Head. This brought coxswain William Harvey of Newhaven a silver medal. The second resulted from the breaking in half of the vast 20,125-ton tanker *World Concord,* flying the Liberian flag. The third was the saving of the sole survivor of the South Goodwin lightship by the crew of an American helicopter. In the last two cases, other Services were closely involved, the *World Concord* being attended for some time by the aircraft-carrier *Illustrious,* which was then on her last commission.

The *World Concord,* in ballast out of Liverpool. bound for Syria, broke in two in hurricane-like conditions where so many ships have come to grief—in the Irish Sea. To make things more difficult, there were men on both parts. The captain and six of the crew were forward; the remainder, thirty-five in all, were aft. The engines were also aft, and they continued to propel the ship, or what remained of her, though there was no one to control them. This did not make for ease of approach.

The first the life-boatmen knew of what was happening was at 5.58 a.m., when the station at St David's, Pembrokeshire, was given the ship's position, and a report that the *Illustrious* was near her; she was then close to the Smalls lighthouse. Anticipating a request for life-boats by the captain of the carrier, maroons were fired, and the local crew assembled. The signal duly came, and shortly after 8 o'clock the *Civil Service No. 6* was at sea.

At 9.15 the *Illustrious* reported the after part of the tanker to have reached about 16 miles NNW of the South Bishop lighthouse. Two and a half hours later, the St David's coxswain had the errant in view. Then came the consideration of how rescue should be attempted. It was not made any simpler by the fact that of those on board, 34 were Greek and one Egyptian, and that their knowledge of English was non-existent. At the time, the seas were such that when the life-boat was in the trough of a wave her crew could not see the tanker's masts, while on the *Illustrious* the life-boat could be kept regularly in view only on the radar screen.

Careful reconnaissance convinced William Watts-Williams, the St David's coxswain, that it was essential for the Jacob's Ladder on the tanker to be shifted, otherwise there could be little hope of the men being taken off successfully. By vigorous signs, he made his wishes clear, and after thirty-four separate runs, which took up the best part of an hour, all the men were rescued. The life-boat left for her home station at 12.30.

This service from the Welsh side was matched in Eire. The forepart of the *World Concord*, without benefit of such eccentric power as the after part possessed to give it unguided motion through the water, first drifted towards the coast of Wexford, where the crew at Rosslare Harbour had been alerted. They were at sea all night, and it was not until the early morning that they were able to take off the seven people in the course of fifteen hectic minutes. They brought them back not to their own station but to Holyhead, having been on service for some thirty-six hours.

Both Williams of St David's and Richard Walsh, coxswain of Rosslare, received the silver medal. The two St David's motor mechanics, George Jordan and Gwillym Davies, were given medals in bronze, as was the second coxswain, William Duggan, and the motor mechanic, Richard Hickey, from Rosslare.

The South Goodwin lightship was the second Trinity House vessel to have needed help within a few months, for in September 1953 Thomas Richards of Tenby had made a most skilful rescue of seven men from the St Gowan lightship when her pumps failed and she was in danger of foundering. The South Goodwin case was tragic. During the night of 27 November 1954 the Deal Coastguard reported that he could no longer see her light, and that she was obviously drifting. He received similar information shortly afterwards from the East Goodwin lightship.

Coxswain Arthur Verrion of Ramsgate got his boat to sea by 1.40 a.m. The wind was then blowing so hard that the maroons could not be heard, and the crew had to be warned individually. Walmer had also been warned to stand by, but here the storm had raised a shingle bar on the beach of such a formidable size that it took an hour's hard slog to clear it, so the crew was held in reserve. The Dover men also put to sea in the dark against the force of the south-south-west gale, but daylight showed that the effort was too late. The lightship by that time was lying on her beam ends on the Sands she guarded, and she could actually be made out from Walmer.

The Walmer boat was launched at dawn and got to within two or three hundred yards of the wreck, but the crew could see no sign of life. Their opinion was confirmed a little later on by an SA-16 Albatross helicopter, piloted by Captain Howard L. Richard, which went up from the 66th Air Rescue Squadron of the United States Air Force, stationed at Manston. But as Captain Richard was not entirely satisfied that all hope of rescue had gone, another helicopter was flown off at 9 o'clock, by which time the wind was slightly less fierce. This time, to his astonishment, the pilot saw a solitary figure on the side of the wreck. It was that of Ronald Murton, a 22-year-old birdwatcher employed by the Ministry of Agriculture and Fisheries, who had managed to make his way on deck and was clinging to what was left of the superstructure.

The normal minimum height for a successful pick-up by the type of helicopter flown was, at that time, fifty feet. The pilot, Captain Curtis F. Parkins, descended to thirty feet and a successful rescue was made. Captain Parkins accepted the Institution's silver medal for his gallantry. The other members of the crew, Major Paul L. Park, Captain Willis R. Kusy and Airman 1st Class Elmer H. Vollman were each presented with the Institution's thanks inscribed on vellum, at the Annual General Meeting held in March 1955. It had been well over a century since awards had been made by the Institution to masters of United States ships, and great interest was expressed in the whole episode. This was the first occasion on which a helicopter had been able to make a rescue when life-boats actually present were unable to do so.

The helicopter ('chopper' in the vernacular) had come to stay, and would play an increasingly valuable part in sea rescue. Regular exercises soon formed a part of life-boat training in areas where helicopters could be made available for the purpose. One of the first took place in September 1955 off the Humber, where crews from several stations joined in, but on eleven occasions during the previous year there had been co-operation on actual service, and this soon became almost routine.

Sea-air co-operation was once again discussed at the seventh International Life-boat Conference in June of the same year.

This time the Portuguese were hosts. As meetings were held at Estoril, near the estuary of the Tagus, the delegates, who included the Secretary and the Chief Inspector, had the chance to see conditions for life-boat work on the magnificent Atlantic beaches of the country of Vasco da Gama and the early Discoverers.

Perhaps it was the splendour of the setting which drew representatives from so many countries, for this was a truly world-wide gathering. It included a welcome return of the Russians, after an absence of nearly thirty years. Twenty-two nations were represented, the largest number which had ever attended. Delegates came from Belgium, Canada, Chile, Denmark, the Dominican Republic, Egypt, Finland, France, Germany, Great Britain, Greece, Italy, Japan, the Netherlands, Norway, Poland, Portugal, Spain, Sweden, Turkey, the U.S.S.R. and the United States.

The subjects considered ranged from Government subsidies (very few countries except Britain and Holland were wholly without help from State or municipal sources), through life-belts and other personal equipment to telecommunications, medical and physiological problems of life-saving, and to the most effective types of distress signal. With so much to ponder, it was perhaps all the more remarkable that so much was enjoyed. But when the representatives of great Powers, not ordinarily so friendly, sit down together to consider objectively matters of benefit to humanity in general, nothing but good may be expected.

One personality whose absence from the Conference was noted with great regret was Sir Godfrey Baring. It is certain that he, who had attended a long succession of such events, would have been there had his health allowed. As matters then stood he was well over eighty, not in the best of health, and was on the point of giving up the Chairmanship of the Committee of Management in favour of Earl Howe, who succeeded him in 1956.

Baring had been an ideal Chairman, in so far as tact, kindliness, assiduity, enthusiasm and a proper sense of the value of time must always be the principal ingredients required in that position. His tenure of thirty-three years had been the longest in the history of the Institution, and the two men most nearly comparable with him had been Thomas Wilson, the first Chairman, and Sir Edward Birkbeck, who had guided the Committee for a quarter of a century—which included the strain of the Parliamentary Inquiry of 1897.

Between the years 1923 and 1956 there had been the multifarious events of the Centenary. Some 29,000 lives had been saved at sea, as the result of over 20,000 operational launches. Since the end of the Second World War the Institution had replaced half its fleet, the grand total in 1956 being 175 boats on station, with 19 in reserve. When Baring resigned, the hundredth life-boat had been built for the Institution by Messrs J. Samuel White of Cowes and was in service at Aberdeen, and the 87th boat to be built since the war, the *Duke of Montrose*, destined for Arbroath, was nearing completion. The total cost of the post-war boats alone had been £1,750,000, a staggering sum in terms of earlier figures for construction.

Baring continued to maintain his interest in the Institution, and as he died the year following his resignation as Chairman he might fairly have claimed to have spent the better part of a lifetime in guiding its affairs, as well as those of the Isle of Wight, of whose County Council he was Chairman for over half a century. He and Lord Mottistone had rivalled one another in their zest for the life-boat service; incidentally, they had also been rivals as candidates for Parliament, for in 1900 Baring had been beaten by Colonel Seely, as Lord Mottistone then was, in an election to represent the Island. Baring won the seat six years later.

Earl Howe, Baring's successor, was a very different type of man. Earlier in his life he had been a racing motorist of international renown, and his interest in the technicalities of life-boats, particularly their motive power, was anything but amateur. He had served since 1919 on the Committee of Management, and had been its Deputy Chairman since 1946. Among his other distinctions he had commanded the battalion of the Royal Naval Division, named after Admiral Lord Howe, in Belgium in the First World War and had also served in the Fleet flag-ship, H.M.S. *Queen Elizabeth*. He held the rank of Commodore in the Royal Naval Volunteer Reserve and was as much at home on sea as on land. His wife was the Chairman of the Central London Women's Committee, and there could be no doubt as to whether the sterling tradition which Baring had carried on would be maintained. Future policy guidance could not have been in more active hands, and this was very soon made clear in the attitude which was taken by the Institution towards the aid given by helicopters.

At first, the idea was mooted that the helicopter had made the life-boat superfluous. A moment's thought would have demolished it, yet it persisted, and it is still not quite dead. Helicopters, with their speed and their ability to hover, can do remarkable things, outside the capability of any life-boat: so much so, that a special sub-committee of the Committee of Management under the chairmanship of Commander F. R. H. Swann was appointed with the purpose of ensuring that every means was taken to improve liaison—one of the first steps being the gradual fitting of VHF radio equipment which would enable communication to be direct. But the Institution could never aspire to build and operate its own helicopters, which would demand full-time service on a scale far beyond its means. The helicopters used in rescue work were those of the armed forces and, as was stated in answer to more than one question in the House of Commons, their primary task concerned Service personnel, though they were gladly put at the disposal of other organizations whenever this was possible. They were particularly welcomed by the injured, for, as a doctor wrote from knowledge gained afloat, 'the relief obtained when becoming airborne on the way to a helicopter, after being carried in a shelter on board a buoyant life-boat, had to be experienced to be appreciated'.

As it was not generally realized that helicopters flew under certain handicaps (none of which applied to life-boats), it was not long before the Ministry of Transport and Civil Aviation saw fit to issue an official memorandum of advice to yachtsmen, explaining what could, and could not, be expected.

At the time of issue, early in 1957, there were three types of helicopter in use, the Sycamore and the Dragonfly, which could rescue two people, and the Whirlwind, which could rescue six or seven. But, it was emphasized, helicopters could not operate more than about sixty miles from their base, and their range was strictly limited. That is to say, they could never be expected to 'stand by', as life-boats were accustomed to do, sometimes for many hours and occasionally for days and nights at a stretch. Moreover, they could not operate satisfactorily by night, or in fog, and they did not usually fly in winds exceeding 45 knots. Yachtsmen in trouble were also warned that a helicopter's slipstream might, under certain circumstances, actually capsize a yacht if carrying sail.

What the Ministry was actually saying was that no yachtsman could expect the same sort of service from a helicopter as from a life-boat, and no service at all in some conditions, such as darkness, storm and high winds, in which many of the more outstanding life-boat rescues had been achieved. Perhaps such extensions of helicopter ability would come, but they were not immediately in sight.

In general terms, the Institution's attitude towards helicopters was that it was eager for use to be made of every possible means of saving life at sea, new or old. In the past, it had itself employed the steam-tug to aid its work, and it had adapted the rocket-line to its particular needs. It would do the same with any other invention or development, since its objects were purely altruistic. Shared experiences by helicopter and life-boat men soon eliminated any element of doubt as to whether or not their services were mutually exclusive. The only serious rivalry was the natural one which arose from seeing which could do the most with the means at its disposal.

A good instance of teamwork occurred off the Norfolk coast at the end of October 1956 when the steamship *Wimbledon*, 1,598 tons, was reported to be in trouble 13 miles north of Cromer light. The signal came through to Sheringham at 8.30 a.m. when it appeared that the *Wimbledon* was trying to reach Blakeney, and that the SS *Eleanor Brooke* and the SS *Sydenham* were standing by.

At the time there was a gale from the north-west, but Coxswain H. E. West launched the *Foresters' Centenary*, a Liverpool-type boat, without delay. When he reached the *Wimbledon* he was told that her captain had been washed overboard, but had been picked up by the *Eleanor Brooke*, though he did not live. The mate in charge of the *Wimbledon*, when contacted by West at about 10.15 a.m., said that he hoped to anchor, if he could, in the lee of the Blakeney over-falls, but his ship, loaded with coal, was in a bad way and it was doubtful if she would last.

Meanwhile, a helicopter, flying in winds well beyond what was the normal limit, had taken a doctor from the shore and put him on board the *Eleanor Brooke* to do what he could for the *Wimbledon*'s master. At this stage, realizing that there was little hope of saving the *Wimbledon*, the Sheringham life-boat took off eight of her crew, who were then transferred to the SS *Blyth*, which was by now also standing by. Coxswain West then requested the help of the life-boat at Wells, first to bring out more petrol for his own boat, and then to take the doctor and the *Wimbledon*'s captain ashore.

The mission of the Wells boat was completed by 1.56 p.m. after which West took off the remaining ten men from the ship in trouble. By the time the rescues were completed the sea was such that no ropes would hold between the life-boat and the steamer, and the Sheringham motor mechanic, E. C. Craske, was up to his armpits in water. He had had to hold his radio-telephone above his head at times to keep it dry, and six feet of the life-boat's fender had been damaged or torn away. The silver medal awarded to West and the bronze one to Craske had certainly been well earned that autumn day.

* * *

On 25 November 1956, a few weeks after the rescues from the *Wimbledon*, there was an incident of a much more light-hearted sort. It could well have been planned, though those concerned say it was chance. It happened to be a Sunday, and the Dover life-boat *Southern Africa* was at sea with the BBC. The idea was to give a picture of the work of a life-boat crew for a children's programme on television, so the producer, Peter Webber, his technicians, and commentator Raymond Baxter were embarked.

All went well, out and home again, but when nearing station on the return journey the coxswain was warned by radio-telephone that a motor-boat, the *Mayflower*, seemed to be in difficulties near the South Foreland, where her owner had been fishing.

At the time there was a moderate south-west breeze, and when the life-boat reached the scene the crew found the *Mayflower* dangerously close inshore and unable to make headway against wind and tide, though her engine was working. The owner, when hailed, said he would be only too glad of a tow, and a line was passed. The *Southern Africa* arrived back at Dover just in time for the trip and the episode to be shown that evening. It was nothing sensational, but at least the television team had not made their trip without incident, and the little glimpse of what the life-boats did came across with unexpected punch.

More dramatic by far was the Thurso fire, which occurred a fortnight later. No one knows to this day quite what happened, but during the night of 10 December, life-boat and boathouse at the Caithness station were totally destroyed. The boat was a brand new 47 ft. Watson type. She had been named *Dunnet Head* (*Civil Service No. 31*) by the Queen Mother the previous summer. Her cost had been £32,500, while the cost of replacing the boathouse was likely to be £23,000. Although the area was sparsely inhabited, a very high average of £1,500 annually was contributed by local efforts, and the loss was felt most keenly. It was borne entirely by the Institution. This was because as far back as 1932 the Committee of Management had decided that insurance should not be continued, the reason being 'excessive premiums being paid, and that the risk of damage or destruction by fire or other causes was actuarially less than the rates of premium applied'. The experience of nearly a quarter of a century had shown the decision to have been right. On balance, the Institution's funds were healthier as a result.

With organizations, as with people, misfortune sometimes serves as a stimulus. So does the need for enough revenue to cover losses and to sustain the work in hand. It was so in this case, and that services continued so satisfactorily and indeed were expanded was owing to the fact that, in every region as well as at headquarters, there were so many who found inspiration in help to the life-boat cause.

One such person was Bella Mattison, known throughout the north of England as 'Bella the Life-boat Lady' who at the age of seventy-seven announced that she would at last have to give up her voluntary work for the Institution. Bella had long since been awarded the gold brooch for her efforts, and when the time came for her to retire it was announced that, single-handed, she had contributed the remarkable total of £4,000, mostly in very small sums.

Bella was of the true breed of the Cullercoats fishwives, all of whom had at one time or another served as life-boat launchers. She had been born at North Shields, and after her marriage had settled in the fishing village where she 'carried the creel' on her back, the harvest of her family's nets and lines, dressed in the traditional costume which included skirts of varied hue and a silken shawl which was the envy of most strangers. Bella had collected for well over thirty years and she was, alas, the only survivor of her kind. It was appropriate that she had taken the part of Grace Darling at a pageant staged at the Albert Hall. She lived to receive the British Empire Medal in the Birthday Honours, 1963.

The retirement of Commander Michelmore as Chief Inspector in June 1958 almost coincided with the entry into service of a new type of life-boat. This was called the Oakley, after the Institution's principal designer. She was 37 feet long, weighed between nine and ten tons, and cost £26,500. It was thought that she would be transportable by a new type of carriage which had recently come under test. Although the cost was high—£3,365—the carriage was found satisfactory for use not only on sand or shingle beaches, but on mud flats.

The first Oakley life-boat was built by Messrs William Osborne of Littlehampton, following a model made by Messrs Saunders-Roe for extended tank tests at Cowes. She was self-righting, the method being the transfer of 1½ tons of water ballast into a righting tank on the port side beneath the engines, which were twin Perkins PM4 diesels. The boat could right itself in six seconds and would drain in twelve seconds. Trials on service proved so satisfactory that the Oakley soon became one of the standard boats, and remains so today.

What the future held in the way of strange calls had been shown by an incident in the West Country a few months earlier. Shortly before dusk one day, signs were apparent that a 60-foot-high drilling tower, which had been erected off Hinkley Point in Bridgwater Bay, Somerset, was in a dangerous state of imbalance. The Minehead life-boat *Fifi and Charles* was launched at 6 p.m. in a north-westerly breeze and took off seven men. It would not be many years before crews would be called upon to undertake rescues of a similar kind among the oil rigs soon to become familiar in the North Sea and elsewhere.

Another portent, indicating an increasing foreign presence in what the Admiralty were once accustomed to describe as 'Home Waters', was a rescue made in the autumn of 1958 from the Soviet trawler *Urbe*. The vessel was believed to have had a crew of twenty-five. This was several times the number that a British ship of equivalent size would have carried. She was reported to have sunk, during the night of 16 October, on or near the Holm of Skan, an uninhabited rocky islet north-east of Unst in the Shetlands.

The *Urbe* was one of a fleet of about thirty Russian trawlers, and the distress signal had come from the parent ship *Tomsk*. At this time, incidentally, over 22 per cent of all launches by life-boats were still concerned with fishermen. This was 2½ per cent higher than calls from merchantmen of every kind, and 4½ per cent higher than those from private yachts and boats.

The conditions in the north were bad on the day in question. There was a full gale blowing, and when the Lerwick life-boat, the *Claude Cecil Staniforth*, a new 52 ft. Barnett-type, was launched at 9.32 p.m., she had well over fifty miles of rough going before her coxswain could hope to make any rescues, and this in the teeth of the wind.

During the early hours of 17 October Coxswain John Sales put in at Baltasound to embark Mr Andrew Mouat as local pilot. Shortly afterwards, Sales realized all too clearly that he was in the Russian fishing area, because his starboard screw became fouled by a net. On reaching the Holm of Skan, he anchored in ten fathoms about forty yards from the beach, and scanned the place with his searchlight. This revealed three Russians sheltering near a pillar of rock. The second coxswain, William Sales, fired a rocket and the men were taken off by line. The operation was completed by 5.20 a.m.

Among the survivors was the Russian skipper, who had just enough English to indicate that there was one other man on the Holm, but whether he was alive, dead, or too badly injured to be taken off without assistance was not clear. Coxswain Sales therefore made for Norwick with the intention of taking on board a 10-foot local boat, with which he returned to the Holm. There, Mr Mouat and three of the life-boat crew searched the rock without success, though two dead bodies were found in the sea, and the *Urbe* herself was discovered, only her bow and masts being above water.

The captain of the *Tomsk* was anxious, almost frantically so, that the Russians should be sent to him without being landed, but the Lerwick coxswain was advised not to comply as it was feared that the life-boat would be damaged in making the transfer. Mr Mouat was landed at Baltasound shortly after mid-day, and the life-boat was back at Lerwick by the evening.

Sales, who had been without sleep for over forty hours, received the silver medal for this service, Mr Mouat being given one in bronze. All members of the crew were presented with what, since 1955, had become known as 'medal service certificates'. These were awarded by the Institution whenever a coxswain had received a medal in respect of a particular service, unless this had been granted for an entirely individual act of gallantry. The *Urbe* rescues were accorded praise from the official Soviet press, and the Russian fishermen rejoined their compatriots as soon as the sea became calmer.

There was a welcome Soviet presence once again at the eighth International Life-boat Conference. This time it was held at Bremen, between 23 and 25 June 1959. The British delegation was led by Earl Howe, and the West German hosts, wishing to pay him and his colleagues a compliment, arranged for an orchestra to play Haydn's 'Oxford' Symphony at the opening ceremony. Handel's 'Water Music' would have been equally appropriate, since on this occasion, as at some of the earlier Conferences, there were a number of life-boats present. They included a British example, the Barnett-type *Ethel Mary*, destined for Ballycotton. She was in charge of Commander E. W. Middleton, the Superintendent of the Boreham Wood depot, and had a crew drawn from members of the Institution's staff. Life-boats from Poland, Norway and Sweden were also on show, and the West Germans demonstrated a large 'rescue cruiser' which carried a smaller, daughter boat. They had become one of the small group of nations whose life-boat service was entirely unsubsidized, since, having experienced State control, they had deliberately reverted to voluntary status. An excursion was made down-river to Vegesack, which was considered to be the birthplace of their Society.

Seventeen delegations were present. They came from Belgium, Canada, Denmark, Finland, France, Germany, Great Britain, Holland, Iceland, Japan, Norway, Poland, Portugal, Spain, Sweden, Turkey and the U.S.S.R. The United States Coast Guard sent a paper for discussion, so that once again it was a gathering which could be considered really world-wide.

The Dutch, as always, were full of ideas, and they submitted a proposal that as helicopter–life-boat co-operation was now so general, life-boats should have orange upper-works to facilitate recognition from the air, or should fly a yellow flag. The Russians gave up-to-date information about their rescue services, and the American paper dealt with the use of plastic material for life-boats and for some of their equipment. European experience had not always shown that man-made substances justified what was claimed for them, and Captain Holter of Norway raised a laugh when he remarked: 'Before you go in for plastics—touch wood!'

As at all earlier Conferences, the proceedings were in English, and it was agreed that the system by which the R.N.L.I. acted as a central secretariat continued to be a great success. The final meeting brought a request that the next Conference should take place in Great Britain, and although Lord Howe had no power to agree to this proposal on the spot, he made it clear that he would be delighted to put it before his Committee.

* * *

Some of the best-known life-boat rescues have taken place during the month of October. This was so in 1959, when the first gold medal awarded for ten years went to Coxswain Richard Evans of Moelfre, when bronze medals were won by life-boatmen of Islay and Fraserburgh, and when many other notable services were recorded, including rescues by the boats at Mallaig and Beaumaris.

The weather on 27 October 1959 was exceptionally bad, and this was the day on which many stations were alerted. In the particular part of the Irish Sea where the Moelfre life-boat usually operated, conditions suddenly became critical. This was owing to the fact that what had started as a south-westerly gale became more than ordinarily menacing when the wind veered to the north. It blew with such force that there were gusts of up to 104 m.p.h. and waves 25 feet from crest to trough were reported.

The coaster *Hindlea* of Cardiff, 506 tons, which was on a run between Manchester and Newport, Monmouthshire, in ballast, had anchored in Dulas Bay to shelter when she had to face this change in wind direction. The confused sea and the deteriorating conditions soon made her situation critical. By 11.50 a.m. the coastguard had reported that she was dragging her anchor and nearing the shore. Her engines were in use to keep her head to sea, but they were obviously not enough and it was clear that she would soon founder.

Coxswain Evans got the 41 ft. *Edmund and Mary Robinson* away within a few minutes of the alarm, but the crisis was such that he felt he could not wait for all his regular men to assemble and he went off with a crew of five, one of whom, Hugh Jones, had not been on operational service before.

By 1.55 p.m. the *Hindlea* was within 200 yards of the rocks, and the captain gave orders to abandon ship, though there was not much hope for the boat she carried. Fortunately, the Moelfre coxswain arrived on the scene before any attempt could be made to launch her, and then ten separate runs—each of great hazard—were necessary to take off the five-man crew. It was remarkable that there were no serious injuries during the rescue. The life-boat was scarcely away before the *Hindlea* smashed against the rocks, and it was many hours before the sea subsided.

A tremendous strain had been thrown on the coxswain and the motor mechanic, Evan Owens, due to the size of the waves and the unpredictable motion of the steamer. Coxswain Evans received the gold medal, Owens was given the silver, and the remaining crew members, Donald Francis, Hugh Owen and Hugh Jones the bronze. Hugh Owen's was in fact a second service clasp, for he was a veteran of an earlier rescue, for which two gold medals had been given. It was that of October 1927, when William Roberts and Captain Owen Jones made their rescues from the ketch *Excel*. By coincidence, the earlier episode had occurred on the same day of the month.

So impressed was the Board of Trade by the reports of the *Hindlea* that a submission was made to the Queen that all members of the Moelfre crew who had taken part should receive the Sea Gallantry Medal. This rare distinction was presented by Her Majesty to the five men at Buckingham Palace in the summer of 1961, nearly two years after the event. It is noteworthy that the gold medal rescues of 1949 and 1959 had both been made in veteran life-boats. The Jersey boat was 25 years old and the Moelfre boat had been built in 1938. Both had petrol engines.

Conditions in the Sound of Islay on the day of the Moelfre exploit were almost as difficult as those farther south. Coxswain James Gillies was faced with an exceptionally tricky launch, and the rescues he made by rocket-line from a vessel in trouble near Black Rock Buoy taxed all his skill. His boat was the *Charlotte Elizabeth*, a 45 ft. 6 in. Watson-type.

At Fraserburgh, on the other side of Scotland, there were rain squalls accompanying the gale, visibility was poor, and when fishermen were seen to be in trouble (with the regular coxswain at sea with them), the experienced motor mechanic, Frederick Kirkness, got together a scratch crew to man the *Duchess of Kent*, a Watson-type boat named in honour of the President, and put out with Mr Alec Duthie, a local fisherman, in charge. At one stage the life-boat was twice spun round by the seas but, nothing daunted, Duthie took off two men from the *Ocean Swell*. Two boats were lost on that part of the coast during the day, and the medals given to Kirkness and Duthie were in recognition of their great initiative as well as their valour.

In December, within a few weeks of these Welsh and Scots rescues, the Torbay crew were in the news as the result of saving a man on a Dutch lighter which had driven aground in high seas after being cast off by a tug which was herself in trouble. Coxswain Henry Thomas was awarded the silver medal, and a third service clasp went to the motor mechanic, Richard Harris, who had taken part in two notable war-time rescues.

Next day, 8 December, it was reported that the North Carr lightship was dragging her cable, and the Broughty Ferry life-boat, under Coxswain Robert Grant's command, was launched to go to her help. The *Mona*, also a Watson-type had been built in 1935 and so was pre-war, but she was in perfect condition. The sea at the time was such that navigation buoys had been driven from their position by the south-easterly gale, and during the hours of darkness the *Mona*'s signals suddenly ceased. The life-boat had capsized, drowning all her crew.

The tragedy drew immediate response. Within a few days there were forty applications to join the Institution's service, and a fund inaugurated by the Lord Provost of Dundee quickly grew to a total of £90,000, which was typical of Scots generosity in life-boat matters. At a Procurator-fiscal's inquiry, the Sheriff-Substitute, Mr J. B. W. Christie, after quoting the famous sentence from St John: 'Greater love hath no man than this, that a man lay down his life for his friends', added the sentence:

> It seems to me that when men reach that standard in their deeds and actions they are beyond the realm of comment by lesser men like us. When one hears a story such as we have heard today, the only fitting thing we can do is just to listen in respectful silence.

The men of the North Carr lightship were not left to their fate. Rescue was achieved by helicopter by Flight-Sergeant Breach of 228 Squadron, R.A.F. who was awarded the Alan Marsh medal by the Royal Aeronautical Society.

* * *

At the Annual General Meeting held in the spring of 1959, Lord Howe had been able to announce that while the revenue of the Institution had exceeded a million pounds, administrative costs continued at a figure which he believed to be 'a great deal lower than the cost of any other charity in this country'.

This was a bold claim, but successive Secretaries and their staffs had been well aware of the need to maintain the tradition that they were the servants rather than the masters of the coastal stations. Any idea that the London headquarters was top-heavy could quickly be dispelled by the charts which appeared from time to time in the pages of the *Life-boat*. These showed, in terms understandable by all, just where the money went. By far the greatest proportion was spent on construction and maintenance, on remuneration of life-boat men, and on pensions to dependants of those who had lost their lives on service.

No one had been more aware of the need to keep internal expenditure down than Colonel Burnett Brown, who had spent nearly thirty years, war service apart, in supervising such matters. But during his term of office, from 1931 to 1947 as Deputy Secretary, and from 1947 in full charge, administrative complexities had grown side by side with revenue, so that by 1958 he needed full-time help. Lieutenant-Colonel Charles Earle, formerly of the Grenadier Guards, was taken on as Secretary-designate. He succeeded to the post of Secretary in the summer of 1960, but resigned during the course of the following year.

The decade beginning in 1960 was to be invigorating and it was not inappropriate that it should have begun with a birth. On 5 February 1960, late at night, the life-boat *R. A. Colby Cubbin No 3* was launched at Barra, in the Outer Hebrides, to take an expectant mother to South Uist. The child was safely delivered during the course of the journey, the first incident of its kind recorded as having taken place on board a British life-boat. When the news was announced the French Society, in offering congratulations, recalled that in 1939 a similar event had occurred on board the *Jean Charcot* of the Ile Molène, and that the parents of the infant had included 'Charcot' among his baptismal names.

One of the more exciting events of the same year was yet another October rescue. This was an instance of co-operation with the Navy which had some unusual features. It began when, during the early hours of the 22 October, the station at Portrush, County Antrim, was warned that the Greek steamer *Argo Delos* of Piraeus, 10,392 tons, had gone ashore on the islet of Torbeg, which was about a mile from the Inishtrahull lighthouse, due north of the mainland of Ireland.

The *Lady Scott* (*Civil Service No, 4*), a 46 ft. 9 in. Watson boat, was launched at 3.5 a.m. with Samuel Cunningham in charge. At 5.58 he made contact with the officer commanding the frigate *Leopard*, which was standing by the doomed ship. Cunningham made some dummy runs to see how best he could take off the men, and had a ladder in position by 8.15 a.m. He then decided to wait until the sea, which was confused and had a rise and fall of about fifteen feet, gave him a better chance to succeed in taking men off without serious danger of losing them in the process, or risking grave damage to his boat.

Meanwhile, unknown to Cunningham, a helicopter had landed a naval party on the forecastle of the *Argo Delos*, to establish communication with the *Leopard*. The actual rescues, which were difficult because the Greeks had to jump backwards off the ladder into the waiting arms of the life-boatmen, took altogether one and three-quarter hours. Success was achieved partly by helicopter, partly by the life-boat, and partly by the frigate. Ropes would not hold; a propeller of the *Lady Scott* became fouled, and altogether it was an operation demanding great skill.

Cunningham and his men were fourteen hours away. He himself was given the Institution's silver medal, his second coxswain, Robert McMullan, receiving one in bronze. The ship's company of H.M.S. *Leopard* were so impressed by the seamanship of the life-boat crew that they presented silver tankards to all who had taken part. The incident had been complicated, as it had been with the *World Concord* six years earlier, because few of the Greeks knew enough English to obey directions precisely. As it was, one of them fell into the sea, though he was got on board with only minor injuries.

Three days later, two silver medals were won by men not in the Institution's service, for a brave rescue in a privately owned dinghy. This took place not out at sea, but on the river Severn, after two small tankers, the *Arkendale* and the *Wastdale*, both loaded with fuel, had collided near the dock entrance at Sharpness. There was fog at the time and the vessels, locked together, drifted out of control until they hit a bridge. This collapsed and held them firmly together by its debris, which included a massive stretch of railway line. Fire had broken out in the ships, one of which contained petrol, and it seemed very doubtful whether any of those who had remained on board could have survived. Thomas Carter, another tanker captain, helped by Mr Charles Henderson, a carpenter from Glasgow, determined to make sure. They commandeered the dinghy and, at extreme risk from the conflagration, the pair managed to pick up a seaman, after efforts lasting nearly two hours. The survivor was in bad shape, but still living.

Just before Christmas that same year, an episode of a most unusual kind occurred at Chicken Rock lighthouse, off the southern coast of the Isle of Man. At 10 o' clock on the morning of 23 December the tower was shaken by an explosion, and flames soon spread. At the time, the crew of three men were in the upper rooms. They were trapped; and to avoid being burnt alive, they slid down from the balcony to the rock face by rope. There they were faced with a rough sea, bitter cold, and a rising tide. The day was overcast and, as they had had no chance to give those ashore notice of their plight, their prospect seemed grim. Fortunately they were able to reach the lower deck of the lighthouse.

The Coastguard station had realized that there was a possible emergency, and had alerted the life-boat station at Port St Mary. The R. *A. Colby Cubbin* was soon away, in charge of Coxswain Gawne, but as he neared the reefs he found that he could not approach closer than a hundred yards. A line was sent across, and by means of a breeches-buoy one of the lighthouse-keepers, who had been injured, was got aboard the life-boat, though not before a wave had tipped him into the sea, from which he was pulled by the crew. It was then apparent that it would not be possible to rescue the other two men by the same method, and it was also clear that the injured man needed expert attention. A signal was sent to Port Erin, where the life-boat was launched, the coxswain making for Chicken Rock to stand by.

As soon as Coxswain Gawne had landed the injured man he returned to Chicken Rock, but it was not until after 6 p.m., long after dark that, with the weather moderating, he was able to take his boat through the reefs to complete the rescue. This was one of the various occasions when a life-boat was able to bring help to the lighthouse men serving Trinity House.

The year 1961 was the second running in which the Institution had to report itself as being overdrawn. Revenue had not equalled expenditure, and reserves were called upon. Although this was so, there was a great deal to show for what had been a large outlay. Five new boats had entered service, at a cost of £185,000, and two substantial slipways, at the Lizard and Selsey, had been completed for £167,000. There was also news of valuable equipment—automatic lights for life-jackets, echo-sounders; and the Superintendent Engineer, Commander R. A. Gould, was able to announce the first successful change-over, on a life-boat already in service, from petrol to diesel engines.

From the earliest experiments with diesels, dating back to 1932, the type had given nothing but satisfaction. So much so, that since 1952 no petrol engines had been fitted into boats at the builder's yards, although the many in service continued to do everything required of them, and often exceeded all reasonable expectations in what strains they could withstand.

The earlier diesels had been 4-cylinder Admiralty Coventry supercharged 2-strokes, which developed 50 h.p. at 2,000 revolutions per minute. Twenty-four boats had been given this type, or a 3-cylinder variant developing 20 h.p. at 1,600 revolutions per minute. Then had followed three boats fitted with Perkins P4s, developing 43 h.p. at 2,000 revolutions per minute. It was, however, plain to the technical staff that if a regular commercial type of engine could be employed, economies must result. In particular, the difficulty of having to make occasional spare parts in the Depot would be avoided. During 1954, two standard Gardner diesels were tested, and they proved so satisfactory that they were adopted by the Institution.

The change from petrol in boats already on station produced

problems but it was thought that solutions would be found. The boat chosen for trials belonged to Port Erin, Isle of Man. She had been built with two 36 h.p. petrol motors. These were exchanged for a pair of 47 h.p. diesel engines with good results, though the type of propeller had to be changed. The range at full speed was increased from 64 to 94 miles. The engines were also fitted with controls which enabled the coxswain to operate the throttle from his wheel, leaving the motor mechanic free, when necessary, for other duties below.

The converted boat sailed to Ramsgate on 28 October 1961; thence up the east coast to Gorleston, to the Humber, Teesmouth, Berwick-on-Tweed and Aberdeen. Later a passage was made through the Caledonian Canal to Oban and Campbeltown, and thence south to the home station. The trip took just under a fortnight, covered 889 miles, and showed fuel consumption to be 3.88 gallons per hour. This was a distinct improvement on the boat's original performance, and the various Inspectors under whose eye she came reported her good behaviour in a sea-way. Incidentally, she met her share of rough weather.

There were two notable losses during the course of the year: Commander S. W. F. Bennetts, twice decorated for war service in destroyers and submarines, died suddenly in April. He was succeeded as Chief Inspector by Lieutenant-Commander W. L. G. Dutton, who had been fifteen years in the service of the Institution, and whose experience elsewhere included two years in the Merchant Navy and five years in minesweepers. A few months later Lieutenant-Colonel Charles Earle was succeeded as Secretary by Stirling Whorlow. This was the first time that the post had been filled from within the ranks of the existing staff. Stirling Whorlow had completed over thirty years with the Institution, eight of them as Assistant Secretary. Not long after his appointment, a coxswain was elected to the Committee of Management, which was also strengthened by Captain R. E. Cowell, the Marine Superintendent of the P & O Lines.

The coxswain concerned was P. Denham Christie of Tynemouth, who was a Director of Swan Hunter and Wigham Richardson, the shipbuilders, and of the Wallsend Slipway and Engineering Company. This was not the first occasion on which a serving coxswain had been on the controlling body, Lord Mottistone having set a precedent. It cannot be said that either of these men was representative of their exceptional breed, but they both could bring special knowledge to bear on the affairs of the life-boat service.

There were some notable feats accomplished during the course of the year. In September occurred the first rescues from a hover-craft; then, on successive days in November, there were rescues from a Royal Fleet Auxiliary and from a small coaster. The hovercraft, VA 3–001, ran between Rhyl and Hoylake, and on the night of 17 September she broke adrift from her moorings while awaiting a tug from Liverpool. The crew of three who were on board tried to get her out to sea, where she could perhaps have ridden out the rising storm with the use of her engines, but this proved impossible. At 1.14 a.m., on a very dark night, the Coastguard alerted the Rhyl life-boat station and Coxswain Harold Campini launched the 35 ft. 6 in. Liverpool-type boat *Anthony and Robert Marshall* with great difficulty, because of the high wind and heavy spray.

The men on the hovercraft were got to safety within seven minutes of the craft hitting the local promenade, for she had been close inshore. As she had 250 gallons of kerosene in her tanks, the fire brigade stood by, though they were not needed. The coxswain received the Institution's silver medal.

So did Coxswain Sidney Cann of Appledore in Devon for rescues from the Royal Fleet Auxiliary *Green Ranger*. This tanker, of 3,500 tons, had drifted ashore near Long Peak Beach, three miles south of Hartland Point, when a tow-line from the tug *Caswell* parted in a Force 9 gale. The Clovelly life-boat also put out, but the Appledore crew, with their larger boat, a 47 ft. Watson, had slightly more sheltered water, and were able to rescue the crew by breeches buoy.

Next day, 18 November, Coxswain Thomas Fawcus of Blyth saved two men from the motor vessel *Paullgate* of Hull, and, with the help of his bowman, J. D. Kerr, prevented the ship from running ashore near the entrance to the Tyne.

Further south, at Seaham, the *George Elmy*, a Liverpool-type boat, had been launched to go to the help of a coble, the *Economy*, only the day before. Five men were picked up, in winds gusting up to 80 miles an hour, but shortly afterwards the life-boat was seen to capsize, thirty feet from the end of the south pier at the entrance to the harbour. The crew of five were all drowned, and so were all but one of the fishermen who had been taken from the coble.

The verdict at the inquiry could have stood for a number of such tragic episodes. It ran:

> The life-boat was hit by successive waves from heavy seas when broadside to wind and tide in the confused broken water at the entrance to the harbour. These conditions were further aggravated by the backwash and undertow from the breakwaters.

A local fund for the benefit of the dependants of Coxswain John Miller and his men reached over £48,000, and the Institution's flag hangs in St John's Church, Seaham, to commemorate the gallantry shown that day. By this stage in its history, the pensions paid by the R.N.L.I. to widows of all crew members who lost their lives on duty had become based on those applicable to Chief Petty Officers of the Royal Navy.

8

Inshore Life-boats

Undoubtedly the great event of the 1960s was the introduction of what were known at first as Inshore Rescue Boats (IRBs). Since 1972, the type has been officially designated Inshore Life-boat (ILB), which exactly describes the purpose served.

Such a project had long been in contemplation by the Committee of Management, in view of the fact that so many incidents took place comparatively close to beaches or cliffs, where the main requirement was often initiative and speed rather than the more elaborate process of firing maroons, assembling a life-boat crew, and launching the life-boat itself, with all that this entailed in the way of attention from those on shore.

A start was made during the summer of 1962 when a scheme was put into operation, with the collaboration of the Ministry of Transport, by which a register was kept of owners of small craft, willing to act in sea-rescue, along the stretch of coast between Selsey Bill and Swanage, and in the Isle of Wight. Whilst on service, those who had registered would be entitled to the same remuneration as regular life-boat crews, and, as had always been the case with rescues by boats other than those of the Institution, those concerned became eligible for awards on the same scale as was applicable to members of the R.N.L.I.'s service. The experiment was successful. Twenty-three calls were notified within two months, and a number of others which those concerned did not consider worth reporting. Eleven rescues were made.

During the summer of 1963 the area within which registration took place was extended to include the whole coast between Berwick-on-Tweed and Weymouth. By that time the first of the Institution's own Inshore Rescue Boats were in operation at Aberystwyth, Atlantic College, South Wales, Gorleston, Redcar and Wells, Norfolk. These were inflatable, and were made from a tough nylon material, proofed with neoprene. A 40 h.p. outboard motor mounted on a wooden transom gave a speed of 20 knots or more. They were 15 ft. 9 in. long, had a beam of 6 ft. 4 in., and could be handled by a two-man crew, with two helpers to launch them where necessary. They were essentially for summer use, and as the first batch fulfilled expectations, others were placed at Mudeford in Hampshire, Southwold in Suffolk, West Mersea in Essex and Whitstable in Kent. It was a Welsh boat which had the honour of making the first rescues, when, on 3 June 1963, three people and a dog were brought to safety after being cut off by a rising tide.

Concurrently with these small craft, a new type of Oakley life-boat was put into service. She was a cabin boat; her length 48 ft. 6 in. She was of 27 tons, and had a speed of 9 knots. She was built by Messrs William Osborne of Littlehampton, and was self-righting by means of the transfer of 2¾ tons of water ballast, on the same principle as had proved successful in the 37-foot type from the same designer.

The boat was named *Earl and Countess Howe* in honour of the Chairman and his wife, and she was sent to Leith for the ninth International Life-boat Conference, which was held in Edinburgh in June 1963. She was destined in due course for Yarmouth, Isle of Wight, and was equipped with a Decca radar set of a new type. This was paid for out of a fund raised, a few years earlier, to signalize the centenary of the birth of Joseph Conrad.

Lord Howe presided at the Annual General Meeting that year, and also at Edinburgh. In London he gave an indication of the future scope of the Inshore Life-boats; and he also introduced as a speaker Mr Christie of Tynemouth, who delivered a speech on the work and outlook of a coxswain, which included observations of lasting value.

Although he spoke on behalf of what was a somewhat unusual Tynemouth crew, in that it was far more miscellaneous than those in some parts of the country, particularly in the north, including as it did a builder's foreman, a policeman, a joiner, a carpenter, a printer and a shipyard manager, Mr Christie said he scorned the idea, so often presented to him, that they were a bunch of amateurs.

> Volunteers, certainly, with all the advantages of the volunteer, but there is nothing amateurish about their work: trained as a team, trusting each other, and with boats and gear on which they can rely, you won't find crews to touch them anywhere in the world.

Mr Christie then spoke of the actual tasks, and the states of feeling, of life-boat coxswains, including 'the quickening of the heart if the phone rings at an unusual time, so that it is actually a relief when a call does come'. In summing up the qualities required, Mr Christie said that a coxswain

> . . . needs vision to weigh up a situation, self-discipline to take the unpopular decision, moral courage to face uninformed criticism ashore and not to let it affect his judgement, and the organizing ability to keep the crew keen, efficient and happy during long periods of inactivity between calls.

In its entirety the speech could almost be regarded as a blue-print of what was required. For good measure he included instances of false alarms and other unamusing aspects of the life. He would have endorsed Lord Mottistone's statement, made many years earlier: 'The intense joy of the thing achieved, when the rescued men are safely on board, is almost the most wonderful thing in human experience.'

On the same occasion Captain G. E. Barnard, Deputy Master of Trinity House, touched on the sadder side of the Institution's record, and made a very shrewd point in saying that: 'When we consider the sort of weather conditions, and the many services carried out, it is not perhaps surprising that there has been an occasional casualty: it is much more surprising that there have been so few.'

It was certainly extraordinary that there had been no fatal casualties in the rescues by the Guernsey life-boat which had taken place a few months earlier, when the complexity of the circumstances are considered.

During the afternoon of 5 February 1963 the crew at St Peter Port had been summoned, on a report that the Norwegian motor vessel *Johan Collett* was in trouble about fourteen miles west-north-west of Les Hanois lighthouse. It was blowing a gale at the time, and the wind was still rising.

Coxswain Petit was well out at sea within an hour of the warning, in the 52-foot Barnett boat *Euphrosyne Kendal*. The *Johan Collett*, of 1,995 tons, was bound from Tunis to Ghent with a cargo of zinc concentrates; this had shifted and given her a dangerous list to starboard. At five o'clock her master managed to transfer eleven of his crew to the SS *Bonnard*, which was standing by, and these men were landed later at Ostend. Shortly afterwards three more were picked up from a rubber raft by another merchant ship. At about 6 o'clock the South African frigate *President Kruger* arrived on the scene, and the merchantmen proceeded on their way. Petit and his men were at hand by 6.30, though the gale, which was from the south-east, had become very violent, with driving snow, and severe icing was building up on the life-boat's wind-screen. There was a long swell, with waves about fifteen feet from trough to crest. Visibility, with the help of the searchlight, was at best poor, and sometimes negligible.

The *Johan Collett* was lying stopped, her port beam to the wind, and was waiting for a tug from Cherbourg. As conditions grew steadily worse, the Master asked Petit to take off the Chief Engineer and two young apprentices. After five runs in the darkness, and with the help of the searchlight from the frigate, these rescues were made.

At 10.41 the French tug arrived, together with the aircraft-carrier H.M.S. *Ark Royal*. Seven separate attempts had to be made before a towing-line could be secured. This took over an hour and a half of concentrated and dangerous effort. As there were six people still on board the motor vessel, and as the wind had risen to Force 10 on the Beaufort scale, the Master decided, shortly after midnight, to abandon ship, although she was still under tow at about three knots. Once again helped by the *President Kruger*'s searchlight, Petit made six more runs, and everyone was taken off, although one seaman fell twenty feet into the life-boat and the Master himself, in jumping, hit the outside of the guard-rail and was nearly lost.

It was 1.17 a.m. on 6 February before the life-boat's weary crew were at last able to head for their home station, where they arrived five hours later. In addition to the gold medal for the coxswain, his son, John Petit, who held a master-mariner's certificate, and who had helped his father throughout with conspicuous ability, received one in bronze, as did the motor mechanic, E. C. Pattimore. Hubert Petit was also given a gold medal by the Norwegian Life-boat Society, the first of its kind to have been bestowed for a rescue operation. The Institution sent an official Letter of Thanks to Captain M. R. Terry Lloyd for his valuable help in the *President Kruger*.

* * *

The Edinburgh Conference of 1963, which was opened by the Duchess of Kent, was a very special occasion. It was the second time that delegates had met in the United Kingdom. Seventeen nations were represented: Belgium, Chile, Denmark, Eire, France, West Germany, Great Britain, Holland, Iceland, India, Japan, Norway, Poland, Portugal, Sweden, the U.S.A. and the U.S.S.R. Five of the Institution's boats were on view at Leith. Others had sailed from Germany, Norway, Sweden and Holland.

This time the emphasis was on life-boat development, papers coming from Britain, Norway, Holland and the United States. Representatives from Iceland, Japan, Sweden and Brittany described their inshore rescue methods, and were eager to have reports of the experiments then proceeding. A film was shown by the United States Coast Guard which featured a new type of 44 ft. steel boat of which much was hoped. Both the Institution and the two Dutch Societies showed great interest in this, and their inquiry was soon followed up.

At the port there was a capsize demonstration staged with a 37 ft. Oakley life-boat. By way of contrast the *Zetland*, which had been built in 1800 and was kept at Redcar as an historical relic, had been sent north for the occasion.

In only one way was the occasion sad. It was the last life-boat gathering of any size to be attended by Lord Howe. He was in ill health and he did not, in fact, long survive the Conference, for he died the following year at the age of eighty. He had been the most encouraging Chairman. During the course of his long term on the Committee of Management, which he had joined soon after the First World War, he had visited every single life-boat station, and his expert knowledge was valued by the crews, many of whom were known to him personally.

Lord Howe's successor, Captain the Hon. V. M. Wyndham-Quin, RN, had been his deputy for eight years, and had been on the Committee of Management since before the Second World War. Earlier in life he had crossed the Atlantic three times under sail. He had made himself familiar with most aspects of the Institution's work, particularly on the practical side. His daughter, Lady Egremont, was active in the affairs of the Ladies Life-boat Guilds which had long been an important means of fund-raising.

Two Deputy Chairmen were appointed. One was Air Vice-Marshal Sir Geoffrey Bromet, who had served at one time as

Lieutenant-Governor of the Isle of Man, and was thoroughly imbued with the Hillary tradition. The other was Commander F. R. H. Swann, who was to play an increasing part in the Institution's affairs, being a small boat sailor and also experienced in finance. Commander Swann was the only officer of the Royal Naval Volunteer Reserve to have been given command of an aircraft carrier during the Second World War, and he was later to become Commodore of the Royal Cruising Club. He had served on all the main sub-committees, including that concerned with boats and construction of which he was Chairman from 1960–9.

It was the new Chairman and Commander Swann, accompanied by two other members of the Boat and Construction Committee and Lieutenant-Commander W. L. G. Dutton, Chief Inspector of Life-boats, who visited the United States in January 1964 to go further into the possibilities of the steel life-boat which had been discussed at Edinburgh. They had a productive trip, and were so impressed by what they saw that the Committee of Management ordered one of the boats for extended trials. The Chief Inspector returned to the States for further investigation, and to arrange for the craft to be shipped to England. She was self-righting, and had a maximum speed of 15·3 knots, which was well above that of the Institution's boats of equal size. Incidentally, the United States Coast Guard, many years earlier, had wished to acquire a Watson cabin boat for testing, but the transaction had been vetoed by the U.S. Government.

During the course of his visit, Wyndham-Quin was able to announce that the Institution had decided to name one of its new boats after the late President of the United States, John F. Kennedy, whose recent murder had shocked the world, and that it would be stationed in the Irish Republic, whose Government warmly supported the idea. President Kennedy had had a notable career as a naval officer, and as sailing had been one of the passions of his life, the gesture was appropriate.

At the first Annual General Meeting over which he presided, in 1964 Wyndham-Quin gave details of some memorable rescues. Another medal, this time in silver, had gone to the Mumbles station. Coxswain Lionel Derek Scott had taken off members of the crew of the Dutch motor vessel *Kilo* during the early hours of 18 November 1963, when her deck cargo of sodium drums had begun to explode, so that the ship was in imminent danger of catching fire and becoming a total loss. Rain and high seas added to the difficulty of the rescue.

There was also a Scots silver medallist, Coxswain Daniel Kirkpatrick of Longhope, who on the night of 3/4 January 1964 took off nine men from the Aberdeen trawler *Ben Barvas*, which had gone ashore on the Pentland Skerries. The rescues were made by breeches buoy in the heavy and confused seas so often encountered in that area. This was Kirkpatrick's second silver medal.

Even with steel for life-boats in prospect, it was sad for the technical staff to learn that the firm of J. Samuel White of Cowes were giving up wooden boat construction, and that, although they would complete the 134th craft ordered by the Institution, she would be the last. A connexion which had extended for well over a century could not be severed lightly, particularly as 'White boats' had long been renowned for their workmanship. Yet wood, as the principal constructional material, might at last be on its way out, for the experience gained from the American purchase proved most instructive. Trials off every type of coast, including that of Holland, and extending over some five thousand nautical miles, convinced the experts that steel life-boats were likely to prove so valuable in service that a batch of six were ordered from Messrs Brooke Marine of Lowestoft, at a total cost of £158,700. Once more, life-boats were to be built in that part of East Anglia from which, in the past, so many had come. They were not, in fact, the first steel craft to be ordered by the Institution, for the steam life-boats had been of this material. The new 44 ft. boats, which became known as the Waveney class, had other advantages besides steel construction, including speed and manoeuvrability.

Another extension of activity concerned 70-foot steel boats, which were also in contemplation. These would be the largest yet built for the British rescue service. Two experimental examples were ordered from Messrs Yarrow of Scotstoun, Glasgow, one of them from the designs of R. A. Oakley, the other from those of John Tyrrell of Arklow, County Wicklow. Models had undergone satisfactory tests at Cowes, and the first was completed in September 1965 at the cost of £57,000, which was met out of the resources of the Civil Service Fund. This boat had powerful twin Gardner diesels, which gave her a full speed of 11·14 knots, at which her range was 650 miles. If necessary, the crew could sleep on board, and—significant refinement—she could carry inflatable boats. One was powered by a 33 h.p. outboard motor the other, much smaller, had one of 18 h.p.

Two former officers of the Institution just lived to hear news of these developments. One was J. R. Barnett, who attained his century, though he died a few months before the Yarrow boat was completed. The other was Admiral of the Fleet Sir Henry Oliver, who also reached a hundred years of age, and who between 1932 and 1944 had been Chairman of the Boat and Construction Committee. Mr Barnett had been gratified to hear that two boats of his design had been ordered from Messrs Groves and Guttridge of Cowes, for service in Italy. Two officers and seven petty officers went through an intensive course of life-boat training at Torbay and the Lizard before taking them over.

If age and experience were rightly honoured, they were epitomized in these two men, so different in attainments, and in the veteran of seventy-nine, Mr Jack Hawkes of Ramsgate, who had served in his station's life-boat at Dunkirk in 1940, and who returned with a party to that famous port in the summer of 1965, to revisit the scene of wartime endurance.

But it was largely to youth that the Institution must look if it was to continue to flourish. A letter had appeared in the *Life-boat* suggesting the formation of a Life-boat Enthusiasts Society. This had come from inland, from John Francis of Petts Wood, Orpington, Kent, and by the close of 1965 the idea had been translated into reality. The society attracted as its Honorary Archivist Grahame Farr of Portishead, Bristol, the author of a number of standard histories of life-boat stations, particularly those of the West Country, and a widely recognized authority on the whole subject of sea-rescue.

There was plenty going on to fire the imagination, at sea as in the building-yards. There was, for instance, the second bronze medal service performed by Coxswain Henry Nicholas of Sennen Cove, Cornwall, then aged sixty-two, after a Belgian trawler had gone ashore at Land's End. His first bronze medal had been earned at the age of seventeen when he had taken part in a rescue on the Longships. There was a fourth bronze medal to Coxswain

Patrick Power of Dunmore, for rescues from the Dutch motor vessel *Jan Bronz* which went on the rocks near Ardnamult Head, and a similar award, also for the fourth time, to motor mechanic Richard Harris of Torbay, for standing by the Danish vessel *Northwind*, a feat of endurance which brought the coxswain a silver medal.

Each week, summer and winter, the record of both the larger and the inshore life-boats (which were now coming into use in certain areas most of the year) held proof that there was as much incident and excitement in the rescue field as ever there had been. Each year, the total of launches seemed to increase, and so far from the life-boat being outmoded, all the evidence was the other way, the crucial difficulty being neither lack of enthusiasm nor a dearth of willing helpers, but galloping costs.

One of those who had had cause to realize this was Richard Oakley, for when he retired in the summer of 1966 he could look back upon the whole great period of modernization, with its attendant expense and complexity. Mr Oakley had been employed originally by the firm of S. E. Saunders Ltd, who had built some of the finest of the earlier powered boats. He had joined the Institution's service in 1928, having worked on a prototype cabin life-boat which had been seen at the Wembley Empire Exhibition in 1924, and then made a memorable journey by road to Southampton on a trailer drawn by a steam traction engine. Mr Oakley had become Surveyor in 1940 and, after the introduction of the two life-boats of his own design, the 37 ft. boat of 1958 and the larger 48 ft. 6 in. boat of 1963, he had been appointed Naval Architect, a fit successor to such men as J. R. Barnett and G. L. Watson. In view of his attainments, it is not altogether surprising that an Irish schoolgirl, when she composed an essay on life-boats, stated that they were constructed 'either of steel or of oakley'.

There were indeed other materials besides steel and 'oakley' in prospect, particularly for new types of small, fast craft, with which experiments were going forward. Messrs Osborne of Littlehampton built a wooden prototype for display on the R.N.L.I. exhibit at the Boat Show at Earls Court early in 1967 of what became known as the Hatch boat. The design had been produced by G. N. Hatch, the Institution's senior draughtsman. It was for a craft 20 ft. 6 in. long, with a beam of 6 ft. 11 in. She

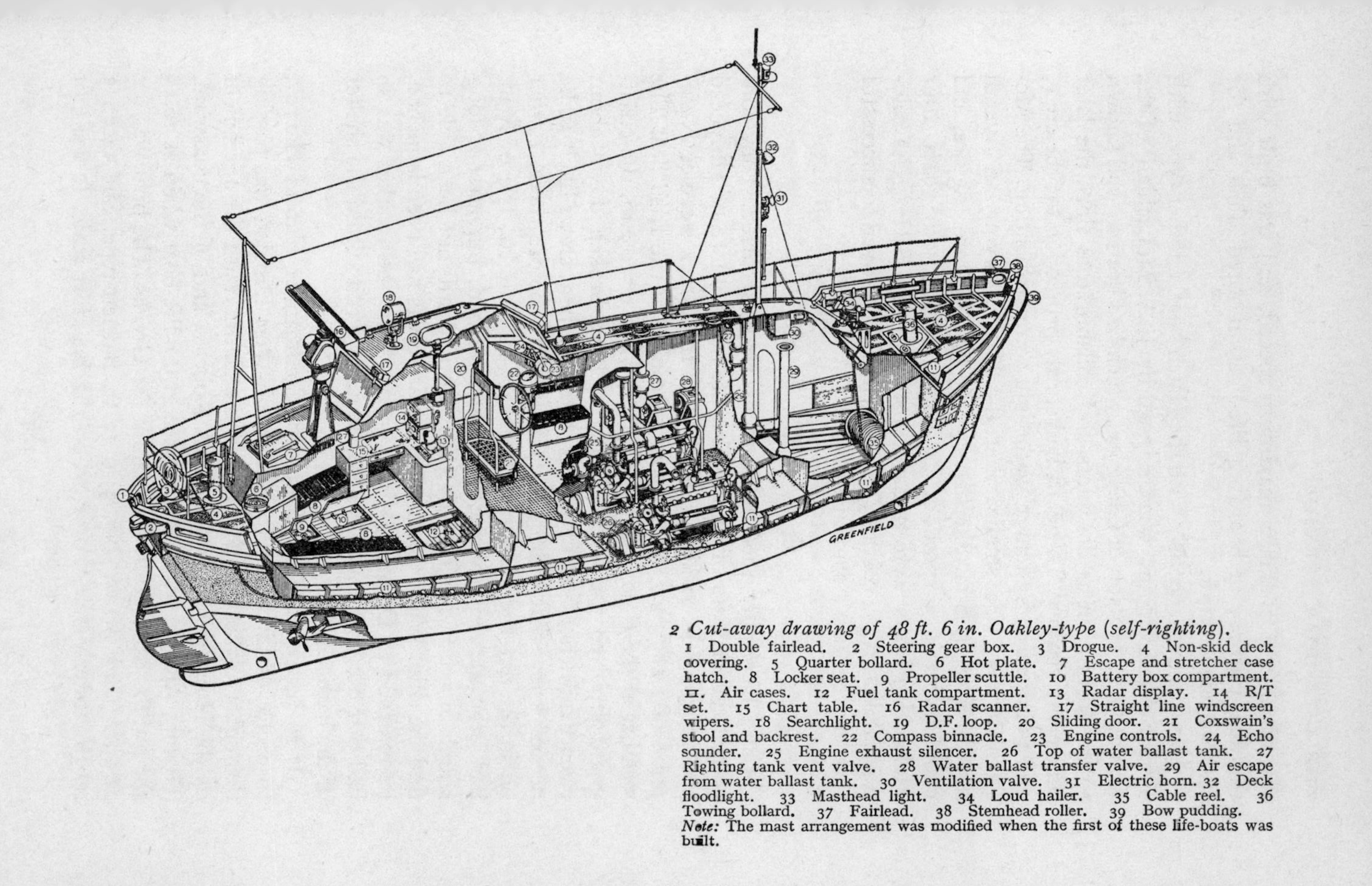

2 *Cut-away drawing of 48 ft. 6 in. Oakley-type (self-righting).*
1 Double fairlead. 2 Steering gear box. 3 Drogue. 4 Non-skid deck covering. 5 Quarter bollard. 6 Hot plate. 7 Escape and stretcher case hatch. 8 Locker seat. 9 Propeller scuttle. 10 Battery box compartment. 11. Air cases. 12 Fuel tank compartment. 13 Radar display. 14 R/T set. 15 Chart table. 16 Radar scanner. 17 Straight line windscreen wipers. 18 Searchlight. 19 D.F. loop. 20 Sliding door. 21 Coxswain's stool and backrest. 22 Compass binnacle. 23 Engine controls. 24 Echo sounder. 25 Engine exhaust silencer. 26 Top of water ballast tank. 27 Righting tank vent valve. 28 Water ballast transfer valve. 29 Air escape from water ballast tank. 30 Ventilation valve. 31 Electric horn. 32 Deck floodlight. 33 Masthead light. 34 Loud hailer. 35 Cable reel. 36 Towing bollard. 37 Fairlead. 38 Stemhead roller. 39 Bow pudding.
Note: The mast arrangement was modified when the first of these life-boats was built.

was capable of 26 knots maximum speeed, and was built with the dual purpose of boarding life-boats moored afloat and for inshore rescue work.

Almost simultaneously with the Hatch boat, another type, with similar characteristics, was designed by J. A. McLachlan, of the firm of G. L. Watson of Glasgow, which had been so well known to the Institution as designers and collaborators since the later nineteenth century. This craft had sturdy protection for the crew, and an ingenious system of watertight compartmenting. The McLachlan boat was smaller that the Hatch, having an overall length of 18 ft. 6 in. She had two 60 h.p. inboard engines, and could maintain a speed of 20 knots. Within two years, four McLachlan boats were under construction in GRP (glass reinforced plastic) at a cost of £3,400 each. They proved so successful that they became a standard design.

* * *

On 2 December 1966 memorable events occurred. They concerned the services of two Welsh life-boats, those of Holyhead and Moelfre, in making rescues from the Greek steamer *Nafsiporos*, of 1,287 tons, which was in trouble in the Irish Sea. The weather at the time was terrible, and when at 10 a.m. the coastguard reported the Greek vessel to have broken down about twenty miles north of Lynas Point, the life-boat crews likely to be needed knew that a difficult task could be before them. Earlier on in the day the Honorary Secretary at Douglas, Isle of Man, had been alerted and the life-boat launched, but after a long search in poor visibility the coxswain had still not been able to find the ship. When told that other life-boats had been launched, he returned to Douglas, where by that time the weather was so bad that the boat could not be rehoused, even within the shelter of the harbour.

It so happened that Lieutenant-Commander Harold Harvey, Inspector of Life-boats for the North-West District, was passing through Holyhead at the time of the alarm. With the agreement of the Honorary Secretary, T. B. Roberts, and of the coxswain, Thomas Alcock, he took his place in the life-boat when at 10.30 she put to sea to go to the help of the Greeks. The boat was the *St Cybi* (*Civil Service No.* 9) a 52 ft. Barnett-type. She faced a north-westerly gale, Force 10 on the Beaufort scale. It was not until some three hours later that she made contact with the ship, which was then being circled by Shackleton aircraft of R.A.F. Coastal Command.

By that time there was another life-boat involved. This was the 42 ft. Watson from Moelfre, the *Watkins Williams*, commanded by Coxswain Evans, who had been at the rescues from the *Hindlea*, seven years before. Evans had originally been called to the help of the motor vessel *Grit*, but his services had not been needed, and he was back at Moelfre when the call came for the *Nafsiporos*. The ship was clearly in a bad way, and when news of her came through she was said to be heading for Port Lynas, though her position was uncertain.

There was a Russian ship, the *Kungurles*, standing by the *Nafsiporos*, and the seamanship of her master was such that at one time he had actually been able to get a tow-line aboard the Greek ship. Early in the afternoon, this had parted.

The time of crisis came shortly before 4 p.m. when daylight had almost gone and when the *Nafsiporos*, rolling to an angle of 35 degrees amid waves which were sometimes 35 feet from trough to crest, and in winds of the order of 100 miles an hour, tried to anchor about a quarter of a mile west of West House Rock, in less than six fathoms of water. A grim situation was complicated still further by the fact that there was a ship's boat hanging loosely from a davit, and neither Alcock nor Evans, whose life-boats were now in company, could make it clear to the captain that if lives were not to be imperilled still further, and unnecessarily, his crew must cut this boat away from the falls.

On an early approach to the *Nafsiporos* by the Holyhead boat, the steamer's counter crashed against the port quarter of the life-boat, inevitably doing some damage, though this was not crippling. Later, the life-boat was swept towards the steamer just as her stern reared out of the water, and for some terrifying seconds her screw revolved close above the heads of the life-boatmen.

It next became apparent that the Greek sailors were too terrified to leave their ship. That being so, every man who could be spared would be needed on the life-boat's deck to prise the men away. It was at this stage that Coxswain Alcock made a decision which required much moral courage. Knowing that he could be most useful in the work of physical rescue, he asked Lieutenant-

Commander Harvey to take the wheel for him, and this was done, with the approval of the crew. Then everyone available set about the extremely difficult task of wrenching the Greeks from their holds. After several runs, five men were got on board the life-boat.

What was possibly the worst moment of all was when the swaying loose boat on board the steamer suddenly crashed down on to the deck of the Holyhead life-boat. Thanks to shouted warnings and to sheer good luck, there were no casualties from this mishap, though some structural harm occurred. Even as the debris was being cleared, in went the Moelfre boat under Coxswain Evans and took off ten more Greeks. The captain and three others refused to leave the ship, which was later taken in tow by the Dutch tug *Utrecht*.

Both the life-boats returned to Holyhead, after one of the finest rescues since the war. The Committee of Management decided that the award of two gold medals was justified. One went to Coxswain Evans of Moelfre, which made him the only living man to have won this highest of life-boat distinctions twice: the other went to Lieutenant-Commander Harvey, who became the first Inspector ever to have received the gold medal. Three silver medals were bestowed: one on Coxswain Alcock of Holyhead, the others on the motor mechanics of the two boats, Eric Jones of Holyhead and Evan Owens of Moelfre. The remaining members of both crews received bronze medals.

Coxswain Evans retired not long after the episode. He stated: 'Often I wondered whether I was doing the right thing. I risked making a widow of my wife and leaving my three children fatherless, for the sake of some sailors I had never met. Yet I'd do it again, and there is not a life-boatman who would disagree with me.'

The tug *Utrecht*, which had been concerned in the aftermath of the December rescues, provided a connecting link with an event of three months later. This was the stranding of the 61,000-ton tanker *Torrey Canyon* on the Seven Stones Rocks, in the area of sea between Cornwall and the Isles of Scilly, in broad daylight and after warning that she was standing into danger. The wreck occurred at 9 a.m. on 18 March 1967, or very soon after, and within hours it had become not merely national but world news, for it seemed likely that damage caused to marine and sea bird life, and to coastal amenities, through seeping oil, would be on an unparalleled scale, and extend to France and Ireland.

Within a few minutes of the disaster, the *Guy and Clare Hunter*, the Watson-type boat stationed at Hugh Town, St Mary's, Isles of Scilly, was launched under the command of Coxswain Lethbridge. The weather was not severe, and at first Lethbridge's main duty was to provide liaison between the *Utrecht*, which was standing by in the expectation of salvage, and the *Torrey Canyon*.

Oil began to seep from the tanker shortly after 1.30 p.m. and within an hour it was spreading rapidly. There was no immediate danger to human life, but Lethbridge stood by the ship from within a short time of her striking to early the next morning. Then, as the wind was rising and there was an increasingly difficult oily swell, he took off nine men, one of whom fell into the sea but was hauled back. Others were winched off by helicopter.

During the afternoon of 19 March the St Mary's boat was relieved by the life-boat from Penlee. The two crews then took turns to stand by until, on 21 March, the *Torrey Canyon* was on fire after being bombed, and clearly about to break up, when no more could be done. The Isles of Scilly crew were 54 hours at sea, and the Penlee men 30 hours. Although no hazardous rescues were made or were necessary, the members of the *Torrey Canyon*'s crew who were taken to St Mary's subscribed £31. 7. 0. so that a plaque could be placed in Hugh Town to commemorate the service. This was a gesture of appreciation, not nearly so common as it might be, which was valued by all concerned.

The case of this tanker, and the calls which East Anglian, North Country and Scottish stations were receiving when North Sea oil-rigs appeared to be in danger, made it apparent that oil was likely to present life-boat stations with some tricky problems.

Coxswain Lethbridge and his men were again in the news not many weeks later when, on 22 May, they went to the help of the motor yacht *Braemar*. It was a service that kept them at sea for 27 hours, and ended in Mount's Bay.

The *Braemar* reported trouble in her engine-room when she was 28 miles into the Atlantic beyond Bishops Rock. The life-boat was launched at 6.48 a.m. in a rising sea. By 9 a.m. when contact was made, the yacht's power had failed altogether and she was drifting about 13 miles from Wolf Rock. The motor ship *Trader* was standing by, and shortly after midday she got a tow-rope to the *Braemar*, but this parted in the heavy seas. Then the life-boat took over, and towed the cripple as best she could until 7.53 when the *Braemar*'s captain, thinking that without the use of mechanical pumps his vessel was likely to sink, asked Lethbridge to take off most of those on board.

This was a matter of great difficulty in the state of the sea, but eventually 15 were dragged on board the life-boat, leaving the captain and two others still in the *Braemar*. Towing was resumed, although by that time the wind was estimated as having reached Force 10. In the end the yacht was brought safely to Cornwall, but it had been touch and go, and the feat was not achieved without cost, for one of the rescued men died of heart failure.

Lethbridge was awarded the Institution's silver medal; the second coxswain, Ernest Guy, and the motor mechanic, William Burrow, earning a bronze. As was usual in such cases, the remainder of the crew received Medal Service Certificates.

Some way north of where the *Braemar* nearly came to grief, at Padstow, a station with an eventful history, there had been major changes. The place itself presented operational difficulties because of the problem of siting a launching platform which would be usable at every stage of wind, tide and weather. Scientific measurements of wave patterns and behaviour extending over two years were made before the Institution felt justified in embarking on a project which, like those at Selsey and the Lizard, would cost a great deal.

It was eventually decided to build a new station at a cost of £114,600 in Mother Ivey's Bay, Trevose Head, the earlier station at Hawker's Cove having to be closed owing to the silting of the harbour. A life-boathouse and slipway were built on the foreshore near the foot of the cliffs, which at that point are about a hundred feet high. The life-boat was to be launched down a 240-foot slipway, after a new road had been constructed, a quarter of a mile long, from the coastguard station to the top of the cliff. The great expense had been incurred because of the problems of silting in the area.

The composer Malcolm Arnold wrote a 'Padstow Life-boat March' in honour of the occasion. This was performed in June 1967 during the course of the BBC's International Festival of Light Music at the Royal Festival Hall, the composer conducting. The life-boat service had been celebrated or commemorated in

Princess Marina, Duchess of Kent, President, R.N.L.I. 1943–68, with Coxswain Richard Evans at Moelfre, 1960

The Duke of Kent at Bembridge, Isle of Wight

Goblet, over 12 inches high, engraved by Honoria D. Marsh. Acquired in 1964 by the Calouste Gulbenkian Foundation, Lisbon, to benefit the R.N.L.I.

Queen Elizabeth II, with Commander F. R. H. Swann, Chairman, R.N.L.I. and (*right*) Lieutenant-Commander W. G. Dutton, Chief Inspector of Life-boats, at Henley, July 1972, on board the *Royal British Legion Jubilee* life-boat

Captain Nigel Dixon, R.N., Secretary, R.N.L.I.

Young members of the Blue Peter team, with records of lives saved by Blue Peter life-boats

The Fraserburgh life-boat (*background*) at the moment of capsize, 21 January 1970

Modern life-boat types: 70 ft. Clyde, steel

44 ft. Waveney, steel

McLachlan Inshore Life-boat

Inshore Life-boat

Commemorative medals, designed by John Crittenden and issued by Messrs Slade Hampton, to signalize the 150th anniversary in 1974 of the founding of the R.N.L.I.

many ways: in writing, painting, sculpture, the film, the drama, television, but it was some time since it had attracted a composer.

* * *

Britain had been host at two out of the nine International Life-boat Conferences held so far. In 1967 the French, who had arranged the second in 1928, presided at another. This, the tenth Conference, was organized by the Société Centrale de Sauvetage des Naufragés under their President, Vice-Admiral d'Harcourt. It was held at Dinard and St Malo, with an addendum at Jersey, between 5 and 8 June. The British delegation was led by the Deputy Chairman, Commander Swann.

Sixteen nations sent representatives, and every one of them, except New Zealand, had sent delegations before. The full list was Belgium, Canada, Denmark, Finland, France, the German Federal Republic, Britain, Holland, Iceland, Japan, New Zealand, Norway, Poland, Sweden, the U.S.A. and the U.S.S.R. It was a special pleasure to welcome New Zealand, which operated a sea-rescue service somewhat on the lines of the R.N.L.I.

There was much to see, including a French life-boat from St Servan and others from Britain, Norway, Denmark, Germany (whose boat incorporated the 'daughter boat' principle of a large craft carrying a smaller one inboard, a pioneering step which had been taken up elsewhere), and from Sweden and Holland.

The papers covered electronics as applied to the life-boat service; there was one on inflatable boats; and the Institution's Secretary, Stirling Whorlow, was particularly interesting on the art of fund-raising, although this necessity applied only to a proportion of the delegates, others receiving state or municipal subsidy. The matter was growing more important than ever to the Institution, since the ambitious programme of building and modernization which had been embarked upon was leading to a situation where it was becoming necessary, in some years, to draw upon reserves. What Mr Whorlow could not say, having in mind the presence of representatives of Iron Curtain countries, was that there had actually been occasions when contributions had been refused! This had been so when, after the defection of Guy Burgess to Moscow, he had suggested that a four-figure fee which he had been offered by a Sunday newspaper should be given to the R.N.L.I. The Institution declined the money. The reason for so doing, that the organization would not be willing to accept money arising from treason, was scarcely open to dispute. What was much to everyone's credit was that, as the result of the way in which the matter was handled by the Press, money, exceeding the amount refused, was contributed to the revenue.

On 11 July, a few weeks after the international conference had dispersed, a reception was held at St James's Palace to celebrate the completion by Princess Marina, Duchess of Kent, of twenty-five years as President. She was presented by Captain Wyndham-Quin with the Institution's gold medal, a singular mark of appreciation. There was, indeed, much to appreciate, for it was almost half a century since the Royal Family had first begun to take an immediate part in the affairs of the Institution. The enthusiastic way in which the Prince of Wales, then his brother the Duke of Kent, and finally the Princess, had fulfilled their duties, by their continuous interest in the affairs of the Institution, its staff and crews by many visits to life-boat stations for naming ceremonies, and attending a whole succession of Annual General Meetings, had never slackened. What this meant to those who served the life-boats, was shown the following year, in the concern which was shown when the news became known that the Princess was gravely ill.

Captain Wyndham-Quin resigned from the Chairmanship in 1968, though he remained on the Committee of Management. His duties were taken over by Admiral Sir Wilfrid Woods, who thus became the first flag-officer to preside over the policy-making body.

Admiral Woods had served in submarines in the Second World War, and on the staff of the Commander-in-Chief, Mediterranean. From 1960 to 1962 he had been Commander-in-Chief, Home Fleet and NATO Commander-in-Chief, Eastern Atlantic. His last naval appointment had been Commander-in-Chief, Portsmouth, and Allied Commander-in-Chief, Channel. He had been Commodore of the Royal Naval Sailing Association since 1963, and his exceptional experience was to be of great value to the Institution during the four years of his tenure.

At the Annual General Meeting on 9 April 1968 he had something pointed to say on the matter of salvage, about which there was widespread misconception.

Whatever the circumstances the Institution never makes a salvage claim. Our crews, however, have a legal right to do so, in common with all seamen. Actually but few claims are made, and the sums involved in the aggregate only small. For example, a recent review of twelve life-boat stations from Hastings to Torbay for the period 1955–1965 revealed that of 360 services which might have resulted in property salvage claims, salvage was, in fact, claimed on only 36 occasions—one in ten—and the average amount received by each crew member over the period was five shillings per annum.

The annual average of salvage claims is only 5 per cent of the total number of effective services carried out in the course of the year, and even so on many occasions the 'claim' really is only an agreement that the crew shall receive a few pounds a man. You will realize, therefore, how groundless is the fear of salvage claims from the Institution. Yet I know that boat owners have on occasion not rewarded, or even thanked, life-boat crews who have saved their boats for fear of this being interpreted as an admission that salvage has been performed.

Just a week before the Meeting, Coxswain Daniel Kirkpatrick of Longhope had made yet another fine rescue, which for the third time won him the Institution's silver medal, which made him unique among living life-boatmen.

During the early hours of 1 April 1968 the coastguard reported to the Honorary Secretary of the Longhope station that the Grimsby trawler *Ross Puma* was ashore on the Orkney island of Hoy. At the time, the wind was from the north-west and was approaching gale force. It was extremely cold, with heavy sleet and snow. The 47 ft. Watson boat *T.G.B.* put out at 2.56 a.m. and at 3.30 contact was made by radio-telephone with the trawler, which came into view by searchlight a quarter of an hour later. The *Ross Puma* had stranded on the Little Rackwick Shoals, only about fifty yards from the shore, from which the cliffs rose three or four hundred feet. She was rolling and pounding heavily, and the crew was frequently swamped by seas breaking over the vessel. There were three life-rafts alongside, but as the *T.G.B.* drew near, one of these broke adrift.

Coxswain Kirkpatrick anchored to windward of the vessel. Eighty fathoms of cable were veered, and the life-boat came to within twenty yards of the trawler's starboard quarter. Attempts to take off the crew by rocket line failed; the life-boat herself received some damage from the rocks but, after forty minutes' hazardous work in the darkness, all fifteen fishermen were brought to safety by making use of the two remaining life-rafts.

Trawlermen could well have considered Kirkpatrick as their particular benefactor, for all three of his silver medal services had been concerned with them. The first had taken place in 1959, when he had saved fourteen men from the trawler *Strathcoe*. The second was in 1964 when, as already described, he had rescued fifteen from the *Ben Barvas*. In its display of seamanship, the third incident was the equal of the others.

Kirkpatrick's was one of the last outstanding services to be reported to Princess Marina as President. She had long been accustomed to follow the news from the stations, and she had engaged herself to name the new life-boat at Padstow, but was too ill to make the journey. The ceremony was attended by her son, who read her speech, and who thus continued an association with the Institution which had been begun by his father before the Second World War.

Princess Marina died on 27 August 1968, to the great sorrow of all who knew her. On the day of her Memorial Service, R.N.L.I. flags flew at half-mast, and crews, staff and helpers were all represented at Westminster Abbey.

9

Later Events

The year 1969 was to bring both encouragement and sorrow to the Institution. It opened well, with the formation, announced on 2 January at the International Boat Show at Earl's Court in London, of the Yachtsmen's Life-boat Supporters Association, which was to become familiar as the 'Y.L.A.' The launch was by Sir Alec Rose, who had recently completed his memorable voyage round the world. He said:

> The question which I think we should all now ask ourselves is whether boat owners are doing enough for the R.N.L.I. Some of course are, but it has to be admitted that a great many are not. Now an opportunity is being presented to every man, woman and child who owns a boat or who takes pleasure in going out in boats to give to the Royal National Life-boat Institution the help it so badly needs in order to maintain the wonderful volunteer service it has always given.

The Y.L.A. was one of the most important of the new plans for increasing revenue at a time when this question was becoming more urgent every year. Among the first to join was Edward Heath, who was to be outstanding among Prime Ministers in his enthusiasm for sailing. Certainly the trend, which had been evident since the end of the war, for more and more rescues to be concerned with privately owned craft, was increasing. Figures showed that services in this direction had multiplied threefold within the previous few years. In 1968, reported Commander Swann, 'inshore rescue boats alone launched 1,177 times and saved 506 lives, and no less than 61 per cent of these services were to those who seek their pleasure on the sea'. Although the idea behind the Y.L.A. was essentially fund-raising, the fact that members would regularly be sent a copy of the *Life-boat* ensured that they would realize the extent of the services rendered by the Institution, and would know what was going on.

There were, for instance, the new 48 ft. 6 in. Solent-class steel boats, such as had come into service at Lochinver on the west coast of Scotland, and at Rosslare Harbour, County Wexford. There were eight of these built or building at yards in Cowes or Southampton, hence the name. Based largely on the Oakley design, with the same length of hull, they were given natural righting capacity without the necessity of transferring water-ballast, as in their wooden predecessors. They were built for a seven-man crew, and it was estimated that they could carry the weight of about one hundred survivors. The cost per boat was about £70,000, and they were the largest in the current programme.

It is doubtful whether any existing life-boat, except possibly the 70 ft. type, would have stood up to the battering which capsized Coxswain Kirkpatrick and the Longhope *T.B.G.* on the night of 17 March 1969. The boat had been launched to go to the help of the Liberian vessel *Irene* which had gone aground on the east coast of South Ronaldsay, the crew eventually being rescued by the coastguard by means of breeches buoy.

The Longhope men were Daniel Kirkpatrick, Second Coxswain James Johnston, Bowman Raymond Kirkpatrick, Motor Mechanic Robert Johnston, Assistant Mechanic James Swanson, John Kirkpatrick, Robert Johnston and Eric McFadyen; a typically close-knit group. Robert Johnston, aged sixty-two, was the oldest man on board, and two of his sons were in the boat. Coxswain Kirkpatrick, three times silver medal winner, also had two sons with him.

The maroons went off at 7.40 p.m. and the *T.G.B.* was at sea twenty minutes later. There was a south-easterly gale in the Pentland Firth, estimated at the time as Force 9, with a rough sea and heavy swell. Rain and snow flurries reduced visibility.

At 8.40 the Longhope men gave their position as three miles south-east of Cantick Head lighthouse. At 9.20 the head keeper at Pentland Skerries lighthouse sighted the *T.G.B.* in line with the Lother Rocks, which were about two miles away from him. At 9.35 the same man, and his two assistants, saw her stern light to the eastward about a mile away. That was the last time Kirkpatrick and his men were known to be alive. Their reporting signal had been received a few minutes earlier by Wick radio.

The 70 ft. *Grace Paterson Ritchie*, stationed at Kirkwall, had put out at 8 p.m. at the request of the coastguard and at 10.5 p.m. Wick radio was asked to inform both life-boats that conditions alongside the *Irene* had become 'almost impossible'. By that time there were grave doubts about the safety of the Longhope boat, and emergency rescue parties were sent to vantage points on the east coast of South Ronaldsay to search. At 11.5 p.m. the coastguard asked the *Grace Paterson Ritchie* to make for a position south of the *Irene* where, it was hoped, a rendezvous with Kirkpatrick could be made. On her arrival, at 11.15, Staff Coxswain Ian Ives fired a parachute flare but there was no answering signal from Kirkpatrick.

It was then agreed that a search should be made at daylight with the help of aircraft. This was done. An R.A.F. Shackleton from Kinloss and a naval helicopter from Lossiemouth co-operated with the *Grace Paterson Ritchie* and with the Stronsay, Thurso and Stromness life-boats, all of which put out on the morning of 19 March. It was not until 1.40 p.m. that the Thurso men sighted the Longhope life-boat, upturned, four miles south-west of Tor Ness. They took her in tow to Scrabster Harbour, escorted by the Stromness life-boat. The difficult and painful journey was not completed until 8.55 that evening.

Only seven bodies were recovered, six of them with life-jackets on. The door of the port side of the wheel-house was found open, and it is probable that the missing man, James Swanson, was either lost overboard before the capsize or that his body floated out through the open door.

The findings of the inquiry held by the Institution were that correct action had been taken by all concerned; that the condition of the hull and machinery of the boat at the time of launching was in all respects first class; and evidence suggested that the boat capsized shortly after 9.35 p.m. on 17 March while proceeding eastwards between South Ronaldsay and Mickle Skerry lighthouse, after being overwhelmed by 'very high seas and maelstrom conditions'. The most likely position for these conditions to be met would have been where the flood tide running south down the east coast of South Ronaldsay meets the east-going stream north of the Pentland Skerries, which is about the position where the boat was last seen. The findings agreed closely with those of the Procurator-fiscal's inquiry held at Kirkwall on 10 June.

It so happened that the day before the disaster, Raymond Baxter had made an appeal on BBC television, and Brigadier J. W.

H. Gow, a member of the Committee of Management, a radio appeal in Scotland on behalf of the Institution. The result, in direct response, was overwhelming—£43,000, or more than ten times the sum raised in answer to a similar appeal in 1961. London Life-boat day occurred on 19 March, and newspaper placards all over the metropolis reported news of the progress of the search for the Longhope men. A fund was launched by the Lord-Lieutenant of Orkney, and as the result of the interest of the Press, notably the *Daily Mirror* and the *Daily Express* in London and the *Daily Record* in Scotland, a further £13,000 was subscribed for the Institution. It had been made clear that appreciation of those engaged in the work of rescue at sea was as great as ever, even though it needed a shock to produce a special response.

As for the spirit obtaining among life-boat families, this was expressed by Mrs Margaret Kirkpatrick, wife of the dead coxswain and mother of two members of his crew. When asked whether she would wish her remaining son to join the service she said: 'If he should want to go on the next Longhope life-boat, I will not stop him or try to.'

* * *

At the end of what proved to be a very busy summer, an episode occurred at Amble, Northumberland, which led to the award of the first gallantry medals bestowed for a service by an Inshore Life-boat.

On 29 September 1969, at 6.30 in the morning, the coastguard was watching a yacht entering the harbour in a heavy swell. He had a maroon ready to fire, as he thought help might be needed. It was—though not by the yacht. R.A.F. pinnace No. 1386 capsized as she approached from the north. The maroons went off, and the Honorary Secretary of the station, L. J. Matthews, called out the Inshore Life-boat while the regular life-boat crew were assembling.

The ILB, manned by Robert Stewart and Andrew Scott, went off at 6.34 and made for the pinnace at full speed. So did the 46 ft. Watson-class life-boat *Millie Walton*, which got away five minutes later. Coxswain William Henderson included some men in his crew who were not experienced in rescue work, in order to avoid delay.

The ILB spotted two men clinging to a life-buoy and took them on board only twelve minutes from the first alarm. The crew then searched for the captain of the pinnace and others, one or more of whom might have been trapped in the hull. A message was sent, by way of a seine-net vessel, asking for skin divers, and as the rescued men were in a poor state, Stewart and Scott returned to harbour where they could be looked after.

Within two minutes of the rescues by the ILB, Coxswain Henderson had reached the scene. He found a man clinging to the bottom of the pinnace, with seas breaking over him continuously. He was hauled aboard. By this time a helicopter was carrying out a search, in the course of which another man was picked up. Henderson understood that taps could be heard inside the hull of the pinnace, so he tried to right her by means of the grapnel line, but this could not be done. He therefore decided to tow the upturned craft into the harbour as quickly as possible.

The tow-line parted shortly after Henderson had successfully negotiated a line of heavily breaking water, but it was re-secured. By 7.10 the ILB had picked up two skin divers and had joined the *Millie Walton*, but the men were unable to get beneath the pinnace because of the tide and the heavy swell. They were hauled back exhausted.

With the help of a seine-net vessel, the pinnace was brought as far as the harbour bar, but there the mast and derrick struck bottom. The tow-line parted, and nothing further could be done until the wreck had been washed behind the south pier, a position from which she was unlikely to shift.

At 10.30 a.m. naval divers who had been flown from Rosyth, together with the life-boat crew, carried cutting gear across the rocks, went out to the wreck, and by 11.15, nearly five hours after the accident, the experts had succeeded in cutting through the bottom of the pinnace, and had released the survivor trapped inside, fortunately with enough air to keep him alive. Three men were still missing, and a search for them was made by the Amble and Newbiggin life-boats, though little hope was felt that they could be still alive. Their bodies were eventually found among the rocks near the shore.

Coxswain Henderson, and James Stewart, a member of his crew who had been outstanding in his efforts to secure the original tow, which had been an operation of much difficulty, received the bronze medal, as did the two who had manned the ILB. It had been an unusual type of service, notable for the speed and co-ordination which had been apparent throughout.

Some two months after the affair at Amble, Coxswain William Sheader of Scarborough won a silver medal for a rescue which in some ways recalled the extraordinary feat of Coxswain Cross of the Humber in the early days of the Second World War. It occurred so close inshore that at times there were only five feet of water, or less, beneath the life-boat's keel.

Shortly after noon on Sunday, 23 November 1969 it was reported that the converted ship's life-boat *Sheena* had overturned in South Bay and that the occupants were in the sea. The 37 ft. Oakley *J. G. Graves of Sheffield* was launched within five minutes of the alarm and made for the bay in overcast conditions, in a north-easterly wind of Force 6, and rough seas.

To reach the one survivor he could see, Sheader had to take his boat within a rock-strewn area, with breaking waves, and with the certainty that if his boat capsized she would not be able to right herself as there was insufficient depth of water. As it was, she filled several times, and a heavy growth of kelp could well have fouled the screws. The man was hauled aboard thirteen minutes from the time of the alarm and eight minutes from when the life-boat went out. He was in such poor shape that he was landed at once, after which Sheader put to sea again to look for another survivor. He too was got aboard and rushed to hospital, but his condition was such that he died soon afterwards.

Later the life-boat put out for the third time to look for yet another man reported missing, but he could not be found. By that time, weather conditions had much deteriorated, and two fishing boats nearing the harbour entrance were escorted in, one of them, with a flooded engine, under tow. The whole incident showed perfect teamwork.

Three other events marked the year. The first was the agreement of the Duke of Kent to take over the Presidency, although as a serving officer of the Army it would obviously not be possible for him to give as much time to the cause as he would have wished. The second was the retirement of Stirling Whorlow after eight years as Secretary and forty years on the staff of the Institution, to which, as a colleague wrote, 'he gave all he had to give'—and this was a very great deal. He was succeeded by Captain Nigel Dixon, RN, who since 1967 had been Personal Assistant to the Chief Inspector of Life-boats. The third was the establishment, at Cowes, of a repair centre and depot for the Inshore Life-boats, which became as busy, and as essential, as the depot at Boreham Wood.

* * *

On 21 January 1970 there occurred one of the saddest episodes in the history of the Institution. This was the loss, just over ten months after the Longhope tragedy, of the entire crew of the Fraserburgh life-boat, with the exception of a single man, Jackson Buchan. There were many witnesses of the accident, and of the exceptionally large wave which was the cause of the loss; and such was public concern that when the news became known, Goronwy Roberts, Minister of State, Board of Trade, stated in the House of Commons that a formal investigation would be held, under the provisions of the Merchant Shipping Act of 1894. The Institution was glad of this decision and submitted an account of its own inquiry to the Board of Trade. As a result of these proceedings, the life-boat service came under as careful a scrutiny as it had received since the Parliamentary Report of 1897.

The Sheriff Principal, Frederick W. F. O'Brien, QC, presided at sessions which were held from 5 to 12 October at the Sheriff Court House, Aberdeen. He was aided by three Assessors.

The circumstances were that on the evening of the previous 20 January the Danish motor fishing vessel *Opal* sailed from Buckie, Banffshire, and set course for the Fladden fishing grounds. At about 10.30 p.m. it was found that the engine-room was flooding, and the pumps failed. The master reported his position to Skagen radio, Denmark, at about 5 a.m. on 21 January, and asked if help could be had from other Danish ships in the vicinity, though he did not then consider his ship to be in immediate danger.

Wick radio heard from Skagen that the *Opal* was taking in water and needed help with pumping, and asked whether anything could be arranged. The Wick and Peterhead coastguards were told of the situation, and the Honorary Secretary of the Peterhead life-boat station reported that although there was no pump available, the life-boat would be launched if necessary for life-saving. Peterhead coastguard contacted Fraserburgh coastguard, who then told the acting Honorary Secretary, Coxswain John C. Stephen, of the mishap, and the need for a pump and prompt assistance.

Stephens tried to get hold of a pump; meanwhile he warned his motor mechanic and his assistant, the boat being afloat in the south basin because of alterations being made to the shore accommodation. At 6 a.m. maroons were fired and the crew assembled, although, not unexpectedly, it had proved impossible to get a pump. The life-boat *Duchess of Kent*, a 46 ft. 9 in. Watson-type, cast off at 6.30 a.m. with the wind south-south-west and Force 6 to 7.

The decision to launch at once was correct, for a few minutes after the maroons had gone off, Skagen radio reported that the state of the *Opal* appeared to be critical. At 6.32 Wick radio sent out a 'Mayday' signal, requesting immediate assistance by all means available, and this was repeated.

At 8.39 a.m. Stephens gave his estimated time of arrival at the scene of the casualty as 11 a.m. Nine minutes later the Russian ship *Victor Kingisepp* reported herself as being twelve miles from the *Opal* by her radar, and at 9.17 Skagen radio reported that another Russian ship was actually alongside. By 10.6 the *Victor Kingisepp* was nearby, and her master reported that four vessels, two of them Russian, were standing by. This news was not transmitted directly to the life-boat, nor was information, received earlier, that a helicopter had taken off one of the Danish crew, leaving three on board.

By 11 a.m. Stephens was approaching the *Opal*, and ten minutes later he reported that she was under tow from a Russian trawler, the *Iwa*, on a course heading into the wind. That was the last message to come from him. At this time the wind's strength was Force 8 to 9, with waves averaging 15 to 16 feet, with occasional waves of twice that height.

The life-boat approached the *Opal* from the west, then altered course to starboard and reduced speed until she was on the *Opal*'s port beam and on a parallel course. Stephens was heard by Jackson Buchan to say that he would go ahead in order to read the name or number of the towing ship. The evidence seemed to suggest that he had either increased or was increasing speed when the life-boat was struck by a very large breaking wave on her port bow and was overwhelmed. It appeared that the bow was lifted high into the air and the life-boat capsized bow over stern with some transverse inclination to starboard. She lay capsized with her starboard side visible to those aboard the *Opal*.

The Russian trawler *Iwa* continued on her course with the *Opal* in tow, while the life-boat floated bottom upwards. The sole survivor swam to, and contrived to scramble aboard the capsized craft. He was picked up, after twenty minutes, by one of the Russian trawlers, and despite his ordeal maintained liaison between the rescuing vessels and the shore. Simultaneously the *Victor Kingisepp* approached, and her men made strenuous efforts, at great personal risk, to right the life-boat. She was eventually righted at 2.31 p.m. but the four members of the crew trapped inside were dead. A fifth was not found.

The *Victor Kingisepp* took the life-boat in tow and made for Buckie. Next day the bodies were transferred to Buckie life-boat, the *Duchess of Kent* being handed over to the Buckie crew and towed into harbour at about 5 p.m. on 22 January. Besides the coxswain, the others who lost their lives were the motor mechanic, Frederick A. Kirkness, and crew members William Hadden, James R. S. Buchan and James Buchan. Kirkness's body was never recovered.

The findings of the Court were unequivocal, and they would have held good for a whole succession of similar accidents to life-boats and their crews. 'The *Duchess of Kent*', said the Report, 'was well equipped and in a seaworthy condition when she sailed on her last mission. No vessel can be guaranteed to survive all possible sea conditions and this life-boat was unfortunate to encounter a very large wave which overwhelmed her. No blame for the disaster can be attributed to her coxswain and crew or to the R.N.L.I. The Court emphasizes that life-boat rescue operations are, and always will be, extremely hazardous.'

To the objection made in some quarters that operational limits should have been placed on the use of certain types of boat, the Court's view was 'that it is impossible in practice to formulate such limitations, as there is an infinite variety of combinations of wind, sea and tide in any given locality. Decisions as to launching are best entrusted to the judgment of experienced seamen on the spot.'

At the Annual General Meeting held on 8 April 1970, which was attended by Rear-Admiral B. Yashin and Captain L. Kousmin of the Soviet Embassy, and Mr Hans Kuhne, Minister at the Danish Embassy, Admiral Sir Wilfrid Woods said:

> I would like to pay tribute to the courage, determination and fine seamanship displayed by the captains of the two Soviet fishing vessels which rescued Mr Jackson Buchan, the survivor, and did all that was possible to rescue the others.

The Meeting was asked to stand in silence to honour the memory of the five men who had lost their lives.

* * *

From time to time even the most specialist journals require a new look. Usually this leads to regret on the part of well-established readers, but the idea is largely to attract the young. Certainly the *Life-boat*, which for some years had contented itself with a modest format and a sky-blue cover with the R.N.L.I. badge at the top, was due for a change. In January 1971 the size of page was expanded, a sea-going personality appeared on the front, and a letter was printed from 10 Downing Street wishing the Institution well. Mr Heath, the Conservative Prime Minister, yachtsman as he was, had a natural interest in the work, but his Labour Party predecessor had not been without it. Mr Harold Wilson was well known to the life-boat crew at St Mary's, Isles of Scilly, and he had received members, when they came to London to receive awards, with generous hospitality.

The first number of the *Life-boat* in the new guise certainly contained news to match the occasion. First in importance were the published accounts of the inquiry into the Fraserburgh disaster, and the repercussions in the Press at home and abroad.

More cheerful in tone, there were encouraging reports from the recently formed Life-boat Enthusiasts' Society, which was announced as being 'basically concerned with the collection and collation of historic information, and also the recording of up-to-the-minute life-boat trends and developments' all over the world. The Yachtsmen's Life-boat Supporters' Association announced that membership stood at well over six thousand, and that it was growing fast. The first member from Poland had recently been enrolled, a fact which Joseph Conrad would have relished.

An item of special interest overseas was the holding of an International Air and Surface Search and Rescue Seminar in New York City. This took place between 26 and 29 October 1970. Life-boat and rescue organizations from many countries were represented, Commander D. B. Cairns, R.N.R., Staff Inspector, Life-boats, attending on behalf of the Institution.

Scarcely was this event over, when a practical example of co-operation in rescue work was given. The Institution's part began with an emergency flight to East Pakistan by a small team, sent to help with the work of flood relief. Four men were concerned: Lieutenant E. D. Stogdon, R.N.V.R., Staff Inspector, Life-boats; Mr Michael Brinton, a mechanic from East Cowes; and two volunteers from the Littlehampton Inshore Life-boat crew, Mr R. Cole and Mr C. J. Pelham.

Twenty inflatable Inshore Life-boats, with a number of spare engines, were assembled within thirty-six hours at the Boreham Wood depot and flown from Stansted, Essex, to Dacca on 21 November 1970, as the result of an urgent appeal from the Red Cross. The team was away until 8 December, working at first in the south-east sector of the affected area in co-operation with parties from the Royal Navy and from the United States armed forces. Local crews were instructed in managing the life-boats, and at one stage three were used to tow an Army pontoon barge, laden with relief supplies. For their work in the stricken area, the team received the Thanks of the Institution inscribed on vellum.

The eleventh International Life-boat Conference was held between 16 and 20 May 1971, in the United States. It was the first time that such a meeting had been arranged on the far side of the Atlantic. Twenty-one nations were represented at New York City, newcomers being the delegates from the Bahamas, an island cluster conveniently near at hand; the Philippines, and South Africa. The R.N.L.I. team consisted of Admiral Sir Wilfrid Woods; Commander F. R. H. Swann, the Deputy Chairman; the Secretary, Captain Nigel Dixon; Commander Peter Sturdee, representing the Chief Inspector; the Public Relations Officer; and Lieutenant E. D. Stogdon. The British Coastguard sent its Chief Inspector, Lieutenant-Commander J. A. Douglas, RN, and the hosts were the United States Coast Guard, the Chairman being Vice-Admiral Thomas R. Sargent III, Assistant Commandant.

Papers and discussions were arranged at the Hotel Commodore, the programme being varied by visits to the Coast Guard station at Fire Island, and the base at Governor's Island. Among the demonstrations at Fire Island, delegates saw a U.S. 40 ft. boat in operation, also an 18 ft. self-righting 'daughter-boat' brought over by the German Life-boat Society, and the Institution's 21 ft. Inshore Life-boat. The British example was in charge of Lieutenant Stogdon, not long returned from Pakistan, and it aroused much interest. Christened the *Atlantic 21*, it was semi-inflatable with a wooden bottom, fitted with inflatable buoyancy sponsons, and equipped with radio and navigation lights, giving it a night capability. It was powered by twin 40 h.p. outboard engines giving speeds up to 28 knots with a three-man crew.

New types of rescue craft were described by the North and South Holland Life-boat Society, the Swedish Society, and the R.N.L.I. The principal Dutch boat discussed was a fast rescue launch built at the yards of Messrs Vosper Thornycroft at Porchester, Hampshire, and completed in 1969. With a top speed of 28 knots she was believed to be the fastest life-boat of her kind in Europe. The boat was based on a standard Keith Nelson design for a 40 ft. glass reinforced plastic hull, similar to one built the previous year for the R.N.L.I., which had been powered for a more modest maximum speed of 18 knots. The main task of the Dutch boat would be rescue in all but the worst weather, the design being particularly useful for searching a large area in conditions of poor visibility.

The Swedish paper described a 46 ft. rescue boat with a speed of 19 knots. One of the R.N.L.I. papers was on the prototype 52 ft. life-boat built at Littlehampton, which was then undergoing extensive sea trials.

The most important paper from the United States was one from Peter A. Silvia, Chief of the Boat Technical Section at the Coast Guard headquarters. He pointed out that there was little direct competition between the various boat-building materials, the properties of each of which suited a different type of boat and service.

Wood was not favoured, said Peter Silvia, except for boats

owned by 'die-hard timber sailors with the time and money to invest in upkeep, or for boats which were considered expendable, such as those of the U.S. shrimp fleet, with an average life of five years'. Fibreglass reinforced plastic was excellent for boats in light to moderate service, where speed and appearance were important. In the hands of a careful operator, a well-built fibreglass boat should last indefinitely and require little attention. Aluminium was well suited for boats in moderate to rough service, where speed was important and where occasional major damage must be expected. Steel was best for rough service, where speed, appearance and corrosion were secondary considerations. Its main advantage was that it could stand up under extreme abuse, but it was twice as heavy as fibreglass or aluminium. The only overlap in suitability was in the case of fibreglass and aluminium. Even there, the right decision should not be difficult. 'If a small weight penalty can be accepted, and if many boats are to be built, fibreglass is the choice. If the duty is severe, and ease of major repair and adaptability are important, or if few are to be built, then aluminium is the choice.'

While there was much of interest on the technical side which emerged from the meetings, the most valuable paper, historically, was the one presented by the Institution's Public Relations Officer Patrick Howarth. This was on 'Exchange of Information between Life-boat Societies'. It summarized the results of all the Conferences since the first, held in Great Britain in 1924.

The upshot of the discussion which followed was that it was proposed to establish an international technical journal, provided funds could be obtained from some trust or foundation. It would take the form of a periodical to be published in the English language, the editorial board to have representatives from at least five life-boat Societies. The Institution, the United States Coast Guard, and the French, Netherlands and Swedish Societies were willing to appoint members to the editorial committee.

Before the delegates dispersed, they expressed a wish that the twelfth Conference, which was due to take place in 1975, should be held in Finland.

That a move in the direction of the Baltic was appropriate was shown just a year after the gathering in New York. Captain H. Hansson, Director of the Swedish Life-boat organization, who was a guest speaker at the Annual General Meeting of the R.N.L.I.

in 1971, was shortly to retire and was made an Honorary Life Governor. He was a moving spirit behind a conference held at Malmö between 29 and 31 May 1972 of voluntary life-boat societies, the first of its kind ever to be arranged. Besides the host nation, Finland, the Åland Islands, the Federal Republic of Germany, Great Britain and Ireland, the Netherlands, Norway and Spain sent delegates.

The R.N.L.I. delegates led by Commander Swann sailed via Holland, Bremerhaven, the Kiel Canal and Copenhagen in a 52 ft. 'Arun' prototype life-boat which had recently been shown to the public at Lambeth, on Thames-side. She was self-righting, with a maximum speed of 19 knots, derived from twin engines each of 375 h. p. She was built at Littlehampton in the yards of William Osborne. The previous autumn this boat had done sea trials off the coast of Spain, following a visit to London by a Spanish delegation. Spain had recently set up a new voluntary life-saving society, to be known as the Spanish Red Cross of the Sea. The crew of the prototype were able to provide familiarization exercises to men of the new Society.

The delegates at Malmö unanimously affirmed their belief in the economy and efficiency of a voluntary system of life-saving, but recognized that in some countries there was a case for financial support from central and local governments, as was so in some of the countries represented. Admiration and gratitude were expressed for the voluntary work done by women in different countries in raising funds for their rescue organizations.

The R.N.L.I. boat returned by way of Gothenburg, Oslo, Kristiansand and Stavanger, the voyage ending at Kirkwall on 10 June. She was due to take up operational duties replacing one of the 70 ft. boats which was due for periodical survey.

Meetings nearer home than New York or Malmö had brought a welcome return of the family of the Duke of Kent. The Duchess had been present at the Annual General Meeting of 20 April 1971, which had been held, for the first time, in the Royal Festival Hall. The following year, on 18 May, the President himself had attended, and had presented awards. On that occasion the Chair was taken by Commander Swann, who had recently succeeded Admiral Sir Wilfrid Woods as Chairman of the Committee of Management, two Deputy Chairmen being appointed, the Duke of Atholl and Major-General R. H. Farrant. Admiral Woods had

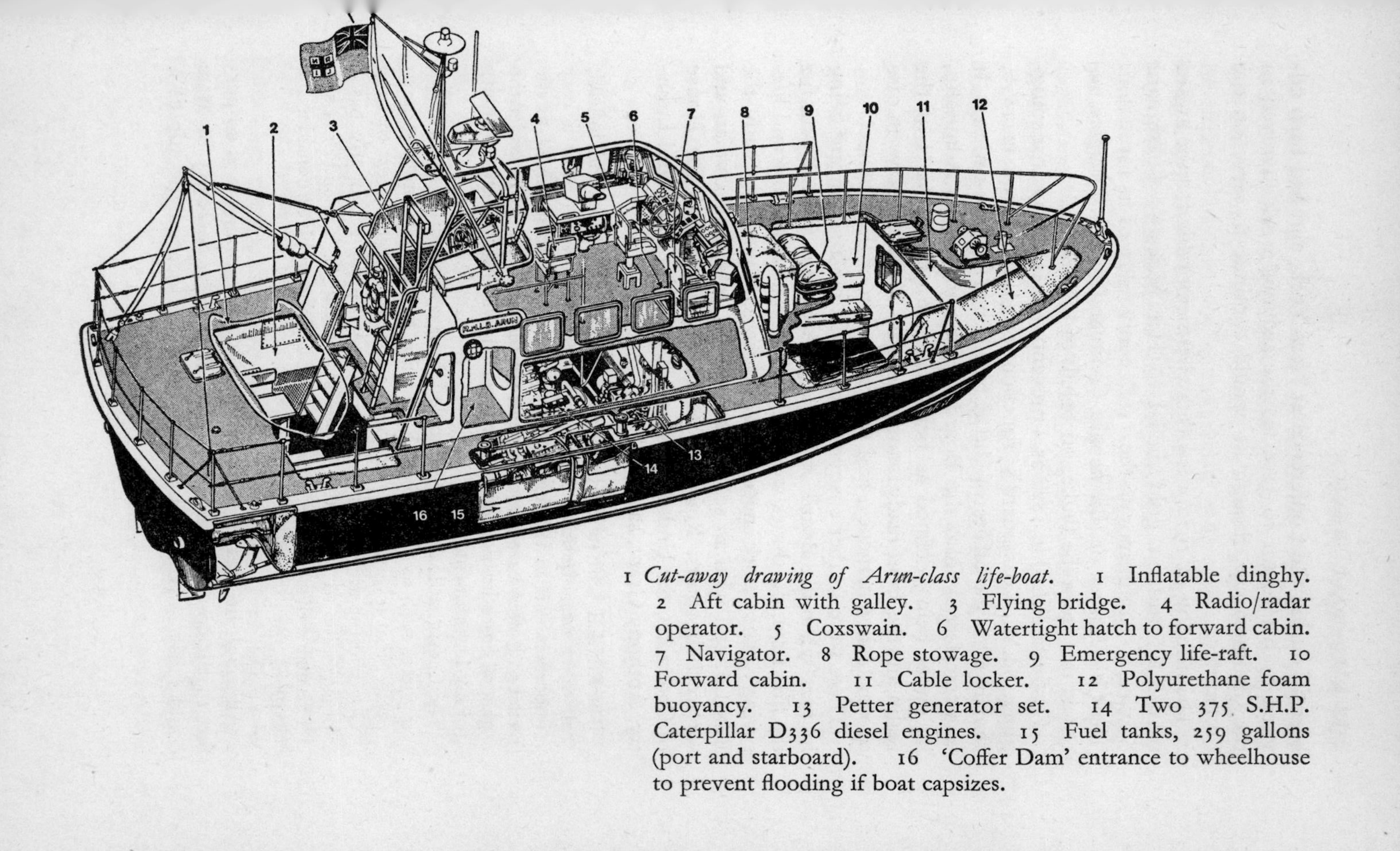

1 *Cut-away drawing of Arun-class life-boat.* 1 Inflatable dinghy. 2 Aft cabin with galley. 3 Flying bridge. 4 Radio/radar operator. 5 Coxswain. 6 Watertight hatch to forward cabin. 7 Navigator. 8 Rope stowage. 9 Emergency life-raft. 10 Forward cabin. 11 Cable locker. 12 Polyurethane foam buoyancy. 13 Petter generator set. 14 Two 375 S.H.P. Caterpillar D336 diesel engines. 15 Fuel tanks, 259 gallons (port and starboard). 16 'Coffer Dam' entrance to wheelhouse to prevent flooding if boat capsizes.

been ill during the Conference at New York, and had been advised by his doctor to give up the arduous work involved in the Chairmanship, though he would continue to serve on the Committee.

The meeting of 1972 was otherwise memorable for the award of the Institution's gold medal to Her Majesty's Coastguard Service, to commemorate the 150th anniversary of its formation. The Chief Inspector, Lieutenant-Commander J. A. Douglas, received this from the Duke, on behalf of his Service.

First established in 1822 as a preventive measure against smuggling, H.M. Coastguard's function radically altered in 1856, shortly after the affairs of the R.N.L.I. had been re-ordered. It was transferred from the Board of Customs to the Admiralty, its duties being defined as being defence of the coasts of the realm, and the 'more ready manning of Her Majesty's Navy in case of war or in emergency, and the protection of the revenue'.

There were further changes, one of the most significant being in 1925 when the Board of Trade took over control. Then, for the first time, the duties were defined as 'coast-watching and life-saving'. The work necessitated close co-operation with the R.N.L.I. and with all sea-rescue services, including civilian and service helicopters. Referring to the Coastguard in the House of Commons, the Under Secretary of State for Trade and Industry, Anthony Grant, said:

> The R.N.L.I. with its life-boats and inshore rescue boats and, indeed, all other organizations including ships at sea which play a very important part in this emergency activity, are all involved in the vital and often hazardous work of sea-rescue. They work under the general co-ordination of the Coastguard, which is the responsibility of my Department. . . .
>
> The Coastguards do a remarkable job of co-ordinating the various services, such as the R.N.L.I. and the R.A.F., but nothing is so perfect that it cannot be improved, and it is in that context that the Government are prepared to look carefully for a properly based organization to deal with all aspects of rescue, be it inland or at sea. This may well take time, as such considerations involve a considerable study. . . .

Although he was right to emphasize that nothing was so perfect that it could not be improved, the Under Secretary of State could fairly have added that it had never needed the stir of a major disaster to alert the rescue organizations into considering how best they could attune themselves to ever-changing conditions.

* * *

A man who was much in the news, while these more general events were unfolding, was Coxswain Derek Scott of the Mumbles in Wales. He had won the Institution's silver medal for rescues from the Dutch vessel *Kilo*, as already described, in addition to a British Empire Medal. On 12 April 1971 he made a very brave individual rescue, for which he received a second service clasp.

At 9.46 a.m. on the day concerned, Scott heard that a boy was in the sea, clinging to an upturned boat off the Mumbles slipway. Realizing that every second mattered, and leaving his wife to call out the Inshore Life-boat crew, he crossed the road to where a dinghy was lying. This was just over 10 feet long, with a 4 h.p. outboard motor.

Embarking in this craft, Scott was told by onlookers on Mumbles pier that the boat had drifted towards Mumbles Head. Off the Head there was a very confused sea, with breaking crests, and waves up to ten feet high.

Scott found the boy in the tide-race, exhausted. With great difficulty he headed the dinghy towards him, several times having to throw himself forward to prevent the dinghy being capsized bow over stern. When he reached the boy, Scott tied him to the dinghy with a line. Then he removed the engine, to clear a space to haul him aboard over the transom. This proved impossible until the dinghy's stern began to sink in the trough of a wave. Scott and the boy then landed backwards in the dinghy, and the boy was secured inboard. When the Inshore Life-boat arrived on the scene, the boy was transferred to it.

Later in the year Scott received recognition under the Institution's James Michael Bower Endowment Fund and the Maud Smith Bequest. It was scarcely surprising that he was invited to attend a 'Men of the Year' luncheon held at the Savoy Hotel on 10 November: for in addition to his other awards Scott had received a testimonial from the Royal Humane Society in 1959 for rescuing the crew of an upturned boat, and the Institution's bronze medal in 1968 for services to men of the sand-dredger *Steepleholme*.

If Scott's saving of the half-drowned boy was an instance of personal initiative rather than collective endeavour, it showed how quickly an emergency could arise, and how diverse could be the nature of the problems faced by those trained in sea-rescue. Two other instances were to occur not long afterwards, one in Orkney, and the other off that old haunt of the life-boat men, the Goodwin Sands.

The northern incident took place at Kirkwall, where the Institution's 70 ft. *Grace Paterson Ritchie* was afloat. Early in the morning of 8 November 1971, Staff Coxswain Robin Dennison heard that the Danish fishing vessel *Clupea* had broken adrift from the pier, and was aground to the east. The wind at the time was Force 10, gusting to Force 12, with a very rough sea and a heavy swell, which made conditions in the harbour extremely bad. The pier itself was awash, and three other Danish vesssels were pitching alongside in a dangerous way.

Shortly after the grounding of the *Clupea*, a second vessel, the *Kami*, broke adrift and grounded inside the *Clupea*. By skilful use of breeches buoy equipment, the Coastguard were able to hold both vessels, and thus prevent them from being driven farther ashore.

With weather conditions deteriorating, the general situation had by now reached a critical state. The two remaining fishing boats were breaking their moorings frequently, and there was immediate danger that they would break adrift altogether, and carry away the rescue lines which were aboard the two stranded boats.

At 9 a.m. Dennison decided to tow the two boats which were still moored to the pier to safety, and he thereupon took the life-boat out of harbour, a Danish seaman being aboard as interpreter. The Danish vessels, *Rosslau* and *Anne Stranne*, were taken clear of the pier, and later hove to. Dennison was then free to consider the best action to help the stranded boats.

He decided that the safest method of saving the crews was by towing the vessels off. He fired a rocket to the pier, and by this means passed a messenger rope to the Coastguard, who attached a tow-line to the securing line of the *Clupea*, which by this time had no power at all, and had sustained damage to her steering gear. The life-boat managed to tow the vessel to the *Rosslau*, which took over from her. The process was repeated with the *Kami*, and none too soon, as she was being heavily pounded.

The whole operation was successfully completed by 1.20 p.m. and the four ships were then able to proceed under their own power. Dennison advised the captains to take shelter at Shapinsay, and the life-boat was returned to her berth. Dennison was awarded the Bronze medal, and Service Certificates were sent to his crew of six.

The episode off the Goodwin Sands occurred on 24 May 1972. It involved exceptional local knowledge on the part of the Walmer coxswain and crew, which they may be said to have possessed almost from birth.

After a Coastguard report that a yacht was in trouble in the neighbourhood of the South Goodwin Light Vessel, and that she was firing flares, the life-boat was launched at 4.20 a.m. on a bleak day. The wind was south-south-west, its strength Force 8; visibility was poor, with mist and rain; and it was almost low water. The Coastguard had also reported that the yacht, with its engines broken down, was in very rough water and being driven towards wrecks. Although he was unable to see the flares, Coxswain Henry Brown deduced that she was in fact likely to be near the wreck of the *Luray Victory*, near the South Goodwin Buoy, and not the South Goodwin Light Vessel.

Soon after altering course in that direction, the crew saw a flare, and established radio contact with the yacht. By 5.30 a.m. the life-boat men found that the craft in trouble was the 21-ton ketch *Nell*. She was being driven on to the South Caliper Sands, and was seen to be touching bottom in the trough of the short, steep seas.

Brown, seeing that there was no time to be lost, made a first approach along the lee side, and put two of his own crew aboard. Three members of the yacht's crew were taken off, before the rolling of the *Nell* forced the life-boat to go astern. The yacht was hitting the bottom regularly, and rolling heavily to port. Brown took the lifeboat to her starboard side for a second attempt, losing three guard-rail stanchions in so doing. The life-boat was herself now bumping the bottom; nevertheless, two more people were taken off, with only about a hundred yards between the *Nell* and the wreck.

As the owner was reluctant to leave the yacht, Brown decided to try to tow her out of danger. At first he met with no success, and for twenty minutes no progress whatever was made. Brown then decided that he must take off the owner, also his two crew members and, having nothing to lose but the tow-rope, he put his engines full ahead. To the surprise of all present, the tow held, and the *Nell* was pulled clear of the Sands. The life-boat then towed her to Dover, where she arrived safely at 7.35 a.m.

The crew of the yacht certainly owed their lives to the local knowledge of the Walmer coxswain, who realized that she must in fact be three miles to the north-east of where she was believed to be, and was thus able to save her, as well as those on board, before she was pounded to pieces. Brown received the Thanks of the Institution inscribed on vellum, and his crew of six were given vellum Service Certificates for their work that day.

* * *

It had been an odd fact that whereas successive kings and queens had been Patrons of the Institution ever since its foundation, and that Queen Victoria had presented two life-boats, no reigning sovereign had ever named a life-boat until Queen Elizabeth II did so at Henley on 17 July 1972. The day was brilliant.

The boat concerned, the *Royal British Legion Jubilee*, belonged to the 48 ft. 6 in. 'Solent' class, with a displacement of 28 tons, a maximum speed of 9 knots, and a range, at this speed, of 127 miles. She had been built by Messrs Camper & Nicholson at Southampton, and had done trials in Spanish waters. There, off Corunna, she had proved her capabilities when her crew discovered the trawler *Carmen Vilarino* aground off Pragueira Point, in thick fog. The life-boat took off the trawler's crew of seven, who had taken to their raft. Lieutenant G. R. Cooper, R.N.R., the Inspector in charge of the operation, was able to complete the good work by saving the trawler.

There were many touches of colour at the ceremony, such as the appearance of the Queen's Bargemaster and her Watermen in their scarlet uniforms and peaked velvet caps, and there was the impressive drill of the Legion's standard bearers; but what was most significant was the way in which the life-boat had been provided. The sum received from the British Legion had been over £51,000. This had been handed over, in December 1971, to the Duke of Kent, as President of the R.N.L.I. It represented all but £19,000 of the cost of construction, the balance coming from the funds of the Institution. An appeal had been made to mark the fiftieth anniversary of the foundation of the Legion, and each member had been asked to subscribe not less than five new pence.

The boat had already proved herself, and it was in fact the third time during the year that a life-boat newly completed rendered service in rescues immediately after being on station. For on 22 May 1972 an Inshore Life-boat of the 18 ft. class designed by J. A. McLachlan, of which four others had then been built, had arrived at Oban for operational evaluation. Within two days she had saved three young people from a dinghy which was in trouble off Greag Island. Four days afterwards a man and a woman were rescued from the rocks after their craft had got into difficulties near Dunstaffnage Bay, the woman being unconscious and needing artificial respiration.

Then in October, very shortly after her naming at Littlehampton, the prototype of the 52-foot Arun class, which had been paid for with gifts from Miss Alice M. Johnston of Guildford and Birds Eye Foods Ltd, sailed for Guernsey. Within hours of arrival, on Friday 13th and in a north-easterly gale, the boat had gone to the help of a French trawler which was aground on the Roches Douvres, 25 miles from the French coast. Coxswain John Petit and the Guernsey men got to the scene just as the trawler was beginning to break up. The crew, which had taken to two dinghies, were soon safely aboard the *Arun*. John Petit had succeeded his father as coxswain and had been with him in the rescues from the *Johan Collett* nearly ten years earlier.

Christmas duty in 1972 proved arduous for the men of the life-boat at Islay, Inner Hebrides. A call came at 4.15 in the morning of Christmas Day to go to the help of the coaster *Raylight* of Greenock which was in trouble in a Force 9 gale. The ship's engines had broken down and a tug, summoned to try a tow, had had to put back owing to the weather conditions. No better luck attended a motor fishing vessel, or a German ship which, although she got a hawser across with the help of the life-boat, had to abandon her task when her screw became fouled.

At the onset of darkness, with the weather deteriorating still further, the *Raylight*'s master decided he must abandon ship. He and his two-man crew boarded a life-raft, from which they were picked up by the life-boat only 30 feet away from the shore. The life-boatmen did not return to their station until 8 p.m. on Christmas evening, having been away for over sixteen hours. Even then it was to a temporary berth, and they had to muster again on Boxing Day to put their boat back on its own moorings. Acting Coxswain Malcolm Mackay received the bronze medal, and appropriate certificates were awarded to the crew.

* * *

As it is sometimes alleged that the Institution has been slow to adopt new methods in design and techniques, certain considerations need to be remembered in regard to its building programme over the years. The paramount factor is of course the safety of life-boat crews, which means that no design or equipment could be adopted as standard until it had been exhaustively proved. The second is the sheer size of the fleet, consisting of about 160 boats with a life of 25 years if normally afloat, or 30 if housed ashore, followed by a few more on relief duties.

It was not feasible to scrap or dispose of more than the annual replacements, which in past years averaged about five boats. The number of suitable building yards is limited, and enlarging the programme formidable in cost. Safety apart, a further restriction on design is imposed by the fact that some two-thirds of the fleet must either be launched down slipways, from transporters or, in rare cases, down a beach. Until lately it was the policy of the Institution that life-boats, so far as possible, should be interchangeable. Accordingly, most boats could be launched down a slipway. This entailed a standard midship section and hull form, with propellers in protective tunnels. With such limitations it was almost impossible to improve speed.

The point seemed to have been established that a self-righting capability was necessary in all newly built life-boats. As a result, the intention was stated of having a completely self-righting fleet by 1980 at the latest. Meanwhile, some of the larger non-self-righting boats were made self-righting by structural alterations, and were fitted with an inflatable air-bag with an automatic valve, effective in the event of capsize. Trials of this invention were carried out at Cowes, in co-operation with the British Hovercraft Corporation.

The 37 ft. Mark I Oakley life-boat, which could be launched from a slipway or a transporter and which went into service in 1938, was the first of a type which was to figure prominently in the modern fleet. In a later modification there were notable improvements; chief among these was that the self-righting characteristic was achieved not, as in the Mark I, by the transference of water-ballast, but because, by virtue of her profile, the boat was unstable in the capsized position. Oakley's larger boat, the 48 ft. 6 in. class, first seen at the Scottish Conference of 1963, has been modified to enable the coxswain to steer from amidships.

The delegation visiting the United States in 1964 had been much impressed by the sea-keeping qualities of the 44 ft. steel life-boat favoured by the Coast Guard service. At that time some thirty of this type had been built by the U.S. Coast Guard in their yard at Curtis Bay on the Chesapeake. Among the characteristics of this boat were high speed and a self-righting capability, whilst their twin Cummins diesel engines gave good power for towing.

The opportunity of acquiring one of these boats for the Institution was a useful time-saver in the process of evolving a faster home product. The American boat proved a great success, as the result of which six were ordered of a similar pattern, but with an aluminium instead of a steel deck.

The Institution's own designers then drew up plans for a 50 ft. boat basically of the American type, but with slightly greater speed – 17 knots, produced by two General Motors engines, each of 390 h.p. It was planned that the first of the class should be stationed afloat at Falmouth. The 50 ft. boats would be only slightly less fast than the Arun class, with a service speed of 18·8 knots. Future Arun boats, which will be constructed of Glass Reinforced Plastic (GRP) will have rather more power than that of the prototype, and will have a lower deck-line. The hulls are virtually unsinkable, so many spaces being filled with polyurethane.

The development of Inshore Life-boats has, from the nature of the case, been faster than progress with conventional life-boats. The rigid-hull 18 ft. design of 1968 by McLachlan followed the inflatable craft of six years earlier. She has proved a good sea-boat, and can reach a speed of 22 knots with petrol engines, or 18½ knots with diesel. Her chief disadvantage over the inflatables is weight, which prevents a launch down an open beach. The McLachlan and the Atlantic 21-types have a night capability, and the latter, which are powered by two 40 h.p. outboard motors, can maintain a speed of 28 knots.

Such a progressive building programme shows an awareness by the Committee of Management of where existing equipment most needs improvement, also confidence in its future. The best disposition of the Institution's fleet is indicated by a regular stream of data useful for planning operations. The enormous value of such information was emphasized by a Coast Review Working Party which was set up in the earlier 1960s under the chairmanship of Admiral Sir William Slayter.

The entire coastline of the United Kingdom and Ireland was covered; every life-boat station was examined, and the records of every casualty over a ten-year period. Current service records are now computerized.

A system such as this is essential to the efficient deployment of the life-boat fleet. It is fully in line with the ideas expressed in an official Report on Search and Rescue, which appeared in 1970. As a result of the observations therein, a Search and Rescue Committee was set up by the Department of Trade and Industry, the R.N.L.I. being at present the only non-official body represented. The role of the Institution in Search and Rescue is therefore fully established, and the cover for which it is responsible is defined. The Committee is also invaluable as a forum for the exchange of information between, for example, the Institution and the Coastguard, which now controls its own helicopter service.

* * *

The complexity and cost of the Institution's building programme reflected ever-increasing demands. It entailed such an amount of business for the Committee of Management that steps were taken to try to ease some of its burden. An Executive Committee was appointed in 1970; flexibility was introduced into the hours of meeting so as to give more opportunity to men who could not always spare time in the mornings from their own concerns; and a firm of management consultants was invited to make a detailed assessment of the organization and operations.

These consultants were given wide terms of reference, to include investigation of the relationship of the Institution to other bodies engaged in marine search and rescue; the functions of the permanent staff; fund-raising methods; and the advantages and drawbacks of office and depot organizations.

The resulting report endorsed the soundness of the operational plans, and suggested administrative changes which were agreed. The first was that more opportunities should be given to associate voluntary workers with decision-making. This would be done through area committees. If these bodies gained sufficient support, they would be entitled to provide a number of members to serve on the Committee of Management, whose composition would thus be varied; some members being elected by the Governors of the Institution at the Annual General Meeting; others by the new area bodies, and others by co-option. In line with this recommendation, there would be greater decentralization, with fuller responsibility given to area staffs, who would have more direct budgetary control and more involvement in publicizing activities.

The headquarters staff would in future consist of one Division and four Departments. The Chief Inspector of Life-boats would be in charge of the Division, which would concern itself with operations and their technical support. The business of the Departments would be Fund-raising; Finance; Public Relations; and Personnel. The report drew attention to the fact that the burden of work had nearly trebled during the previous eight years, whereas the staff had increased by only one-third.

Perhaps the most radical recommendation concerned the future site of the head office and of the depot at Boreham Wood. It was agreed that, with the exception of a small office which would continue in London, both the administrative headquarters and the depot would be moved to the provinces. Shortly afterwards, in October 1972, it was announced to the Press that a site had been bought at Poole, Dorset, and that a move thereto would be made very gradually over the course of the next few years. It was expected that the cost of the project would be covered by the sale of former properties and through economies brought about by rationalization.

The consultants paid handsome tribute to the great services rendered by voluntary workers; and of the crews of the life-boats they wrote: 'In these people, their calibre, experience and enthusiasm, lies much of the Institution's strength.'

* * *

In the long history of the Institution, one factor has been constant: the success of its work has depended upon a steady revenue. Apart from legacies, and from substantial outright gifts, funds are raised by the assiduity and skill of staff members whose main duty it is to ensure that the flow never dries up.

The principle is that in every fund-raising region, of which there are thirteen, including Scotland and Ireland, there is a full-time District Organizing Secretary helped by one or more assistants. The function of these Organizers is to look after Financial Branches of the area. There are over two thousand of these in the United Kingdom and Ireland.

Money is raised through the energy and ingenuity of local committees, most of whose members are women. Those who work for regional offices are responsible to the fund-raising staff at headquarters. They are themselves supported by the Boreham Wood depot, which supplies them with display material, collecting boxes, miniature flags—everything they need for their appeals.

Over the decades, thousands of people of every age and condition have by their sustained efforts ensured that the R.N.L.I. remains efficient on a voluntary basis, with no interference from outside. It would be easy to collect material for a separate volume given solely to fund-raising, and it would be full of incident and humour. For experience has shown that the two ways by which money is most easily attracted is through a wave of sympathy such as is felt after a tragedy at sea, or, in times of less stress, by putting people into a cheerful frame of mind, so that they give with pleasure.

Over the years, the pages of the Institution's journal have been full of accounts of lively fund-raising. Moreover, although it is tirelessly reiterated that this is a cynical age, with no time for hero-worship, any collector knows that there is a reservoir of goodwill among the general public. This is drawn upon year by year with impressive results.

Earlier examples of fund-raising have been referred to, notably the achievements of Sir Charles Macara and the organizers of the Saturday Life-boat Fund which was the outcome of his zeal. Inspiration continues, not least among the young, who seize every opportunity, and even enlist the help of their pets, to further the cause they have adopted. One of the more notable of many recent examples was the Blue Peter Appeal. This was made on 5 December 1966 and called for 60,000 paperback books. The response was so great that the 250,000 books sent in paid for four inshore life-boats. These were stationed at Littlehampton, Beaumaris, North Berwick and St Agnes. The young sponsors have since kept a tally of the operational launchings of the boats and of the lives they have saved.

Currently, races of all kinds, sponsored walks and swims, auctions of antiques are widely favoured. Their popularity will doubtless continue and expand. On a different level, the growth of the Yachtsmen's Life-boat Supporters Association produces an increasing income. An appeal to a wider public was made in 1972 with the launching of Shoreline (incorporating the Y.L.A.), designed to attract regular support by offering Associate Membership; Membership and Governorship; Life Membership and Governorship, through a graduated scale of subscription. A single gift of £60 or more makes the donor not only a Governor of the Institution, but carries voting rights at the Annual General Meeting.

The lessening value of money affects the Institution, as it must every charitable body. Since the end of the Second World War it has not proved possible to build up substantial reserves. In view of the scope of the programme, with a target of some ten new boats a year to achieve a fully self-righting fleet by 1980, this is a state of affairs likely to continue. Twenty years ago, the cost of running the organization was between £600,000 and £700,000 annually. Today it is over £3,000,000, so that the fund-raisers have a stiff problem in keeping pace with inflation. The task is never easy and efforts are never relaxed.

Great encouragement is found in the continuance of outright gifts of money for the provision of life-boats by organizations, firms and individuals. Moreover, there is a sustained attitude of generosity on the part of many suppliers of equipment and commodities essential for life-boatmen. Notable examples have been the gift of lubricant, for all types of machinery, by

Messrs Duckham, and of brandy by Messrs Martell. Incidentally, spirits are administered in strict accordance with rules laid down by the Institution, and are never given to those with head wounds or those who are unconscious from immersion.

It is heartening that legacies steadily increase. Income from legacies is of course imponderable, being subject to the fluctuations of the stock market, but it has always provided a substantial part of the revenue. Those who have the cause at heart thus continue their support long after they have themselves passed away.

Such is the state of things as the Institution prepares to celebrate its 150th anniversary. Sir William Hillary's aims remain as sound as when he made them known. Those who took up his work share his enthusiasm. The quality of the life-boat crews, and of those who provide the means to enable them to do their work, is as high as ever – and of the continuing need for their services there is massive evidence. By the time of the Centenary in 1924 the R.N.L.I. had saved the lives of nearly 60,000 people from death by drowning. During the last fifty years, that number has grown to nearly 100,000.

In practical terms, how is it all achieved?

At the end of the nineteenth century, when Charles Dibdin, that supremely devoted Secretary, was being examined by the Parliamentary Committee appointed to look into the affairs of the R.N.L.I., he referred more than once to the 'Green Book'. Green was then, and is still, the colour favoured for the cover of the regulations which govern the work of the Life-boat service, from the formation of local branches down to the responsibility for cleaning up a life-boat when she returns from sea.

Branches are of two kinds: station branches, in places where life-boats are maintained, and financial branches, which are found throughout the United Kingdom and Ireland. Liaison is particularly close when, as often happens, both kinds of branch operate in the same area. Financial branches meet some of the day-to-day running expenses incurred by the local station branch, remitting any surplus funds to headquarters.

There are also Ladies' Life-boat Guilds, dedicated to fund-raising. Sometimes they work in conjunction with a station or financial branch, sometimes in direct contact with District Organising Secretaries. It is an essential condition of membership that a gift should be made to the funds, and that some form of personal service should be undertaken each year.

District organizing secretaries throughout the country exist to help branches in the activities of fund-raising. Within this field, they correspond to the operational staff, and to the inspectors of life-boats who supervise the technical side of the Institution's work.

In a station branch, in addition to a president, chairman, honorary secretary, honorary treasurer and at least four other annual subscribers, it is usual to invite the inspector of Coastguard, the local officer of Coastguard, the harbour master, the customs officer, Lloyd's agent or sub-agent, and the senior police officer to join the committee. The honorary secretary undertakes the management of the station, conducts correspondence with headquarters and, in normal circumstances, after receiving notice of a casualty or an emergency from the Coastguard, gives orders for assembling the crew and launching the life-boat. The form of summons is still by maroon, with the telephone as an essential supplement. Maroons have the advantage of giving visible and audible warning to station helpers such as shore signalmen, shore attendants, winchmen and launchers. They can be particularly useful when, as sometimes happens, telephone lines are torn down by gales.

The normal complement of a life-boat consists of a coxswain, a second coxswain, a motor mechanic who doubles as radio operator, an assistant motor mechanic, and as many other hands as may be necessary and available to manage the boat at sea in any particular emergency. About seven men usually embark, and they perform duties as directed by the coxswain. Formerly each life-boat crew included a bowman, who was in line of succession for coxswain, and who, when afloat, had charge of the anchor and cable. Since 1968 the rank has been allowed to lapse.

At every life-boat station there is kept a list of 'enrolled members of the life-boat crew'. This allows a generous margin for contingencies. For instance, where it is usual to proceed to sea on a service call with a crew of six or seven, there may be as many as fifteen or more who could fill their places. There is competition for the privilege of crew membership, and the list is drawn up by the honorary secretary in consultation with the coxswain.

Coxswains and second coxswains receive annual retaining fees, as do certain others such as the head launchers at stations where a transporter is used, shore signalmen, and winchmen. The winchman's duty can be intricate. With a slipway, a life-boat is launched by releasing a pin with a hammer-blow. The return requires considerable power from the winch motor, and sometimes it is necessary to await a suitable state of tide and sea before the boat can be re-housed. Meanwhile, she rides to a mooring.

The coxswain not only takes charge at sea, but is responsible for the efficiency, good order and cleanliness of the life-boathouse and slipway as well as the life-boat and her gear. After a service or exercise he supervises the hosing-down of the boat and all ropes, life-belts and other equipment with fresh water. He is also responsible for the care of the emergency provisions which are kept in each life-boat, primarily for the use of survivors.

Motor mechanics, who on some stations also serve as coxswains, are usually full-time servants of the Institution, other crew members being part-time. It is the mechanic who, more often than not, becomes the guide to those who visit a life-boat station with the idea of learning something about its work. These visits can be impressive. One of the first things which may strike a member of the public is the orderliness and the readiness of every object, from the spotless life-boat herself, fuelled for instant call, down to the rows of clothing, life-jackets and sea boots at hand for that sudden emergency—as often as not in winter darkness, with a high sea roaring at the bottom of the slipway.

Stations which operate an inshore life-boat only are, in general, organized in a similar way, but on a smaller scale, and with younger crews. They usually call on the service of about six or seven people, with helpers as available.

Every life-boat station has a history, recorded not only in the minute books of the local committee, but on boards in the life-boathouse itself, and in photographs and other memorials. Most stations with any length of service have attracted their own historians, and the growing library of their work is one of great fascination. Stations with exceptional records are the pride of their district—Ramsgate for instance, which in May 1973 brought its total of lives rescued to 2,000, with Great Yarmouth and Gorleston and Holyhead not far behind; Whitby, with a record of six gold medal services associated with it; Cromer; Douglas, Isle of Man, with its links with Hillary; old-established Scots and Irish stations like Montrose, Arbroath and Howth. Very rightly, such places become objects of pilgrimage among those to whom the sea has a strong appeal.

It is natural enough to think of the life-boat service in a romantic way, but those who run it are entirely matter-of-fact. The life-boatman in his orange protective clothing, turning out on a wild night on his errand of mercy is a disciplined specialist bred to the sea or deeply familiar with its ways, with exceptional local knowledge, and with trust between him and his fellows. He is a crew member because he wants to be; because, in a great many cases, there is a life-boat tradition in his family; and because he believes that what he is risking his life for is worth while. Every life-boatman is sustained by the full resources of the Institution, and nearly always by a home where the womenfolk are equally ready to serve the cause.

The R.N.L.I. is regarded, throughout the world, as the parent of all voluntary life-boat societies. It has created for itself a seemingly inexhaustible fund of respect, affection, and goodwill. Delegations from abroad continue to look to it for example and advice, and its status is unique. Sir William Hillary made a far greater contribution to the progress of humanity than he could ever have known. He generated enormous power for good, not only in his own country but in others which have been glad to follow his lead.

The coxswain and crew on service; the organizers of life-boat days and special events; the little girl selling flags with her pet beside her, are backed by an organization which for a century and a half has worked tirelessly to become efficient in all its activities. The R.N.L.I. continues to devise new means to its selfless end, and to give the brave and skilful men, who serve in the same spirit as their predecessors, the best equipment.

10

Postscript

In at least two ways, both of them serious, this 150th Anniversary history is incomplete. Even during the time when it is in course of production, a succession of launches will have been made. Rescues will have been achieved or attempted, and a hundred and one events may have occurred which to some degree will affect the future. Omissions are inevitable, however much they may be regretted. But what may not be so readily understood or forgiven is the emphasis given to particular areas, stations or people. With such a wealth of information to draw upon, selection becomes necessary or the narrative expands to an impossible size. If the proportions should seem wrong to some, it is possible that they will be more approved by others. What is plain is that much has been omitted which it would have been a pleasure to include.

As regards the future, there are those who are uneasy about the voluntary principle continuing to be applied to the life-boat service. It is nearly eighty years since the matter of State control was raised at the Parliamentary Inquiry of 1897. The answer was given in no faltering terms; but in that distant era many organizations depended on private charity, including the great hospitals. Social and economic conditions have since then radically changed.

Critics take their stand on at least two notions. Why, they say, should a service whose effort is for the benefit of all seafarers depend on the goodwill of charitable people, many of whom give only casually? And if, by good management, the work, under such a system, is done well and economically, could it not equally be so if it were put under official control?

Defenders of the voluntary principle need to be armed with arguments. One of the many variegated and sometimes grotesque comments they often hear is that costly boats and equipment are used infrequently, and that they represent so much idle capital, even though, when called upon, they may be needed desperately. Another is that, as the crews are for the most part not full time, they have too little chance during the course of exercises, which are often held under comparatively favourable conditions, to weld themselves into a team in that exceptional sense which can be so necessary to meet emergencies.

The historian's business is to assess what has been achieved under the prevailing system and, where necessary, to note shortcomings. Being composed of fallible human beings, the Institution's staff, and its committees, are as liable to err, in matters of administration as well as in the execution of their task, as any other group of people. But the sum of achievement over the last century and a half speaks so eloquently that there can be no doubt of its value and the power of its example.

On the mitred caps of grenadiers, the picked men of the earlier British infantry regiments, there was an embroidered motto, *Nec aspera terrent* (Difficulties do not daunt us). What was true of the grenadiers has always been true of the life-boat service, and it has applied as much in the realm of policy as in the face of the sea.

Not the wisest can tell what the future may hold. But what is quite beyond argument is that the Institution's record is unsurpassed by any comparable body. It has been achieved by courage, skill, and the eagerness to give.

Appendix I

GOLD MEDAL AWARDS

The list of Gold Medals awarded by the R.N.L.I. includes 'Second Service Clasps' where indicated. Ranks are given as at the time of the service concerned. S.C. = Service Clasp.

Name and Rank where appropriate	*Station where appropriate*	*Casualty where appropriate*	*Date of Award*
H.M. King George IV		Honorary	14 May 1825
H.R.H. The Duke of York		Honorary	14 May 1825
His Grace the Archbishop of Canterbury		Honorary	14 May 1825
Fremantle, C. H. Captain, R.N.	Christchurch	Unknown Swedish Brig	10 July 1824
Clarke, Joseph Lieutenant, R.N.	Birling (Eastbourne)	Brig *Juno*	8 Dec. 1824
Hillary, Sir William Baronet		Awarded as Founder. (Sir William Hillary's later awards were bestowed for gallantry)	10 March 1825
Manby, G. W. Captain		Presented as a testimony of the great utility of his life-saving apparatus	10 March 1825
Bennett, C. G. Captain, R.N.	Lyme Regis	Ship *Unity*	5 Jan. 1825
Grandy, S. Lieutenant, R.N.	Portsmouth	Ship *Admiral Berkeley*	9 Feb. 1825
Randall, Henry Lieutenant, R.N., Coastguard	Elie N.B.	Ship *Devoran*	9 Feb. 1825
Peake, Thomas L. Captain, R.N.		Ship *Admiral Berkeley*	2 March 1825
De St Croix, Mr P.	St Helier	*Fanny* of St Malo	27 July 1825
De St Croix, Mr Francis	St Helier	*Fanny* of St Malo	27 July 1825
De St Croix, Mr Jean	St Helier	*Fanny* of St Malo	27 July 1825
Morris, John Rowe Captain, R.N., Coastguard	Newcastle, Ireland	Ship *Richard Pope*	5 April 1826

Name and Rank where appropriate	*Station where appropriate*	*Casualty where appropriate*	*Date of Award*
Wilson, Thomas Member of Parliament		Chairman—1824–52	18 April 1826
Joy, McGeorge Master, H.M. Cutter *Mermaid*	Holy Island	Ship *John & Jessie*	13 Sept. 1826
Else, Lieutenant, R.N.	Fowey	Ship *Providence*	18 Oct. 1826
Bowen, C. H. Lieutenant, R.N.	Fraserburgh	*Rose* of Wick	31 Jan. 1827
Lindsay, James Lieutenant, R.N.	Fort George	Sloop *Lively*	7 Feb. 1827
Jobson, Christopher Lieutenant, R.N., Coastguard	Arbroath	Ship *Alice*	28 March 1827
Matthews, R.B. Lieutenant, R.N.	Lowestoft	*The Lord Duncan*	24 Oct. 1827
Hillary, Sir William (2nd S.C.) Baronet	Isle of Man	Ship *Fortroendert*	16 Jan. 1828
Blois, J. R. Captain, R.N.	Glynn, Ireland	Steamer *Venus*	20 Aug. 1828
Brunden, J. Lieutenant, R.N. Chief Officer of Coastguard	Boulmer	Schooner *Triton*	10 Dec. 1828
Lloyd, Sam Lieutenant, R.N., Coastguard	Ballycotton	Brig *Capricho* (Spanish)	18 Feb. 1829
Broad, William Lloyd's Agent	Falmouth	Brig *Sarah*	10 June 1829
Lingard, John Lieutenant, R.N.	Whitby	Brig *Esther*	19 Aug. 1829
Hutchison, H. Lieutenant, R.N.	Kingshorn	Brig *Duke*	11 Nov. 1829
Graham, Philip Captain, R.N.	Walmer	Brig *Mountaineer*	10 Feb. 1830
Johnson, W. W. P. Lieutenant, R.N.	Walmer	Brig *Mountaineer*	10 Feb. 1830
Walls, Wm. Stephen Lieutenant, R.N.	Walmer	Brig *Mountaineer*	10 Feb. 1830
Jones, Richard Lieutenant, R.N., Coastguard	Whitby	Brig *Smalls*	10 Feb. 1830
Prattent, John Lieutenant, R.N.	Hastings, H.M. *Hyperion*	Lugger *La Constance* (French)	10 March 1830

Name and Rank where appropriate	*Station where appropriate*	*Casualty where appropriate*	*Date of Award*
James, Horatio Lieutenant, R.N.	Hastings, H.M. *Hyperion*	Lugger *La Constance* (French)	10 March 1830
Hillary, Sir William (3rd S.C.) Baronet	Isle of Man	Sloop *Eclipse*	27 Nov. 1830
Hillary, Sir William (4th S.C.) Baronet	Isle of Man	Steamer *St George*	15 Dec. 1830
Robinson, Robert Lieutenant, R.N.	Isle of Man	Steamer *St George*	15 Dec. 1830
Manby, G. W. Captain (2nd S.C.)		For his method for forcing boats from a beach through a heavy surf	15 Dec. 1830
Jones, Richard (2nd S.C.) Lieutenant, R.N., Coastguard		Sloop *Northfield*	5 Jan. 1831
James, William Lieutenant, R.N.	Falmouth	Brig *Le Bon Père*	5 Jan. 1831
H.M. King William IV		As Patron	30 March 1831
Earle, E. C. Lieutenant, R.N.	Rye	Brig *Fame*	4 May 1831
Steane, John Lieutenant, R.N.	Rye	Brig *Fame*	4 May 1831
Turner, Charles Lieutenant, R.N.	Fraserburgh	Sloop *Janet*	1 June 1831
Leigh, Thomas Lieutenant, R.N., Coastguard	Winterton	Brig *Annabella Colm*	21 Sept 1831
Parey, R. M. Lieutenant, R.N.	Rye	Fishing boat *L'Arnée*	25 Jan. 1832
Leigh, Thomas (2nd S.C.) Lieutenant, R.N., Coastguard	Winterton	Ship *Crawford Davison*	24 April 1833
Sumner, W. Richard Surgeon	Formby, Liverpool	Pilot Boat *Good Intent*	12 Dec. 1833
Snell, George Lieutenant, R.N., Coastguard	Dungeness	Brig *Pioneer*	29 Jan. 1834
Randall, Henry (2nd S.C.) Lieutenant, R.N., Coastguard	Anstruther	Schooner *Wanderer*	21 May 1834

Name and Rank where appropriate	*Station where appropriate*	*Casualty where appropriate*	*Date of Award*
Owen, William Master Mariner	Holyhead	Ship *Plutarch* (American)	7 Oct. 1835
Williams, Rev. James	Holyhead	*Active Sarah*	7 Oct. 1835
Somerville, John Lieutenant, R.N., Coastguard	New Romney	Brig *Industry*	28 Oct. 1835
Cox, H. Lieutenant, R.N., Chief Officer, Coastguard	St Andrews	Schooner *Tid* of Dundee	28 Oct. 1835
Jelland, W. John Master Mariner	*The Agendria* (at sea)	*Francis Speight*	10 March 1836
Walsh, W. Martin Master Mariner	Wexford	Ship *Glasgow* (American)	16 Aug. 1837
Essell, William Folkes Lieutenant, R.N., Coastguard	Carnsore	Sloop *Anne and Elizabeth*	28 Feb. 1838
Stark, Peter Lieutenant, R.N., Coastguard	Broughty Ferry	*Ranger of Perth*	21 March 1838
Rymer, D. Lieutenant, R.N., Chief Officer Coastguard	Berwick	Schooner *Margaret of Dundee*	9 May 1838
Hoed, W. Francis Philip Master Mariner	Netherlands Ship *Phénomene*	Ship *Columbia* of Liverpool	6 June 1838
Browne, P. R., Captain	Dundrum	Schooner *Bloom*	15 Nov. 1838
Britain, G. S. Lieutenant, R.N.	Whitby	Brig *Jupiter* of Whitby	15 Nov. 1838
Ross, Thomas Captain, R.N., Inspecting Commander Coastguard	Swords District, Ireland	Brig *Gainsborough*	9 Jan. 1839
Symmes, H. A. S. Lieutenant, R.N.	Isle of Wight	Brig *Claire* (French)	9 Jan. 1839
Lett, S. J. Lieutenant, R.N., Chief Officer of Coastguard	Rosslare, Ireland	Ship *Ariadne*	9 Jan. 1839
Thompson, R. K. Chief Officer, Coastguard	Clogher Head	Schooner *Minerva*	17 April 1839

Name and Rank where appropriate	*Station where appropriate*	*Casualty where appropriate*	*Date of Award*
Collins, John Master Mariner	American ship *Roscius*	Ship *Scotia*	8 Jan. 1840
Metherall, R. R. Lieutenant, R.N., Coastguard	Youghal	Brig *Medora*	15 April 1840
Sewell, H. J. Lieutenant, R.N., Coastguard	Newcastle (Co. Down)	Smack *Sarah*	9 Nov. 1840
Marsh, Digby Captain, R.N., Coastguard	Brighton	Brig *Mary*, Schooner *Sir John Seale*, Brig *Offerton*	17 Dec. 1840
Macnamara, Timothy Lieutenant, R.N., Coastguard	Littlehampton	*Billy Boy Victoria.* Sloop *Lively*	17 Dec. 1840
Steel, W. Charles Coastguard	Scilly	Steamer *Thames*	4 March 1841
Quadling, W. B. E. Chief Officer, Coastguard	Courtmacsherry (Co. Cork)	Brig *Salona*	13 April 1842
Vicary, William Lieutenant, R.N., Coastguard	Atherfield, Isle of Wight	Brig *George*	8 Feb. 1843
Bulley, John Lieutenant, R.N., Coastguard	Atherfield, Isle of Wight	Brig *George*	8 Feb. 1843
Britton, John Master Mariner	At sea. American ship *Rochester*	Ship *Dorchester*	30 July 1845
Bulley, John (2nd S.C.) Lieutenant, R.N., Coastguard	Atherfield, Isle of Wight	Ship *Llanrumney*	10 Feb. 1848
Pym, R. E. Lieutenant, R.N.	Whitby	Fishing boat *Harm* of Christchurch	5 Nov. 1848
Goss, Thomas Lieutenant, R.N., Coastguard	Dunmanus	Ship *Mountaineer*	16 Jan. 1851
Davies, George Captain, R.N.	Penzance	Brig *New Commercial* of Whitby	30 Jan. 1851
Howard, T. R. Commander	Penzance	Brig *New Commercial* of Whitby	30 Jan. 1851
Palmer, George Member of Parliament	Nazing Park, Essex	In consideration of the services of the life-boats built on his plan	3 March 1853

Name and Rank where appropriate	*Station where appropriate*	*Casualty where appropriate*	*Date of Award*
Ludlow, Isaac Captain	At sea. American ship *Monmouth* of New York	Ship *Meuadan*	5 Jan. 1854
Hamilton, H. A. Chief boatman, Coastguard	Balbriggan	Brig *Tregiste* of Trieste	2 Dec. 1858
Peake, James H.M. Dockyard	Devonport	Designer of the life-boat of the Institution	3 Feb. 1859
Rodgers, Joseph Seaman *Royal Charter*	Anglesey	Steamer *Royal Charter* of Liverpool	3 Nov. 1859
Cobb, Rev. Charles	Dymchurch	Lugger *Courrier de Dieppe* of Dieppe	17 Jan. 1867
Perrott, Sir Edward G. L. Baronet		Presented for his long and most valuable services as Chairman of the Preparatory Committee of the Institution	7 March 1872
Elyard, Captain Honorary Secretary at Broadstairs Branch	Broadstairs	Schooner *Lion* of Goole	6 April 1876
Cubitt, Wm. Son of Hon. Sec.	Bacton	Schooner *Richard Warbrick* of Fleetwood	5 Feb. 1880
Torrens, John Lieutenant, 2nd Dragoons	Poolbeg	Schooner *Robert Brown* of Wavenpoint	6 Jan. 1881
Fish, Chas. E. Coxswain	Ramsgate	Ship *Indian Chief* of Liverpool	25 Jan. 1881
Chapman, Thomas Chairman, F.R.S.		Chairman, 1873–83	5 April 1883
Ward, Vice-Admiral John Ross Chief Inspector of Life-boats		Served the Institution 1852–83	7 June 1883
Fish, Charles E. (2nd S.C.) Coxswain	Ramsgate	On his retirement	8 Oct. 1891
McCombie, Thos. Master of Irish lights	Dublin	Ship *Palme* of Finland	9 Jan. 1896

Name and Rank where appropriate	Station where appropriate	Casualty where appropriate	Date of Award
Haylett, James Late Assistant Coxswain	Caister	Services during 50 years, and at accident to No. 2 Life-boat	9 Feb. 1905
Rees, Daniel Solicitor	Barry	Yacht *Firefly*	11 July 1907
Owen, Milliani Coxswain	Holyhead	S.S. *Harold* of Liverpool	12 March 1908
O'Shea, Rev. John Michael	Ardmore	Schooner *Teaser* of Montrose	13 April 1911
Langlands, Thomas Coxswain	Whitby	S.S. *Rohilla*	12 Nov. 1914
Smith, Robert Coxswain	Tynemouth	S.S. *Rohilla*	12 Nov. 1914
Burton, Captain H. E. Hon. Superintendent of Motor-boat	Tynemouth	S.S. *Rohilla*	12 Nov. 1914
Blogg, Henry George Coxswain	Cromer	S.S. *Fernebo*	9 Feb. 1917
Howells, John Coxswain	Fishguard	Schooner *Hermina* of Rotterdam	17 Dec. 1920
Swan, John J. Coxswain	Lowestoft	S.S. *Hopelyn* of Newcastle	17 Nov. 1922
Fleming, Wm. G. Coxswain	Gorleston	S.S. *Hopelyn* of Newcastle	17 Nov. 1922
North and South Holland Lifeboat Society		Centenary of that Society	18 Nov. 1924
South Holland Life-saving Society		Centenary of that Society	18 Nov. 1924
Jones, Captain Owen Volunteer Life-boatman	Moelfre	Ketch *Excel* of Poole	17 Nov. 1927
Roberts, William Second Coxswain	Moelfre	Ketch *Excel* of Poole	17 Nov. 1927
Blogg, Henry George (2nd S.C.) Coxswain	Cromer	Dutch oil tanker *Georgia*	15 Dec. 1927
Patton, Robert Coxswain	Runswick	S.S. *Dispenser* of West Hartlepool	8 March 1934
Sliney, Patrick Coxswain	Ballycotton	Daunt Rock Lightship	12 March 1936
Cross, Robert Coxswain	Humber	S.T. *Gwith* of Grimsby	14 March 1940
Boyle, John Coxswain	Arranmore	S.S. *Stolwyke* of Rotterdam	17 April 1941

Name and Rank where appropriate	*Station where appropriate*	*Casualty where appropriate*	*Date of Award*
Blogg, Henry George (3rd S.C.) Coxswain	Cromer No. 1	S.S. *Oxshott*, S.S. *Gallois*, S.S. *Deerwood* and S.S. *Paddy Hendly*	11 Sept. 1941
McLean, John B. Coxswain	Peterhead	S.S. *Runswick*, S.S. *Fiora* and S.S. *Saltwick*	12 March 1942
Bennison, Lieut. W. H. Coxswain	Hartlepool	S.S. *Hawkwood* of London	12 March 1942
Murphy, Patrick Coxswain	Newcastle (Co. Down)	S.S. *Browning* of Liverpool	21 May 1942
Cross, Robert (2nd S.C.) Coxswain	Humber	H.M.T. *Almondine*	11 Feb. 1943
Gammon, William J. Coxswain	The Mumbles	H.M.C.S. *Cheboque*	14 Dec. 1944
King, Thomas J. Coxswain	St Helier, Jersey	Yacht *Maurice Georges* of Jersey	8 Dec. 1949
Evans, Richard M. Coxswain	Moelfre	M.V. *Hindlea*	10 Dec. 1959
Petit, Capt. Hubert Ernest Coxswain	St Peter Port	Norwegian M.V. *Johan Collett*	11 April 1963
German Life-boat Society	Bremen	On the occasion of the Centenary in 1965	10 Dec. 1964
French Central Life-boat Society	Paris	On the occasion of the Centenary in 1965	10 Dec. 1964
Harvey, Lieut-Cdr. Harold Inspector of Life-boats	Holyhead	Greek M.V. *Nafsiporos*	12 Jan. 1967
Evans, Richard M. Coxswain	Moelfre	Greek M.V. *Nafsiporos*	12 Jan. 1967
Marina, Princess H.R.H. Duchess of Kent		To mark the 25th Anniversary of her appointment as President	12 Jan. 1967
H.M. Coastguard		To mark the 150th Anniversary of foundation of Coastguard in 1822.	9 Feb. 1972

Appendix II

PRINCIPAL OFFICERS

1 Patrons

Successive Sovereigns have been Patrons of the Institution since King George IV in 1824.

2 Presidents

The Earl of Liverpool, 1824–8
The Fourth Duke of Northumberland, 1851–65
The Sixth Duke of Northumberland 1866–99
H.R.H. Albert Edward, Prince of Wales (King Edward VII), 1900–1
H.R.H. the Duke of York and Cornwall, afterwards Prince of Wales (King George V), 1902–10
The Seventh Duke of Northumberland, 1911–18
H.R.H. Edward, Prince of Wales (King Edward VIII), 1919–36
H.R.H. Albert, Duke of York (King George VI), 1936
H.R.H. the Duke or Kent, 1936–42
H.R.H. Princess Marina, Duchess of Kent, 1943–68
H.R.H. The Duke of Kent, 1969–

3 Chairmen of the Committee of Management

Thomas Wilson, M.P., 1824–52
Alderman William Thompson, M.P., 1852–3
Thomas Baring, M.P., F.R.S. 1854–73
Thomas Chapman, F.R.S., 1873–83
Sir Edward Birkbeck, Bart., M.P., 1883–1908
Colonel Sir Fitzroy Clayton, K.C.V.O., 1908–1911
Earl Waldegrave, P.C., 1911–23
Sir Godfrey Baring, Bart.. K.B.E., 1923–56
Commodore the Earl Howe, P.C., C.B.E., 1956–64
Captain the Hon. V. M. Wyndham-Quin, R.N., 1964–8
Admiral Sir Wilfrid Woods, C.B.E., K.C.B., D.S.O., 1968–72
Commander F. R. H. Swann, O.B.E., R.N.V.R., 1972–

4 Secretaries

(at the head of the full-time administrative staff)

Thomas Edwards, 1824–50
Richard Lewis, 1850–83
Charles Dibdin, 1883–1910
Sir George Shee, 1910–31
Lieutenant-Colonel C. R. Satterthwaite, 1931–47
Colonel A. D. Burnett Brown, 1947–60
Lieutenant-Colonel Charles Earle, 1960–1

Stirling Whorlow, 1961–9
Captain Nigel Dixon, R.N., 1970–
(From 1970 the title became 'Director and Secretary')

5 Chief Inspectors of Life-boats

(at the head of technical and operational staff)
Commander (later Vice-Admiral) J. Ross Ward, 1852–83
Captain the Hon. H. W. Chetwynd, R.N., 1883–93
Commander St Vincent Nepean, R.N., 1893–1909
Commander Thomas Holmes, R.N., 1909–19
Captain H. F. J. Rowley, R.N., 1919–30
Commander E. D. Drury, R.N., 1930–8
Lieutenant-Commander P. E. Vaux, R.N., 1939–51
Commander T. G. Michelmore, R.N.R., 1951–8
Commander S. W. F. Bennetts, R.N., 1958–61
Lieutenant-Commander W. L. G. Dutton, R.N.R., 1961–

6 Life Vice-Presidents

Air Vice-Marshal Sir Geoffrey R. Bromet, K.B.E., C.B., D.S.O., D.L.
C. G. Freke, Esq., C.I.E.
Sir Arnet Robinson

7 Honorary Life Governors

This is the highest honour which the Institution can confer on honorary workers. It was instituted in 1922, to be conferred only in recognition of long and very distinguished services, and to be accompanied by the presentation of a vellum signed by the President of the Institution.

Living holders of the honour	*Appointed*
The Lady Dorothy D'Oyly Carte	January 1934
Mrs R. H. Edmondson, B.A.	January 1946
Miss Pattie Price	June 1948
Mrs Dorothy Abel Smith, O.B.E.	December 1949
Mrs Miles Thornewill	October 1953
Mrs Graham Goodson	November 1954
John S. Duncan, M.B.E., J.P.	January 1958
Mrs R. M. Lloyd	January 1961
Mrs D. J. Wilkes	January 1964
Lieutenant-Commander H. Th. de Booy	February 1964
B. V. Howell, M.B.E.	January 1965
R. H. Mahony, Esq.	January 1967
Captain G. B. Piggott, D.L., J.P.	January 1967
S. Valentine, M.B.E., B.L.	January 1967
Sir Philip Hay, K.C.V.O., T.D.	January 1967
Air Marshal Sir Brian Baker, K.B.E., C.B., D.S.O., M.C., A.F.C.	January 1971
Alderman Miss Mary Conway Burton	January 1972

Mrs Constance Noyce	January 1972
Captain H. Hansson	May 1972
David Chapel, M.B.E., T.D.	May 1973
Mrs Graham Doggart	May 1973
Prof. William Flexner, Ph.D.	May 1973

8 Vice-Presidents

The Duke of Atholl
Sir Charles C. Baring, Bart., D.L., J.P.
The Archbishop of Canterbury, P.C.
The Marquis Camden, D.L., J.P.
L. C. H. Cave, Esq.
P. Denham Christie, Esq., B.Sc.
Raymond Cory, Esq.
Major-General Ralph H. Farrant, C.B.
Brigadier J. W. H. Gow, C.B.E., D.L., J.P.
Admiral Sir Angus Cunninghame Graham, K.B.E., C.B.
Commander H. G. P. Grenfell, D.S.C., R.N.
Geoffrey Hale, Esq., M.B.E., M.B., B.Ch.
Lieutenant-Commander The Hon. Greville Howard, V.R.D., R.N.R.
Rear-Admiral Sir Edmund Irving, K.B.E., C.B.,
Major The Lord Killanin, M.B.E., T.D., M.A., M.R.I.A.,
R. Leigh-Wood, Esq, D.L.
The Duke of Northumberland, K.G.
The Duke of Portland, K.G.
Captain R. E. D. Ryder, V.C., R.N.
Commander F. R. H. Swann, O.B.E., R.N.V.R.
N. Warington Smyth, Esq, O.B.E.
Admiral Sir Wilfrid Woods, G.B.E., K.C.B., D.S.O., D.L.
Captain the Hon. V. M. Wyndham-Quin, R.N.

Treasurer: The Duke of Northumberland, K.G.
Deputy Treasurer: D. A. Acland

9 Committee of Management

The President The Vice-Presidents The Treasurer
Commander F. R. H. Swann, O.B.E., R.N.V.R.. *Chairman*
The Duke of Atholl
Major-General Ralph H. Farrant C.B. } *Deputy Chairman*
H.R.H. The Prince Philip, Duke of Edinburgh, K.G.
D. A. Acland, Esq.
Captain Sir George Barnard
Surgeon Captain F. W. Baskerville, C.B.E., L.M.S.S.A., R.N. Rtd.
William T. Bishop, C.B.E., F.R.I.C.S.
A. Burn, Esq.
J. H. B. Chapman, C.B., C.Eng., F.R.N.I.A., R.C.N.C. Ltd.
Philip G. Clarke, Esq.
Philip Colville, Esq., M.B.E.

Vice-Admiral Sir Peter Compston, K.C.B.
W. P. Courtauld, Esq.
Lieut-Colonel R. Crawshaw, O.B.E., T.D., D.L., M.P.
Commander M. Cunningham, Assoc. R.I.N.A., R.N.
Maldwin Drummond, Esq., J.P.
Sir Knowles Edge, Bart., J.P.
Major-General Ralph H. Farrant, C.B.
Marshal of the R.A.F. Sir John Grandy, G.C.B., K.B.E., D.S.O.
Peter Guinness, Esq.
G. Harrison, Esq.
Vice-Admiral Sir Arthur Hezlet, K.B.E., C.B., D.S.O., D.S.C., D.L.
Rear-Admiral D. J. Hoare, C.B., M.I.Mech.E., M.R.I.N.A.
R. G. Hollond, Esq.
Robin Knox-Johnston, Esq., C.B.E.
Frank Lemass, Esq.
W. F. G. Lord, Esq.
Clayton Love Jnr.
Captain Sir Charles McGregor, Bart.
P. V. MacKinnon, Esq. O.B.E.
Rear-Admiral M. Morgan Giles, D.S.O., O.B.E., G.M., M.P.
Marquis of Normanby, M.B.E.
Peter D. Odlum, Esq.
H. A. W. Oughton, Esq,. O.B.E.
Lieutenant-Commander P. E. C. Pickles, M.B.E., J.P., R.N.V.R.
E. G. E. Rayner, Esq.
Air Marshal Sir Anthony Selway, K.C.B., D.F.C.
J. K. Shipton, Esq.
Lieutenant-Commander Jeremy Tetley, R.N. Rtd.
Michael Vernon, Esq.

Ex Officio

The Lord Mayor of London
The Admiral Commanding Reserves and Director-General of Naval Recruiting
The Deputy Master of Trinity House
The Hydrographer of the Navy
The Chairman of Lloyd's
The Master of the Honourable Company of Master Mariners
The Chairman of the Baltic Exchange

10 Administrative and Organizing Staff

Director and Secretary: Captain Nigel Dixon, R.N.
Chief Inspector of Life-boats: Lieutenant-Commander W. L. G. Dutton, O.B.E., R.D., R.N.R.
Deputy Director: J. R. Atterton, M.B.E.
Public Relations Officer: Patrick Howarth
Finance Secretary: J. R. Barnett, F.C.I.S.

Appeals Secretary: V. C. Frank
District Appeals Secretary: Commander E. F. Pritchard, R.N.
Membership Office: G. R. Walton

11 Operational and Technical Staff

Secretary (Operations Division): M. S. Porcher, C.M.G., O.B.E.
Chief Staff Officer (Technical): Symington Macdonald, B.Sc.. F.R.I.N.A., M.I.Ess., S.N.A.M.E.
Chief of Operations (Designate): Commander D. B. Cairns, R.D., R.N.R.
Staff Officer Operations: Captain R. M. Dabbs
Staff Officer (Technical): Lieutenant-Commander H. E. Over, C.Eng., M.I.Mech.E., A.M.B.I.M., R.N.
Superintendent of Depot: Lieut.-Commander H. H. Harvey, V.R.D., R.N.R.
Staff Officer Inshore Life-boats (Technical): Lieut. E. D. Stogdon, R.N.V.R.
Resident Engineer (Littlehampton): J. G. Groves

12 Regional Co-ordinators

North: Miss I. E. Morison
West (Designate): Commander P. D. Sturdee, O.B.E., R.N.

13 Regional Inspector of Life-boats

Scotland: Commander P. F. Gladwin, R.D., R.N.R.

14 Inspectors of Life-boats

No. 1 Division (Scottish Region): Flight Lieutenant T. F. Notman, R.A.F.
No. 2 Division (Scottish Region): Lieutenant A. M. Woodroffe, R.N.R.
No. 3 Area: Lieutenant-Commander H. F. Teare, R.D., R.N.R.
No. 4 Area: Lieutenant-Commander R. S. Porchmouth, C.D., R.C.N.
No. 5 Area: Lieutenant-Commander A. W. Tate, R.N.
No. 6 Area: Lieutenant-Commander D. J. Wilford, R.N.R.
No. 7 Area: Lieutenant-Commander G. R. Cooper, R.N.R.
No. 8 Area: Lieutenant-Commander P. F. B. Roe, R.N.
No. 10 Area: Lieutenant-Commander B. Miles, R.N.R.

15 District Organizing Secretaries

Scotland: Miss E. M. Lloyd-Jones
North-East: K. Thirwell
Midlands: Colonel J. T. Benn, O.B.E.
East: G. E. Price
London, North of the Thames: J. R. F. Sims
London, South of the Thames: P. Holness
London, City: H. J. Berry
South-East: I. Wallington
Southern: A. K. Oliver
South-West: A. R. Dickinson
Wales: Miss T. H. Ashe
North-West: Major James G. Disley
Ireland: Lieutenant-Colonel D. H. Clark, M.C., G.M.

Appendix III

PRESENT AND PAST STATIONS OF THE ROYAL NATIONAL LIFE-BOAT INSTITUTION

Hon. Secretaries and Coxswains appear as in the latest (1973) edition of the R.N.L.I. Year Book. Life-boat names are in italics.

An asterisk denotes that there is an Inshore Life-boat, sometimes additional to the regular life-boat.

The closure of stations, as recorded in this list, is always a matter of extreme regret. It is sometimes made inevitable by changing circumstances, such as the fact that, with the increased range of modern life-boats, certain stations can serve a larger area.

Station	*County*	*Date when station was established or taken over by the Institution*	*Date closed*
Aberdeen*	Aberdeen	1802	
Hon. Secs., Captain B. Atkinson and R. M. Addison; Coxswain, Albert Bird (*Ramsay-Dyce*).			
Aberdovey*	Merionethshire	1837	1931 (I.L.B. 1963)
Hon. Sec., Major J. G. Richards, M.B.E.			
Abergele	Denbighshire	1868	1869
Abersoch*	Caernarvonshire	1869	1931 (I.L.B. 1965)
Hon. Sec., David Fletcher-Brewer.			
Aberystwyth*	Cardiganshire	1862	
Hon. Sec., Gwym Martin, D.F.M.			
Ackergill	Caithness	1878	1932
Aith	Shetlands	1933	
Hon. Sec., John D. Garrick J.P.; Coxswain, Kenneth Henry (*John and Frances Macfarlane*).			
Aldeburgh	Suffolk	1824	
Hon. Sec., D. J. Owen; Coxswain, Reuben Wood (*The Albert and Patience Gottwald*).			
Alderney	Channel Islands	1869	1884
Alnmouth	Northumberland	1853	1935
Amble	Northumberland	1842	
Hon. Sec., John Matthews; Coxswain, John Connell (*Millie Walton*).			
Angle	Pembrokeshire	1867	
Hon. Sec., Major J. N. S. Allen-Minehouse; Coxswain, William Holmes (*Richard Vernon and Mary Garforth of Leeds*).			

Station	*County*	*Date when station was established or taken over by the Institution*	*Date closed*
Anstruther	Fife	1865	
Hon. Sec., Captain W. Anderson; Coxswain James Jack (*The Doctors*).			
Appledore	Devonshire	1825	
Hon. Sec. Ivor Wickersham; Coxswain Desmond Cox (*Louisa Anne Hawker*).			
Arbroath *	Angus	1803	
Hon. Sec., Captain J. Small; Coxswain, Douglas Mathewson (*The Duke of Montrose*).			
Ardmore	Co. Waterford	1858	1895
Ardrossan	Ayr	1869	1930
Arklow	Co. Wicklow	1826	
Hon. Sec., J. Tyrrell; Coxswain, Michael O'Brien (*St Andrew, Civil Service No.* 10).			
Arran Lamlash*	Bute	1970	
Hon. Sec., Captain K. M. Rore.			
Arranmore	Co. Donegal	1883	
Hon. Sec., Bernard Gallagher; Coxswain, Owen Kavanagh (*T.G..B.*).			
Atherfield	Isle of Wight	1890	1915
Atlantic College, St Donat's Castle*	Glamorgan	1963	
Hon. Sec., John L. Lipscombe.			
Ayr	Ayr	1802	1932
Bacton	Norfolk	1857	1882
Balbriggan	Co. Dublin	1875	1898
Balcary	Kirkcudbright	1884	1931
Ballantrae	Ayr	1871	1919
Ballycotton	Co. Cork	1858	
Hon. Sec., D. O'Sullivan; Coxswain, Michael Walsh (*Ethel/Mary*).			
Ballywalter	Co. Down	1866	1906
Baltimore	Co. Cork	1919	
Hon. Sec., Rodger de Quincy; Coxswain, John Collins (*Sarah Tilson*).			
Bamburgh Castle	Northumberland	1786	1898
Banff (*see* **Whitehills**)			
Bangor*	Co. Down	1965	
Hon. Sec., W. E. Hay.			
Barmouth*	Merioneth	1828	
Hon. Sec., Captain T. R. F. Addie; Coxswain, Evan Jones (*The Chieftain*).			
Barmston	Yorkshire	1884	1898

Station	*County*	*Date when station was established or taken over by the Institution*	*Date closed*
Barra Island	Outer Hebrides	1931	

Hon. Sec., Hugh N. Morrison, M.B.E.; Coxswain, John MacLeod (*R. A. Colby Cubbin No. 3*).

Barrow*	Lancashire	1864	

Hon. Sec., T. Downing; Coxswain, Robert Charnley (*Herbert Leigh*).

Barry Dock	Glamorgan	1901	

Hon. Sec., Captain J. D. Harries; Coxswain Francis Tinsley (*Arthur and Blanche Harris*).

Beaumaris*	Anglesey	1891	

Hon. Sec., M. L. Booth; Coxswain William Pritchard (*Field-Marshal and Mrs Smuts*).

Bembridge*	Isle of Wight	1867	

Hon. Sec., Arthur P. Weaver, B.E.M.; Coxswain, Peter Smith, B.E.M. (*Jack Shaylor and the Lees*).

Berwick on Tweed*	Northumberland	1835	

Hon. Sec., Lieutenant-Commander G. Gibson; Coxswain, Henry Crombie (*William and Mary Durham*).

Bideford (*see* **Appledore**)

Blackpool*	Lancashire	1864	

Hon. Sec., Frederick L. Burton; Coxswain, Jim Stanhope (*Edgar, George, Orlando and Eva Child*).

Blackrock (Dundalk)	Co. Louth	1859	1935
Blakeney	Norfolk	Before 1825	1935
Blyth*	Northumberland	1826	

Hon. Sec., Dr Reginald Carr; Coxswain, Samuel Crawford (*Winston Churchill. Civil Service No. 8*).

Borth*	Cardiganshire	1966	

Hon. Sec., T. Aran-Morris

Boulmer	Northumberland	1825	1968
Bournemouth*	Hampshire	1965	1972 (I.L.B. 1972)

Hon. Sec., Commander Anthony D. Casswill, R.N.

Brancaster	Norfolk	1874	1935

Braunton (*see* **Appledore**)

Bridgwater	Somerset	1836	Before 1850
Bridlington*	Yorkshire	1824	

Hon. Sec., Arthur W. Dick; Coxswain, John King (*William Henry and Mary King*).

Brighstone Grange	Isle of Wight	1860	1915
Brighton*	Sussex	1824	1931 (I.L.B. 1965)

Hon. Sec., H. C. Mileham

Brixham (*see* **Torbay**)

Station	*County*	*Date when station was established or taken over by the Institution*	*Date closed*
Broadstairs	Kent	1868	1912
Brooke	Isle of Wight	1860	1937
Broughty Ferry*	Angus	1830	
Hon. Sec., Captain R. W. Forbes and James T. Potter; Coxswain, Alick MacKay (*The Robert*).			
Buckhaven	Fife	1900	1932
Buckie	Banff	1860	
Hon. Sec., P. Kurray; Coxswain, Thomas Garden (*Laura Moncur*).			
Buddon Ness	Angus	1961	1894
Bude*	Cornwall	1837	1923 (I.L.B. 1966)
Hon. Sec., S. W. Whateley			
Bull Bay	Anglesey	1868	1926
Burnham	Somerset	1866	1930
Burnham-on-Crouch*	Essex	1966	
Hon. Sec., G. B. Law			
Burry Port	Carmarthenshire	1887	1914
Cadgwith	Cornwall	1867	
Cahore	Co. Wexford	1857	1916
Caister	Norfolk	1857	1969
Calshot	Hampshire	1972	
Hon. Sec., Colonel P. N. Keymer M.C.; Coxswain, William Jones (*Ernest William and Elizabeth Ellen Hinde*).			
Camber (*see* **Rye**)			
Cambois (*see* **Blythe**)			
Campbeltown	Argyll	1861	
Hon. Sec. J. P. McWhirter; Coxswain, David Farmer (*City of Glasgow II*).			
Cardigan*	Cardiganshire	1849	1932 (I. L. B. 1970)
Hon. Sec., Captain J. B. James			
Carmarthen (*see* **Ferryside**)			
Carnsore	Co. Wexford	1859	1897
Carrickfergus	Co. Antrim	1896	1913
Castletown	Isle of Man	1856	1922
Cemaes	Anglesey	1872	1932
Cemlyn	Anglesey	1828	1919
Chapel	Lincolnshire	1870	1898
Chapman's Pool	Dorset	1866	1880
Chichester Harbour (*see* **Selsey**)			
Christchurch	Hampshire	1802	No record
Church Cove (*see* **Lizard**)			

Station	*County*	*Date when station was established or taken over by the Institution*	*Date closed*
Clacton-on-Sea*	Essex	1878	
Hon. Sec., Lieutenant-Commander C. J. White R.N.V.R.; Coxswain, Charles Bolinbroke (*Valentine Wyndham-Quin*).			
Cleethorpes (*see* **Humber Mouth**)			
Clogher Head	Co. Louth	1899	
Hon. Sec., Mrs Marie C. Hoy; Coxswain, Michael Kirwan (*George and Caroline Ermen*).			
Cloughey-Portavogie	Co. Down	1885	
Hon. Sec., Captain M. Rutherford; Coxswain, John Donnan (*Glencoe, Glasgow*).			
Clovelly	Devonshire	1870	
Hon. Sec., Captain A. G. Sowman, C.B.E.; R.N.; Staff Coxswain, James Hunter (*Charley H. Barrett. Civil Service No. 35*).			
Conway*	Caernarvonshire	1966	
Hon. Sec., Richard H. Jones.			
Corton	Suffolk	1869	1879
Courtmacsherry	Co. Cork	1825	
Hon. Sec., J. O'Dwyer; Coxswain, John Barry (*Helen Wycherley*).			
Courtown	Co. Wexford	1865	1925
Coverack*	Cornwall	1901	1972 (I.L.B. 1972)
Hon. Sec., Lieutenant-Commander C. E. Sheen, D.S.C., R.N.; Coxswain, Vivian Carey (*William Taylor of Oldham*).			
Crail	Fife	1884	1923
Craster*	Northumberland	1969	
Hon. Sec., J. W. Robson			
Cresswell	Northumberland	1875	1944
Criccieth*	Caernarvonshire	1853	1968 (I.L.B. 1968)
Hon. Sec., Glyn Humphreys.			
Crimdon Dene*	Co. Durham	1966	
Hon. Sec., T. P. Reynolds.			
Cromarty	Ross & Cromarty	1911	1968
Cromer*	Norfolk	Before 1835	
Hon. Sec., Dr Paul S. Barclay, M.C., T.D.; Coxswain, Henry Davies, B.E.M. (*Ruby and Arthur Reed*).			
Cruden Bay (*see* **Port Erroll**)			
Culdaff	Co. Donegal	1872	1913
Cullercoats*	Northumberland	1852	1969 (I.L.B. 1969)
Hon. Sec., Alan Rankine.			

Station	*County*	*Date when station was established or taken over by the Institution*	*Date closed*
Dartmouth	Devonshire	1878	1896
Deal (*see* **North Deal**)			
Derrynane	Co. Kerry	1844	After 1850
Donaghadee	Co. Down	1910	
Hon. Sec., D. T. McKibbin; Coxswain, James Bunting (*Sir Samuel Kelly*).			
Donna Nook	Lincolnshire	1829	1931
Dornoch Firth and Embo	Sutherland	1886	1904
Douglas	Isle of Man	1802	
Hon. Sec., Captain T. H. Corteen; Coxswain, William Corran (*R. A. Colby Cubbin No 1.*).			
Dover	Kent	1837	
Hon. Sec., H. W. Andrews. Coxswain, Arthur Liddon (*Faithful Forester*).			
Drogheda	Co. Louth	1856	1926
Dublin (*see* **Poolbeg**)			
Dunbar*	East Lothian	1808	
Hon. Sec., William Gilmour; Coxswain, Robert Brunton (*Margaret*).			
Duncannon	Co. Wexford	1869	1886
Dundalk (*see* **Blackrock**)			
Dundee (*see* **Broughty Ferry**)			
Dundrum (*see* **Newcastle**)			
Dungarvan (*see* **Helvick Head**)			
Dungeness	Kent	1826	
Hon. Sec.; G. L. Bates; Coxswain, Tom Tart (*Mabel E. Holland*)			
Dun Laoghaire	Co. Dublin	Before 1825	
Hon. Sec., J. E. de Courcy Ireland; Coxswain, Eric Offer (*John F. Kennedy*)			
Dunmore East	Co. Waterford	1884	
Hon. Sec., J. S. Power; Coxswain, Stephen Whittle (*Dunleary II*).			
Dunwich	Suffolk	1873	1903
Easington	Yorkshire	1913	1933
Eastbourne*	Sussex	1822	
Hon. Sec., Alderman Cecil F. Baker, J.P.; Coxswain, Derek Huggett (*Beryl Tollemache*).			
Eastney*	Hampshire	1965	
Hon. Sec., Dr Ian T. McLachlan.			
Exmouth*	Devonshire	1803	
Hon. Sec., W. L. C. Smith; Coxswain, Brian Rowsell (*City of Birmingham*).			
Eyemouth	Berwick	1876	
Hon. Sec., Captain P. W. Gibson; Coxswain, Alexander Dougal (*Louise Stephens*).			

Station	*County*	*Date when station was established or taken over by the Institution*	*Date closed*
Falmouth	Cornwall	1867	
Hon. Sec., Captain F. H. Edwards; Coxswain, Walter West (*Lilla Maures, Douglas and Will*).			
Fenit	Co. Kerry	1879	1969
Ferryside	Carmarthenshire	1835	1960
Fethard	Co. Wexford	1886	1914
Filey*	Yorkshire	1823	
Hon. Sec., Philip Hodgson; Coxswain, Thomas Jenkinson (*Robert and Dorothy Hardcastle*).			
Fishguard	Pembrokeshire	1822	
Hon. Sec., N. O. Mabe; Coxswain, Glyn Bateman (*Howard Marryat*).			
Flamborough	Yorkshire	1871	
Hon. Sec., T. Woodhouse, O.B.E., J.P.; Coxswain, George Pockley (*Friendly Forester*).			
Fleetwood*	Lancashire	1859	
Hon. Sec., Richard T. Willoughby, T.D.; Coxswain, Roy Mitchinson (*Ann Letitia Russell*).			
Flint*	Flintshire	1966	
Hon. Sec., K. R. G. Parkington.			
Folkestone	Kent	1893	1930
Formby	Lancashire	1894	1919
Fowey	Cornwall	1859	
Hon. Sec., Captain J. G. Wilson, D.S.C., R.D., R.N.R.; Coxswain, James Turpin (*Deneys Reitz*).			
Fraserburgh	Aberdeen	1831	1973
Hon. Sec., Captain J. Carter.			
Galway Bay	Co. Galway	1927	
Hon. Sec., The Very Rev. Father O'Morain; Coxswain, Coleman Hernon (*Joseph Hiram Chadwick*).			
Giles Quay	Co. Louth	1879	1912
Girvan	Ayr	1865	
Hon. Sec., Captain J. W. Brown; Coxswain, William Coull (*James and Barbara Aitken*).			
Gourdon	Kincardine	1878	1969
Gt. Yarmouth and Gorleston*	Norfolk	Before 1825	
Hon. Sec., J. S. Ling; Coxswain, John Bryan (*Khami*)			
Greencastle	Co. Donegal	1864	1928
Greenore	Co. Louth	1894	1920
Greystones	Co. Wicklow	1872	1896
Grimsby	Lincolnshire	1868	1927

Station	*County*	*Date when station was established or taken over by the Institution*	*Date closed*
Groomsport	Co. Down	1858	1920
Guernsey (see **St Peter Port**)			
Happisburgh*	Norfolk	1965	
Hon. Sec., B. E. Trett.			
Hartlepool*	Co. Durham	Before 1825	
Hon. Sec., P. A. I. Farquhar.			
Harwich*	Essex	Before 1836	
Hon. Sec., Captain J. D. Gibson; Coxswain, Peter Burwood (*Margaret Graham*).			
Haisborough	Norfolk	1866	1926
Hastings*	Sussex	1858	
Hon. Sec., J. J. Adams; Coxswain, John Martin (*Fairlight*).			
Hauxley	Northumberland	1852	1939
Hayle	Cornwall	1866	1920
Hayling Island	Hampshire	1865	1924
Helensburgh*	Dunbarton	1965	
Hon. Sec., Alfred E. Thurgood.			
Helvick Head	Co. Waterford	1859	1969
Hendon Beach (*see* **Sunderland**)			
Hilbre Island	Cheshire	1848	1939
Holyhead*	Anglesey	1828	
Hon. Sec., Tudor B. Roberts; Coxswain, William Jones (*St Cybi, Civil Service No. 9*).			
Holy Island	Northumberland	1802	1968
Hope Cove	Devonshire	1878	1930
Hornsea	Yorkshire	1854	1924
Horton and Port Eynon*	Glamorgan	1968	
Hon. Sec., D. H. Farmer.			
Hove (*see* **Brighton**)			
Howth*	Co. Dublin	Before 1825	
Hon. Sec., J. Norman Wilkinson, D.S.C.; Coxswain, Gerald McLoughlin (*A.M.T.*).			
Hoylake	Cheshire	1803	
Hon. Sec., W. E. Kirkbride; Coxswain, Harold Triggs (*Thomas Corbett*).			
Humber	Yorkshire	1810	
Superintendent Coxswain, Robertson Buchan (*City of Bradford III*).			
Humber Mouth* (Cleethorpes)	Lincolnshire	1965	
Hon. Sec., Stanley R. Meakings.			
Huna	Caithness	1877	1930
Hunstanton	Norfolk	Before 1825	1931
Hurst Castle	Hampshire	1824	No record

Station	*County*	*Date when station was established taken over by the Institution*	*Date closed*
Hythe	Kent	1876	1940
Ilfracombe	Devonshire	1828	
Hon. Sec., Lieutenant-Commander C. D. Hines D.S.M., R.N.; Coxswain, David Clemence (*Lloyd's II*).			
Irvine	Ayrshire	1834	1914
Islay	Inner Hebrides	1934	
Hon. Sec., Neil MacMillan; Coxswain, Donald McPhee (*Francis W. Wotherspoon of Paisley*).			
Isle of Arran (*see* **Kildonan**)			
Isle of Purbeck (*see* **Kimmeridge and Chapman's Pool**)			
Isle of Whithorn (*see* **Whithorn**)			
Jersey, St Catherine's*	Channel Islands	1969	
Hon. Sec., Captain R. S. Taylor.			
Jersey (*see* **St Helier**)			
Johnshaven	Kincardine	1890	1928
Kessingland	Suffolk	1867	1936
Kildonan	Isle of Arran, Bute	1870	1902
Killybegs	Co. Donegal	1941	1945
Killough	Co. Down	1901	1914
Kilmore	Co. Wexford	1847	
Hon. Sec., J. T. Sutton; Coxswain, James Bute (*Lady Murphy*).			
Kimmeridge	Dorset	1868	1896
Kinghorn*	Fife	1965	
Hon. Sec., Dr R. M. L. Weir.			
Kingsdown	Kent	1866	1927
Kingsgate	Kent	1862	1897
Kingstown (*see* **Dun Laoghaire**)			
Kinsale	Co. Cork	Before 1825	No record
Kippford*	Kirkcudbright	1966	
Hon. Sec., John McKay.			
Kirkcudbright	Kirkcudbright	1862	
Hon. Sec., Dr R. N. Rutherfurd; Coxswain, George Davidson, D.S.M., B.E.M. (*Mary Pullman*).			
Kirkwall	Orkney	1972	
Hon. Sec., Captain W. S. Sinclair; Staff Coxswain in command (*Grace Paterson Ritchie*).			
Largs*	Ayr	1964	
Hon. Sec., J. T. Watt			

Station	*County*	*Date when station was established or taken over by the Institution*	*Date closed*
Lerwick	Shetland	1930	
Hon. Sec., Magnus M. Shearer. Coxswain, George Leith (*Claude Cecil Staniforth*).			
Little and Broad Haven*	Pembrokeshire	1967	
Hon. Sec., Elson G. Phillips.			
Littlehampton	Sussex	1884	1921 (I.L.B. 1967)
Hon. Sec., Peter Cheney.			
Littlehaven	Pembrokeshire	1882	1921
Littlestone-on-Sea*	Kent	1966	
Hon. Sec., J. K. Boardman.			
Liverpool	Lancashire	Before 1802	No record
Lizard—Cadgwith	Cornwall	1859	
Hon. Sec., L. A. Britton; Coxswain, Maurice Legg (*The Duke of Cornwall. Civil Service No. 33*).			
Llanaelhaiarn	Caernarvonshire	1883	1901
Llanddwyn	Anglesey	1840	1907
Llandudno*	Caernarvonshire	1861	
Hon. Sec., Thomas Taylor; Coxswain, Meurig Davies (*Lily Wainwright*).			
Llandulas	Denbighshire	1869	1932
Llanelly (*see* **Pembury**)			
Lochinver	Sutherland	1967	
Hon. Sec., P. W. Hay; Coxswain, David McBain (*George Urie Scott*).			
Londonderry (*see* **Greencastle**)			
Longhope	Orkney	1874	
Hon. Sec., J. M. F. Groat; Coxswain, John Leslie (*The David and Elizabeth King and E.B.*).			
Looe	Cornwall	1866	1930
Lossiemouth	Moray	1859	1923
Lowestoft	Suffolk	1801	
Hon. Sec., M. W. Chapman; Coxswain, Thomas Knott (*Frederick Edward Crick*).			
Lydd (*see* **Dungeness**)			
Lyme Regis*	Dorset	1826	1932 (I.L.B. 1967)
Hon. Sec., Major-General R. W. Jelf, C.B.E.			
Lymington*	Hampshire	1965	
Hon. Sec., K. C. G. Bacon, M.M.			
Lynmouth	Devonshire	1869	1944
Lytham-St Anne's*	Lancashire	1851	
Hon. Sec., John Kennedy; Coxswain, Arthur Wignall (*Sarah Townsend Porritt*).			

Station	*County*	*Date when station was established or taken over by the Institution*	*Date closed*
Mablethorpe*	Lincolnshire	1851	
Hon. Sec., William D. Stoney.			
Machrihanish	Argyll	1911	1930
Mallaig	Inverness	1948	
Hon. Sec., A. A. McLellan; Coxswain, Charles Henderson (*E.M.M. Gordon Cubbin*).			
Margate*	Kent	1860	
Hon. Sec., Noel Richard Kingston; Coxswain, Alfred Manning (*North Foreland. Civil Service No. 11*).			
Maryport	Cumberland	1865	1949
Methil (*see* **Buckhaven**)			
Mevagissey	Cornwall	1869	1930
Middlesbrough	Yorkshire	1858	1895
Milford Haven (*see* **Angle**)			
Minehead*	Somerset	1901	
Hon. Sec., Commander E. R. Tyndale-Biscoe, R.N.; Coxswain, Stanley Rawle (*B.H.M.H.*).			
Moelfre*	Anglesey	1830	
Hon. Sec., Thomas Owens; Coxswain, William Roberts (*Watkins Williams*).			
Montrose	Angus	1800	
Hon. Sec., J. M. D. Smith; Coxswain, James Paton, B.E.M. (*Lady McRobert*).			
Moray Firth (*see* **Nairn**)			
Morecambe*	Lancashire	1966	
Hon. Sec., Sam Baxter.			
Morthoe *or* **Morte Bay**	Devonshire	1871	1900
Mostyn	Flintshire	1835	1851
Mudeford*	Hampshire	1965	
Hon. Sec., Ken Durham.			
Mullion	Cornwall	1867	1908
Mumbles*	Glamorgan	1866	
Hon. Sec., E. G. Beynon; Coxswain, Derek Scott, B.E.M. (*William Gammon—Manchester and District XXX*).			
Mundesley	Norfolk	Before 1825	1895
Nairn	Nairn	1878	1911
Newbiggin	Northumberland	1851	
Hon. Sec., A. D. Manley; Coxswain, Edward Dawson (*Mary Joicey*).			
New Brighton	Cheshire	1863	
Hon. Sec., Captain W. P. Duguid; Coxswain, William Morris (*Norman B. Corlett*).			
Newburgh	Aberdeen	1828	1965

Station	*County*	*Date when station was established or taken over by the Institution*	*Date closed*
Newcastle	Co. Down	1835	
Hon. Sec., Captain the Earl of Roden, R.N; Coxswain, Michael Leneghan (*William and Laura*).			
Newhaven	Sussex	1803	
Hon. Sec., R. K. Sayer, M.B.E.; Coxswain, Edgar Moore (*Kathleen Mary*).			
Newlyn	Cornwall	1908	1913
Newport	Pembrokeshire	1884	1894
Newquay*	Cornwall	1860	1945 (I.L.B. 1965)
Hon. Sec., Lewis J. C. Billingham.			
New Quay*	Cardiganshire	1864	
Hon. Sec., Captain Cosmo Jones; Coxswain, David Evans (*Birds Eye*).			
New Romney	Kent	1861	1928
Northam Burrows (*see* **Appledore**)			
North Berwick*	East Lothian	1860	1925 (I.L.B. 1967)
Hon. Sec., Lieutenant-Commander J. D. Tweedie, R.N.V.R.			
North Deal	Kent	1865	1932
North Deal Reserve	Kent	1915	1921
North Sunderland*	Northumberland	1827	
Hon. Sec., R. H. Reay; Coxswain, Robert Douglas (*The Edward and Mary Lester*).			
Oban*	Argyll	1972	
Hon. Sec., N. E. Budge.			
Ormes Head (*see* **Llandudno**)			
Padstow	Cornwall	Before 1825	
Hon. Sec., H. H. Lobb; Coxswain, Anthony Warnock (*James and Catherine Macfarlane*).			
Pakefield	Suffolk	1840	1922
Palling	Norfolk	1852	1930
Peel*	Isle of Man	1828	1972 (I.L.B. 1972)
Hon. Sec., Captain A. D. Watterson. I.L.B. (*Helena Harris—Manchester and District XXXI*).			
Pembery *or* **Pembury**	Carmarthenshire	1863	1887
Penarth	Glamorgan	1861	1905
Penlee and Penzance	Cornwall	1803	
Hon. Sec., D. L. Johnson; Coxswain, William Richards (*Solomon Browne*)			
Penmon	Anglesey	1832	1915

Station	*County*	*Date when station was established or taken over by the Institution*	*Date closed*
Penrhyndu	Merioneth	1844	1853
Peterhead	Aberdeen	1965	
Hon. Sec., W. A. P. Cormack; Coxswain, Alexander Birnie (*James and Mariska Joicey*).			
Piel (*see* **Barrow**)			
Pill*	Somerset	1971	
Hon. Sec., Pilot J. Rich, M.I.N., M.N.I.			
Plymouth*	Devonshire	1803	
Hon. Sec., Raymond H. E. Sainsbury; Coxswain, John Dare (*Thomas Forehead and Mary Rowse*).			
Point of Ayr	Flintshire	1894	1923
Polkerris (*see* **Fowey**)			
Poolbeg	Co. Dublin	1820	1959
Poole*	Dorset	1865	
Hon. Sec., Major John Showell-Rogers, R.M.; Coxswain, Reginald Brown (*George Elmy*).			
Port Askaig (*see* **Islay**)			
Port Ellen (*see* **Islay**)			
Port Erin	Isle of Man	1883	
Hon. Sec., R. Rimington; Coxswain, Peter Woodworth (*Matthew Simpson*).			
Port Erroll	Aberdeen	1877	1921
Port Eynon (*see* **Horton**)	Glamorgan	1884	1916
Porthcawl*	Glamorgan	1860	1902 (I.L.B. 1965)
Hon. Sec., John Blundell.			
Porthdinllaen	Caernarvonshire	1864	
Hon. Sec., J. E. Roberts, M.B.E., J.P.; Coxswain, Thomas Moore (*Charles Henry Ashley*).			
Porthleven	Cornwall	1863	1929
Porthoustock	Cornwall	1869	1942
Porth Rhuffydd	Anglesey	1891	1904
Port Isaac*	Cornwall	1869	1933
Hon. Sec., Raymond M. Harris.			
Portloe *or* **Portlor**	Cornwall	1870	1887
Portland	Dorset	1826	1850
Port Logan	Wigtown	1866	1932
Portmadoc (*see* **Criccieth**)			
Portpatrick	Wigtown	1877	
Hon. Sec., J. Campbell; Coxswain, Andrew Mitchell (*The Jeanie*).			

Station	*County*	*Date when station was established or taken over by the Institution*	*Date closed*
Portrush	Co. Antrim	1860	

Hon. Sec., W. R. Knox, C.B.E., M.M., J.P.; Coxswain, Robert McMullan (*Lady Scott. Civil Service No. 4*).

Port St Mary*	Isle of Man	1896	

Hon. Sec., J. Hudson; Coxswain, John Gawne, B.E.M. (*R.A. Colby Cubbin No. 2*).

Port Talbot (Aberavon Beach)*	Glamorgan	1966	

Hon. Sec., David F. Aubrey.

Purbeck Island (*see* **Chapman's Pool**)

Pwllheli*	Caernarvonshire	1891	

Hon. Sec., Captain D. C. Evans; Coxswain, William McGill (*Anthony Robert Marshall*).

Queensferry*	West Lothian	1967	

Hon. Sec., Captain J. F. Kersley.

Queenstown	Co. Cork	1866	1920
Ramsey	Isle of Man	1829	

Hon. Sec., B. T. Swales; Coxswain, Lawrence Gawne (*James Bell Ritchie*).

Ramsgate*	Kent	1802	

Hon. Sec., K. F. Speakman; Coxswain, Thomas Cooper (*Michael and Lily Davis*).

Red Bay*	Co. Antrim	1972	

Hon. Sec., Captain T. L. Scollay.

Redcar*	Yorkshire	1802	

Hon. Sec., Frank Cockcroft; Coxswain, Ronald Dixon (*Sir James Knott*).

Rhoscolyn	Anglesey	1830	1929
Rhosneigr	Anglesey	1872	1924
Rhyl*	Flintshire	1852	

Hon. Sec., John M. Owen; Coxswain, William Hunt (*Har-Lil*).

Robin Hood's Bay	Yorkshire	1830	1931
Roe Island (*see* **Peel**)			
Rogerstown	Co. Dublin	1874	1882
Roker (*see* **Sunderland**)			
Rosslare Harbour	Co. Wexford	1838	

Hon. Sec., C. G. Miller; Coxswain, Richard Walsh (*R. Hope Roberts*).

Rosslinks (*see* **Holy Island**)			
Rossglass	Co. Dublin	1825	1835
Runswick	Yorkshire	1866	

Hon. Sec., H. Roddom; Coxswain, Colin Harrison (*The Royal Thames*).

Station	*County*	*Date when station was established or taken over by the Institution*	*Date closed*
Ryde	Isle of Wight	1869	1923
Rye	Sussex	1803	1901
Rye Harbour*	Sussex	1803	1928 (I.L.B. 1966)
Hon. Sec., Humphrey Lestocq.			
St Abbs	Berwick	1911	
Hon. Sec., E. Greene; Coxswain, James Wilson, B.E.M. (*Jane Hay*).			
St Agnes*	Cornwall	1968	
Hon. Sec., C. J. Whitworth.			
St Agnes	Scilly Isles	1890	1920
St Andrews	Fife	1800	1938
St Anne's (*see also* **Lytham-St. Anne's**)	Lancashire	1881	1925
St Bees*	Cumberland	1930	
Hon. Sec., Captain James Gibbons, D.S.C.			
St Brides (*see* **Littlehaven**)			
St David's	Pembrokeshire	1869	
Hon. Sec., W. Llewellyn; Coxswain, William Morris (*Joseph Soar, Civil Service No. 34*).			
St Helier	Jersey	1884	
Hon. Sec., Captain R. S. Taylor; Coxswain, Michael Berry (*Elizabeth Rippon*).			
St Ives*	Cornwall	1840	
Hon. Sec., Captain E. Kemp; Coxswain, Thomas Cocking (*Frank Penfold Marshall*).			
St Mary's	Scilly Isles	1837	
Hon. Sec., Captain A. J. Jenkins; Coxswain, Matthew Lethbridge (*Guy and Clare Hunter*).			
St Peter Port	Guernsey	1803	
Hon. Sec., Captain J. C. Allez; Coxswain, John Petit (*Arun*).			
St Sampsons (*see* **St Peter Port**)			
Salcombe	Devonshire	1869	
Hon. Sec., W. P. Budgett; Coxswain, John Griffiths (*The Baltic Exchange*).			
Saltburn	Yorkshire	1849	1922
Scarborough*	Yorkshire	1801	
Hon. Sec., Major R. F. Soper, M.B.E.; Coxswain, William Sheader (*J. G. Graves of Sheffield*). (Inflatable: *Young People of Scarborough*)			
Scilly Isles (*see* **St Mary's**)			
Seaham	Co. Durham	1970	
Hon. Sec., Leslie Hood; Coxswain, Arthur Farrington (*The Will and Fanny Kirby*).			
Seascale	Cumberland	1875	1895
Seaton Carew	Co. Durham	Before 1835	1922

Station	*County*	*Date when station was established or taken over by the Institution*	*Date closed*
Seaton Snook	Co. Durham	1907	1909
Selsey*	Sussex	1861	
Hon. Sec., Desmond Cockayne; Coxswain, William Jones (*Charles Henry*).			
Sennen Cove	Cornwall	1853	
(Temporarily non-operational)			
Sheerness*	Kent	1972	
Hon. Sec., Captain D. Gibbons. Coxswain, Charles Bowry (*Gertrude*).			
Sheringham	Norfolk	1839	
Hon. Sec., J. R. Bell; Coxswain, Robert West (*The Manchester Unity of Odd Fellows*).			
Shoreham Harbour*	Sussex	1865	
Hon. Sec., John C. Harrison; Coxswain, John Fox (*Dorothy and Philip Constant*).			
Sidmouth	Devonshire	1869	1912
Silloth*	Cumberland	1860	(1896 I.L.B. 1967)
Hon. Sec., Michael Saul.			
Skateraw	East Lothian	1907	1943
Skegness*	Lincolnshire	1825	
Hon. Sec., F. N. Ball; Coxswain, Kenneth Holland (*Charles Fred Grantham*).			
Skerries	Co. Dublin	1854	1930
Solva	Pembrokeshire	1869	1887
Southend Cantyre	Argyll	1869	1930
Southend-on-Sea*	Essex	1879	
Hon. Sec., P. G. Garon, M.C., G.M.; Coxswain. Peter Gilson (*Greater London II. Civil Service No. 30*).			
Southport	Lancashire	1860	1925
Southsea	Hampshire	1886	1918
Southwold*	Suffolk	1852	1940 (I.L.B. 1963)
Hon. Sec., John Adnams.			
Spurn (*see* **Humber**)			
Staithes	Yorkshire	1875	1938
Stonehaven*	Kincardine	1867	1934 (I.L.B. 1967)
Hon. Sec., James Elliot.			
Stornoway	Isle of Lewis, Hebrides	1887	
Hon. Sec., Captain Alexander Mackay; Coxswain, Roderick Maclean (*The James and Margaret Boyd*).			
Stromness	Orkney	1867	
Hon. Sec., Captain J. Allan; Coxswain, Alfred Sinclair (*Archibald and Alexander M. Paterson*).			

Station	*County*	*Date when station was established or taken over by the Institution*	*Date closed*
Stronsay	Orkney	1909	1972
Hon. Sec., Andrew Burghes; Coxswain, James Stout (*The John Gellatly Hyndman*).			
Studland	Dorset	1826	1852
Sunderland*	Co. Durham	1800	
Hon. Sec., Captain William W. White; Coxswain, John Todd (*William Myers and Sarah Jane Myers*).			
Sutton	Lincolnshire	1844	1913
Swanage	Dorset	1875	
Hon. Sec., Captain D. A. N. Aldridge; Coxswain, Ronald Hardy (*R.L.P.*).			
Swansea (*see* **Mumbles**)			
Teesmouth	Yorkshire	1911	
Hon Sec., E. R. Copeman; Coxswain, William Carter (*Sarah Jane and James Season*).			
Teignmouth	Devonshire	Before 1825	1940
Tenby*	Pembrokeshire	1852	
Hon. Sec., G. Reason-Jones; Coxswain, Joshua Richards (*Henry Comber Brown*).			
Theddlethorpe	Lincolnshire	1864	1882
Thorpeness *or* **Thorpe**	Suffolk	1853	1900
Thurso	Caithness	1860	
Hon. Sec., Captain A. A. Munro; Coxswain, Gilbert Reid (*The Three Sisters*).			
Tighnabruiach	Argyll	1967	
Hon. Sec., Dr George L. Thomson.			
Tobermory	Hebrides	1938	1947
Torbay*	Devonshire	1866	
Hon. Sec., Alderman Frederick W. H. Park, M.B.E.; Coxswain, Kenneth Gibbs (*Princess Alexandra of Kent*).			
Torquay	Devonshire	1876	1923
Totland Bay	Isle of Wight	1885	1924
Tranlee Bay (*see* **Fenit**)			
Tramore*	Co. Waterford	1858	1924 (I.L.B. 1964)
Hon. Sec., Finian P. Mongey.			
Tre-Arddur Bay*	Anglesey	1967	
Hon. Sec., Tudor B. Roberts.			
Troon	Ayr	1871	
Hon. Sec., T. M. Brown; Coxswain, Edward Brooks (*Connel Elizabeth Cargill*).			
Tynemouth*	Northumberland	1862	
Hon. Sec., Kenneth Middlemiss; Coxswain, Robert Burnton (*Tynesider*)			
Tyrella	Co. Down	1860	1899

Station	*County*	*Date when station was established or taken over by the Institution*	*Date closed*
Upgang	Yorkshire	1865	1919
Valentia	Co. Kerry	1864	

Hon. Sec. P. J. Gallagher; Coxswain Dermot Walsh (*Rowland Watts*).

Walmer*	Kent	1856	

Hon. Sec., Alderman Cavell; Coxswain, Henry Brown (*Charles Dibdin. Civil Service No. 32*).

Walton and Frinton	Essex	1884	

Hon. Sec., R. Oxley, J.P.; Coxswain, Frank Bloom (*Edian Courtauld*).

Watchet	Somerset	1875	1944
Wells*	Norfolk	1869	

Hon. Sec., Lieutenant David J. Case, R.N.V.R.; Coxswain, David Cox (*Ernest Tom Neathercoat*).

West Hartlepool	Co. Durham	1869	1906
West Kirby*	Cheshire	1966	

Hon. Sec., W. E. Kirkbride.

West Mersea*	Essex	1963	

Hon. Sec., Lieutenant-Commander Maurice W. Bond, R.N.R.

Weston-super-Mare*	Somerset	1882	

Hon. Sec., Clifford Smith.

Westport	Co. Mayo	1857	1860

West Wittering (*see* **Selsey**)

Wexford (*see* **Rosslare**)

Weymouth	Dorset	1869	

Hon. Sec., Kenneth H. Mooring Aldridge; Coxswain, Alfred Pavey (*Frank Spiller Locke*).

Whitburn	Co. Durham	1830	1918
Whitby*	Yorkshire	1802	

Hon. Sec., Eric Thomson; Coxswain, William Harland (*Mary Ann Hepworth*).

Whitehaven	Cumberland	1804	1925
Whitehills	Banff	1860	1969
Whitelink Bay	Aberdeen	1878	1905
Whithorn, Isle of	Wigtown	1869	1919
Whitstable*	Kent	1963	

Hon. Sec., B. E. Hardy, M.I.C.E.

Station	*County*	*Date when station was established or taken over by the Institution*	*Date closed*
Wick	Caithness	1895	
Hon. Sec., Captain M. D. MacKenzie; Coxswain, Donald McKay (*Princess Marina*).			
Wicklow	Co. Wicklow	1857	
Hon. Sec., James L. Kavanagh; Coxswain, Charles Byrne (*J. W. Archer*).			
Winchelsea (*see* **Rye Harbour**)			
Winterton	Norfolk	1857	1924
Withernsea	Yorkshire	1862	1913
Woodbridge Haven	Suffolk	1801	1852
Workington	Cumberland	1886	
Hon. Sec., R. Atkinson; Coxswain, Albert Brown (*Manchester and Salford XXIX*).			
Worthing	Sussex	1852	1930
Yarmouth (*see* **Gorleston**)			
Yarmouth*	Isle of Wight	1924	
Hon. Sec., L. W. Noton; Coxswain, David Kenneth (*The Earl and Countess Howe*).			
Yealm River	Devonshire	1878	1927
Youghal	Co. Cork	1839	
Hon. Sec., Commander B. K. C. Arbuthnot, D.S.C., R.N.; Coxswain, Christopher Hennessy (*Grace Darling*).			

Appendix IV

TYPES OF OFFSHORE LIFE-BOAT NOW IN SERVICE

Clyde 70 ft. steel
Arun 52 ft.
Barnett 52 ft.
Thames 50 ft. steel
Solent 48 ft. 6 in. steel
Oakley 48 ft. 6 in.; 37 ft.
Beach 42 ft.; 41 ft.
Waveney 44 ft; steel
Keith Nelson 40 ft. glass reinforced plastic
Rother 37 ft.
Liverpool 35 ft. 6 in.

TYPES OF INSHORE LIFE-BOAT

INFLATABLE
also 21 ft.
19 ft.
18 ft.
17 ft.

Appendix V

PRINCIPAL AWARDS OF THE INSTITUTION

For operational service:

Gold Medal: Instituted 1824
The Institution's highest award for gallantry in sea-rescue. Very occasionally given as a mark of distinction to corporate bodies or individuals. Total of gold medals and clasps awarded, to 1973, 132

Silver Medal: Instituted 1824
Total of silver medals and clasps awarded, to 1973, 1,499

Bronze Medal: Instituted 1917
Total of bronze medals and clasps awarded, to 1973, 562

Thanks Inscribed on Vellum

Medal Service Certificates: Instituted 1955
Awarded to crew members in rescues which have justified the giving of medals to individuals in the boat or boats concerned.

Note. Holders of the Institution's medals, if wearing the uniform of the Armed Services, wear the blue ribbon on the right breast, as in the case of certain other life-saving awards. (One of Sir William Hillary's medals, now belonging to the Institution, has, by way of contrast, a red ribbon.) The dolphin clasp attaching the medal to the ribbon is noteworthy. When the ribbon alone is worn, holders of the gold medal show on it a miniature of Hillary's head: this miniature also signifies the award of second service clasps or bars for acts of gallantry following the first for which a medal was given.

For services to the Institution:

Honorary Life Governorship: Instituted 1921

Gold Badge: Instituted 1912
Awarded in recognition of at least twenty years' exceptionally good service. A bar (instituted 1956) may be awarded after further service, normally of not less than five years.

Silver Badge: Instituted 1956
Normally given to Honorary Secretaries after ten years' service as such, and for equivalent work.

Gold and Silver Brooches:
Awarded to women for exceptional services to the Institution, with bars as appropriate.

Framed Records of Thanks: Instituted 1918

Framed Letters of Thanks signed by the Chairman of the Committee of Management: Instituted 1966

Appendix VI

ANNUAL RECEIPTS

1824..£9,706
1825..£9,826
1826..£3,392
1827..£1,269
1828..£1,234
1829..£1,324
1830..£2,425
1831..£835
1832..£984
1833..£1,615
1834..£2,227
1835..£806
1836..£788
1837..£899
1838..£554
1839..£743
1840..£1,582
1841..£729
1842/9..not recorded.
1850..£354
1851..£758
1852..£2,468
1853..£703
1854..£1,885
1855..£1,744
1856..£4,983
1857..£5,327
1858..£6,112
1859..£10,633
1860..£14,027
1861..£15,092
1862..£14,825
1863..£21,101
1864..£31,917
1865..£28,932
1866..£41,718
1867..£39,305
1868..£31,668
1869..£14,409
1870..£25,711
1871..£28,140
1872..£27,331
1873..£31,740
1874..£33,500
1875..£39,835
1876..£33,801
1877..£42,442
1878..£34,493
1879..£30,125
1880..£38,507
1881..£36,419
1882..£43,117
1883..£40,250
1884..£44,810
1885..£47,035
1886..£43,044
1887..£56,970
1888..£50,813
1889..£42,700
1890..£42,523
1891..£65,295
1892..£58,527
1893..£56,550
1894..£73,526
1895..£81,159
1896..£117,036
1897..£81,569
1898..£108,625
1899..£105,176
1900..£101,184
1901..£107,293
1902..£105,454
1903..£112,704
1904..£118,507
1905..£114,007
1906..£121,073
1907..£103,793
1908..£115,303
1909..£126,215
1910..£97,322
1911..£113,352
1912..£110,908
1913..£122,966
1914..£111,813
1915..£139,606
1916..£146,948
1917..£150,844
1918..£181,003
1919..£151,025
1920..£185,903
1921..£174,501
1922..£91,399
1923..£180,014
1924..£241,780
1925..£235,818
1926..£211,964
1927..£228,975
1928..£299,263
1929..£311,054
1930..£319,434
1931..£264,040
1932..£268,588
1933..£294,916
1934..£309,584
1935..£321,861
1936..£293,915
1937..£308,015
1938..£349,882
1939..£284,153
1940..£356,321
1941..£386,836
1942..£495,775
1943..£528,726
1944..£563,507
1945..£609,294
1946..£588,541
1947..£619,944
1948..£689,125
1949..£577,638
1950..£741,863
1951..£655,861
1952..£739,708
1953..£775,040
1954..£864,235
1955..£837,675
1956..£1,001,209
1957..£997,848
1958..£1,118,684
1959..£973,322
1960..£1,023,629
1961..£1,234,909
1962..£1,355,792
1963..£1,530,541
1964..£1,695,282
1965..£1,598,334
1966..£1,721,485
1967..£1,521,124
1968..£1,819,887
1969..£2,173,508
1970..£2,419,259
1971..£2,501,380
1972..£3,123,277

Appendix VII

R.N.L.I. HOUSE FLAG AND ENSIGN

The original flag of the Institution was made in about 1884 by Miss Leonora Frances Margaret Preston, sister of one of the Committee of Management. It is made up of the Red Cross of St George, edged with blue on a white field. The letters R.N.L.I. are placed one in the centre of each canton. In the centre of the flag is a yellow crown, above a yellow anchor.

In December 1964 the Ministry of Defence issued a Warrant authorizing the Institution's boats to fly a Red Ensign defaced by its house flag.

The life-boat fleet is registered in London. When stationed in the Irish Republic, life-boats fly the Irish Tricolor.

Appendix VIII

CHRONOLOGY INDEX OF SOME IMPORTANT EVENTS

1771 Bamburgh Castle sea-rescue organization in being (p. 12).
1786 Bamburgh administrators commission Lionel Lukin to convert a coble for rescue work (p. 13).
1790 Henry Greathead's *Original* life-boat in service at South Shields (p. 12).
1823 Hillary's Appeal for a national sea-rescue service (p. 4).
1824 'National Institution for the Preservation of Life from Shipwreck' established (p. 8).
1838 Grace and William Darling's rescues from the *Forfarshire* (pp. 14–17)
1839 Founding of the Shipwrecked Fishermen and Mariners Royal Benevolent Society (p. 17).
1851 Great Exhibition, and the Fourth Duke of Northumberland's Presidency (p. 21).
Competition for designs of efficient life-boats (p. 27).
1852 First issue of *The Life-boat Journal* (p. 35).
1854 Change of name to 'Royal National Life-boat Institution' (p. 38).
Subsidy from the Board of Trade (relinquished 1869) (p. 38).
1860 Charter of Incorporation (p. 38).
1874 Publication of Richard Lewis's *History of the Life-boat* to mark the jubilee of the Institution's foundation (p. 44).
1890 First steam life-boat in service (p. 71).
1897 Parliamentary Inquiry into the affairs of the Institution (p. 62).
1904 Headquarters moved from Adelphi to Charing Cross Road (p. 77).
1909 Motor life-boats in service (p. 80).
1914 Rescues from the hospital ship *Rohilla* at Whitby (pp. 91–5).
1924 Centenary of the foundation. (pp. 114–21).
First International Life-boat Conference, in London (pp. 115, 119).
British Empire Exhibition, Wembley (p. 117).
1928 Second International Life-boat Conference, Paris (p. 129).
1929 Introduction of radio-telephony in life-boats (p. 135).
1930 Headquarters established at Grosvenor Gardens (p. 132).
1932 Third International Life-boat Conference, in Holland (p. 133).
1934 Experiments with diesel engines (p. 135).
1938 Fourth International Life-boat Conference, at Gothenburg (p. 142).
1939 Opening of the Boreham Wood Depot (p. 147).
1940 Services of life-boats at Dunkirk (pp. 153–8).
1947 Fifth International Life-boat Conference, at Oslo (p. 174).
1951 Life-boats shown in the Festival of Britain (p. 182).
Sixth International Life-boat Conference, in Belgium (p. 183).
R.N.L.I. undertakes to act as International Secretariat (p. 183).
1955 Seventh International Life-boat Conference, in Portugal (p. 195).

1956 Introduction of VHF/radio-telephony for communication with helicopters (p. 197).
1959 Eighth International Life-boat Conference, in Bremen (p. 203).
1963 Ninth International Life-boat Conference, in Edinburgh (pp. 215–18). Inshore Life-boats established (p. 214).
1964 Inauguration of Life-boat Enthusiasts Society (p. 221).
1967 Tenth International Life-boat Conference, France (p. 229).
1969 Establishment of Yachtsmen's Life-boat Supporters' Association (p. 233).
1970 Official Inquiry into the loss of the Fraserburgh life-boat (p. 241).
1971 Eleventh International Life-boat Conference, in New York (p. 245).
1972 Conference of Voluntary Life-boat Societies, in Malmö (p. 245). Naming of the Life-boat *Royal British Legion Jubilee* by H.M. Queen Elizabeth II (p. 252).
1974 150th Anniversary of the Foundation of the Institution.

Note. Thanks are due to A. W. Neal of Operations Division R.N.L.I. for information included in Appendix I; to S.E. Bartholomew and Adrian Batten for Appendices V, VI and VII; and for illustrative material to Christopher Elliott.

Select Bibliography

The bibliography of the life-boat is enormous, and even a list which included histories of particular stations, many of which are admirable, would be extensive. It is not possible to be inclusive, but the works listed below, chronologically, are those which have proved most valuable in the writing of this history.

Greathead, Henry: *Report of the Evidence and other Proceedings in Parliament respecting the Invention of the Life-boat*. Hansard, London, 1804.

A summary had appeared in the *Naval Chronicle* Vol. VIII (1802). In the *Naval Chronicle* Vol. IX (1803), illustrated particulars of Greathead's life-boat and transporter were included. Details of Greathead's life, and of Lloyd's part in the establishment of early rescue stations, appear in *The History* of *Lloyd's* by F. Martin, Macmillan, London, 1876.

Lukin, Lionel: *The Invention, Principles of Construction and Uses of Unimmergible Boats*. Nichols, London, 1806.

Hillary, Sir William: *An Appeal to the British Nation, on the Humanity and Policy of Forming a National Institution for the Preservation of lives and Property from Shipwreck*. Whittaker, London, 1823.

This pamphlet (the title-page of which is reproduced following page 36), contains the essential aims of the Institution.

Hillary, Sir William: *A Plan for the Construction of a Steam Life Boat, also for the Extinguishment of Fire at Sea*. Whittaker, London, 1824.

The original manuscript is in the Institution's archives.

Palmer, George: *A New Plan for Fitting all Boats, so that they may be made secure, as Life-boats*. Richardson, London, 1836

Report of the Committee appointed to examine the Life-boat Models submitted to compete for the Premium offered by the Duke of Northumberland. Clowes, London, 1851.

Lectures on the Results of the Great Exhibition of 1851, delivered before the Society of Arts, Manufactures and Commerce. Bogue, London, 1852.

Includes Captain Washington's lecture on 'The Progress of Naval Architecture . . . and on Life-boats.'

The Life-boat or *Journal of the National Shipwreck Institution*, 1852–4.

The Life-boat or *Journal of the Royal National Life-boat Institution* (1855, continuing).

The official journal of the R.N.L.I. contains accounts of all the principal rescues, of ceremonies, technical developments, and the current history of the rescue service in general. It is the basis for any detailed survey, and contains information otherwise only to be found in individual station records.

Ballantyne, R. M.: *The Life-boat: A Tale of our Coast Heroes*. Nisbet, London, 1864.

This story, popular in its day, is once again to be in print, with an Introduction by the Duke of Atholl, Deputy Chairman of the Institution. It is mainly set in Deal, Kent, and it is full of authentic information about the work of the life-boats of the day. In *Ballantyne the Brave*, by Eric Quayle (Hart-Davis, London, 1967), particulars are given of Ballantyne's work for the cause, which resulted in the presentation of a life-boat to the station at Port Logan, Fife, Scotland.

Lewis, Richard: *A History of the Life-boat and its Work*. Macmillan, London, 1874.

This book marked the jubilee of the founding of the Institution. It was written by the Secretary and includes information on the tactics of sea-rescue.

Report from the Select Committee on the Royal National Life-boat Institution, 15 July 1897. Command Paper no. 317: H.M.S.O. 1897.

The result of the work of investigation, submitted to the House of Commons by the Committee appointed to examine every aspect of life-boat affairs. It is the most thorough inquiry of its kind ever to have been made.

Lamb, Sir John Cameron: *The Life-boat and its Work*. Clowes, London, 1911.

Methley, N. T.: *The Life-boat and Its Story*. Sidgwick and Jackson, London, 1912.

Macara, Sir Charles: *Recollections*. Cassell, London, 1921.

Includes an account of the author's work in originating Life-boat Saturdays and other ways of arousing public enthusiasm for the life-boat cause. *Sir Charles W. Macara: A Study of Modern Lancashire* by W. Haslam Mills (Sherratt and Hughes, Manchester 1917), is biographical.

Dawson, Major A. J.: *Britain's Life-boats: The Story of a Century of Heroic Service*. Hodder and Stoughton, London, 1923.

The official history, published in the autumn before the Centenary in 1924. With an Introduction by the Prince of Wales (later Edward VIII), and a Foreword by Joseph Conrad. The corrected manuscript of the Foreword is in the Institution's archives.

Seely, Major-General J. E. B.: *Launch: A Life-boat Book*. Hodder and Stoughton, London, 1932.

The author (later Lord Mottistone), had served as a coxswain as well as on the Committee of Management of the Institution.

Barnett, J. R.: *Modern Life-boats of the Royal National Life-boat Institution*. Blackie, Glasgow, 1933. Revised edition 1950.

A technical account, by the Consulting Naval Architect to the Institution.

The Life-boat in Verse: An Anthology Covering a Hundred Years. Selected and with a Commentary by Sir John Cumming and Charles Vince. Hodder and Stoughton, London, 1938.

Carr, H. G.: 'Flags of National Life-boat Societies.'

An article in the *Mariner's Mirror: The Journal of the Society for Nautical Research*, Vol. 25, No. 2, April 1939.

Hillary, Richard: *The Last Enemy*. Macmillan, London, 1942.

Includes a description of the author's rescue by the Margate life-boat after he was shot down in the Battle of Britain.

Vince, Charles: *Storm on the Waters: The Story of the Life-boat Service in the War of 1939–45*. Hodder and Stoughton, London, 1964.

The author was Publicity Secretary of the Institution during the war, and for many years on its staff.

Cumming, Sir John: *Literature of the Life-boat*. Royal National Life-boat Institution, 1947.

A greatly extended edition of a bibliographical and general account of the evolution of the life-boat, and of sea-rescue. The original material was published during 1936 and 1937 and it was enlarged in 1947. It remains valuable for its survey of the earlier literature, both in books and in periodicals.

Howarth, Patrick: *The Life-boat Story*. Routledge and Kegan Paul, London, 1957.

With an introduction by Princess Marina, Duchess of Kent, President of the Institution. This work, by the Institution's Public Relations Officer, was followed by *How men are Rescued from the Sea* (Routledge and Kegan Paul, 1961). This also includes brief accounts of Trinity House, the Coastguard Service and the Air-Sea Rescue organization.

Jolly, Cyril: *Henry Blogg of Cromer: Greatest of the Life-boat Men*. Harrap, London, 1958.

Elder, Michael: *For Those in Peril: The Life-boat Service*. John Murray, London, 1963.

Owen, David: *English Philanthropy: 1660–1960*. Oxford University Press 1965.

A documented survey which places the Institution's work within the general framework of charitable activities.

Hornby, W. M. Phipps: 'Grace Horsley Darling 1815–1842: Northumbrian Heroine.'

This article appeared in the *Mariner's Mirror: The Journal of the Society for Nautical Research*, Vol. 54, No. 1, February 1968. There have been a number of lives of Grace Darling, few of them satisfactory. This is a brief, reliable guide to the facts of the rescue of 1838.

Nightingale, Benedict: *Charities*. Allen Lane, London, 1973.

A survey of the whole range of British charities, including a consideration of the Royal National Life-boat Institution and its problems.

Farr, A. D.: *Let Not the Deep: The Story of the Royal National Life-boat Institution*. Impulse Books, Aberdeen, 1973.

General Index